The South
Services

)ok is the first full history of South African intelligence and provides
'ed examination of the various stages in the evolution of South Afri-
elligence organisations and structures.
ering the apartheid period of 1948–1990, the transition from apart-
o democracy of 1990–1994, and the post-apartheid period of new
gence dispensation from 1994–2005, this book examines not only
artheid government's intelligence dispensation and operations, but
iose of the African National Congress, and its partner, the South
n Communist Party (ANC/SACP) – as well as those of other libera-
iovements and the "independent homelands" under the apartheid
. Examining the civilian, military and police intelligence structures
perations in all periods, as well as the extraordinarily complicated
ieid government's security bureaucracy (or "securocracy") and its
ires and units, the book discusses how South Africa's Cold War
on" influenced its relationships with various other world powers,
ially where intelligence co-operation came to bear. It outlines South
's regional relationships and concerns – the foremost being its activ-
n South-West Africa (Namibia) and its relationship with Rhodesia
gh 1980.
ially, it examines the various legislative and other governance bases
e existence and operations of South Africa's intelligence structures –
periods – and the influences that such activities as the Rivonia Trial
ie end of the history) or the Truth and Reconciliation Commission
ie other end) had on the evolution of these intelligence questions
ighout South Africa's modern history.
iis book will be of great interest to all students of South African pol-
intelligence studies and international politics in general.

K in A. O'Brien has served for a number of years as a senior advisor to
Western government and critical infrastructure sectors on public security
and intelligence matters. He is currently a senior analyst with the Government of Canada. He has a PhD in International Politics (Security Studies)
from the University of Hull.

Studies in Intelligence Series
General Editors: Richard J. Aldrich and Christopher Andrew
ISSN: 1368–9916

British Military Intelligence in the Palestine Campaign 1914–1918
Yigal Sheffy

British Military Intelligence in the Crimean War, 1854–1856
Stephen M. Harris

Signals Intelligence in World War II
Edited by David Alvarez

Knowing Your Friends
Intelligence inside alliances and coalitions from 1914 to the Cold War
Edited by Martin S. Alexander

Eternal Vigilance
50 years of the CIA
Edited by Rhodri Jeffreys-Jones and Christopher Andrew

Nothing Sacred
Nazi espionage against the Vatican, 1939–1945
David Alvarez and Revd. Robert A. Graham

Intelligence Investigations
How Ultra changed history
Ralph Bennett

Intelligence Analysis and Assessment
Edited by David Charters, A. Stuart Farson and Glenn P. Hastedt

TET 1968
Understanding the surprise
Ronnie E. Ford

Intelligence and Imperial Defence
British Intelligence and the defence of the Indian Empire 1904–1924
Richard J. Popplewell

Espionage
Past, present, future?
Edited by Wesley K. Wark

The Australian Security Intelligence Organization
An unofficial history
Frank Cain

Policing Politics
Security intelligence and the liberal democratic state
Peter Gill

From Information to Intrigue
Studies in Secret Service based on the Swedish Experience 1939–45
C.G. McKay

Dieppe Revisited
A documentary investigation
John Campbell

More instructions from the centre
Christopher and Oleg Gordievsky

Controlling intelligence
Edited by Glenn P. Hastedt

Spy Fiction, Spy Films and Real Intelligence
Edited by Wesley K. Wark

Security and Intelligence in a Changing World
New perspectives for the 1990s
Edited by A. Stuart Farson, David Stafford and Wesley K. Wark

A Don at War
Sir David Hunt KCMG, OBE (reprint)

Intelligence and Military Operations
Edited by Michael I. Handel

Leaders and Intelligence
Edited by Michael I. Handel

War, Strategy and Intelligence
Michael I. Handel

Strategic and Operational Deception in the Second World War
Edited by Michael I. Handel

Codebreaker in the Far East
Alan Stripp

Intelligence for Peace
Edited by Hesi Carmel

Intelligence Services in the Information Age
Michael Herman

Espionage and the Roots of the Cold War
The conspiratorial heritage
David McKnight

Swedish Signal Intelligence 1900–1945
C.G. McKay and Bengt Beckman

The Norwegian Intelligence Service 1945–1970
Olav Riste

Secret Intelligence in the Twentieth Century
Edited by Heike Bungert, Jan G. Heitmann and Michael Wala

The CIA, the British Left and the Cold War
Calling the tune?
Hugh Wilford

Our Man in Yugoslavia
The story of a Secret Service operative
Sebastian Ritchie

Understanding Intelligence in the Twenty-First Century
Journeys in shadows
Len Scott and Peter Jackson

MI6 and the Machinery of Spying
Philip H.J. Davies

Twenty-First Century Intelligence
Edited by Wesley Wark

Intelligence and Strategy
Selected essays
John Robert Ferris

The US Government, Citizen Groups and the Cold War
The state–private network
Edited by Helen Laville and Hugh Wilford

Peacekeeping Intelligence
New players, extended boundaries
Edited by David Carment and Martin Rudner

Special Operations Executive
A new instrument of war
Edited by Mark Seaman

Mussolini's Propaganda Abroad
Subversion in the Mediterranean and the Middle East, 1935–1940
Manuela A. Williams

The Politics and Strategy of Clandestine War
Special operations executive, 1940–1946
Neville Wylie

Britain's Secret War against Japan, 1937–1945
Douglas Ford

US Covert Operations and Cold War Strategy
Truman, secret warfare and the CIA, 1945–53
Sarah-Jane Corke

Stasi
Shield and sword of the party
John C. Schmeidel

British Intelligence and the Arab Revolt
The first modern intelligence war
Polly A. Mohs

Exploring Intelligence Archives
Enquiries into the secret state
Edited by R. Gerald Hughes, Peter Jackson, and Len Scott

US National Security, Intelligence and Democracy
The Church Committee and the war on terror
Edited by Russell A. Miller

Intelligence Theory
Key questions and debates
Edited by Peter Gill, Stephen Marrin and Mark Phythian

East German Foreign Intelligence
Myth, reality and controversy
Edited by Thomas Wegener Friis, Kristie Macrakis and Helmut Müller-Enbergs

Intelligence Cooperation and the War on Terror
Anglo-American security relations after 9/11
Adam D.M. Svendsen

A History of the Egyptian Intelligence Service
A history of the Mukhabarat 1910–2009
Owen L. Sirrs

The South African Intelligence Services
From apartheid to democracy, 1948–2005
Kevin A. O'Brien

The South African Intelligence Services

From apartheid to democracy, 1948–2005

Kevin A. O'Brien

LONDON AND NEW YORK

First published 2011
by Routledge
2 Park Square, Milton Park, Abingdon, Oxon OX14 4RN

Simultaneously published in the USA and Canada
by Routledge
711 Third Avenue, New York, NY 10017

Routledge is an imprint of the Taylor & Francis Group, an informa business

First issued in paperback 2012

© 2011 Kevin A. O'Brien

The right of Kevin A. O'Brien to be identified as author of this work has been asserted by him in accordance with sections 77 and 78 of the Copyright, Designs and Patents Act 1988.

Typeset in Baskerville by Wearset Ltd, Boldon, Tyne and Wear

All rights reserved. No part of this book may be reprinted or reproduced or utilised in any form or by any electronic, mechanical, or other means, now known or hereafter invented, including photocopying and recording, or in any information storage or retrieval system, without permission in writing from the publishers.

British Library Cataloguing in Publication Data
A catalogue record for this book is available from the British Library

Library of Congress Cataloging-in-Publication Data
O'Brien, Kevin A.
The South African intelligence services: from apartheid to democracy, 1948–2005/Kevin A. O'Brien.
p. cm.
1. Intelligence service–South Africa–History. 2. National security–South Africa–History. 3. South Africa–Politics and government. I. Title.
JQ1929.I6O37 2010
327.1268009'045–dc22
2010017317

ISBN13: 978-0-415-43397-6 (hbk)
ISBN13: 978-0-203-84061-0 (ebk)
ISBN13: 978-0-415-53524-3 (pbk)

For my girls

Contents

List of illustrations   xi
Acknowledgements   xii
List of abbreviations   xvi

1 Introduction: South African intelligence in revolution and counter-revolution 1948–2005   1

2 The birth of South Africa's intelligence capability and the rise of the "securocracy", 1948–1972   13

3 "Total Strategy" and the "securocratisation" of the government, 1972–1978   41

4 Hydra: the rise of the national intelligence and counter-revolutionary structures, 1978–1983   63

5 Carrot and stick: the domestic COIN paradigm, 1980–1985   95

6 The assassins' web: the growth of counter-revolutionary warfare intelligence, 1979–1985   116

7 Crossing the Rubicon: "the gloves come off" for a total counter-revolutionary strategy, 1985–1990   138

8 Negotiating a settlement: reform and retrenchment for all, 1990–1994   172

9 Progress and problems: South Africa's new intelligence dispensation, 1994–2005   204

x *Contents*

10 Conclusion: still fighting the war – the legacy of
    South Africa's intelligence history   233

    Notes   237
    Bibliography   276
    Index   296

Illustrations

Figures

2.1	National Intelligence (1969–1978)	27
3.1	Military Intelligence Division (1976–1990)	55
3.2	SADF Special Forces (1972–1990)	61
4.1	National Intelligence (1980–1990)	67
4.2	State Security Council structures (c.1985)	73
4.3	ANC–SACP–MK structures (1982)	79
4.4	National Security Management System (c.1984)	85
4.5	SSC and NSMS structures	89
5.1	South Africa's covert structures (c.1986)	102
5.2	SAP Security Branch (c.1983)	105
7.1	The assassins' web (c.1986)	157
9.1	RSA Intelligence structures (1996)	213
9.2	RSA Intelligence structures (2003)	224

Tables

Table 5.1	SAP Security Branch sections (c.1985)	107
Table 5.2	C1 assassinations and killings (examples)	112–113
Table 7.1	Statistical analysis of terrorist incidents (July 1976–April 1990)	139
Table 7.2	MK incidents (1976–1987)	142
Table 9.1	South African intelligence personnel (1994–1995)	208

Map

Map 1.1	South Africa (including homelands) 1990	4

Acknowledgements

This work is the product of a number of years of dedicated research. While a portion of it is drawn from my PhD dissertation (University of Hull, 2001), other sections are the product of research conducted on various aspects of South Africa's intelligence dispensation both before and since my PhD; equally, a significant amount of new research – covering particularly the pre-1960 and post-1990 periods – has also been done in support of this book. As such, it spills across the last 16 years of my life as a research analyst – and is, therefore, the product of not just my efforts but also of those around me who supported, assisted, tolerated, encouraged, relaxed with, critiqued, and, above all, believed in me.

In terms of academic thanks, this must first and foremost go to Colin S. Gray for the advice, counsel, support, guidance and enduring patience with a student who thought he knew better than others what he was doing – and for putting him right, gently but firmly, many times. I am similarly grateful to Justin, Ernie, Billy, Simon, Neena and the boys for the chats, the meals and drinks, and (with the late, lamented Hilaire McCoubrey) the debates on security studies and international law. I must also thank particularly Andrew Rathmell for his understanding, time, assistance, critiques and overall support in this and other efforts over the years – and particularly through a rather difficult time near the end of my PhD. From all those who critiqued my work on South Africa, an exceptional thanks must be made to Stephen Ellis for the debates, time and assistance, as well as some of the inspiration for this work. In this regard, I must also thank Chris Alden, Annette Seegers, Peter Batchelor, Robert Henderson, Brandon Hamber, Piers Pigou, Guy Lamb and others who have offered their expert guidance and insights along the way – as this study is a reflection on their excellent work on security and politics in the apartheid state, and the evolution of these factors into the post-apartheid era. Equally, further support and critique in developing my ideas came from a number of colleagues in the academic study of intelligence – including Stuart Farson, Peter Gill, Mark Phythian, David Charters, Loch Johnson, Kevin O'Connell, Shlomo Schpiro, Hans Born, and – particularly – the leadership of the Canadian Association for Security and Intelligence Studies

(CASIS) over the last two decades, who afforded me a forum many times to air my evolving assessments of this topic. My students at both the University of Hull and King's College London – from 1997 to 2009 – were also excellent sounding-boards for many of the points explored in this book. I must thank the University of Hull for the Brynmor Jones Studentship and the Vice-Chancellors' Award which afforded me the time to concentrate on the PhD portion of this study; the Department of Politics and Asian Studies (University of Hull) for the Doctoral Fellowship and the opportunity to teach. This book would not have gotten where it did without the support from all my colleagues throughout the PhD, too many to name, for the companionship, debates, beers and suffering. Looking back along the road from whence I've come, I must also thank Alex Morrison for getting me on to the wider path in the first place and affording me the opportunity (in many ways), and Doug Scoyne, Jennifer Milliken and Edith Klein for setting my academic interests alight originally and making it interesting enough to pursue professionally, for which I am forever grateful.

In terms of the many government, intelligence, military and other public persons who assisted – in a variety of ways – with this study, two individuals in particular must be mentioned first and foremost: A.B. for the initial push and the on-going encouragement throughout the process, and the Tall Colonel for the inspiration, wonder and encouragement, even though I learned more than he ever intended; I would wish him to consider this a good accounting. In a similar vein to the Colonel, I must thank the Good General for not pulling back the curtain entirely, forcing me to find the door; in the same way, I must also thank an anonymous SANDF brigadier who, unbeknownst to me at the time, gave me more than I could have wished for. Bennie and Barry – each in their own way – made it ever more interesting as my investigations progressed. Colin's insights into the street-level activities of South African intelligence operatives in Britain also provided an extremely useful OPFOR understanding for those having to deal with the fall-out from apartheid's overseas covert operations. In addition, there were a number of journalists, researchers and other members of the public in South Africa, Britain, the United States, and the Netherlands who helped me in times of difficulty – while anonymous, their contribution must be acknowledged with gratitude.

While one driver for this book is academic, the other is personal: in examining the South African security forces in their evolution over the past two decades, I met numerous members of both the apartheid and ANC security forces, and wanted to understand the context and environment in which they developed their strategies and carried out their operations, during a period in human history which shall be looked back upon as regrettable, despicable, and – perhaps – even avoidable. Certain individuals in particular, and the conversations which I have had with them over the past decades, drove this desire to understand. It is largely for this reason that I chose this topic to glean as much insight into as possible – I am hoping that those insights will prove useful to others, both those who experienced the events discussed in this book and those who have merely watched them with interest. In that light, I must thank one former covert operator for his insights into "the disease" that afflicted so many former apartheid-era operatives – known collectively (and colloquially) as "the I-don't-remember disease"; while facetious, this pointed me towards one of the main challenges (and – occasionally – dangers) in developing an academic study of a topic that remains very much alive for those who lived through its story. In this sense, and most importantly, this study would not exist in the form it does – perhaps not at all – if it were not for the many interviewees and the hard-learned-but-never-forgotten lesson they taught me that one person's academic research is another person's life, livelihood and possession. Ultimately, it was the review and critique (and not a small amount of direct criticism, at times tinged with the legacy of personal experiences under apartheid) that came from many of those involved – on both sides – in South Africa's dirty wars, as well as the transition from apartheid to democracy and the efforts to develop a "new dawn" in South Africa's intelligence dispensation, that strengthened my resolve to see this story – one which will never be complete – told. This book is better for those critiques, no matter how harshly put at times. To that end, I particularly owe a great deal of thanks to W.M. for his good-natured tolerance of my stumblings and fumblings, his personal insights on many of the harder issues, and his invaluable advice on where to stride and when to keep low and move fast. In a similar manner, I must particularly thank Tony for trusting me enough to let me in.

Most importantly, I must express my heartfelt thanks to my wife Rachel – and, particularly in the final months of researching and writing the final study, Cate and Maggie – without whose patience, good nature, understanding, support, care, love and countless arguments about international politics and law (!) I could never have made it through the process (with herself always involved in a similar one); and to my family for being understanding about my choices and supporting me in them, even when they never really could understand what exactly it was that I was doing. I must not forget my friends, especially Susan and Don for being there – always; Steve for showing me how it was done – and being there when I needed him for the best task of all; Omar for the Leonard Cohen and for walking alongside of me, at least part of the way; Nino for the refuge and the humour; Darling for the talks – the endless talks – and the insights which kept me sane; Cols for challenging me and leading me onwards with her own achievements; and all collectively for giving me the courage to make the first leap. I must also thank D.C. for the humorous insights into the PhD process and what comes of life after the PhD; Greg for the never-ending support on other efforts which allowed me the mental and temporal space to finish this one, alongside his cutting insights into contemporary security challenges; and my other friends, too many to name, for seeing me through it all, sticking by me throughout the process and the many peaks and valleys that accompanied it all.

I am also grateful to my editor – Andrew Humphrys – and Editorial Assistants – Rebecca Brennan, Emily Kindleysides, and Katie Gordon – for their patience *in extremis* with me for the completion of this study, as well as their guidance along the way. I must also thank Richard Aldrich and Christopher Andrew for not only agreeing to support this study as part of their Studies in Intelligence series with Routledge, but also for the many discussions about intelligence studies and practice over many years. Finally, I must acknowledge Routledge/Taylor & Francis for the kind permission to re-use in this book portions of four previous articles that I have written: "Counter-intelligence for Counter-revolutionary Warfare: The South African Police Security Branch", *Intelligence and National Security* 16:3 (Autumn 2001); "Special Forces for Counter-revolutionary Warfare: The South African Case", *Small Wars and Insurgencies* 12:2 (Summer 2001); "The Use of Assassination as a Tool of State Policy: South Africa's Counter-revolutionary Strategy 1979–1992 (Part II)", *Terrorism and Political Violence* 13:2 (Spring 2001); and "South Africa's Evolving Intelligence and Security Structures", *International Journal of Intelligence and Counterintelligence* 9:2 (Summer 1996).

Finally, and most curiously, I must pay my debt to David Cornwell for the inspiration many years ago, which has never wavered – may this go some way towards the reality of your world.

Abbreviations

ANC	African National Congress
ANC-DIS	African National Congress Department of Intelligence and Security
ANC-NAT	African National Congress Department of National Intelligence and Security
ANC-NEC	African National Congress National Executive Committee
APLA	Azanian Peoples' Liberation Army
Caprivis	*Inkatha* supporters trained for hit-squad activities by DMI
CCB	Civil Co-operation Bureau (SADF)
COIN	Counter-insurgency
COSATU	Congress of South African Trade Unions
CSADF	Chief, SADF
CSI	Chief of Staff, Intelligence (SADF)
DCC	Directorate Covert Collection (SADF)
DCI	Directorate of Covert Information (SADF)
DG	Director-General
DMI	Military Intelligence Division (SADF)
DP	Democratic Party
DST	Directorate Special Tasks (SADF)
EMLC	Electronic magnetic logistical component
FRELIMO	*Frente de Libertação de Moçambique* (Front for the Liberation of Mozambique)
Geveilstaf (GVS)	Joint Security Staff (Afrikaans acronym)
GIKOM	*Gesamentlike Inligtingskomitee* – Joint Intelligence Committee (Afrikaans acronym)
GIS	*Gesamentlike Intelligensiesentrum* – Joint Intelligence Centre (Afrikaans acronym)
GOC-SF	General Officer Commanding, Special Forces (SADF)
GOS	*Gesamentlike Operasionele Sentrum* – Joint Operations Centre (Afrikaans acronym)

IFP	*Inkatha* Freedom Party
KIK	*Koördineer Inligting Komitee* – Co-ordinating Intelligence Committee (Afrikaans acronym)
KOMKOM	*Kommunikasiekomitee* – Communications Committee (Afrikaans acronym)
KZN	KwaZulu-Natal
KZP	KwaZulu Police Force
MK	*Umkhonto we Sizwe* – Spear of the Nation, the military wing of the ANC/SACP
MPLA	*Movimento Popular de Libertação de Angola* (Popular Movement for the Liberation of Angola)
NCM	National Co-ordinating Mechanism
NIS	National Intelligence Service
NP	National Party
NSCS	National Security Co-ordination Structures
NSMS	National Security Management System
PAC	Pan-Africanist Congress
PIDE	*Polícia Internacional e de Defesa do Estado* (International Police for the Defence of the State), Portugal
PLAN	People's Liberation Army of Namibia
RENAMO	*Resistênçia Naçional Moçambicana* (Mozambican National Resistance – also MNR)
RSA	Republic of South Africa
SACP	South African Communist Party
SADF	South African Defence Force
SAP	South African Police
SAP-CCID	South African Police Crime Combating and Investigation Division
SAP-CIS	South African Police Crime Intelligence Service
SAP-SB	South African Police Security Branch
SEMKOM	*Staatkundige-Ekonomiese-en-Maatskaplikekomitee* or Constitutional/Economic/Welfare Committee (Afrikaans acronym)
SSC	State Security Council
Stratkom	Strategic Communications Branch, State Security Council (Afrikaans acronym)
SWAPO	South-West African People's Organisation
TBC Special Forces	Transkei, Bophutatswana and Ciskei Special Forces
TBVC	Transkei, Bophutatswana, Venda, and Ciskei
TBVCDF	TBVC Defence Forces
TBVCPF	TBVC Police Forces
TBVIS	Transkei, Bophutatswana and Venda Intelligence Services
Trewits	*Teen Rewolusionêre Inligting Taakspan* (Counter-

	revolutionary Targeting Committee) (Afrikaans acronym)
UDF	Union Defence Force (1910–1957)
UDF	United Democratic Front (1976–1990)
UNITA	*União Nacional para la Independência Total de Angola* (National Union for the Total Independence of Angola)
VEIKOM	*Veiligheidskomitee* – Security Committee (Afrikaans acronym)
ZANLA	Zimbabwe African National Liberation Army
ZANU	Zimbabwe African National Union
ZAPU	Zimbabwe African People's Union
ZIPRA	Zimbabwe People's Resistance Army

1 Introduction

South African intelligence in revolution and counter-revolution 1948–2005

> Who will believe that your course is just when your behaviours are so unjust?
>
> Unknown sixteenth-century French peasant

On 12 September 1989, two men checked-into the Palace Hotel in Lucerne, Switzerland. Using the names Michael James and Jacobus Maritz, they were in Switzerland illegally – travelling on false passports, false documentation and under cover-names – but decided that the risk was acceptable, given the enormity of what they were about to embark upon. Waiting nervously in their rooms for their contacts – John and Jack Simelane – they considered the possibility that they, or their contacts, could be killed in the process of the meetings, or – possibly even worse – detected and exposed by the Swiss authorities, or the American, British, French or West German intelligence services. As the evening wore on, the Simelane brothers arrived at the hotel, and asked for James' and Maritz's suite. Approaching their door cautiously in case James or Maritz were waiting to shoot them down in their turn, the Simelane brothers turned the corner into the room, and stopped: standing before them were James (in reality, Mike Louw, the deputy director of South Africa's National Intelligence Service) and Maritz (in reality, Maritz Spaarwater, its chief director of operations), with nervous looks on their faces. Entering the room, John Simelane (in reality, Thabo Mbeki, a leading member of the African National Congress' National Executive Council) and Jack Simelane (in reality, Jacob Zuma, the deputy head of the ANC's National Intelligence Department) grinned in relief. "Well...", sighed Mbeki, "here we are, bloody terrorists and for all you know fucking communists as well." The group broke-up in laughter, thereby starting the first moves by the intelligence services of both the apartheid state and its principal opponent of negotiating a settlement towards the end of apartheid, and a democratic future for all South Africans.[1]

Introduction

Since 1994, South Africa has moved down the path towards a multi-racial, representative democracy based on non-racialism and the concept of "one man, one vote". In reaching this point, the country has moved from a political system where a single party – composed of representatives of the white Afrikaner minority in South Africa – dominated politics for 45 years, to a political system where a single party – composed of representatives across the "colour bar" in South Africa – completely dominates politics. While promoting a vision of national co-operation with other political parties in the country, the African National Congress (ANC), which achieved electoral victory in April 1994 during the country's first all-race elections, is of such political strength – in a not-dissimilar manner to the power of the Afrikaner-dominated National Party during apartheid,[2] but under altogether different circumstances – that it has been able to dictate largely the terms of the ensuing transition.

This transition has been a difficult one – yet, relatively smooth when considering comparative examples in other African countries and the alternative futures confronting its crafters in 1990. However, a number of very serious issues confront the new government and its supporters, issues which are being dealt with as well as possible in light of the staggering effect that some of them have. While the successive ANC-led governments since this transition have succeeded generally in dealing with many of the same type of problems faced by their predecessors in Africa who underwent decolonisation or moved from white-minority to black-majority rule, in attempting to deal with these problems, new ones have been created, some of which appear insurmountable based on current attempts to deal with them.

Many of these challenges surround South Africa's ever-evolving intelligence dispensation – and, in the post-apartheid era, reflect many of the same issues with that dispensation that confronted (and, by-and-large, were ignored by) the apartheid state's political and security leadership. As such, it must be borne in mind from the start that South Africa's approach to intelligence today evolved out of the intelligence dispensation which existed under the apartheid regime; as such, this dispensation has both the unique characteristics for a democratic system, and the failings and foibles of a transitional state following liberation. In many ways, it could be said that not only South Africa's history, but also its viability as a country and a society has been – to varying degrees over the period from 1910 to 2005 – dictated and influenced by its intelligence dispensation. As Sanders notes,

> Since the early 1960s, South Africa has been a land infested with spies. Some intelligence operatives are essentially civil servants, others are freelance traders in information … over the last half-century, the ten-

tacles of intelligence stretched far and wide ... espionage, however incoherent and dishonest, is part of the glue that has held apartheid and post-apartheid society together.[3]

This is true as much for the apartheid era as it has been for the period since South Africa's democratic transition in 1994 – and while that transitional period can now be said to be over, many problems from that transition remain, and continue to evidence societal and political fall-out for South Africa today.

Overview: South Africa's evolving national intelligence and security establishment

This study grapples with those issues – with a long-view approach to understanding how and why they have evolved (in terms of South Africa's intelligence dispensation as a whole), what impact and influence they have had on South Africa's society and politics across its modern history, and what lessons may be learned from these understandings for the future.[4] As such, this study's primary period of interest is that from 1961 – the year in which South Africa's first formal national intelligence capability was established since the founding of the modern South African state in 1910, therefore effectively the beginnings of its post-colonial intelligence history, and the year after the ANC launched its "armed struggle" against the apartheid state – through 2005 – the year that saw the most recent set of amendments to that dispensation introduced by the government in Pretoria. It is, however, impossible to strike a clean starting-point at 1961 – given the influence that intelligence in the decades prior to that year had on the intelligence dispensation long after that year. Therefore, this study takes significant account of developments in that dispensation from 1939 particularly – and 1948, the year that apartheid was introduced in South Africa – in order to understand this evolution in long-view. Equally and clearly, South Africa's intelligence history did not freeze in 2005 and many significant events have continued to unfold even to the point of writing (2010), as is discussed in Chapter 9's Postscript – but with this last round of legislative amendments to the dispensation (which do not reflect on the 2009 Presidential Decrees forming the State Security Agency – see Chapter 9) occurring in 2005, an end-point must also be dictated.

The impact of South Africa's political history on its security

While space prevents a discussion of South Africa's history generally, a brief appreciation is required.

This history centres on the struggle between the Dutch-descended people of South Africa (known as Afrikaners) and all other ethnic groups which have inhabited or controlled South Africa at various points throughout its history, including

4 *Introduction*

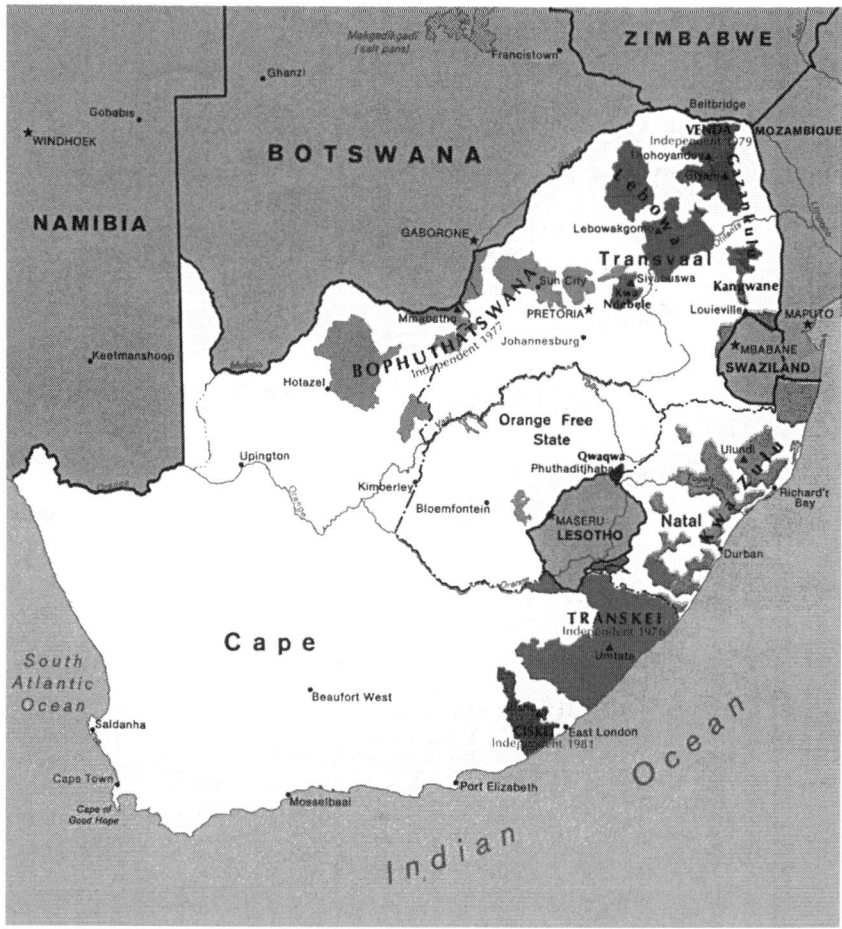

Map 1.1 South Africa (including homelands) 1990 (source: CIA World Factbook).

confrontations between those of English descent and the Afrikaners. One of the single biggest misunderstandings with regard to South Africa's past is that Afrikaner antipathy towards the English is as strong, if not perhaps greater than, their belligerence towards the various black tribes of the region, as Allister Sparks has pointed out in his remarkable study *The Mind of South Africa*.[5]

When the National Party (NP) was elected to power in 1948 and declared the policies of apartheid ("separateness"), it did so with the view that these were necessary in order to ensure the survival of the Afrikaner nation in a country where it was thought that black majority-rule would lead to genocide against the Afrikaner nation, and where the English could never be trusted. Thus, the National Party (hand-in-hand with the

Dutch Reformed Church in South Africa) represented the political and cultural aspirations of the Afrikaners as "white Africans" in a country filled with black Africans.

The English were not, however, the biggest problem confronting the Afrikaners. From the beginning (1911, with the Union of South Africa, followed one year later by the founding of the ANC on 8 January 1912), it was the black tribes of South Africa that constituted the biggest perceived threat to Afrikanerdom. Over the course of the twentieth century, this view evolved to such a degree that, by the 1970s, the state believed that it was faced with a "total onslaught" by the liberation and revolutionary forces confronting it, both in South Africa and regionally – through the network of Communist guerrilla movements aligned with the Soviet Union and Cuba, fighting South Africa and its allies across Southern Africa. This twin rubric of a "black tide" sweeping the Afrikaners to their extinction in South Africa, while "black communism" would accomplish the same with their cultural and religious beliefs, drove the NP to confront these movements with every means at their disposal – and pushed it to decide that the only possible response that it could give to this "total onslaught" was to prepare a "total strategy" to confront it. Within this context, the National Party government implemented policies which reflected two forms of confronting its adversaries: overt, military confrontation; and clandestine-covert confrontation, which will form the major focus of this study's consideration of the apartheid era and the transition from it.

From the point-of-view of the ANC and other national liberation movements, South Africa had been placed under the yoke of colonial occupation by Dutch (Boer) settlers more than three centuries previously. These Boers (and, later, the British) implemented racist policies to ensure that the black tribes who provided the labour and thus economic success to the white settlers, would remain subservient to them in perpetuity. Thus, the termination of these racist policies (which were developed during South Africa's Union period and, by 1948, culminated in the one policy of apartheid) and the removal from political and economic power of those that propagated them was the aim of the liberation movements. They believed that, in pursuing this aim, due to the nature of their opponent, an armed struggle was morally justified.

Within this history, it will be noted – as a starting-point for this study – that South Africa's security establishment began to evolve almost immediately following the National Party election victory in 1948; it would not, however, begin to coalesce into a truly comprehensive security architecture until the late 1960s. The apartheid regime did not have an independent intelligence service until 1961 – the year that Republican Intelligence (RI) was founded, and the year following the launch of an "armed struggle" by the ANC, the South African Communist Party (SACP) and their jointly organised *Umkhonto weSizwe* ("Spear of the Nation" or MK, the guerrilla army founded in June 1961 by Nelson Mandela); this was significant because the British, in their dominion capacity up to 1961 (the year that South Africa declared itself a republic and withdrew from the Commonwealth) did not allow it to have one, for reasons which will be outlined. It was, however, the events of the Sharpeville Massacre on 21 March 1960 and the subsequent launch of the ANC/SACP "armed struggle" – alongside similar efforts by the Pan Africanist Congress (PAC, a radical black militant offshoot of the ANC), and the African Resistance Movement (ARM, a group of radical-left whites whose bombing campaign between 1962 and 1964 mobilised the security establishment against such future action) – which prompted the apartheid leadership to realise that they had insufficient security and intelligence capabilities to confront these threats, and so move to remedy this over the decade. Even then, a truly effective security intelligence service (as distinct from the intelligence interests of the South Africa Police and the defence forces) did not exist until the establishment of the Bureau for State Security (known as BOSS) in 1969.

Consequently, during the period from 1960 to 1990 (the year in which the transition to a post-apartheid South Africa began) – and under the successive leadership of Prime Ministers Hendrik Verwoerd and B.J. (John) Vorster, and Presidents P.W. Botha and F.W. de Klerk – South Africa was a security state, one which used intelligence extensively to directly target its opponents both internally and externally. While nominal political authority and power rested with the elected ministers who composed the Cabinet, this was not the reality of the situation. By 1970, the true centre of power resided in the central security structures of the government – led by the State Security Council (SSC); while the Cabinet oversaw and acquiesced to all major decisions affecting the country, the SSC was the "super-Cabinet". In its sessions, the members of the SSC made all recommendations and decisions which affected the governing of the country; ultimately, bodies such as the SSC ran the policies of "Total National Strategy" and "Total Counter-revolutionary Strategy" that ran South Africa. The authority of the wider Cabinet would not be restored effectively until De Klerk came to power in 1989.[6]

Intelligence in South Africa must, therefore, be seen in light of the role that it played in supporting and driving the counter-revolutionary strategies, structures and operations of the apartheid state, alongside the role it played for the exiled ANC and SACP particularly in their efforts to overthrow that state through revolutionary means. In the post-apartheid era, intelligence has continued to play a significant role in supporting the ANC's continued efforts at introducing revolutionary change to South Africa, in many senses of the word.

Revolution, counter-revolution, and South Africa's intelligence dispensation

It is also worth noting that in a number of senses South Africa has, in effect, been a revolutionary state since the election victory of the Afrikaner-dominated National Party in 1948. First, with the establishment of the apartheid state in 1948, the National Party and its allies (in other, more conservative Afrikaner movements and parties) sought to revolutionise the nature of the South African state to protect Afrikaner culture and political dominance – not only against the black, coloured or Indian populations that comprised the overwhelming majority of the state's population, but also against the legacy of British control of South Africa for the first half of the twentieth century. Equally, as noted, the principal liberation movement – the ANC and its ally, the SACP – had determined in 1960 that an "armed struggle" was the only option it now faced, in attempting to overthrow the apartheid order and government in South Africa. It, therefore, began its own revolutionary efforts, which it pursued over the following three decades; this revolutionary approach led to the development of a counter-revolutionary strategy within the apartheid state's security apparatus, which – following the 1976 Soweto Uprising and by the middle of the 1980s – saw a symbiosis of revolution and counter-revolution both inside and outside South Africa. While this conflict calmed during the negotiated settlement concerning a post-apartheid state and society, it did not abate entirely, with continued ANC/SACP efforts to use covert, revolutionary means to overthrow the government in Pretoria during the course of the negotiations supporting the settlement. Finally, following the short, transitional period involving a Government of National Unity – combining the National Party and the ANC – from 1994 to 1997, an assessment of the post-apartheid intelligence dispensation within the wider politics pursued by the ANC demonstrates a continued revolutionary *and* counter-revolutionary pursuit by the ANC, as – in an inherently paradoxical fashion – it both attempts to create a transparent and accountable intelligence and security dispensation under democratic principles, and at the same time attempts to ensure that its hold on the reins of power, at both the political and bureaucratic levels of the state, remains unthreatened for years to come.

In the apartheid era – which forms the balance of this study's focus – the pursuit of a counter-revolutionary strategy against its opponents involved the use of intelligence for five key facets, each of which formed a portion of the apartheid state's national security policy and strategy. The first of these was the targeting of the state's opponents – somctimes for assassination, sometimes for discrediting and intimidating, and sometimes for recruiting as double-agents and moles within the national liberation movements confronting the apartheid state. The focus of this targeting was both within the apartheid state – including, in this sense, South-West

Africa, which remained a South African "protectorate" until its independence in March 1990 – and external to the state, including not only across Southern Africa but also in the United Kingdom and Europe. Intelligence was also central – second, and directly related to the first – to the relationships that Pretoria maintained with the governments of the "Frontline States" in Southern Africa (which included Angola, Botswana, Mozambique, Tanzania, Zambia, and Rhodesia/Zimbabwe), as well as with Lesotho and Swaziland. Prior to the Portuguese coup in 1974 and the transition in Rhodesia from white-minority rule in 1979, the governments in Luanda, Salisbury/Harare and Maputo were staunch allies of South Africa engaged collectively in a multi-dimensional conflict against liberation movements across the sub-continent; following these transitions and the consequent loss of these alliances, however, Pretoria found itself opposed by virtually every government in the region and without regional allies to support its own counter-revolutionary programmes against the ANC and its allies – indeed, many of these newly independent states now supported the ANC, explicitly or implicitly. As a result, South Africa poured pressure on all of these states – sometimes very directly (such as in Angola) and sometimes more indirectly (as in Zimbabwe, Mozambique, Lesotho and Swaziland particularly) – to curtail such support. South Africa's intelligence dispensation played a central role in the decision-making on and operational implementation of these relationships.

In the wider context – third – South Africa's intelligence needs were also positioned within the global anti-Communist paradigm of the Cold War. Supported, sometimes overtly but more heavily covertly, by its intelligence relationships with the United States (US), the United Kingdom (UK), West Germany and Israel – as well as other anti-Soviet states – South Africa saw itself as a bulwark against Communist expansion in Southern Africa. This position, which was supported somewhat by the fact that virtually every national liberation movement in Southern Africa was supported by the Soviet Union and/or China, was brought into stark relief with the Cuban intervention in Angola in 1975 in favour of the first post-colonial government in Luanda. While the United States and the United Kingdom may not have seen the same linkage between the apartheid system and the Cold War paradigm that Pretoria did, both countries did view South Africa as an intelligence ally in the Cold War conflict, and provided significant covert support to Pretoria between 1975 and 1990.

While the focus of this study will be on these three key contexts for apartheid South Africa's intelligence dispensation, its intelligence efforts also supported two other key areas: fourth, its efforts at overcoming the anti-apartheid sanctions regime placed against it over the course of the 1970s and 1980s; and, fifth, the development of its nuclear-weapons programme, most importantly through its covert relationship with Israel. These aspects will be considered where they relate to the first three contexts. In considering how each of these three aspects related to the apartheid state's counter-revolutionary strategy, while political action forms the overwhelming part of any counter-revolutionary warfare strategy, this study focuses specifically on how the intelligence dispensation was formed and used to support the military-security aspects of counter-revolutionary warfare, and even more specifically the elimination of insurgent structures – a euphemism for assassination; the political aspects will, of course, be discussed as extremely relevant but will not be examined in the same depth as the military. In terms of the South African case, this means that, while the political, economic and social reform initiatives of the government were emphasised in the revolutionary and counter-revolutionary strategies of each side, these shall only be discussed where related to the counter-revolutionary military initiatives of the government.

Intelligence and the targeting of the state's opponents

Assassination was developed as a tool of state policy in South Africa, and the national security architecture which developed under apartheid was geared significantly towards this end. Assassination was rarely used as a singular act, but resulted from a mechanised and systematised process whereby problems were reported, targets were selected, and operations implemented to remove those targets (via their "permanent removal from society" through assassination or through less lethal means such as detention without trial or banning) as a threat to the state. Such operations were carried out by a variety of units, some of which were specifically tasked with assassinations; their methods included poisoning, letter-bombs, "rigged" grenades, and direct targeting.

In a manner of speaking, these structures were extremely efficient in dealing with their opponents and achieved a high success rate against those targeted; in the end, however, this programme of selective assassination achieved little in halting the drive towards multi-party, non-racialist democracy. Over the course of the late 1980s and into the early 1990s, these units slowly ranged out of control: from what began as "the white man's war to preserve his status in Africa", it rapidly decayed into "a rampage of murder, mayhem and sabotage, continuing long past the twilight of white rule".[7] This has come to be one of the principal questions raised time and again: who was responsible for ordering and authorising such operations? This point will be answered later in the study.[8]

Therefore, in order to successfully implement the apartheid state's counter-revolutionary strategies, the clear support of the intelligence community as a whole had to be guaranteed in South Africa; however, this support was neither uniform nor would it turn out to be guaranteed throughout this evolution of South Africa's national security capabilities – themselves diverse and often disharmonious. In an effort to secure this "guarantee", first Vorster – as minister of justice and then prime minister – and, later, Botha appointed security chiefs to run the intelligence dispensation who would be loyal to them personally; at the same time, each prime minister championed one of the country's intelligence services. Under Vorster, this would be the South Africa Police Security Branch and its Bureau for State Security (BOSS),[9] while under Botha this would be the Department of Military Intelligence (DMI) of the South African Defence Force (SADF). Each would demonstrate significant power and sway over the rest of the intelligence dispensation in their times; it would only be with De Klerk's accession to the presidency that the civilian intelligence service – the National Intelligence Service (NIS) – would gain supremacy. In this sense, the strong central role of the South African intelligence community in both the policy-making process of the state security apparatus and the decision-making of the Cabinet (partly through its growing subservience to the state security structures) has been clear. During this time, the apartheid government continuously reformed the intelligence dispensation of a country engaged in a counter-revolutionary strategy against a number of national liberation movements, based both domestically and externally. In the late 1980s, when change was to come to the apartheid system, the support of the intelligence community – or, indeed, its active opposition – would turn out to be crucial to the success of the negotiated settlement which ensued.

Intelligence and the new South Africa

In the transition to the post-apartheid era, the new intelligence dispensation lost this overwhelmingly singular focus on defeating these liberation movements, and took on a more traditional appreciation of a wider-range of threats and risks to both South Africa's state and its society. A significant aspect of this new dispensation included a far more robust – at least, on paper – degree of transparency, oversight and public accountability for the intelligence services; however, even with both this widened remit and the introduction of significant oversight mechanisms, the post-apartheid intelligence dispensation continued to suffer from problems. Many of these could be related directly back to not only the legacy of apartheid and its security environment, but also to the deals and compromises reached as part of this transition from apartheid to democracy.

In considering the pursuit of an intelligence function broadly,[10] it can be appreciated that the South African state – across the period of 1948–2005 – demonstrated a capability in all intelligence areas; at the same time, these capabilities were subservient to the political requirements and strategies of the day. In that sense, while the intelligence requirements of the state – in both the apartheid and post-apartheid eras – were both dictated by the political leadership and the security environment of the period, and – in a number of senses – skewed and corrupted by those political views, it was only during the transitional period of 1990–1996 that a real effort was made to make the intelligence dispensation truly subservient to the overall public good; even then, this effort would by-and-large founder by the end of the 1990s. This theme – of the twisting and corrupting influence that state politics has had on South Africa's various intelligence dispensations since 1948 – will be notable throughout this study.

Dealing with South Africa's intelligence history

The history of South Africa's intelligence dispensation is obviously vast and complex. Given a stated focus on the relationship between the state, its strategy, its politics and political leaders, its security forces, its people, and the overall intelligence dispensation, this study will not focus pedantically on the technical development of this intelligence dispensation – nor on the day-to-day activities and individual operations of South Africa's intelligence services – but more widely on its central role in supporting all national security, revolution and counter-revolutionary forces in South Africa's modern history. Aiming for an understanding of the long-term trends in policies, strategies, structures and capabilities that – ultimately – underpinned the activities of the intelligence services in both the apartheid and post-apartheid eras, this study will generally not deal with specific plots, cases or the like excepting those that are illustrative of the evolving history of intelligence in South Africa's various eras and political forms. As such, in most cases many more "popular" cases and stories will receive only passing reference – including such examples as BOSS interference (and alleged collusion with MI5) in Britain in the 1970s, and its counter-exile operations in Britain and Europe more broadly; alleged NIS involvement in coup attempts throughout Africa (such as the Seychelles) in the 1980s; the development of South Africa's CBW programme (known as Project COAST) and its intelligence and counter-revolutionary warfare dimensions; or the so-called "coup" attempts against Thabo Mbeki's post-apartheid government (including the so-called "McBride Affair"). In addition, this study will not provide operational histories of any security force unit or agency – as with the examples above, appropriate references will be provided for further readings. In addition, as this study is focused very heavily on South Africa's national security – across all eras – and the role that the intelligence services played in/around it, it takes a far more domestic focus (which does include references to its counter-exile operations against South African exiles abroad, and the role played by intelligence liaison with Britain, the United States and others in supporting those aims) and far less "foreign" focus.

Finally, and in so doing, this study aims to understand the symbiotic nature of action/reaction between, first, the apartheid government and its opponents (particularly in the ANC, its armed wing *Umkhonto weSizwe* and its National Intelligence Department – NAT) in the period from 1948 to 1990; second, the National Party-led government and its security apparatus, slowly ranging out of control, and the ANC's lead negotiators in its revamped Department of Intelligence and Security (ANC-DIS) in the period from 1990–1994; and, third, the new intelligence dispensation, its management by the ANC-led Government of National Unity (and, later, ANC government), and its reactions to the challenges the intelligence dispensation encountered in attempting to fulfil its mandate while dealing with an increasingly visible degree of corruption infecting both its ranks and those of its ANC-dominated government decision-makers in the period after the democratic transition of 1994 – and why successes or failures arose in each of these three eras assessed.

This study will grapple with these complexities in its assessment of how South Africa's intelligence dispensation evolved across these three eras – including the common themes, challenges, failings and trends which emerge and fell across all eras – in understanding how South Africa's intelligence history evolved from apartheid to democracy.

2 The birth of South Africa's intelligence capability and the rise of the "securocracy", 1948–1972

> History shows that penalties do not deter men when their conscience is aroused ... for to men, freedom in their own land is the pinnacle of their ambitions, from which nothing can turn men of conviction aside.
>
> Nelson Mandela, 1964

The past as prologue: South Africa's intelligence dispensation 1910–1948

From the founding of the Union of South Africa in 1910 through to its establishment as a republic in 1961, South Africa did not possess a national intelligence service; such a capability was either provided by Britain or existed in all-but-theoretical form throughout this period. It is for this reason – in tandem with the creation of South Africa's first formalised national intelligence capability in 1961 following the declaration of an armed struggle by the African National Congress and its allies against the apartheid state the year before – that, as noted in Chapter 1, a focus on the development of South Africa's intelligence dispensation starting in 1960 is most significant. Nevertheless, despite this intelligence capability gap which existed prior to 1961, the development of the structures and relationships which would subsequently inform that intelligence dispensation are of considerable importance to understand, not the least of which because of the trends in South Africa's intelligence dispensation which were established in the pre-republican period and have lasted well into South Africa's new, post-apartheid intelligence dispensation in the twenty-first century.

Intelligence prior to 1948

Prior to 1939, South Africa had very few assets and expertise which could be accurately referred to as an intelligence capability. As far back as the late nineteenth century, the fledgling Boer republics – the South African (Transvaal) Republic and the Orange Free State – maintained a limited intelligence capacity. These were generally centred on two individuals:

first, Cornelius Smidt, who had led the "Transvaaler political secret service" against the British following Britain's annexation of the Transvaal in 1877 and through the subsequent First Anglo-Boer War of 1880–1881; and, second, Willem Leyds, who was appointed by President Paul Kruger as State Secretary in 1888. Leyds' primary concern was the growing tensions with Britain through the 1890s, for which he "regularized and expanded the Transvaal intelligence system" as tensions increased, concentrating his efforts on both sending spies into the British Cape Colony, while leveraging Boers living there as agents, and defeating British attempts to do the same into the Transvaal.[1]

Following the 1899–1902 Anglo-Boer War and the founding of the Union of South Africa in 1910, South Africa's intelligence requirements domestically reflected generally the British model of colonial policing for controlling South Africa internally, centred on the South African Police (SAP), which began to develop an intelligence capability in the 1920s; at the same time, its international intelligence needs were met almost entirely by the British security service MI5 – founded in the wake of both the Boer War and the growing concerns over German spies in Britain prior to the First World War – which retained responsibility for intelligence activities across Britain's colonial possessions and dominions, including the Union of South Africa.[2]

Britain's intelligence-driven relationship with Pretoria was not, however, a comfortable one – its historic links to South Africa were predicated, first, on its military relationship with the country throughout the first half of the twentieth century (following the end of the 1899–1902 Boer War and the establishment of the Union of South Africa under British dominion), and – second – on this colonial policing model. Over the course of the mid-twentieth century, however, it began to develop military intelligence requirements concerning both overseas and internal threats that the Union Defence Force (UDF) were ill-equipped to meet. The South African security forces – in the form of the SAP and the UDF, both (and in particular the former) heavily dominated by Afrikaners opposed to British Union rule – looked on Britain's mothering with a combination of envy and anger, with memories of Britain's harsh treatment during the Boer War never far from many minds. Outside of the two world wars periods, Britain resisted almost all efforts by the Union government to develop an autonomous intelligence capability: in 1938, Colonel Pierre de Villiers, Commissioner of the SAP, approached MI5 to investigate the possibility of establishing a "parallel security organization on MI5 lines". Britain refused, concerned that such a service would be used as part of domestic political conflicts, inevitably drawing Britain into these.[3] MI5 was also seriously concerned about the penetration of South Africa's security forces by radical Afrikaner nationalists and Republicans (see below), severely affecting the trust that MI5 could pursue with the SAP particularly. Therefore, this intelligence relationship between London and Pretoria – even prior to 1948 –

was an uncomfortable one; at one point in 1940–1941, the relationship had become so troubled that MI5 considered it was "virtually out of direct touch with internal events in the Union" due to a combination of liaison breakdowns and rivalries between the SAP and military intelligence which destroyed external contacts.[4]

Nevertheless, South Africa's Union government did begin to develop an intelligence capability that, initially, reflected many of the same concerns felt by MI5. Prior to the war, and in the traditional colonial policing model, it was the SAP's Detective Branch which had the intelligence lead – heavily concerned with counter-subversion and counter-intelligence – for the Union government.[5] Within the UDF, conversely, "intelligence" work had been by-and-large something pursued by amateurs – of which many "intelligence officers" were also journalists; indeed, financial constraints had prevented the UDF from expanding its intelligence capabilities prior to the war to "monitor the burgeoning activities of German and Italian agents throughout southern Africa".[6] With the impending threat of war in 1939, the SAP Detective Branch identified one major source of concern – Nazi sympathisers in South West Africa (a former German colony ceded to South Africa's mandate by the League of Nations after the First World War) – and moved to eradicate this threat; conversely, at this time – and significantly until at least the National Party's 1948 election – the threat from "native agitators" was seen to be of a significantly lower concern, not the least of which because the African National Congress (ANC) and the South African Communist Party (SACP) had not yet moved their campaigns into the "armed struggle" phase, which would not occur until 1961 (see below).[7]

The recognition of this threat and its international links – ultimately to focus on its war-fighting needs as part of the Western alliance of forces – also drove the UDF to revamp its fledgling intelligence capability at the outbreak of the war to ensure that both these needs would be met. At the same time, while such external threats were being addressed, Jan Smuts' Union government also had to take account of the growing threat from Afrikaner-nationalist forces (particularly the *Ossewa-Brandwag* (OB), a paramilitary organisation in both competition with D.F. (Daniel) Malan's Afrikaner-dominated National Party and heavily represented in the SAP; and to a lesser degree the Afrikaner *Broederbond*, a Masons-type secret organisation of conservative and nationalist Afrikaners) inside the Union, at least until 1943. MI5, also deeply concerned about Nazi sympathisers within the more radical Afrikaner ranks, focused on both counter-espionage and counter-subversion aimed at detecting such activities within Afrikaner circles. This recognition of deficiencies was matched to a recognition that the SAP was too heavily influenced – the evidence would say infiltrated – by the OB and Republicans, and therefore incapable of providing Smuts' government with independent intelligence and analysis on threats to the Union emanating from the Afrikaner nationalists; the UDF was perceived as a far more "British" institution, and hence the push for UDF intelligence to support the government's requirements.

During the Second World War, however, the seeds of South Africa's future intelligence dispensation would be sewn – and in more ways than one. Recognising these tripartite threats to South Africa's national security, Smuts pursued a hasty reorganisation and concomitant attempt to create a standing intelligence capability within the UDF and SAP. The Department of Military Intelligence (DMI) was created formally in February 1940, following the creation of the director of Intelligence post within the UDF late the previous year.[8] This process was rife with problems, however: the UDF "trained intelligence officers in a hurry for service ... the haste showed", with officers "unable to distinguish fact from fiction", as well as "promot[ing] their own views" in their analysis of events, particularly those tied to Republican politics.[9] At the same time, Smuts established an Intelligence Records Bureau (known as the ICB) whose non-operational responsibilities centred on acting as a "clearing-house for the processing, recording, and transmission of information" received from its membership (the Departments Of Censorship, Military Intelligence, SAP, Railway Police, The Treasury, Immigration, and Customs), as well as to the "Imperial chain of intelligence centres integrating the Union with Singapore, Nairobi, Cairo, and London". The SAP and DMI would have the authorities to pursue counter-subversion and counter-intelligence activities both within and outside South Africa. At the same time, MI5 and MI6 (Britain's Secret Intelligence Service) maintained strong interests in both threats to shipping across the Cape and in any attempts by the German or Italian Fascists to establish networks within South Africa, while the Special Operations Executive (Britain's wartime covert operations unit) operated out of Durban, in a close relationship with the UDF – one intelligence relationship which worked well.[10]

These intelligence requirements would outlast both the war and the post-war period – particularly the need to focus heavily on identifying any signs that an armed uprising by either Afrikaner Republicans or the SACP was imminent – prior to the 1948 election-victory by the National Party, which instituted apartheid.[11] These factors, and most particularly the rivalry in the intelligence sphere between the SAP, the defence force and the government's central intelligence structures and requirements, would feature heavily in South Africa's post-1948 history, especially after 1969.

In December 1945, the relationship between MI5 and the SAP began to thaw as the Union's post-war intelligence requirements began to grow and MI5's concerns over Soviet subversion of the Commonwealth dominions grew, and so an accommodation was sought between London and Pretoria. Indeed, it is possible that Sir Percy Sillitoe, MI5's contemporary Director General (who had previously served in South Africa and Northern Rhodesia), visited Pretoria secretly in mid-1946 as part of efforts to restart this relationship.[12] Yet Smuts' concerns to avoid being seen as subservient to London may have contributed to his intransigence in taking up this opportunity – and so the relationship foundered, again.

The founding of apartheid and the role for national intelligence

During the early days of apartheid – following the 1948 election victory of the Afrikaner National Party and through its evolution when South Africa departed the Commonwealth and declared itself a republic in 1961 – intelligence remained tied to South Africa's relationship with Britain; indeed, the fledgling apartheid government relied almost entirely on British intelligence, although it was loathe to admit it, with the British attempting to exert every influence on South Africa's intelligence concerns. This despite the fact that, as Andrew notes, the National Party's election made it "more difficult to maintain intelligence liaison with South Africa" – indeed, MI5 did not even maintain a Security Liaison Office in Pretoria after 1944 (by 1948, its closest SLO was in Salisbury, Southern Rhodesia), when it dismantled the MI5/MI6 network in South Africa. This problem was significant because, as Chavkin notes,

> South Africa's strengthening racist and expansionist goals of Afrikanerdom—often bundled into an overarching anti-communism—prevented the development of fruitful security intelligence cooperation. Overall, the lack of truly shared security concerns and a deteriorating trust among those involved condemned the viability of this liaison.[13]

Thus, Britain – and MI5 particularly – was in a bind: it wanted South Africa to develop "the same standard of security as ourselves" (as MI5 was already pursuing with the establishment of a security service in Australia) and play a "disciplined" role in the growing anti-communist Western intelligence alliance, but the domestic political dynamic in Pretoria raised significant concerns about implementing such a model.[14] For this reason, following a second visit in November 1949 to South Africa, Sillitoe heavily recommended against allowing the National Party to establish a domestic security service, because of fears over "the improper uses" – i.e. domestic suppression and oppression – that such a service could be put to by the Nationalists. Indeed, in one case – that of Michael Scott, an anti-apartheid cleric based out of the United Kingdom in the early 1950s – Britain would patently balk at sharing any intelligence on the individual with South Africa for exactly this fear. MI5 would, however, continue to see value in an intelligence-sharing – and, more accurately and starkly, paternalistic – relationship with South Africa's new leaders for the purposes of countering Communism. It would be under this guise that continuing intelligence co-operation – in both the security and military spheres – would continue throughout the 1950s, in a relationship that would, through 1960, rise and fall with the attention paid to it by each partner.[15]

Ironically – considering the degree to which the SAP was seen to be heavily infiltrated by hardline Afrikaner nationalists – Sillitoe recommended that, instead of a South African MI5, the SAP Special Branch should be "reinforced and set free from any criminal investigation commitments", while reorganised to "be able to deal efficiently with the problems of (*a*) counter espionage; (*b*) counter communism; (*c*) defensive security", and given "facilities for the interception of communications for counter espionage and security purposes". The SAP Special Branch had been created (out of the SAP's Nazi-hunting Special Staff, created in 1939) only in 1947, when the SAP commissioner recognised the need to create a unit dedicated to political crimes to operate alongside the Detective Branch and Uniform Branch. Partly as a result of Sillitoe's recommendations, the SAP Special Branch (subsequently referred sometimes to by this title and, increasingly into the 1950s, as the Security Branch) was again reorganised to focus on these areas; it also immediately began to receive counter-subversion training from British intelligence.[16] Over the next decade, its role in "the preservation of internal safety" – as laid out in the Police Act (No. 7 of 1958) – meant that, as Seegers notes, "this functional priority meant that Security Branch was the elite of the SAP".[17]

Chavkin has noted that, in comparison to other Commonwealth dominions being assisted by Britain to develop security services, Sillitoe's pushing of such capabilities onto the SAP represented "a step backwards in terms of trust".[18] This differentiating between equipping the SAP Special Branch as a security intelligence organisation and avoiding the creation of an independent security service – given the concerns over the politicisation of such a function – would appear to be disjointed; by 1960, its consequences would come to be felt across South Africa's intelligence dispensation and public safety paradigm.[19] Sillitoe – an enormous influence on South Africa's intelligence architecture and stance – also recommended the "establishment of an interdepartmental security organisation based on the institution of security officers in all vital departments of Government", a body that ultimately was focused on document security, rather than wider security intelligence co-ordination across government departments (a mechanism which, effectively, would not come to exist in South Africa until years later – see below).[20]

One major result from the implementation of Sillitoe's recommendations – which would have ringing consequence for decades to come in South Africa's security establishment – was that Head of Special Branch, H.J. du Plooy, became the de facto chief security and intelligence advisor to the Union government. This immediately both politicised the position and created it as the point at which power predicated on control of the security service – initially the Security Branch and later the Bureau for State Security – would be concentrated in the hands of one individual. In

1960, when du Plooy became commissioner of the SAP, it was his head of Security Branch – Henrik van den Bergh – who would succeed him as *éminence grise* of South Africa's security establishment (see below).

While the SAP's security intelligence interests grew in the 1950s, conversely, DMI became – after 1948 – a shadow of its former self, not the least because Malan's government, acting under the new defence minister, F.C. Erasmus, moved to eradicate Unionist sympathisers from its ranks; after all, DMI had been Smuts' key intelligence service to monitor and counter Afrikaner nationalists, and its files – which Erasmus moved to seize by (literally) the truck-load – contained a great deal of useful political intelligence and embarrassment for Smuts' now-Opposition United Party. By the end of this blood-letting – notably, an outcome not reflected in the same transitionary process from one governance system to another in 1990–1994 (see Chapter 8) – DMI was reduced to six full-time officers.[21] At the same time, Erasmus declared to Parliament – in August 1948 – that, first, South Africa's intelligence concerns would become "sovereign", terminating its intelligence-sharing relationship with Britain (at least, in the British direction), while – second – also noting that the UDF's intelligence would "no longer be used to spy on the Opposition", a reference to the United Party rather than the ANC or SACP.[22] As noted above, however, such "sovereignty" would be alternately pursued or ignored, depending on the issue of the day and the degree to which Pretoria's politicians required Britain's assistance – and, by the end of the 1950s with the British public's growing disgust at the policies of apartheid and the government in London finding it increasingly difficult to share intelligence with Pretoria given its internal repression, the intelligence partnership between the two countries was effectively dead. As Chavkin notes, "In the end, South Africa was unable to prevent political interference from disrupting legitimate security intelligence cooperation; the United Kingdom, on the other hand, was unwilling to continue taking the risk".[23] This support would collapse entirely in 1961 with the establishment of South Africa's republic and its withdrawal from the Commonwealth – and, tellingly for the 1970s and 1980s, push Pretoria towards a closer intelligence relationship with both Washington (which was more "realist" in assessing who its friends were in the global fight against Soviet Communism) and Paris (who had become embroiled in its own counter-revolutionary war in Algeria) as it became ever-distant from London.[24]

The ANC, the SACP and the "armed struggle"

While the ANC had existed since 1912,[25] its history of campaigning for universal civil rights and its subsequent confrontation against the state had taken the form (based on policies developed by Anton Lembede, Walter Sisulu and Mandela) of peaceful protest, civil disobedience, strikes, boycotts and similar mass action. It was only following the Sharpeville

Massacre of 21 March 1960 and the consequent banning of the ANC – alongside *Umkhonto weSizwe* ("Spear of the Nation" or MK), the ANC's guerrilla army founded in June 1961 by Nelson Mandela and organised jointly with the SACP (which had itself been illegal since the 1950 *Suppression of Communism Act*, later re-emerging underground in 1953) – the break-away Pan-Africanist Congress (PAC) and its Azanian People's Liberation Army (APLA);[26] and the African Resistance Movement (ARM)[27] under the *Unlawful Organisations Act* on 9 April 1960 that this confrontation changed. The final catalyst was the institution of the *Sabotage Act (General Law Amendment Act,* 1962) and the *Terrorism Act* (1967) which effectively, in the ANC's eyes, terminated all possibilities for peaceful means of resistance.[28] Thus, in this sense, armed struggle was seen to be the only option left open to these "liberation movements".

Black nationalist political ambitions had been turned from their previous policies of non-violent confrontation (based largely on Mahatma Ghandi's philosophy) to one of an underground guerrilla struggle in which the Afrikaner and his establishment were the target. The struggle became militarised as MK began paramilitary strikes against the establishment in the second-half of 1960, while the ANC maintained publicly a policy of non-racialism. In order to accomplish a "more developed and meaningful armed activity of the guerrilla type",[29] a professional military apparatus had to be created to form the core of future guerrilla bands; demonstration had to be made of the fact that the "militant struggle short of armed confrontation" was over; and an "effective method for the overthrow of White supremacy through planned rather than spontaneous activity" had to be developed.[30] In choosing the revolutionary route, the ANC believed that it was "one which holds out the quickest and most fundamental transformation and transfer of power from one class to another".[31]

The ANC's guerrilla strategy[32] took on the mantle of a classic revolutionary war paradigm, based largely on Mao Tse-tung's guerrilla war theories. Overall, its strategy derived primarily from two documents: the first of these is "Operation Mayibuye", a document captured during the police raid on the Rivonia Farm on 11 July 1963 which resulted not only in the capture of most of the internal command of the ANC, but also in a great triumph for the SAP Security Branch and its head, Hendrik van der Bergh;[33] the second is "Strategy and Tactics of the ANC", a position-paper adopted at the ANC's Morogoro Conference in 1969. While the SACP contributed its own thoughts to the armed struggle, this was largely, but not exclusively, done via its alliance with the ANC.

Throughout the 1960s and 1970s, the ANC/MK carried-out an insurgency-style campaign against South Africa, both inside and external to South Africa – some of it through direct action (such as bombings, armed attacks against South African military and establishment targets, the indiscriminate use of landmines and roadside bombs in rural South

Africa, and other guerrilla activities), "armed propaganda" (such as fomenting and supporting the internal unrest and uprisings across South Africa, presenting themselves as a Guevarian "vanguard of the people"), and an international campaign against South Africa. In addition, MK units fought SADF and SAP units directly across the Frontline States, most particularly in Angola. Much of the ANC/SACP's activities across the Frontline States were conducted in co-operation with the liberation movements of Namibia, Zimbabwe, Mozambique, and other Frontline States – with a legacy lasting to this day.

The 1976 Soweto Uprising caught the ANC – as much as the apartheid state – by surprise, and the ANC's leadership spent much of the next decade attempting to regain its prominence of authority as the leading liberation movement for South Africa's black and coloured populations. By the end of 1982, however, a "people's war" looked as far away as a general revolutionary takeover did. In order to inject new life into this aim, the ANC unveiled a new Politico-Military Council (PMC) to replace the old Revolutionary Council. This followed the establishment, in April 1969, of a Department of National Intelligence and Security (NAT – see Chapter 4) as part of an overhaul of the ANC's apparatus. Similarly, a Special Operations Unit and an Intelligence unit were established within MK by 1979. The PMC was designed to emulate exactly the apartheid security establishment, including its committees and sub-units, as a means of "co-ordinating the armed struggle with activity on the labour and political front". Consisting of representatives from MK, NAT, and the political and labour wings of the ANC–SACP–COSATU alliance, its first secretary was Joe Nhlanhla (later the new South Africa's first Minister of the Intelligence Services). It also provided a much more decentralised structure, compared with the ANC Revolutionary Council, in its political, military and intelligence headquarters.[34]

Cawthra has divided the ANC/SACP's struggle into four phases. In the first, from 1961 to 1965, sabotage attacks were the hallmark of operations. In the second, from 1965 to 1976, the ANC/SACP attempted to develop underground structures and train guerrillas abroad, giving little opportunity for attacks inside South Africa. The third phase, from 1976 to 1984 following the Soweto Uprising, saw an upswing in attacks on strategic targets, culminating in the strategy of "armed propaganda" following a visit to Vietnam in 1978 and the quest for a "people's war". Finally, the fourth phase, following the 1984 uprising, stressed the prospects of a general insurrection and "people's war", aiming to "make South Africa ungovernable".[35] To these phases, a fifth should be added covering the period from 1987 to 1990, when the ANC realised that it had been defeated in the military-security realm by the government's draconian security actions, and turned instead to negotiating a settlement with the apartheid government, as well as to increased emphasis on the international sphere as the forum for forcing change in South Africa. These phases will mirror largely the divisions in this study on the apartheid government's approach to intelligence in the period from 1961 to 1990.

Through its ups and downs, in the late 1980s as it was secretly negotiating with the apartheid state the ANC was forced to finally admit that despite all claims to the contrary, MK had failed to overthrow the apartheid state by force, the purpose for which it was intended. The strongest indication of this was that the ANC was never able to establish effective internal underground structures of any duration within South Africa – considered to be Phase One of revolutionary war. This much was clear when the ANC was unbanned in 1990, but was recognised long before; the ANC's "use" of the United Democratic Front (UDF) structures inside South Africa, in this sense, was *not* the same thing as establishing effective internal ANC/MK structures in the way that they intended. This failure – partly due to the ANC/SACP's continuous underestimation of the apartheid government's ability to react strongly and viciously to the "Revolutionary Onslaught"; partly due to the promotion of the armed struggle over all other activities; and partly due to the inability of the ANC/SACP in exile to reach back effectively into the country to lead a revolution – did not, as of 1990, end MK's attempts to overthrow the apartheid state (as will be discussed in Chapter 8).[36]

Establishing the national intelligence function: from Republican Intelligence to BOSS, 1961–1968

From the establishment of the Republic on 31 May 1961 – which also saw South Africa's withdraw from the Commonwealth and, consequently, from its remaining links to British intelligence – until the establishment of the Bureau for State Security (BOSS) in 1969, South Africa's intelligence dispensation could have been called a "limited" function. "Limited" only in the sense that while its whole authority and responsibility rested with one individual – Brigadier "Lang" Hendrik van den Bergh – its capabilities remained fledgling at best. This was largely due to the legacy of South Africa's growth over the first half of the twentieth century, as noted above. This all at a time when militant, often violent, opposition to the apartheid government was growing, in the form of both domestic opposition – centred on the ANC, SACP, MK and APLA (as noted above) – and international condemnation and isolation, as global opposition to South Africa grew in the aftermath of the 1960 Sharpeville Massacre and the 1964 Rivonia Trial of ANC leaders.

A fledgling security intelligence capability: Republican Intelligence

With the loss of its British feed in 1961, the new South African Defence Force (SADF) – created out of the UDF under the *Defence Act* (No. 44) of 1957, which also defined South West Africa as part of South Africa's sovereign military concerns – had to establish a full military intelligence capability. In 1957, with the growth of South Africa's continental interests, the government had established a sub-section for intelligence within the fledgling SADF with responsibilities for collection, interpretation and dissemination of intelligence of both military and strategic value. In July 1962, a Directorate of Military Intelligence (DMI, as opposed to the previous department, which had been more-or-less collapsed after 1948) was established with the above functions alongside wider military intelligence, military security, national strategic intelligence, and counter-intelligence functions.[37] At the same time, DMI's chief, General Retief, proposed that DMI would also become the "Central Intelligence Bureau" with a mandate for both military and domestic intelligence. Vorster rejected this in favour of increasing resources to the fledgling Republican Intelligence (RI) (see below).[38]

The other intelligence actor in South Africa, to this point, was the SAP Security Branch (as noted above). As the new republic developed its security and intelligence function beyond this profile in the 1960s, the principal problem becoming a growing concern was that of effective co-ordination between the intelligence functions of the SAP and SADF, as well as more widely between the two. With the establishment of a military intelligence function in the SADF, the traditional hegemony of the Special Branch over intelligence in South Africa – which had existed since 1910 effectively – was lost. They did not, however, give way easily. Instead, increased rivalry and poorly delineated mandates led to in-fighting within the intelligence community, incidents of spying on each other (an aspect that would continue into the post-apartheid era), and intelligence either not passed-on or (as was the case in the ARM's Johannesburg Station bomb investigation of 24 July 1964) claims that the rival intelligence service had not passed operational intelligence on when it had, in fact.[39] Important and relevant information was withheld by one side from the other; agents of either side were exposed; and political back-stabbing within the government arena grew. If the Republic was to develop the capability to defend itself, which in turn required a strong threat-assessment capability built on strategic intelligence analysis, such problems would have to be terminated.

In 1963, in order to alleviate these problems, the State Security Committee was formed as a central intelligence co-ordinating structure. This failed, however, to end the in-fighting between DMI and the Security Branch, partly due to ineffective administration, and partly due to the fact that it merely served to represent the security forces' interests within the Cabinet, rather than co-ordinating them – but mostly due to the dominance of Security Branch, under Van den Bergh, in all security matters. In response, three years later in 1966, the State Security Advisory Board (SSAB) was formed with the aim of introducing new measures to ensure greater co-ordination of intelligence activities, thus – it was hoped – ending the rivalries.[40] With the same problems as its predecessor, the SSAB also failed to achieve this; this was largely because Vorster did not want to end the dominance of Security Branch[41] as well as due to factors which were to be repeated over the next three decades, including insufficient co-ordinating meeting times for the heads of the security forces both with each other and with their political masters; conflicting agency perspectives; and personality clashes, particularly between Van den Bergh and all others.[42]

While RI – in conjunction with the Security Branch – moved to crush internal resistance, effectively achieving this by 1965, the intelligence dispensation had not been able to move beyond such internal security activities and become an effective intelligence service. It had achieved a small number of notable successes outside of this internal security role – notably the capture of Soviet KGB spy Yuriy Loginov in July 1967, tainted as it was by Loginov's place in the "wilderness of mirrors" created by the CIA's legendarily paranoid counter-intelligence chief James Jesus Angleton[43] – but remained by-and-large incapable of moving beyond police work. In order to compensate for the perception that the republic's intelligence needs were not being met by the fledgling DMI, on 23 August 1968, Verwoerd ordered Van den Bergh – recently appointed as SAP Commissioner – to establish a separate intelligence agency outside of the Security Branch's day-to-day interests which would be responsible for a national intelligence function.[44] Initially, this was formed around RI, established in 1963 and led by Van den Bergh; this unit, as a direct offshoot of the Security Branch, achieved little as it was hampered by the growth of DMI and failing relations with Britain – which had long supported South Africa's intelligence needs. Given RI's fledgling nature, however, throughout this time, South Africa continued to rely on a number of existing intelligence-sharing relationships – including with the United States, Switzerland, Portugal, France, Rhodesia, West Germany, and (later) Israel, as well as remnants of its relationship with the United Kingdom.[45]

The greatest problem facing RI was the fact that, unlike the CIA and SIS on which it modelled itself, it was required to conduct internal security intelligence collection and analysis, something much more akin to the FBI or MI5. Security Branch's failure to act against the sabotage and terrorist actions which had shaken the country since December 1961 was cited as one of the key reasons behind the requirement for an effective internal security intelligence organisation. The 1958 *Police Act* had allowed the Security Police to "undertake the covert collection of information in so far as this was connected with sabotage, subversion, espionage or any other matter relating to the security of the State", but this would not serve to centralise all the security forces' intelligence on internal threats.[46] RI was also seen within political circles as Van den Bergh's vehicle to political success, given his close personal relationship with Vorster. RI's existence in the shadows similarly hampered these activities, although the same qualities enhanced its foreign intelligence-gathering interests.

Therefore, a new agency which could exist outside of the shadows was required to fulfil the needs of the growing security establishment for national security intelligence on internal and external threats. Before this could be effected, however, in September 1966, Prime Minister Hendrik Verwoerd was assassinated in Parliament by a right-wing Afrikaner; Vorster, his Minister of Justice under which the SAP rested, was vaulted into the premiership. The chief of the Security Branch – Van den Bergh, an old confidante of Vorster (and fellow-internee during the Second World War) – was raised in status even further with the accession to power of his boss. Both men "made the matter of internal security their own and rapidly came to appreciate the reciprocal character of intelligence and counterintelligence";[47] this would have a lasting effect on the direction of South African security policy-formulation over the coming two decades. Of all the SAP commissioners from 1960 onwards, five (Generals du Plooy, Prinsloo, Geldenhuys, Coetzee and Van der Merwe) had all served as head of Security Branch or had Security Branch experience. For this reason, "in virtually every significant period of unrest, a former Security Branch head has occupied the post of commissioner of police".[48]

In mid-1968, the Cabinet agreed to the establishment of a centralised intelligence service; this would be the Bureau for State Security – BOSS – constituted subsequently under the 1969 *Public Service Amendment Act* and established formally on 13 May 1969.[49] To assist this, on 28 August, Van den Bergh was directed by Vorster to "commence the setting up of such an organisation",[50] and on 1 October 1968, Van den Bergh was appointed as Vorster's special advisor on state security (instead of SAP Commissioner), a new position under the prime minister's department. This was a prelude to the establishment of the new secret service directly under the prime minister.[51]

Expanding the intelligence establishment: the Bureau for State Security (BOSS)

The Bureau for State Security was officially formed on 13 May 1969 (having been established unofficially under Van den Bergh months previously), with the mandate to

> Investigate all matters affecting the security of the state, to correlate and evaluate the information collected and, where necessary, to inform and advise the government ... [and] to perform such other functions and responsibilities as may be determined from time to time.[52]

While the *Public Service Amendment Act* laid-out the establishment of BOSS, it did not formalise in statute its functions and brief.

Under the subsequent 1972 *Security Intelligence and State Security Council Act*, the mission of BOSS was defined: it would serve as the central evaluation point for all "departmental intelligence" gathered by all departments in the South African government, as well as a central focal-point for South Africa's covert, intelligence-led activities – both domestically and abroad (see Figure 2.1).[53] In conjunction with the SSC structures, it contained collection, processing, analytic, operationalisation and action elements – but it did so in parallel to DMI structures which undertook the same, in support of both South Africa's overall strategy and directed military operations (whether overt, clandestine or covert).

From its inception in 1969, BOSS grew from a small core of 500 personnel to more than 1,000 by 1978.[54] Although little is known about its actual structures, it was reported to have six departments, including Subversion, Counter-espionage, Political and Economic Intelligence, Military Intelligence, Administration, and "National Evaluation, Research and Special Studies".[55] It established close relationships with the Portuguese PIDE and the Rhodesian CIO, all with mutual interests in security in Southern Africa. During the first few years of its life, BOSS continued to benefit from a relationship – albeit an unofficial and uncomfortable one – with British and American intelligence. This relationship was based around intelligence-sharing of information relating to Communist activities of interest to both, as well as training and "best practice" methods for conducting counter-insurgency. The relationship, however, came to an abrupt halt in 1976 when the British government directed the security services and Special Branch to "stop all liaison with South Africa except in matters specially identified as directly advantageous to Britain".[56] It was clear that the British government had become too uncomfortable with this unofficial relationship and, following revelations in British papers in the 1970s, decided to terminate it.

The establishment of BOSS was not, however, without its problems: according to the Potgieter Report (see below), BOSS was to have no executive powers:

> The Bureau merely intends to collect and handle intelligence ... should any form of operational action be required as a result of the intelligence, the Bureau neither desires nor needs any powers to take such action ... operational action following upon intelligence, such as arrest, should be left to the organs of state whose statutory function this is.[57]

Therefore, BOSS was to be solely an organisation for the centralised co-ordination, assessment and dissemination of intelligence; this was not to be the case, however: BOSS would become not only an operational unit alongside the SAP and SADF but would develop into (in many respects) a private intelligence and operations organisation for the prime minister, through his protégé Van den Bergh.

Generally, the new agency engendered jealousy and anger amongst many of the fledgling "securocrats", as Vorster held it up as his favourite

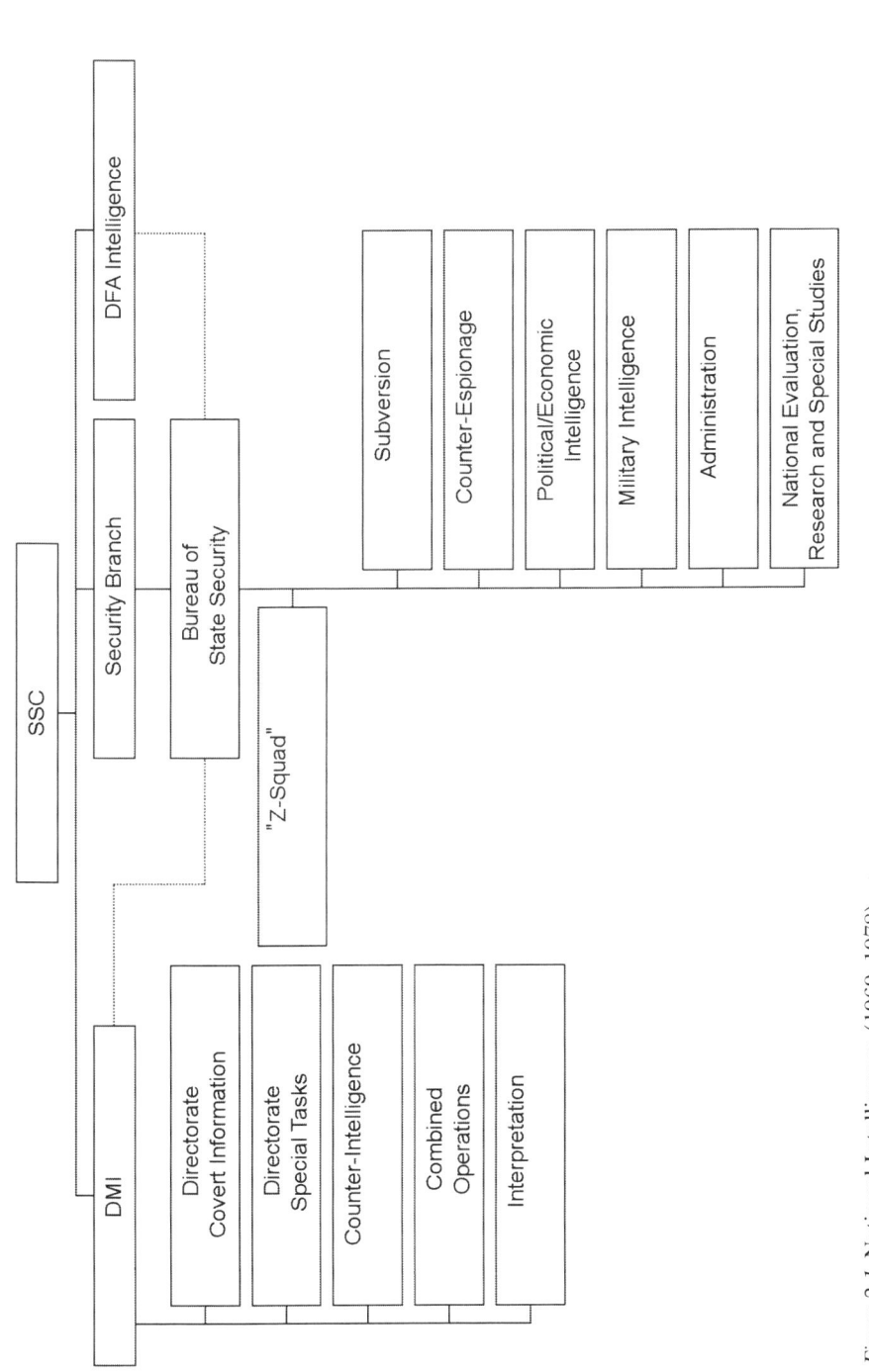

Figure 2.1 National Intelligence (1969–1978).

agency for providing the national intelligence brief, despite moves by Defence Minister Botha to enhance DMI's standing in this regard. Botha and Van den Bergh would even clash in the SSC over rival interpretations of intelligence, each drawing from their own agency. As noted by one observer, "suspicion, competition and duplication often characterise the relationship between South Africa's intelligence agencies".[58] This was made all the worse when DMI was authorised, under the 1972 Act, to "engage in covert counter-intelligence activities within the Republic".[59] Additionally, the Security Branch resented BOSS's intrusion into their area-of-operation (internal security), as well as the recruitment of Security Branch personnel; others within the government saw the new agency as a closed fraternal clique drawn from the Afrikaner *Broederbond*. Even more outrageously, DMI believed that Vorster and Van den Bergh were planning on having BOSS take control of the military intelligence function;[60] although no evidence has been found to support this, the fact that DMI's budget plunged from R830,000 in 1968 to R39,000 in 1969, while the BOSS budget rose from R4,063,000 in 1969 to R12,536,000 in 1974, gave much substance to this suspicion. BOSS even took over DMI's headquarters in 1970.[61] This rivalry reached a head when it was revealed that DMI and BOSS had begun spying on each other; mutual suspicion ran so deep that it was even alleged that BOSS was tapping Botha's telephone in 1977.[62] This would have long-term consequences for South Africa's politics.[63]

The Potgieter Commission

Clashes between the various security chiefs over the pre-eminence of each agency (Security Branch, DMI and BOSS) continued beyond the establishment of BOSS, however. To compensate for this, Vorster formed the 1970 Potgieter Commission (properly called the "Commission to Inquire into Certain Intelligence Aspects of State Security") to produce these guidelines and mission. Viewed as a "foregone conclusion" by General Hein du Toit (the deputy chief of military intelligence) it was seen to be heavily favoured towards Van den Bergh and the Security Branch, a view which its outcome supported.[64]

The Commission took as its starting-point the significant body of strategic thought growing within the apartheid security apparatus – and most particularly within DMI – concerning counter-insurgency tenets and practices. As such, its vision was restricted to appreciating the development of a national security intelligence function within such tenets, heavily predicated on what Seegers has referred to as the "follow the ANC" counter-insurgency imperative to which it stuck.[65] It noted that the continuous confusing of functions between DMI and the Security Branch were presenting a danger to the security of the state, and granted full responsibility for countering the liberation movements' "armed struggle" – or "total onslaught", a phrase used for the first time in the 1971 Report of the Potgieter Commission – to the Security Branch, both within and externally to South Africa, a result which riled DMI to no end.[66] The concept of South Africa's "national security" was also first introduced in the Potgieter Report, which – noting that "enemies were seeking to overthrow the status quo in South Africa" – went on to state that:

> Enemies were active in many spheres ... trying to attack in all fields ... [including] (i) military; (ii) political; (iii) economic; (iv) social; (v) educational; (vi) psychological; (vii) subversive; (viii) terrorism; (ix) sabotage; and (x) espionage ... An onslaught may be made on the security of the State in each of these spheres.[67]

Overall, the "National Security Strategy" of South Africa was built on two premises: first, it was "directly influenced by the ANC's strategy of revolutionary warfare"; second, it was "expected of the RSA security forces to maintain law and order and create a stable environment in which the RSA government could bring about evolutionary political change in the country".[68] Therefore, in the view of the apartheid security bureaucrats (or securocrats as they were known),[69] their strategy flowed from the decision by the ANC to conduct a revolutionary war against South Africa; the internal environment was but an offshoot of this first problem.

As a result of its report, the 1972 *Security Intelligence and State Security Council Act* was struck which laid out the establishment of the State Security Council (SSC) – "under" the Cabinet – as the operational centre of the government's security strategy, and clarified the role of BOSS as the primary security agency of the Republic.

The State Security Council and the rise of the "securocracy", 1968–1972

The SSC first came into being in 1972 following the Potgieter review of the state's security policy-making process; under the *Security Intelligence and State Security Council Act*, it was given the functions

> To advise the government with regard to (i) the formulation of national policy and strategy in relation to the security of the Republic, and the manner in which such policy or strategy shall be implemented and be executed; (ii) a policy to combat any particular threat to the security of the Republic; [and] (b) to determine intelligence priorities.[70]

Its statutory membership included the prime minister; the senior minister of the republic (if not already a member); the ministers of Defence, Foreign Affairs, Justice, and Police; the head of the SADF and SAP; the secretaries for Security Intelligence (later the head of BOSS or the NIS), Foreign Affairs, and Justice; and all others who from time to time were co-opted into its deliberations.[71]

The SSC was viewed by the securocrats as similar to the American National Security Council; while the SSC was but one of four committees reporting to the government, it was by far the most powerful. This is obvious from the fact alone that an SSC representative sat on the other three committees, and that SSC meetings took place twice a week, always before fortnightly Cabinet meetings.[72] Charged with the "formulation and implementation of national policy and strategy in relation to the security of the Republic",[73] it was the hub of discussion and planning for, initially, the "Total National Strategy" and, later, the "Total Counter-revolutionary Strategy" once the conflict moved into this phase; it also ran the National Security Management System (NSMS) which came to govern every aspect of South African society under a security paradigm underpinning and supporting this "Total Strategy" across South Africa and South-West Africa.[74] As an extremely wide range of topics could be construed as having an impact on the "security" of the state, the SSC included consideration of nearly every facet – military, economic, cultural, social, political, etc – of the republic's life. This made it *far* more powerful than the other three Cabinet committees (Cultural Affairs, Economic Affairs, and Social Affairs) and *the* place where effective decision-making and co-ordinating efforts took place within the state security structures.[75] Ultimately, how much the SSC – both as the prime instrument of the executive and as a composite of its component supporting securocrats and members – actually controlled and oversaw the operations of the security forces down to the lowest detail, thereby rendering them accountable for the actions of the intelligence services, remains subject to great contention.[76]

Overall, the securocrats intended the SSC to serve as a "means of ensuring the integrated defence of the state ... placing every single aspect of the affairs of the state under a united and coherent command".[77] Under Vorster, it met sporadically and infrequently, with its deliberations remaining largely subservient to the Cabinet, which remained the principal seat of power; BOSS and Van den Bergh were the real focus of power and influence over security affairs under Vorster, and served as the principal forum for all security-related deliberations in the first half of the 1970s. This would remain the case until Operation SAVANNAH – the invasion of Angola in 1974–1975 – required a centralised body to co-ordinate the covert activities and intelligence angles to this intervention. The SSC presented this forum. With the SADF leading the invasion – and DMI pushing both the strategic underpinnings of the intervention and the intelligence requirements to support it – Botha began to take charge of the SSC, and slowly develop its role and influence over the following years. As a result – as will be discussed in Chapter 3 – the locus of power shifted from the Cabinet to the SSC and, with it, DMI's influence began to grow. Many viewed the Cabinet under Botha as serving no more than a "rubber-stamping purpose" for SSC decisions, often not even being informed of decisions (such as cross-border raids) taken by the SSC prior to their implementation. DMI's (and, larger, the SADF's) influence on the SSC was both extensive and immediately apparent. Lieutenant-General A.J. van Deventer, one of DMI's counter-insurgency specialists and the former commander in Namibia, was the first secretary of the SSC secretariat under P.W. Botha. Appointed in 1979 and serving until 1985, he was then replaced by Lieutenant-General Pieter van der Westhuizen, the former Chief of Staff, Intelligence. Described as "the major power behind Botha's throne",[78] Van der Westhuizen served for three years until Lieutenant-General Charles Lloyd, one of the major proponents of the "win hearts and minds" (WHAM) approach to counter-insurgency, took over until 1990. Within the SSC itself, the deputy secretary throughout the mid-1980s was Major-General J.F. van Rensburg, who also ran the Strategy Branch.[79]

By the late 1970s, the SSC oversaw the covert operations of the apartheid security forces, but its bodies did not always authorise all such operations carried-out by these units; the authority for such operations came from a combination of "policies, strategies, directives, guidelines and instructions issued at the national and departmental level … specific actions and operations were authorised in departmental policies, strategies and directives".[80] Actions such as cross-border raids were justified as "self-defence" by the state; these, however, had to be approved specifically by the SSC, following guidelines established on 12 February 1979. Such actions were divided into: planned operations, cross-border raids (hot pursuit), reconnaissance actions, and clandestine operations. In respect of reconnaissance and clandestine operations, such actions would be difficult to justify in terms of international law and, in respect of clandestine operations, "the scope of these types of top secret operations are unlimited and the rules of international law make no provision for them". The SSC approved the following authorising bodies for the different categories: planned operations – the SSC; cross-border raids (hot pursuit) – head of the SADF; reconnaissance actions – head of the SADF; clandestine actions – "as a result of the far reaching implications that can flow from these types of operations, they can only be authorised at the highest level and the planning and execution must take place on a 'need to know' basis".[81]

Often, a general policy would be placed before the commanders of the security forces, allowing them great latitude in determining what type of operation should occur and who should be targeted. Thus, when it came to the everyday running of these covert units, commanders charged with eliminating the opponents of apartheid had little or no guidance on target selection. Certain killings had to be authorised at the highest levels: for instance, any operation involving cross-border activities (as many did) had to be authorised, or at least acknowledged, at the SSC level; the individual senior commanders of the security forces would give their authority for such operations to be carried-out, but would have to inform the SSC of such activities. Thus, while many of these units operated with the prior knowledge or authorisation of the senior politicians, they were structured to function independent of oversight and supply.

The SSC established a Working Committee in April 1978 directly attached to its structures, which considered intelligence and other information flowing from the state security structures; it was supported by the SSC Secretariat, established in 1979 under Lt-Gen van Deventer. Its purposes were to ensure the provision of co-ordinated intelligence to the security management system, the co-ordination of strategic planning for national security purpose, the co-ordination of the implementation of national security strategies, and the co-ordination of strategic communications.[82] In order to oversee the massive security architecture and programmes that the security management system governed, by the end of the 1970s, the SSC Secretariat included four branches (see Figure 4.2 in Chapter 4). First, the Strategic Planning Branch (SPB) (sometimes called simply the Strategy Branch), responsible for overseeing the national strategy of the apartheid government; it included the "Total Strategy Planning Cell", responsible for "construction of total strategies to counteract manifestations of 'total onslaught'" in co-ordination with the thirteen SSC Interdepartmental Committees (IDCs). Second, the National Intelligence Interpretation Branch (NIIB) was responsible for interpretation of national security intelligence, as well as providing the government with a national intelligence picture derived from materials gathered by all the services (NIS, DMI, Security Branch and Foreign Affairs Intelligence Committee); it ensured "that there is co-ordination between these departments and brings an interdisciplinary approach to intelligence evaluation".[83] Third, was the Administration Branch to run the Secretariat. Finally, the fourth branch was the Strategic Communications (*Stratkom*) Branch, which is discussed further below.

The SSC's securocrats were generally drawn from the SADF and national intelligence (BOSS and, later, the NIS); one account maintains that 70 per cent of its employees were drawn from the former and the remainder from the latter. The Secretariat was run equally by the SADF, SAP and national intelligence; in 1984, Botha stated that 56 per cent of the secretariat personnel were drawn from the NIS, 11 per cent from each of the Security Branch and Foreign Affairs, 5 per cent from the Railway Police, and 1 per cent from the Prisons Service, leaving just 16 per cent from the SADF. By the mid-1980s, the Secretariat had approximately 50 full-time employees.[84] Finally, the National Joint Operations Centre was also run by the SADF.

Intelligence and other information of interest would pass from the various branches of the Secretariat or from the National Joint Management Centre (see Chapters 4 and 7) into the Secretariat, where it would be ordered and passed to the Working Committee for consideration. This intelligence would, in turn, be co-ordinated with other intelligence and information of interest flowing from the other three Cabinet committees (which were governed by the National Welfare Management System) and then passed to the SSC for consideration during its regular or emergency meetings.

Stratkom

Perhaps the most important branch of the SSC Secretariat was *Stratkom*. Not only the nucleus of the apartheid government's counter-revolutionary strategy, it also served as the nexus between the SSC and the various covert units. Where decisions taken in the SSC were communicated, via the SSC Working Committee, to the secretariat and down through the NSMS structures, *Stratkom* devised its own policies and strategies (in co-operation with the NIIB and SPB) for confronting the "Total Onslaught" of the liberation movements. These strategies could include such tactics as "assassinations, attacks on neighbouring countries, economic sabotage, campaigns of character defamation, setting up front companies, propaganda campaigns … the entire gamut of what have come to be known as 'dirty tricks' operations".[85] Once strategies were devised, they would be sent up the chain to the SSC for approval, and then be directed from *Stratkom* to individual units or departments for implementation. In conducting "strategic communications operations", *Stratkom* was also responsible for all propaganda efforts by the state; these were defined as "the planned, co-ordinated execution of an act and/or the presentation of a message to (i) create, maintain or change attitudes, behaviour and ideologies; and (ii) neutralise opposing propaganda".[86]

By 1984, *Stratkom* had 2,650 personnel, 1,930 of which were from the SADF; it was run by Brigadier Peter MacIntyre.[87] *Stratkom* operations were implemented through what became known as "*KomOps*" (for "communications operations" or propaganda). Central to *Stratkom*'s propaganda efforts was the Bureau of Information, separated from the Department of Foreign Affairs in 1986 and reconstituted in the Office of State President (OSP).[88] The Bureau was primarily responsible for "the marketing of national goals".[89] The overall aims of *Stratkom* operations were three-fold: to "discredit the terrorist organisation in Southern Africa, as well as the Cuban and other communist surrogate forces"; to "neutralise the propaganda of the mass media inciting the RSA population against the goals and aims of the RSA government in Southern Africa"; and to "enhance the posture and image of the anti-Marxist Liberation Movements in Southern Africa". Furthermore, there was a differentiation between overt and covert *Stratkom* operations. Overt *Stratkom* comprised "the functions of informing, enhancing the image of, and monitoring State policies openly executed by Departments", while covert *Stratkom* involved exercising "a positive influence in such a way that the involvement of the State is not apparent". To achieve this, the state made "use of individuals and/or organisations which have no obvious ties with the State, but are financially assisted by the State and act according to agree-upon programmes and guidelines emanating from approved strategies".[90]

Counter-intelligence, counter-insurgency and the SAP

While the state's national security architecture and security intelligence capabilities were being developed within both BOSS and the SSC, the apartheid state's security forces were taking the fight to their opponents domestically, across Southern Africa, and internationally. While the SADF generally – and, later, DMI specifically – began to develop both clandestine and covert capabilities to support their counter-insurgency activities, it was the Security Branch and BOSS which took early leads in developing such active capabilities.

For the SAP, counter-insurgency operations had begun with the Security Branch's deployment in Namibia in March 1965; this was in order to combat SWAPO (the South West African Peoples' Organisation), based in the Ovambo region of northern Namibia, which was carrying out a war of liberation, similar to the ANC's in South Africa, through its armed wing the People's Liberation Army of Namibia (PLAN). The SAP's first operation was the successful August 1966 attack on the SWAPO's Ongulumbashe base in Namibia.[91] The SAP was not, however, prepared for a long-term counter-insurgency struggle against SWAPO; most of its training thus far had been in riot control and counter-sabotage, rather than counter-insurgency. This was even more concerning when, by the late 1960s, SWAPO operations increased with their alliance to the newly formed *Movimento Popular de Libertação de Angola* (Popular Movement for the Liberation of Angola or MPLA) in Angola.

Policing the black populations of Southern Africa had largely, previous to the 1960s, been governed by British colonial principles of indirect rule, whereby individual chiefs would be responsible – to the British authorities – for the policing and law-enforcement of their tribal lands. National police forces, and this was no different in South Africa before 1961, were mainly to ensure that "chiefs did not contravene the laws of the central government".[92] When such laws were contravened, either by the chief or his followers, this was perceived as a form of insurgency. In both South Africa and Namibia, following 1961, this type of policing began to change, as rural – and occasional urban – demonstrations began to occur; "security policing" began to dominate, where agitation and rebellion was met with immediate force.

In response to increasing disturbances in 1967, members of the SAP Riot Unit were deployed into Ovambo; while they arrested many suspected SWAPO supporters, they accomplished little in counter-guerrilla operations. These units were withdrawn in May 1968; at this time, there were no more than 600 members of the SAP Namibia Division.[93] In June 1968, the

SAP began formal counter-insurgency training; this included both instructional learning at the Police College and practical experience at the Maleoskop base outside Pretoria. Policemen were then sent to Namibia for no more than three months; in deployment, these counter-insurgency units engaged in search-and-destroy missions against SWAPO guerrillas, acting in co-operation with Security Branch personnel seconded to the counter-insurgency units for interrogation purposes.[94]

The previous year, the South African government had decided to send SAP counter-insurgency personnel to Rhodesia to combat ZANU in its alliance with the ANC. Following joint MK/ZIPRA operations in Rhodesia in August 1967, South Africa became fully involved in Rhodesian counter-insurgency operations. SAP and DMI COIN personnel were also seconded to liaise with the Portuguese in Mozambique and Angola, an approach used earlier with the French in Algeria. By 1974, at least 2,000 SAP personnel were involved in counter-insurgency operations in Rhodesia; at its peak, more than 4,000 SAP personnel were serving in Rhodesia.[95] The justification for this intervention was simple: the SAP was sent "to fight against men who originally came from South Africa and were on their way back to commit terrorism in South Africa".[96] This had been facilitated by a February 1971 agreement between the South Africans, Portuguese and Rhodesians to "establish a joint intelligence steering committee ... provid[ing] for the exchange of intelligence and security information ... and to permit clandestine executive operations on a trilateral basis".[97]

The South African government would take the lessons learned in Rhodesia, Kenya and Namibia – as well as their models for "pseudo-operations" (see below) – to heart over the 1970s and into the 1980s; the experiences of these SAP counter-insurgency personnel in Rhodesia were brought back to support training programmes for police COIN deployments into both South-West Africa and domestically. As a precursor to this, the SAP began to establish counter-insurgency units composed of both black and white personnel; these were for both the limited "hearts and minds" operations of the SAP amongst the Ovambo people (mostly free medical advice and handing out gifts) and to have the ability to operationalise intelligence collected in Ovamboland, partly in order conduct "pseudo-operations" against SWAPO.

Between 1968 and 1972, the South African Air Force and, to a lesser degree, the South Africa Army, assisted the SAP with their counter-insurgency operations; however, with the general strikes in Namibia in 1971–1972, the SAP was at a loss to meet the need for policing. Thus, the SADF became involved; by July 1973, the SAP was forced to withdraw from Namibia temporarily as political violence and the unilateral declaration of independence of Ovambo forced the full entry of the SADF into Namibia. Although a few small SAP counter-insurgency units were lifted from Rhodesia and redeployed into Ovambo in 1975–1976, the SAP were only to return in strength in January 1979 under Operation K (for *Koevoet*), a unit seen as one of the most brutal yet effective specialist counter-insurgency/-terrorism units within the security forces. Combining the intelligence-collection capabilities of the Security Branch with the instant-reaction capabilities of the Special Forces, *Koevoet* was to introduce into the Namibian (and later South African) theatre a unit akin to the Selous Scouts in Rhodesia: a fully combat-capable Security Branch counter-insurgency unit for intelligence collection and operations in Namibia (see Chapter 5).[98]

Active counter-intelligence: turning guerrillas

As Ellis points-out ironically, that where in normal societies policemen were trained to "uphold the law of the land with the minimum use of force", these SAP personnel were being trained in sabotage, assassination, counter-guerrilla warfare and the like.[99] As Vorster was fond of pointing out, "You could not fight communism with the Queensbury Rules".[100] As such, the need for immediate and effective intelligence for counter-insurgency operations was the key lesson learned by the SAP in Rhodesia; according to Ellis,

> The best and most useful intelligence was that obtained from an active guerrilla who, after capture, could be induced to give information on his unit before it had had time even to register his absence. Once such intelligence had been obtained, it would rapidly become obsolete if passed from an intelligence-gathering unit via the central chain of command to an offensive unit, giving the enemy time to move position.[101]

The Rhodesians (and, later, the South Africans) created units which acted on the intelligence that it itself gathered; the most infamous of these was the Selous Scouts, which was partially funded by the SAP Security Branch.[102] The Selous used captured and "turned" guerrillas (who became known as *askaris*, the Swahili word for fighters) operating alongside white special forces personnel in enemy territory to carry-out what were called "pseudo-operations", whereby enemy guerrillas were spoofed into believing that the *askaris* were still at liberty; as a result, large numbers of guerrillas were captured and interrogated. As *askaris* were "turned" over time, they would also provide the security forces with valuable intelligence on the up-to-date internal workings of the insurgent groups; the intelligence gained led to immediate counter-insurgency operations against the guerrillas. The ANC noted the extreme danger of such individuals to its structures, personnel and operations:

> Such infiltrators were given various tasks [as] moles to keep the regime informed on ANC strategies, tactics, intentions and the activ-

ities of leaders. Operational intelligence would also be gathered in order to locate leaders and to accumulate evidence to be used against them in trials ... infiltrators were able to influence the plans adopted by underground cells or MK units with disastrous consequences ... Later, such operational information would be used to prepare for assassinations, the capture and murder of operatives, attacks on homes or ANC installations, and so on.... Most casualties among leaders and activists both within and outside the country derived from such infiltration.[103]

This technique, building on similar British counter-insurgency tactics from Kenya, was probably the most effective in ensuring both the immediate use of tactical intelligence on the battlefield and the introduction of a creeping rot within the guerrilla structures.

As part of the implementation of counter-revolutionary warfare, the Security Branch instituted specialist units to operate against the insurgents. More often than not, these were composed of former ANC/PAC guerrillas who had been "turned" by the police to operate against their former comrades. Emulating the example of the British in Kenya as well as the Rhodesians, these "turned" guerrillas (designated "rehabilitated terrorists" but almost inevitably also referred to as *askaris*) would conduct pseudo-operations against the ANC, PAC and SWAPO, infiltrating these organisations to cause confusion and suspicion, as well as leading unsuspecting guerrillas who had been infiltrated into South Africa or Namibia to their deaths in ambushes, abductions and killings.

Once captured, the guerrilla was faced with two hard choices: either face prosecution, which would most likely result in capital punishment, or work for the security forces; many chose the latter. One of the prime techniques used to "turn" guerrillas was by forcing them to kill an ANC or SWAPO member, either through capture or assassination, in order to implicate them and prevent them from returning to their comrades; however, there were still occasionally *askaris* who did return to the ANC. Often times, the *askaris* who were believed to be considering re-defection would simply be murdered by their officers.[104] These *askaris* developed relationships with anti-government activists inside South Africa and then, following "persecution" by the security forces, "fled" the country to join the liberation movements in exile.[105]

In South Africa, this technique had originally been pioneered by SAP Colonel Att Spengler. In 1963, Spengler established a police farm at Rietvlei, south of Pretoria, at which blacks would be trained to infiltrate the ANC or PAC. Initially, "turned" guerrillas were not used, as it would be easy for their former comrades in exile to recognise them (the size of MK at this time was quite small); in the future, however, these individuals would form the core of the *askaris* used by the SAP.

Targeting opponents: the "Z-Squad"

While the Security Branch began to actively hunt South Africa's opponents in the Frontline States, BOSS also developed its direct targeting capabilities. One such activity – and later an activity pursued by other covert units in the South African security forces – was the surveillance and infiltration of anti-apartheid movements abroad, as well as of individuals engaged in activities against South Africa. Sometimes this was simply to keep tabs on the activities of these individuals and movements,[106] and sometimes – as noted previously – it was in order to target them for elimination. In the 1960s and 1970s, BOSS deployed specialist units for assassination and other covert actions both internationally and domestically; one of these units was known as the "Z-Squad".[107]

The existence of the "Z-Squad" was first confirmed by Gordon Winter, a former BOSS operative in Britain who had fled his service and, in 1981, wrote *Inside BOSS: South Africa's Secret Police*, an exposé of BOSS operations both inside and outside South Africa. The "Z-Squad" was formed in the mid-to-late 1960s, according to Winter, following an idea devised by Van den Bergh in which Security Police began to eliminate ANC sympathisers inside the townships instead of going through the costly and exhaustive procedure of bringing them to trial.[108] While this was never official policy in the Security Branch (or anywhere else at that time), the actions of several members of the Johannesburg Murder and Robbery Squad in killing such individuals inspired Van den Bergh: "there's nothing wrong with that – they kill our chaps, so why shouldn't we kill theirs? It's an eye for an eye, and the Bible says that's all right".[109] In 1979, Van den Bergh testified to the Erasmus Commission as to the effectiveness of BOSS's assassination capability:

> I can tell you here today, not for your records, but I can tell you, I have enough men to commit murder if I tell them to kill ... I do not care who the prey is. Those are the kind of men I have. And if I wanted to do something like that to protect the security of the State nobody would stop me. I would stop at nothing.[110]

These were "men who were willing to use the edge of the sword" for Van den Bergh. Originally composed of five men hand-picked by Van den Bergh, the "Z-Squad" targeted only blacks for the first years of its existence. In 1976, two "Z-Squad" members were seriously injured during a night-attack; Van den Bergh subsequently recruited two further members from the SADF Recces to replace the injured members.[111]

One of the first reported deaths in which BOSS's involvement was suspected was that of Keith Wallace, a former correspondent of the London *Daily Mail* who was alleged to be a long-term BOSS agent. According to one account, Wallace began to work in London in the late 1960s to observe anti-apartheid activists; his relationship with Van den Bergh was, however, "stormy". In 1969, during one of Wallace's visits back to South Africa, Van den Bergh threatened Wallace with dismissal for disobeying orders; Wallace maintained that he would go to the press upon his return to London and expose BOSS's activities there. Shortly after, on 31 January 1970, he was found dead in a London elevator shaft – it was believed that the "Z-Squad" silenced him.[112]

Another assassination was Abraham Tiro, who was killed with a letter-bomb on 1 February 1974 in Gaborone. Tiro had been a leading member of the South African Students' Organisation (SASO) following his expulsion from University of the North in 1972 and from a Soweto high school in 1973 for inciteful behaviour. Fleeing South Africa ahead of an arrest warrant in 1973, he began training activists in Botswana for infiltration back into South Africa; according to Winter, BOSS was aware of his activities and eliminated him.[113] On 12 February 1974, John Dube (better known as Boy Mvemve) was also killed by a letter-bomb in Lusaka. Mvemve had been a founder-member of MK and responsible for planting at least two bombs outside Johannesburg post offices during the 1960s. The "Z-Squad" were believed to have killed him as well; significantly, the letter-bomb had been posted in Lusaka. Other opponents killed by similar methods included Dr Eduardo Mondlane, the former head of FRELIMO, in Tanzania in 1969, and Matt Chitenda, also a FRELIMO leader, in Lusaka in 1971.[114] Finally, the assassination of white academic Dr Richard Turner was believed to have been the product of a "Z-Squad" hit. A lecturer in political science at the University of Natal, Turner was an outspoken critic of apartheid who conveyed this message to his students; for this, he was banned in February 1973. In January 1978, he made indications that he was about to flee South Africa; on 8 January, he was shot by a sniper inside his house. Later, it was alleged that a BOSS agent named Martin Dolinchek was responsible for the killing.[115]

Conclusion

By the early 1970s, Pretoria's intelligence services were maturing, evolving from their security policing origins, missteps and fratricidal in-fighting, and now with the structures and formations which would eventually drive forward the "Total National Strategy" in place, including all intelligence support and activities. As the ANC/SACP gathered strength in exile and formulated a strategy for overthrowing the apartheid state – while, at the same time, the South-West African People's Organisation (SWAPO) launched a guerrilla war against South Africa in South-West Africa (Namibia), and the insurgency against white-minority rule in Rhodesia heated-up – South Africa's governance structures became pinned to national security considerations. While the SSC and BOSS became the hubs around which, respectively, security policy and operational security considerations played-out, other agencies continued to press the dominance of their domains. As BOSS became the dominant security agency domestically, as well as being responsible for overseas intelligence collection and the central analytic and assessments processes, Defence Minister Botha promoted DMI's role as the leading "strategic thinking and formulation" entity in the government. Increased to a division of the SADF in 1970, with joined-up Military Intelligence and Counter-intelligence wings, DMI's dominance of the strategic theory behind the counter-insurgency (later counter-revolutionary warfare) strategy – which came to underpin not only South Africa's domestic security campaign but also informed its strategies in South-West Africa and Rhodesia (and later Angola and the other Frontline States) – led to the rise of not only significant strategic defence-oriented thinking in DMI but also to the rise of an intelligence and special operations infrastructure in the SADF which grew into one of the most complex operational intelligence and clandestine/covert action capabilities ever seen. Replicating a number of other countries' counter-insurgency strategies, the South African government devised its "Total National Strategy" to fight the growing ANC/SACP insurgency, and operationalised the strategy through a growing number of covert "specially tasked" units (such as the BOSS "Z-Squad") developed to fight the insurgency.

When, in 1973, the SAP Security Branch lost the operational lead for COIN operations in South-West Africa – which it had been pursuing since 1965, alongside supporting COIN operations in Mozambique and Rhodesia – due to their limited operational COIN capabilities in the face of both the rising SWAPO threat and insurrections in Ovamboland, DMI-influenced SADF units were given the lead COIN role in South-West Africa, opening South Africa's regional counter-insurgency campaign and dramatically increasing the need for operational and tactical intelligence derived from across Southern Africa. As will be discussed in Chapter 3, the lessons learned, strategies composed and units developed in these regional conflicts outside of South Africa would – by the beginning of the 1980s – be internalised to South Africa as the domestic struggle against apartheid increased dramatically from the mid-late 1970s onwards.

3 "Total Strategy" and the "securocratisation" of the government, 1972–1978

> Intelligence is too damn important and too damn dangerous to be left to the spies or [to the] government.
>
> William Colby (quoted in 1996)

In Chapter 2, the development of the apartheid state's national security architecture and its capabilities to conduct both security intelligence and counter-insurgency activities was outlined. To support all of these elements, and to ensure that the state's entire intelligence capability was geared towards supporting it, a national security strategy was required. This would form initially around the "Total National Strategy" and later, following a significant evolution in both the state's security operations and the ANC's revolutionary onslaught, around a "Total Counter-revolutionary Strategy". As this chapter discusses, these strategies – symbiotically – both became the key determinants of the intelligence requirements of the state, at both operational and strategic levels, and were in turn driven and, to a great extent, determined by the nature of the intelligence dispensation developed by the state. In this sense, the intelligence-led national security strategy of apartheid South Africa became self-sustaining, almost paradoxically losing – it will be argued – the ability to see outside of the security paradigm created by this intelligence paradigm.

The rise of P.W. Botha and the securocracy

By the end of the 1970s, South Africa was facing increasing international isolation, an economic crisis internally, a socio-political and ideological challenge from the liberation movements, and a security threat both internally and externally. In this atmosphere, the idea of a "Total National Strategy" gave the securocrats and politicians an approach that, in theory, could find solutions to all the problems facing the state. The champion of this strategy was P.W. Botha, who – as he rose to power – brought with him the ideas of DMI's security strategy into the premiership. DMI's strategists, who were engorged on the foreign COIN doctrines they had studied, were itching to implement in both South Africa and South-West Africa. While this study will not examine these theories in any depth, it is worth noting that the apartheid securocrats developed their notions of counter-revolutionary warfare and strategy – including its socio-political, economic and military-security elements – within the "Total National Strategy" largely on the basis of the theoretical constructs of André Beaufre, Robert Thompson, David Galula, John McCuen and Samuel Huntington.[1] These theorists provided the central belief, to the securocrats, that intelligence is the primary and central asset for counter-revolutionary warfare – and, while the parameters for these evolved from colonial policing intelligence methods, the highly specialised nature of the South African intelligence architecture was aimed at countering the effects and operations of the ANC and other liberation movements. As such, these theorists were all read widely within the South African security establishment, but relied upon much more heavily by Military Intelligence and the Special Forces. The Security Branch, while recognising the use of such theorists, drew the majority of their lessons for the future from their experiences in the conflicts in Rhodesia and elsewhere in southern Africa. Thus, South African counter-revolutionary warfare doctrine – and the entire basis for the apartheid-era intelligence dispensation and the role it played in supporting the state's strategies – emerged from two not-altogether-complementary schools: that of the theorists and strategists versus those of the policemen who had served in other conflicts.

As a result of this championing, however, DMI rose in power and influence over the SAP and BOSS – a factor which would have serious long-term consequences for both the state and its national security strategy. At the same time, the intelligence processes and structures championed by each of the three services were either championed or shoe-horned into this strategic outlook – with most conforming to the classical COIN approach to intelligence, and very few elements attempting to look outside of this paradigm, at least until the mid-1980s.

Botha's rise and the influence of DMI

By the time Prime Minister Verwoerd appointed Botha to the position of minister of defence in 1966, the SADF had begun to develop as a force quite different from its predecessor, the Union Defence Force. At the same time, the SADF's rivals in the civilian and police intelligence services (as manifested in Republican Intelligence – later BOSS – and the SAP Security Branch) were expanding their influence on the political process, as guided by their masters. Botha's appointment, in April 1966, marked "the birth of the SADF as a corporate actor in domestic politics".[2] Before this, the defence force had been constrained by budgetary neglect, economic crises, political interference in its affairs and the absence of a clearly defined professional identity. The biggest constraint had been its reliance on the British (and other Western states) for materiel, training and intelligence. Much of this had already begun to change by the time Botha became defence minister, such as the termination of the reliance on Britain, but the SADF was still growing as an institution. To reflect these changes, Botha restructured the chain-of-command in the security forces, most significantly perhaps in the SADF. In the mid-1960s, the Defence Staff Council replaced the Supreme Command of the SADF in a move designed to "reflect the influence of USA [sic] military management styles".[3]

By 1975, the beginning of Operation SAVANNAH (the invasion of Angola),[4] Botha had begun to streamline the SADF. This would be completed in later years when – to combat, first, the "Total Onslaught" and, later, the "Revolutionary Onslaught" – the South African Army was divided into three separate functions: conventional forces, counter-insurgency forces, and support/training elements. This move was also driven by the assimilation of the various counter-insurgency theories being propagated by DMI. While the conventional forces were generally involved in the conflicts in Namibia and Angola, the counter-insurgency forces – generally comprising the territorial force inside South Africa – were divided into ten regional commands inside South Africa. Thus, unlike the "border war" in Namibia, "area defence" was key inside South Africa. These counter-insurgency forces, designed to support SAP actions, were composed of part-time SADF forces found in the Commandos and Citizen Force units (the basic reserve force, centred on the light infantry battalion); these were backed up by permanent force members who would respond to crises as and when.[5] These part-time units were given basic counter-insurgency training, including "win hearts and minds" training, for their operations in the rural and urban areas of the country. In certain cases, some units were given specialised anti-terrorist counter-insurgency training, such as that given to the "Hammer" units in the Eastern Cape in the mid-1980s. The significance of this separation of function was felt in a number of different ways. First, it allowed for the complete development of the "Area Defence Policy" (known later as the National Security Management System in its entirety); second, it led to the development of a separate corporate identity (the securocrat notion) in the SADF, as well as in the upper echelons of the security forces as a whole; and, third, it led to the structural expansion of the SADF as a force. Between 1975 and 1990, the SADF more than doubled in size, reaching nearly 100,000 by the end of the 1980s, with 325,000 in the Citizen Force and Reserve.[6]

The importance and significance of this period of Botha's rise cannot be underestimated: from 1975 to 1978, South Africa was suddenly faced with a number of very serious security threats and concerns which had developed, in some cases literally, overnight. The first of these was the growing concern by the security forces about the whole of the Southern African sub-continent. For the SADF, the failure of their strategy to both block the accession to power in Luanda of the MPLA, a Marxist rebel organisation supported from Moscow, following the Portuguese coup in April 1974, and prevent the development of permanent SWAPO bases in southern Angola alongside their MPLA allies, meant now that South Africa was presented on two sides (Angola over Namibia and Mozambique on South Africa's borders) with hostile Marxist governments who were willing to provide shelter and support to the guerrilla movements opposed to South African rule.

The second was the massively increased crisis that this decolonisation process had produced for South Africa's strongest ally in the region, Rhodesia: the independence of Mozambique immediately meant that anti-Rhodesian guerrilla forces could seek haven in and garner support from this country, too, as well as Zambia. Should Rhodesia "fall" to a guerrilla organisation friendly to South Africa's liberation movements, South Africa's own security would be drastically threatened by the loss of – with the end of the Portuguese colonies – the cordon sanitaire upon which it had long counted to hold far off any direct threat to the state.

It is of great note that much of the SADF's counter-insurgency expertise, especially in covert operations, was gained in the experiences of those members of the SADF and SAP who served with the Rhodesian Security Forces – operating alongside the Rhodesian Light Infantry, the Rhodesian Special Air Service, the British South Africa Police and, especially, the Selous Scouts of the Central Intelligence Organisation[7] – during their operations in the 1960s and 1970s against insurgents throughout southern Africa. Equally, the South Africa intelligence establishment benefited greatly from those members of the Rhodesian Security Forces – including all the above – who, upon Rhodesia's transition to Zimbabwe in 1980, crossed into South Africa (under Operation Winter) to join the SADF or SAP and continue prosecuting the anti-apartheid/anti-Communist war from there. This was not surprising, considering not only Pretoria's very close co-operation with Salisbury in like-minded policies, but also as DMI was a principal source of funding for Rhodesian COIN activities and structures.[8] Some of these elements – most particularly, the covert ones – formed the basis for most of the covert intelligence units of the 1980s, including units known alternately as "D40", "Barnacle", the "Civil Co-Operation Bureau", the "Directorate of Covert Collection", and other operational intelligence units which supported South Africa's policy of directed assassination of its opponents.[9] This would, as will be discussed in Chapters 4–7, have a strong impact on both the personnel and tactics of the South African security forces, and especially on their willingness to use assassination and counter-guerrilla operations to "deal with" the personnel and structures of the liberation movements.

Internally, however, the National Party government believed that it had "defeated black radicalism and communism for good, and that all that remained was to encourage the development of a separate system of black politics, to be channelled through institutions designed by planners and politicians in Pretoria". This was to be known as "separate development" whereby all blacks would nominally live in homelands (or bantustans) depending on their tribal origin.[10] The aim of this was to prevent Africans from "causing trouble" to the whites by placing them under African collaborators in the homelands; this would decentralise the need for repression.

This was not to be, however; the third new threat was the 1976 mass uprising in Soweto, which instantly provided thousands of new recruits for MK and, to a much lesser degree, APLA:[11] in the months following the Uprising, thousands of young black South Africans attempted to leave the country illegally to join the liberation movements in exile and undertake training to become part of the armed struggle. This, too, radicalised those who stayed in South Africa (the overwhelming majority) and gave rise to a new level of instability in the townships and throughout various regions of the republic. The SAP were unable to deal effectively with this through "traditional" policing means and began to introduce elements of their counter-insurgency operational doctrine (in the form of "urban counter-insurgency") inside South Africa for the first time. At the same time, the SAP enhanced its "rural counter-insurgency" capabilities throughout the country. In response, Police Minister Jimmy Kruger ordered that the riots "must be broken ... police should react more drastically and with a heavier hand, which would result in more deaths".[12] It was obvious that the state was finding it difficult to handle the opposition.

Taking all of these factors into consideration, between 1975 and 1978, South Africa was indeed confronting a radically new security situation both internally and externally. To meet this concern, an effective strategy had to be developed which would (in the minds of the politicians and securocrats) bring together all the resources of South African society to combat these threats both inside South Africa, in Namibia, against any threat to the Republic's security emanating from the Southern African region, and against its enemies abroad.

The "Information Scandal" and the triumph of Botha and DMI

In 1977–1978, with the "Information Scandal"[13] rocking the South African political establishment – and, consequently, throwing the security establishment into temporary chaos – the SADF began to position itself to be not only the dominant security force (as it, generally speaking, had already become) within the new government, but more importantly the dominant influence on policy-making and -implementation. To ensure this, the SADF had to make sure that their vision of the conflict and the means to combat it was accepted within the national security establishment of the government. This saw a massive change in the politics of South Africa: as Sparks states,

It was the start of a massive militarisation of the South African government, indeed of the whole country. Increasingly the concept of security began to supersede ideology as the dominant political theme, the engine of white mobilisation. More and more it became the new ideology. More and more the locus of decision making and power shifted from the party to the military-security establishment.[14]

The guarantee that this would be so was the triumph of Botha as the new prime minister on 28 September 1978, and the accession to the Cabinet of Magnus Malan as the new defence minister in 1980. Significantly, the "Information Scandal" also signalled the end of the "internationalists" in the National Party government – Vorster, Van den Bergh, and Mulder all resigned – who believed that "it was imperative for South Africa to overcome its pariah status and improve and deepen its ties with the West and conservative African states", while the twin calamities of Angola's collapse and the Soweto uprising had brought white South Africa to the point that it had to "adapt or die". Yet the country – and the apartheid security establishment – was about to head in the opposite direction: Botha's rise brought the military's view to the fore, with some observers believing this constituted effectively a military coup in South Africa, supported by the National Party caucus.[15] As noted by Schrire, however, this was not a "military coup" but an "executive one" – "Botha's government remained structurally and in reality under his political leadership".[16]

It would not just be around the military, however, that Botha would develop his strategy. Using the government (particularly the Office of the Prime Minister) as an institution, Botha developed a "tripartite partnership" which involved the security establishment, the government, and – most importantly – the Department of Constitutional Planning and Development (DCPD), reorganised and resuscitated following the Vorster era.[17] This approach, which Botha held up as a "Total National Strategy" – reflecting the military's push for such a strategy in consecutive *White Papers on Defence* throughout the 1970s, would see to all the needs of the South African state over the coming decade. The security establishment would see to fighting the "Total Onslaught" facing South Africa internally and throughout the region, the DCPD would develop and implement the reform programme which Botha envisioned would solve the socio-political challenge apartheid faced (this would become known as "reform apartheid"), and the government would ensure that the National Party and Botha exerted the influence and pressure where needed throughout the bureaucracy to see through both of these programmes while maintaining the "sham of democracy".[18] In this sense, Botha attempted to "graft the preliminary reform initiatives broached by his predecessor onto the SADF's strategic doctrine".[19]

Developing a "Total National Strategy"

Thus emerged the "Total National Strategy", the "product of a mind-set ... realist, pragmatic, *verlig*, and African".[20] As Williams has pointed out,

> In the chaos and confusion that surround the in-fighting of the 1976–1978 period it was the "Total Strategy" doctrine that was to rise like a clear note above the foray. Its public statements, its Defence White Papers, its media releases and its seminars all emphasise the necessity of political reform, sound economics and a strong military posture as a pre-requisite for stability.[21]

This strategy was based around an orthodox counter-insurgency strategy, defined by Alden as "the introduction of a 'dynamic policy of change' engineered by the state while simultaneously engaging in police work based on an extensive intelligence network".[22] This would differ significantly from the later "Total Counter-revolutionary Strategy" in which "police work" would be replaced by direct lethal military action against the perpetrators of the "Revolutionary Onslaught" and their supporters.

"Total National Strategy" summarised

As noted above, the policy of "Total National Strategy" emerged under Botha during the period of 1971–1975, culminating in its pronouncement in the 1977 *White Paper on Defence*. Alongside Botha, its strongest proponent was SADF chief General Magnus Malan. As noted in Chapter 2, the conceptualisation of national security flowed from the 1971 Potgieter Report and the 1972 *Security Intelligence and State Security Council Act*. From this flowed the "Total National Strategy", first mentioned in the 1973 *White Paper on Defence*, which emphasised the "interaction and inter-dependence of three basic elements: internal policy, foreign policy and defence policy".[23] Subsequently, the state recognised in the 1975 *White Paper on Defence* that it was faced with a "Total Onslaught" by the liberation and revolutionary forces confronting it, both in South Africa and regionally, and that the only possible response to this was to prepare a "Total Strategy" to confront it. Characterising the threat of this "Total Onslaught" as deriving from "its only actual physical expression in the existence of armed elements of banned political organisations accommodated in neighbouring states", it believed that "the threat to the RSA within the ambit of the communist international battle for world domination is also related to the increase and establishment of communist influence and presence in Southern Africa". This supported "attempts [by the banned political organisations] to infiltrate the RSA for the purposes of terrorism, sabotage and subversion with a view to overthrowing the existing order".[24] This threat-perception left little room for questioning.

The 1977 *White Paper on Defence* outlined the "Total National Strategy" as involving "the comprehensive plan to utilise all the means of the state according to an integrated pattern in order to achieve the national aims within the framework of the specific policies".[25] Stating that "the process of ensuring and maintaining the sovereignty of a state's authority in a conflict situation has, through the evolution of warfare, shifted from the purely military to an integrated national action", the conclusions of the Potgieter Commission were further solidified in the 1977 *White Paper* in which it was stated that

> The resolution of a conflict in the times in which we now live demands interdependent and co-ordinated action in all fields – military, psychological, economic, political, sociological, technological, diplomatic, ideological, cultural, etc.... It is therefore necessary that a Total National Strategy be formulated at the highest level.[26]

Significantly, this would also mean the entry of the military into policy-making.

This was a blatant acceptance of the theories of not only Beaufre who, it will be recalled, argued for a "total strategy" to combat any insurgency, but also of similar ideas put forward by McCuen and Thompson; intrinsically, it was a total acceptance of Beaufre's theory of international relations in which political, economic, military and psychological manoeuvres were all strategic manoeuvres. Taking this view further, proponents of the "Total National Strategy" within the SADF believed that the threat to the Republic derived directly from the Soviet Union, which was "waging a total war against South Africa"; there could be no distinction between "internal" and "external" in this conflict, where military and non-military threats blended into one.[27] Therefore, in the context of the South African conflict, this threat did not come from just the liberation and revolutionary movements that were attempting to effect change in South Africa, but also from the states that surrounded South Africa with their communist-inspired liberation movements, especially those movements which were based in Namibia and Angola. In the view of Botha and the securocrats, communist take-overs of Angola, Mozambique and Rhodesia were but stepping-stones to the richest prize of all: South Africa. In order to meet this threat, a method had to be devised which would ensure that all aspects of the state would be geared towards meeting these threats.

No appreciation of South Africa's intelligence history in the 1970s and 1980s can be complete without understanding how (as is noted above) the intelligence dispensation was both child and parent to the national security strategy. In this sense, the apartheid state's intelligence services were the strategic and intellectual godfathers to this strategy and its implementation – the securocrats who controlled the apartheid state, and used the intelligence dispensation to both control that state and target the state's opponents with increasing directness. The first step in this direction had already been taken with the 1972 establishment of the SSC, one aim of which was the co-ordination of a national security doctrine. The next step would be the implementation of what Thompson and McCuen had both argued for, a "national war council" which would co-ordinate and support decision-making and operations at every level. This would become the National Security Management System (NSMS), which will be discussed in Chapters 4–6.

While this paints a picture of the higher-level functions of the intelligence services and their influence on the national strategy, at the operational level and in order to implement the policies of the "Total National Strategy" and "Total Counter-revolutionary Strategy" programmes, the South African security establishment developed a number of highly specialised units within the security structures which were dedicated to the active (and sometimes pro-active) elimination by whatever means necessary of opposition to the apartheid state, both domestically and internationally. These covert structures – which came to be known colloquially as the "Third Force" – were the evocation of the state's intelligence capabilities in action, and reflected one of the most comprehensive cover, intelligence-led counter-insurgency capabilities seen in the twentieth century.

Origins of the "Total National Strategy"

The implementation of the "Area Defence Policy" as part of the reorganisation of the SADF in the late 1960s led directly to the development of, first, the policy of "Total National Strategy" in the early 1970s and, later, the NSMS as the national structural means of overseeing the defence of the Republic against all threats and the responses to those threats. The NSMS was not solely a means for managing this "Total National Strategy"; it was, as Roherty has pointed out, "a revolution in its own right, reflecting the management style of the new prime minister [P.W. Botha], and, more important, the urgency of reform in yet another aspect of Afrikanerdom".[28]

This new "Area Defence Policy" had been in place for many years in the form of Territorial Commands and Military Command Areas generally before Botha reorganised it. However, the new structures placed the emphasis on increasing the intelligence-gathering and intelligence-processing capabilities of the regional security force commands, as well as expanding their operational and logistical capabilities for counter-insurgency operations.[29] As part of this initiative, counter-insurgency training (both rural and urban) became a part of both National Service and Commando/Citizen Force training; by the end of the 1970s, counter-insurgency doctrine and strategy was integral to the training cycles of the SADF.[30] This new training partly led to the expansion of offensive counter-insurgency operations in the mid-1980s, including such operations as

"Hammer" (as discussed in Chapter 6). The most significant aspects of this restructuring was the reorganisation of Military Intelligence:

> DMI was to become Botha's political weapon in his struggles against his adversaries both through its clandestine monitoring of political rivals within the state and the National Party and in the role it played in elaborating and popularising the themes associated with the "Total Strategy" project.[31]

The first public discussion of what was to become "Total National Strategy" emerged during a discussion by General Fraser at the Centre for International Politics at the University of Potchefstroom in December 1968. During this talk, Fraser outlined the future South African counter-insurgency policy, including strong references to the political aspects of such a strategy. This comprised only, however, the military aspects of counter-insurgency. Fraser emphasised time and again that "counter-insurgency must be a carefully co-ordinated system of actions – political, economic, administrative, psychological, police and military",[32] with the political as key. To this end, "Total National Strategy" under Botha would offer four components. The first was a reform package aimed at "resolving some of the structural contradictions of apartheid" which had emerged in the 1970s and at "black resistance which had emerged as a result"; the second was "using the concept of 'reform' to involve sectors in the South African society previously hostile to the National Party government", such as English business or the anti-apartheid press, in the stance against the "Total Onslaught". The third component was "co-opting a class of 'insiders' and using it as a buffer against the frustrations of the vast mass of 'outsiders' " as a means of ensuring total control over society; this was possible because it was generally believed in security circles that "only a small radical elite of 'agitators', 'communists' and 'terrorists' existed, who should be killed", and that the majority of the population was neutral or, at least, not supportive of the liberation struggle. Finally, the last component was the "reorganisation and rationalisation of the state to ensure a more co-ordinated and state-wide approach to formulating strategy".[33] Intelligence – both the product generated by all three agencies, and the national intelligence structures – would support and drive the whole of this.

This strategy would come to be known as "reform apartheid". While it aimed to respond to all the problems perceived by Botha and the securocrats within South Africa, two very serious problems would limit its impact over the proceeding 15 years. The first was that the strategy would never answer effectively (although within the limited mind-set of its implementers it attempted to) the "national political question" of the exclusion of Africans from political power; reflecting on the absolute need to find an alternative political solution to that presented by the liberation movements which would capture the support of the population – as outlined clearly not only in every theory of counter-insurgency but, significantly, also in those examples (such as Malaya) of the successful defeat of insurgencies to which the South African securocrats looked for example. As long as apartheid continued to exist in *any* form, the black majority of the country would be opposed to the government. This was even further exacerbated by the increasing militancy of the black working-class. From the early 1970s, black workers (the heart of South Africa's industrial economy) began to organise themselves, resulting in a series of disastrous strikes between 1972 and 1975, centred on demands for political representation and better conditions. The ideas of this workers' militancy would, in many respects, fuel the greater uprising of Soweto in 1976.[34]

For all these reasons, the National Party's counter-revolutionary strategy could never succeed in the form attempted. The second problem was that, regardless of their acknowledgement that counter-insurgency is 80 per cent political and 20 per cent military, the security elements within both the SADF and SAP appeared unable to confront opposition to the state in any other way except using a heavy-handed military/security repression approach; as noted already, the intelligence picture contributed to this shortcoming. Thus, even in those instances where the socio-political reform aims of the state may have been accepted by the population, this approach by the SADF and SAP undermined – indeed, undid – all such potential successes. This would come back to haunt the security forces by the end of the 1980s.

With the implementation of "Total National Strategy" as the new government's security doctrine, the creation of the national architecture to guide this doctrine began. It was, however, to grow partly out of the downfall of BOSS and the ascendancy of DMI.

The development of DMI

The largest and most influential intelligence agency under apartheid, DMI emerged by the end of the 1970s as the dominant security force element in the NSMS and as the chief securocrat advisor on the policies surrounding the "Total National Strategy". Its significance and influence grew as its chief patron became prime minister in 1978: Botha raised its power above that of BOSS – the favourite of Vorster – and made it the arbiter of state security policy and its implementation in the coming decade. Indeed, as Botha's clique of DMI supporters saw it, BOSS had been "guilty of delivering grossly inadequate 'intelligence'" and that the civilian bureaucrats running the state's security apparatus around the SSC and BOSS were "prone to corruption and ineptitude". As such, Botha saw the need to revamp the SSC and related structures – to support the emerging "Total National Strategy" paradigm – around DMI capabilities and personnel.[35]

As DMI developed throughout the 1970s and into the 1980s, it began to expand its powerbase and capabilities, eventually including all manner of operational capacity far beyond "traditional" intelligence collection. DMI began to function as a force unto itself, both gathering intelligence and acting on it, eliminating the transparency inherent in divided security functions. Throughout this period, its capabilities came to include covert intelligence gathering, clandestine operations (through the Recces, for example), covert operations, contra-mobilisation and the training of surrogate forces, assassination, disruption and destabilisation functions, and counter-intelligence (including counter-espionage).

To understand the power and capabilities that DMI developed before and during this period (from the mid-1970s to the early 1990s when its power was curbed by De Klerk), an examination of the background and development of military intelligence in South Africa is essential.

The expansion of DMI

In the early-to-mid-1970s, DMI was relatively small, with a staff of less than 100, and was believed to be composed of five subsections: besides the Directorates Covert Collection (DCC) and Special Tasks (DST), these included Counter-Intelligence, Combined Operations, and Interpretation. From the late 1970s, it underwent significant expansion, so much so that, by the end of the 1980s, its staff complement was believed to have been a few thousand – partly due to its recruitment of personnel from sectors outside the military, including civilian and police intelligence.

Following the 1978 Coetsee Commission's investigations into the future of the intelligence brief in the South African security forces (as will be discussed in Chapter 4),[36] DMI's structures underwent a significant expansion and reorganisation, the most significant being a structural distinction between strategic and tactical intelligence, with the latter function being organised into parallel staff divisions within each service of the SADF. Following this reorganisation and Coetsee's recommendations, DMI developed three distinct capabilities: strategic intelligence, tactical/operational intelligence and special operations. The division was expanded exponentially to create four new intelligence directorates and, in the early-to-mid-1980s, a separate covert action wing (distinct from the generally clandestine activity of the Special Forces "Recces") to both enhance intelligence collection (through the DCC) and to expand its ability to act on that intelligence (through the Civil Co-operation Bureau – CCB – of Special Forces).[37] These four new directorates included the DCC; Sub-Division, Military Intelligence (SDMI) for strategic intelligence; Sub-Division, Counter-Intelligence (SDCI); and Sub-Division, Communications Operations (after 1985, Sub-Division Intelligence Operations – SDIO).[38] An Intelligence Staff Council was responsible for the co-ordination of policy and comprised: CSI (Chair); Chiefs of Staff Army, Air Force, Navy and Medical Intelligence; chief directors of Military Intelligence, Counter-Intelligence and Intelligence Operation; and the director of the DCC.

In gathering and disseminating strategic intelligence, SDMI was further divided into a number of directorates and "desks", each with specific responsibilities; these included Directorate Southern Africa, which was divided into three sections (West Front: Angola and Namibia; East Front: Zimbabwe, Zambia, Mozambique, Tanzania and Malawi; Home Front: Botswana, Lesotho, Swaziland, Homelands, Subversion, Church Affairs and Terrorism), and the Directorate Rest of Africa/Middle East/Superpowers for most of the rest of the world of direct interest to DMI. There was also established a Directorate Tactical Intelligence, a Directorate Electronic Warfare, a Directorate Foreign Relations, and a Military Information Bureau.[39] The Directorate Foreign Relations oversaw the placement and co-ordination of defence attachés posted abroad while the Military Information Bureau was responsible for determining how much information was shared with the public and in what manner.

Tactical intelligence would be provided by the post-1978 introduction of intelligence elements to each service of the SADF. These included the new Directorates of Chief of Army Staff Intelligence, Chief of Naval Staff Intelligence, Chief of Air Staff Intelligence, and Chief of Medical Staff Intelligence (the South African Medical Service being a separate service of the SADF). The SADF's Signals Intelligence Unit was also included in the tactical intelligence matrix.[40] The intelligence-gathering activities of these directorates were co-ordinated via the Directorate Tactical Intelligence (after 1985, Functional Intelligence) of SDMI, but all maintained a high degree of autonomy, as will be seen with regard to Army Intelligence and Medical Intelligence.

For counter-intelligence operations, SDCI took a very broad interpretation of forces opposing the state, including not only the liberation movements but also the various civic and religious organisations arrayed against apartheid. Thus, SDCI (which was also responsible for vetting and security within the SADF) targeted these organisations for counter-intelligence penetration; its information was fed into the DMI brief as a whole and included in state-level (i.e. SSC and NSMS) decision-making regarding targeting for elimination or neutralisation. It was also responsible for penetrating foreign intelligence services as well as providing military counter-espionage capabilities to the state.[41]

The Sub-Directorate of Intelligence Operations was responsible for "special intelligence projects", including all communications operations (*KomOps*) both domestically and internationally, psychological warfare and propaganda; most importantly, SDIO housed DST 1 and DST 2.[42] SDIO would, subsequently, be closed in 1993 following the Khan Commission's report on all SADF covert projects, many of which were then terminated.[43] Alongside the DCC – responsible for conducting covert operations both inside South Africa and Namibia, and throughout the Frontline States (see

54 *"Total Strategy" and "securocratisation"*

Figure 3.1) – the SDIO was the most important (counter-insurgency and counter-intelligence experts would argue) element in the DMI structure.

DMI, therefore, was one of the central hubs of the apartheid state's covert operational intelligence capabilities, either directly (through the DCC or DST) or indirectly (through entities such as the Army Intelligence "Hammer" unit). Over the next eight years, DMI as a whole developed four separate specially tasked, intelligence-led units for various functions, none of which was overt and all of which would form the core of DMI's counter-revolutionary operations (including assassination). These included the Reconnaissance Commandos (which had been developed in the 1970s but were placed in responsibility to the CSI at this time – see below) largely for clandestine operations externally, although some later undertook covert operations both internally and abroad; the DST, which provided covert support to contra-mobilisation and guerrilla groups regionally and internally; the CCB, which would be the basis for DMI's covert counter-revolutionary activities in the second half of the 1980s and into the 1990s; and the DCC, which would act against opponents of the state through both counter-intelligence operations and pro-active intelligence-gathering operations (meaning the use of political violence, including planning assassinations, to obtain and implement intelligence).

SADF Special Forces: DMI's "eyes and ears"

It is standard practice amongst armed forces the world over to include a specialist element (generally known as "special forces" or "special operations forces") within their ranks.[44] In supporting the conventional activities of the military, special forces have often been called upon to perform both supportive tasks (such as long-range reconnaissance) and what are termed unconventional tasks. In no other situation is this more true than in forces involved in counter-revolutionary warfare (CRW). Throughout the twentieth century, such special forces have been active in Southern Africa's wars since, it could be argued, the Commonwealth Bushveld Patrols in the British South Africa War – fighting guerrilla, terrorist and other irregular forces engaged in revolutionary war or wars of national liberation.

Counter-revolutionary war presents special forces with a number of difficulties. These include separating the insurgents/revolutionaries from the population within which it is active and differentiating between non-combatants and combatants in this milieu; developing intelligence on the nature, location, capabilities, etc. of the insurgent structures which are often based outside the country in which they operate; ensuring the elimination of those structures through a combination of actions; and conducting all of these operations in a clandestine manner, to name but a few. In these situations, special forces generally provide three key functions: counter-revolutionary training and what are termed "hearts and minds" activities (collectively termed "contra-mobilisation"); long-range

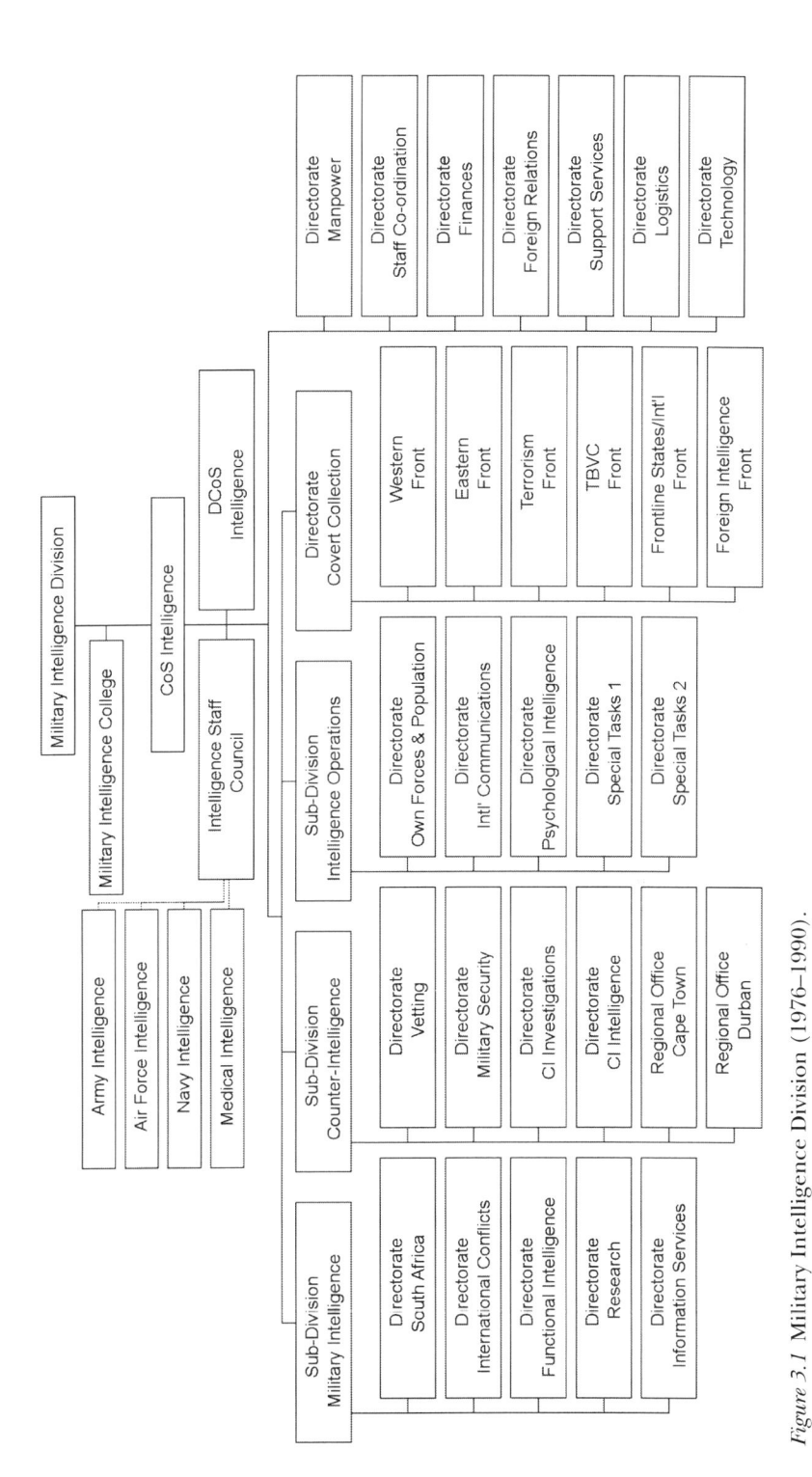

Figure 3.1 Military Intelligence Division (1976–1990).

reconnaissance for both intelligence-gathering and operational purposes; and direct action against the insurgents/revolutionaries.

The difference between such special forces (in other words, those engaging in specialist, sometimes clandestine, operations as a general part of military operations) and "covert operators" emerges in the realm of counter-revolutionary warfare.[45] In a number of contemporary examples where counter-revolutionary warfare was implemented (i.e. Rhodesia's Selous Scouts, Angola's *Flechas*, Vietnam's *Phuong Huong*), *covert* operations were undertaken by specialist military and paramilitary forces for a number of reasons. First, to conduct what are known as "pseudo-operations" – operations where the government forces disguise themselves as the opposing force's guerrilla fighters to carry-out attacks, sometimes involving atrocities, to damage the image of the opposing force in the eyes of the population and internationally.[46] Second, and most important, to allow for what the Americans came to call "plausible deniability" of operations: that the hand of the government cannot be seen to be involved, as this could potentially damage an operation which would otherwise have positive results. Finally, to undertake illegal or extralegal operations against opponents without revealing the hand of the state or to confuse the opponents as to the nature of the instigator.

In the South African case, this was doubly true: specialist units existed in the South African security forces at every level. Alongside the DMI units already noted, as well as various SAP Security Branch COIN/CRW units (explored below and in Chapters 6 and 7) and the remnants of the BOSS covert targeting units (such as the "Z-Squad" and its successors), the SADF Special Forces were utilised for both clandestine and covert operations, but functioned in very different manners. They included the "Recces" (1, 2, 3, 4, 5 and 6 Reconnaissance Regiments) for – generally, but not absolutely – external clandestine operations; the 44 Parachute Brigade Pathfinder Company and 1 Parachute Battalion Pathfinder Unit; 32 Battalion (a light infantry COIN unit developed for the war in Angola and Namibia); and the Civil Co-operation Bureau (CCB). Informally, they also were involved with the Army Intelligence "Hammer" COIN units developed originally in the Eastern Cape Territorial Command, and various Directorates of DMI.[47] Overall, these forces can be divided into three elements: the clandestine (the "Recces" and Pathfinders), the counter-guerrilla (32 Battalion and "Hammer"), and the covert (the CCB and DCC).

The operations of these units were as wide and varied as their composition. While units such as 32 Battalion and the Pathfinders engaged in combat in Angola and Namibia, the Special Forces were tasked with carrying-out a variety of special operations. These included more traditional economic disruption operations against enemy states in Southern Africa, as well as providing clandestine support to other forces. However, a central reason behind the development of Special Forces was that DMI needed operational "eyes and ears": its intelligence-gathering thus far was limited to the development of operational networks or the receipt of intelligence from SAP counter-insurgency operations in Namibia and Rhodesia. In order to both develop a much greater capability to gather intelligence, especially strategic intelligence relating to military operations, *and* (this is central to understanding DMI's absolute role at the centre of the state's counter-revolutionary strategy) to implement operations based on that intelligence, DMI required an operational capability on the ground. The Reconnaissance Regiments provided this capability initially.

As – in a duality that was to call into question the distinction between clandestine special operations and covert counter-intelligence warfare – both the "tip" of the DMI "spear" and, at the same time, DMI's "eyes and ears", the Special Forces were to develop an influence on both operational policy and strategic planning, within both DMI itself specifically and the SADF generally, that went far beyond their size and relative involvement in the border wars. This had little to do with more "traditional" views of specialist forces within the military and much more with the willingness of the political elite to support their role as one of the prime weapons in the counter-revolutionary struggle. In this sense, the apartheid government's reliance on its special forces and specialist capabilities to ensure ultimately the development of "breathing space" to allow for the reform (not removal) of apartheid was ultimately flawed. The power this gave Special Forces and DMI was enormous:

> The influence of the SADF's Special Forces occurred within the context of a deteriorating and increasingly unaccountable political culture, the excessive concentration of power in the executive regions of the state and the veil of secrecy surrounding all military activities under the state of emergency. It also reflected the extent to which an influential faction within the SADF had managed to determine the SADF's strategic and political direction.[48]

This influence and freedom was to give the Special Forces incredible latitude in operations and influence.

In all the examples that the South Africans had drawn on to develop their own views and doctrine of counter-insurgency, specialist military forces had played a central role in conducting the counter-insurgency campaign, including both the military operations and the "hearts and minds" element. This had been the case with the British and their development of the modern (post-Second World War) incarnation of the Special Air Service (SAS) during the Malayan Emergency and in the Arabian Peninsula; with the French and their use of air-mobile forces in both Indochina and Algeria; and with the Americans and their development of Army Special Forces and Rangers for operations in South-East Asia. The US example proved one of the most relevant to the South

58   *"Total Strategy" and "securocratisation"*

African scenario (as far as Western comparative examples were concerned) given the role of the US Navy SEALs units in the Phoenix programme (one of the most directly relevant comparative example to the South African case in terms of the direct-targeting of the insurgent's politico-administrative and military infrastructures) and the Green Berets' contra-mobilisation programmes. Finally, closer to home, the role of the Portuguese *Flechas* ("Arrows") in their counter-insurgency campaigns in Angola and Mozambique also presented an example to learn from.

The most pressing and relevant example of all to the South African military was that of Rhodesia. Throughout the course of the Rhodesian *Chimurenga* (Shona for "liberation war"),[49] four units were key to the Rhodesian counter-insurgency and counter-revolutionary warfare strategies; each would be reflected in the South African security forces by the mid-1980s, once again pointing to the centrality of the Rhodesian example (and the role of Rhodesian personnel in the South African security forces after 1980) as a leader for South Africa. The Rhodesian African Rifles (RAR) would reflect on 32 Battalion and its counter-guerrilla operations in Angola; the Rhodesian Light Infantry (RLI) and Rhodesian Special Air Service (RSAS) would be the benchmarks for the Reconnaissance Regiments; the Selous Scouts would be the model for the development, at the end of the 1970s, of a pseudo-operations and police counter-insurgency element in *Koevoet*; and elements of the RSAS, the Scouts and the Central Intelligence Organisation would form the model for, and contribute personnel to, the Civil Co-operation Bureau's role in counter-revolutionary warfare during the 1980s and into the 1990s.

Origins and development

The development of the SADF Special Forces took place over the period covering the late 1960s to 1986, with a longer-term strategic plan in mind for their continuing development into the 1990s, had the transition post-apartheid not occurred. During the late 1960s, the commanders of the SADF began to realise that, as it currently stood, the SADF lacked a specialist capability to help in implementing the developing counter-insurgency strategy against the opposing forces throughout southern Africa; later, during the early 1980s, this same concern about having the "right tools" would translate into the development of specialist units for counter-revolutionary warfare.

In the late 1960s, the SADF possessed one specialist regiment: 1 Parachute Battalion based in Bloemfontein. This unit was not, however, designed for clandestine operations or long-range reconnaissance of the type foreseen by the SADF General Staff. It was clear from at least two fronts that, sooner or later, the SADF would require strategic reconnaissance units for the provision of operational intelligence, as well as a capability to conduct unconventional operations as part of counter-insurgency. South Africa's security forces were slowly but surely becoming involved in the conflicts developing in Rhodesia and Namibia. This would eventually, it was believed, involve the SADF in a counter-insurgency posture. This would fit perfectly with the SADF's strong belief in the counter-insurgency doctrines which its key thinkers, especially in DMI, espoused. The Parachute Battalion was not generally capable of this type of operation, thus another unit had to be developed. The model for this unit, as its founder later stated, was the British SAS, which offered as a model the three key elements which the SADF believed it would require for future clandestine and covert operations: long-range reconnaissance in war-fighting situations for strategic-intelligence gathering, sabotage against opponent installations and forces, and counter-insurgency/guerrilla capabilities.

From 1971, many DMI operators were trained Special Forces personnel, knowledgeable in clandestine and covert operations. These *Spesmagte* (as they were known in Afrikaans) were active throughout the Operational Area, but should not be confused with the Reconnaissance Commandos: the *Spesmagte* were covert operators. In 1975, as Portugal's colonies became independent, the *Spesmagte* were converted to *Spestake* ("Special Tasks" – see Chapter 6); at the same time, the CSI absorbed the Special Forces function from the Army, thereby integrating under one command the functions of special forces, special tasks, covert paramilitary operations and military intelligence.[50]

The first of these, 1 Reconnaissance Commando, was established by Commandant (later Colonel) Jan Breytenbach at Oudtshoorn on 1 October 1972. Including British and American "advisors" initially (generally former members of the SAS or Green Berets), this unit recruited men from the SADF for specialist training.[51] Over the coming decades, the Recces (and other special forces units) would include nationals not just from South Africa but also British, American, Angolan, Mozambican, Portuguese and other nationalities, contributing to the derogatory label sometimes given the Recces by its critics as "mercenaries". The Special Forces also instituted a continual – and clandestine – training exchange programme between the SADF's Special Forces Division and their opposite numbers in the Federal Republic of Germany, various Latin American countries, Rhodesia and Portugal, and Israel in the early 1970s.[52]

An airborne unit based at Durban, 1 Recce specialised in external landward actions, mainly in the conventional role; predominantly a black unit with white senior officers and with a strength of approximately 1,000, it also integrated members of the RSAS who came south, after 1980.[53] Over the rest of the 1970s, a specialised unit for sea-borne operations (4 Reconnaissance Commando, a relatively small, mainly white unit involved in operations against Angola and Mozambique) was established at Langebaan, while 5 Reconnaissance Commando (an airborne unit specialised in counter-revolutionary warfare, and consisting mostly of black former

60 *"Total Strategy" and "securocratisation"*

Mozambican and Angolan soldiers, as well as former Portuguese officers after 1974 and former Selous Scouts after 1980), which was established at the Duku-Duku camp in Northern Natal, moved to Phalaborwa. By 1980, the Reconnaissance Regiments included these three units, along with 2 Reconnaissance Commando (a Citizen (part-time) Force unit for ex-Recce members which supported Special Forces Headquarters and other Special Forces units), 3 Reconnaissance Commando (composed of former RSAS, Selous Scouts and RLI personnel, and involved in destabilisation operations with DST, later becoming the CCB), and 6 Reconnaissance Regiment (also composed of former RSAS/Scouts/RLI personnel, and subsequently absorbed into 1 Recce).[54] In addition, alongside the Recces, 32 Battalion – formed in 1975 by Breytenbach out of the remains of Daniel Chipenda's faction of the anti-Marxist FNLA (*Frente Nacional de Liberaçao de Angola* or National Front for the Liberation of Angola) which were wandering in chaos throughout southern Angola – engaged in "special operations" in Angola and Namibia;[55] while 44 Parachute Brigade Pathfinder Company also supported Recce operations (see Figure 3.2).

The post of General Office Commanding (GOC) Special Forces was created in October 1974; as the Special Forces rested under the Chief of Staff Intelligence (CSI) function, who reported directly to the chief of the SADF (CSADF) and thereby to the prime minister (later president) via the State Security Council, operationally, the Special Forces were an executive unit and not a line-function of the SADF. This greatly increased their usefulness to the combat effort by ensuring that "their operations, their finances, their location and their identities were kept secret".[56] Headquartered at *Die Gat* ("The Gap/Hole") – a farm outside Voortrekkerhoogte, the SADF's headquarters – the SFHQ included an independent Special Forces Intelligence section to provide intelligence specifically for Special Forces' operations, which interacted closely with DMI's sections for both external and internal operations.[57]

Alongside more conventional roles supporting the SADF in its operations in Angola, the Recces became involved in virtually every clandestine and covert operation that DMI undertook, including (importantly) the training of counter-guerrilla and contra-mobilisation forces both externally throughout the Frontline States and internally in South Africa. This would be one of their two principal operational roles, the other being operations against South Africa's opponents in southern Africa. This second one, which accounted for the majority of Special Forces operations, included sabotage operations against many of the Frontline States, deep-penetration reconnaissance missions in relation to the wars in Angola and Mozambique, "hot-pursuit" operations against ANC and APLA infiltrators as part of counter-terrorist operations, and raids conducted against concentrations of and installations used by the liberation movements as bases for launching operations into South Africa. This would, of necessity, include the direct targeting (either individually or in the guise

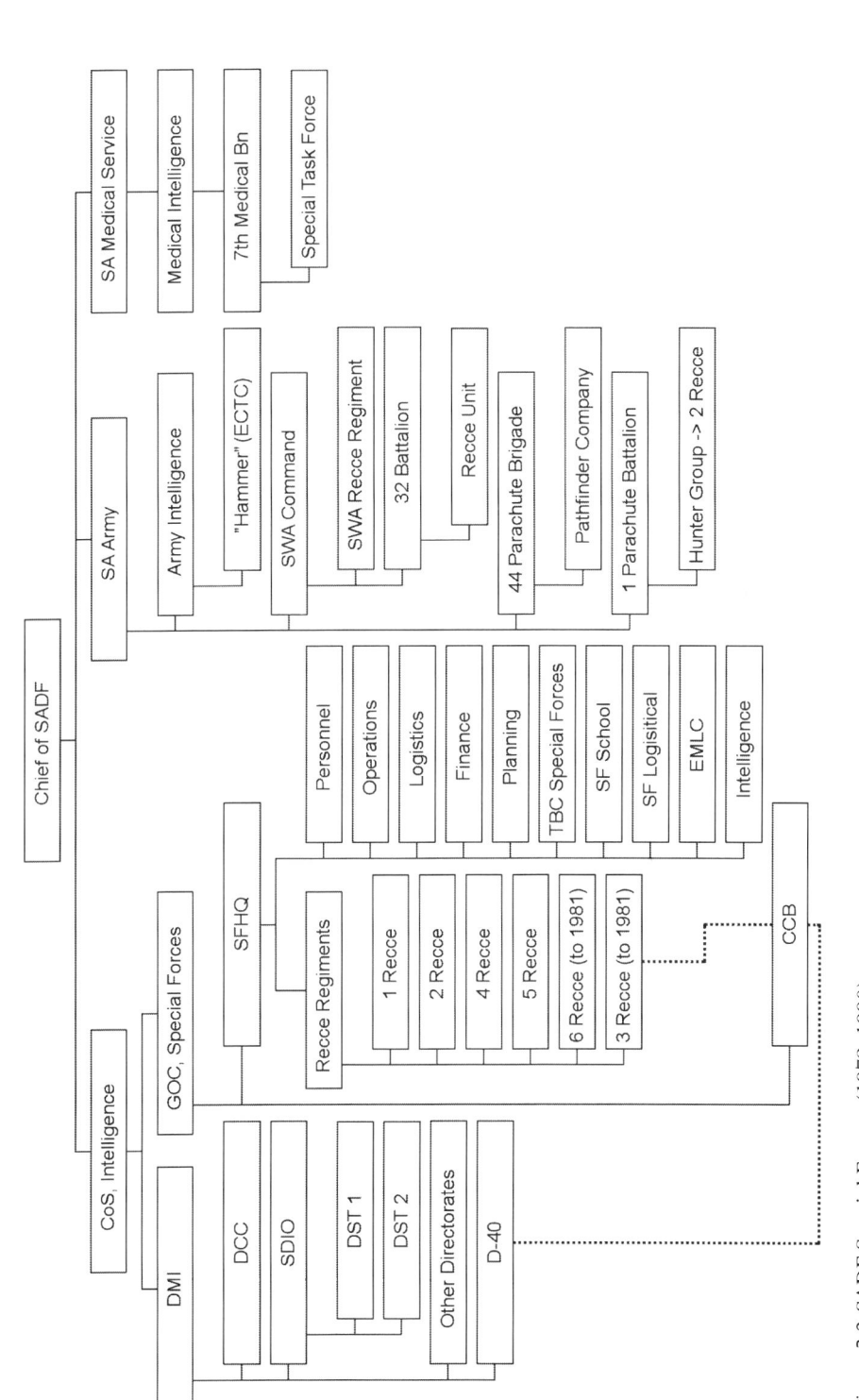

Figure 3.2 SADF Special Forces (1972–1990).

of raids against ANC or APLA targets) of the liberation movements' leaderships.

As, at the end of the 1970s, the apartheid state developed its capabilities in counter-revolutionary warfare against or alongside these covert COIN/CRW units (see chapter 6), the role of the Reconnaissance Regiments was "to inflict the maximum disruption on the enemy of the state by means of special actions".[58] Overall, the Special Forces were used to implement Pretoria's regional destabilisation policies; while successful generally, they must be seen as having succeeded alongside other policies, such as the total economic reliance that the region – including most of the Frontline States – had on South Africa, as well as the other key element of Pretoria's destabilisation strategy, that of contra-mobilisation in the Frontline States implemented by DST (see chapter 6).

Conclusion

Having gained control over the "Total National Strategy" and pushed its dominance of the intelligence brief across the apartheid securocracy, DMI arrived at the end of the 1970s in a dominant position, not the least of which was due to its sponsorship by Botha. While its main rival – BOSS – remained to be dealt with following Botha's accession to the premiership, the SADF would – through the institutions primarily of DMI and Army Intelligence – extend its influence and interests throughout numerous domestic sectors throughout the 1980s. This was partly a reflection of the evolving counter-revolutionary strategy – envisioned but not yet formed by the end of the 1970s, and soon to include both contra-mobilisation and assassination within South Africa – which would be implemented within South Africa's borders during the 1980s, but also of the institutional growth of the SADF as a whole under Botha. DMI exerted considerable influence over many aspects of South African society and policy, especially issues of strategic concern, much greater than its lot should have been. DMI drove strategic and defence doctrine and policy, which in turn guided the NSMS and the "Total National Strategy". As Williams notes,

> DMI not only constituted the powerhouse of SADF policy and thinking but was also the effective "brains" behind much of Botha's administration. In many respects, the role of DMI and its highly intelligent Chief of Staff, Lt General Pieter Van Der Westhuizen, paralleled the influence that Van Den Berghe [sic] and BOSS had exerted on the Vorster administration.[59]

4 Hydra

The rise of the national intelligence and counter-revolutionary structures, 1978–1983

> The protection of the Lord's Kingdom on earth makes the use of the power of the sword a God-given task and calling.
> Dr Niel Barnard, Director-General, National Intelligence Service

Rebirth: the end of BOSS and the rise of the National Intelligence Service

The problem which existed here was a political one: when Vorster, who was both prime minister and minister of justice, took power, he used BOSS as both his eyes-and-ears in the government and as a forum for discussing policy options. For this reason, Van den Bergh was the most powerful leader after Vorster. Thus, BOSS maintained dominance amongst the security forces as the favoured son. However, its chief operational concern traditionally had been directed towards subversion of the state, terrorism, and counter-espionage and counter-intelligence operations, not towards counter-insurgency. Therefore, it was unlikely that BOSS would support both a radical restructuring of the state's security architecture and an enhancement of the counter-insurgency strategy; this would inherently mean a diminution in BOSS's influence in the policy process as other, more pressing priorities were confronted.

BOSS, however, would not survive the 1970s. In 1978, the "Information Scandal" – which involved the Department of Information, under Dr Connie Mulder, using covert funds to influence overseas perceptions of South Africa through the covert purchase of media outlets and publications – rocked South African politics, and resulted in both the end to Vorster's premiership and the rise of Defence Minister P.W. Botha to the leadership in September 1978. With the fall-out directly affecting the state's intelligence dispensation, the period became known as the "Battle for the Intelligence Brief".[1] Within this, two trends were clearly discernible: the effort to centralise and co-ordinate national security intelligence, and the growing dominance of the military in the intelligence brief. This battle was waged partly between the various competing influences to succeed Vorster as prime minister (and, thus, determine which agency would politically dominate the security establishment) but also by BOSS to ensure its own survival. While excuses relating to poor co-ordination of intelligence, corruption, mismanagement and poorly defined briefs were used to justify this repositioning, the ultimate reason for this covert contest of succession was to determine which would become the lead agency under the now-Prime Minister Botha.

There could be little doubt to the answer. DMI had been Botha's "pet thinking shop" on issues of national security throughout his tenure as defence minister; it was only natural that it would become the central body. Wisely, however, Botha (having watched the intelligence agencies throughout the 1970s being used for personal political gain by their masters and, as such, developing an intense institutional rivalry which did little to help the fight against the "Total Onslaught") decided to divide responsibilities for the intelligence brief between the agencies (DMI, BOSS, Security Branch, and Foreign Affairs) which contributed to the overall intelligence picture. DMI would become the lead agency in all respects, but the others would be responsible for clearly defined mandates in combating the "Total Onslaught".

In 1978, the Public Service Commission was committed to "rationalizing" and "cleaning" the government national security apparatus; part of this required significant changes in the overall national security dispensation, as its 1980 report to Parliament (*White Paper on the Rationalisation of the Public Service and Related Institutions*) noted. To eliminate BOSS's potential interference with the new security priorities and to ensure that "Total National Strategy" would be implemented to its fullest, acquiring the fullest support possible from all national resources, Botha bluntly quelled its influence by first bringing about the resignation in 1978 of its head, Van der Bergh, following the "Information Scandal". He was replaced by his deputy, Alexander van Wyk, who led BOSS until the agency itself was restructured and replaced in August 1978. At the same time – and, most tellingly, almost a decade after it first started operating – the *Bureau for State Security Act* (No. 104 of 1978) was tabled at this time, designed significantly to bring BOSS back into the fold after Van der Bergh's years of freewheeling.[2]

In October 1978, Botha appointed one of his protégés, Kobie Coetsee, as the deputy minister of defence and national security (later National Intelligence). At the same time, he appointed him to lead a commission of inquiry to examine options to rationalise the intelligence functions and determine a future course for the strategic intelligence brief, the most important of all.[3] In response, BOSS personnel – perceiving the writing on the wall – began destroying files to prevent them being accessed by either Coetsee's commission or the Erasmus Commission investigating the "Information Scandal". It was clear to them that the future of BOSS was terminal.[4] Coetsee determined (many would argue this was already determined before the commission began its investigations) that the strategic intelligence brief should be given to DMI as a precursor to the development of a new security architecture around it and the SSC. Botha wanted to ensure that "the flow of this intelligence to the National Intelligence Interpretation Branch in the SSC could proceed uninterrupted by other political interests within the State".[5] BOSS's functions in this regard, as they had been responsible for this brief under Vorster, were transferred to DMI and the majority of its senior managers took early retirement.

Williams maintains that, given certain aspects of DMI, it remains a question (especially given future events) whether DMI should have been granted the strategic intelligence brief, for two reasons:

> [First], professional though they were, they were just not equipped to deal with the scope of intelligence-gathering operations previously controlled by BOSS. BOSS had had extensive experience in the field of domestic and regional intelligence operations. They had established an extensive network of operatives within the country, throughout Africa and in the Western world. The decimation of BOSS structures and the elevation of DMI to the apex of the intelligence pyramid severely hampered intelligence operations in forthcoming years, demoralised BOSS officers, threw regional intelligence networks into a state of disarray, and led to a spate of resignation amongst BOSS members.

Second, DMI took a particular view of the world and the various ideological themes that underlay conflict and consensus; it also had a strong belief (born out of its development of "Total National Strategy") that security could be managed in a technocratic manner. Niether of these elements were conducive to effectively understanding the "nuances and complexities of both political and socio-economic processes".[6] However, BOSS had been a police agency, developed largely through policing attitudes towards national security and the place of the criminal (in this case, the agent) within that order. While BOSS had developed mightily in the manner described in the first point above, from the failures to accurately chart such events as the Portuguese coup and its impact upon regional security actors in southern Africa, the attitudes of the Cubans and Soviets to South African intervention in Angola, and the implosion of Rhodesia it was clear that BOSS was neither the agency, nor the type of agency, to which responsibility for strategic intelligence should be left.

Significantly, BOSS, the CIA and the Portuguese security police PIDE had all failed to predict the April 1974 coup in Lisbon; this led to serious recriminations for the relationship between the CIA and BOSS, and ultimately the formal termination of CIA co-operation in 1977 (although US officials would acknowledge later that "some US intelligence agencies ... nevertheless maintained some level of clandestine exchange with the South Africans").[7] The South Africans had, since at least the late 1960s, been covertly supplying the Portuguese with arms, helicopters and pilots; there was even a joint command centre established at Cuito Cuanavale in 1968 to co-ordinate attacks against SWAPO and the MPLA. This was all perceived as a "worthwhile investment" to help safeguard the cordon sanitaire protecting South Africa from hostile African states. There was even a report that DMI had intended transferring arms and supplies to white settlers in southern Angola in September 1974 to fight the insurgents; this was vetoed by Vorster and the supplies were impounded by BOSS at Komatipoort.[8] Additionally, the CIA relied, until the late 1970s, closely on assessments from BOSS (and the PIDE) on Southern African events; such a failing as this left all three services far out of step with preparations for dealing with the consequences of the coup for Southern Africa and meant that the CIA and BOSS, in particular, had to scramble to deal with the new situation in Mozambique and Angola particularly.[9]

It was clear that a non-military, non-police agency with a wider world view and less "biased" opinion of regional events was required to provide this type of strategic intelligence. Botha looked initially to the Department of Foreign Affairs and Information to provide such strategic analysis but this was limited due to the almost entirely overt nature of Foreign Affairs information-gathering means; as well, the department was tainted by the "Information Scandal". The only solution was to do away with BOSS entirely and build a new agency based on "academic" principles of analysis. In its place, therefore, Botha formed the Department of National Security (DONS) in August 1978 that, by 1980, had become the National Intelligence Service (NIS). The power and influence of the NIS was limited to research and analysis of strategic issues; its operational capabilities (such as the "Z-Squads") were by-and-large terminated.[10] Overall, this saw a realignment of the briefs of the individual agencies: the NIS was limited to assessment and analysis, acting (most importantly, though) as the staff for the SSC structures (previously the battleground for rival securocrats from BOSS and DMI), a central player in the National Management Centre and regional Joint Management Centres established under the NSMS to oversee these policies against the liberation movements (see below). DMI gained responsibility over the strategic intelligence brief as well as enhancing its foreign intelligence collection capability and, later, introducing more vigorous domestic counter-intelligence functions through covert units. Finally, the Security Branch – which generally languished throughout the 1970s period of BOSS domination – similarly enhanced its foreign intelligence collection operations but generally had little to do with strategic intelligence assessment (see Figure 4.1).

With the founding of the NIS, Botha selected the young (he was 33 at the time) Dr Lukas Niel Barnard of the University of the Orange Free State, a protégé of Kobie Coetsee, to head the NIS, replacing Alexander van Wyck.[11] Barnard had no experience in intelligence in the least, and was forced to

Figure 4.1 National Intelligence (1980–1990).

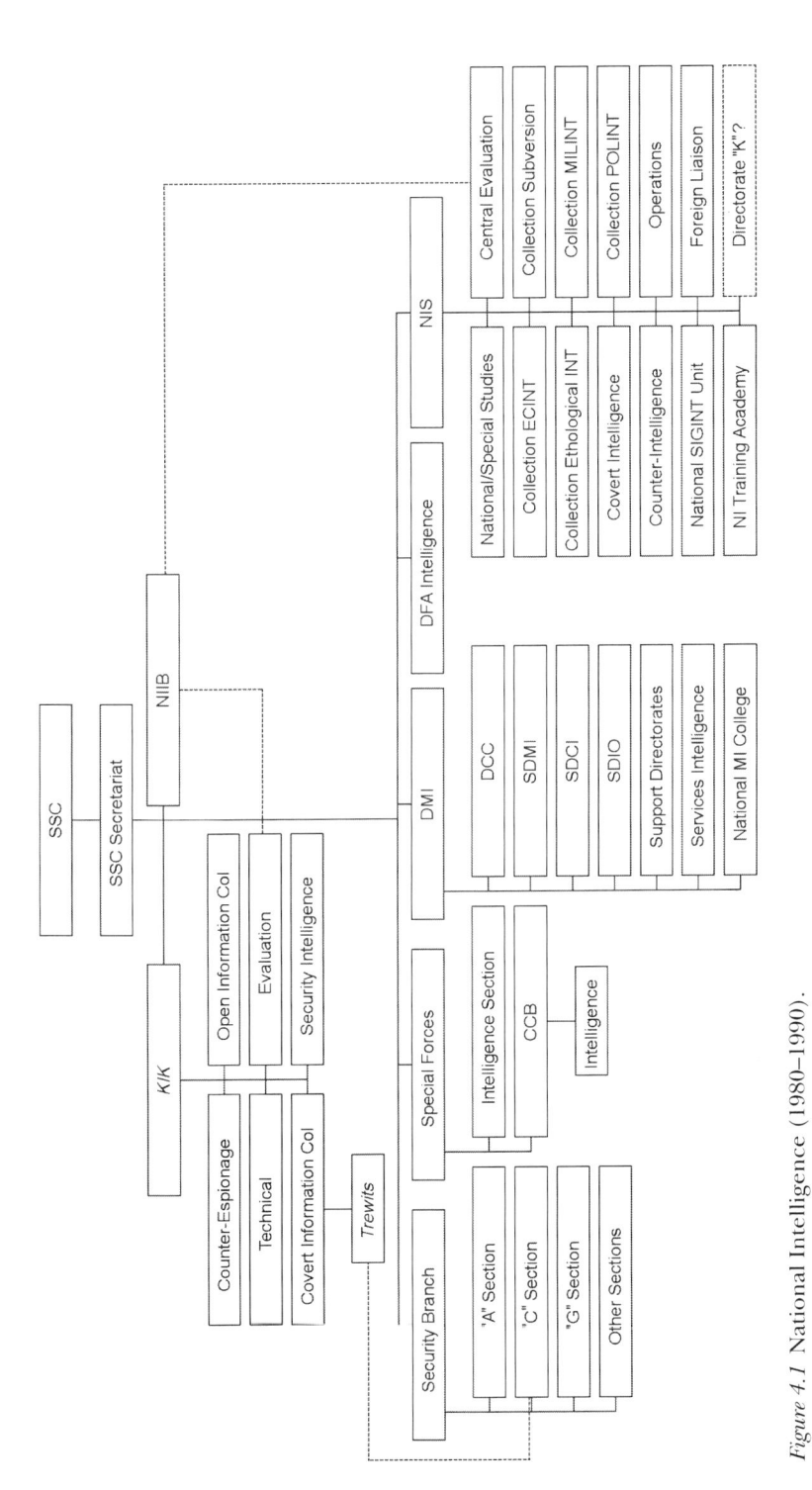

confront an agency in disarray. Many of the old BOSS personnel had left, including most of the management staff, and the institutional philosophy of the agency would require significant shifting if it was to achieve Botha's desire of having an independent civilian intelligence agency capable of providing long-term intelligence analysis for the premier. Botha saw the role of the NIS as being the "supreme co-ordinating and evaluative body within the intelligence pyramid".[12] Barnard was a strong admirer of the CIA's interaction with academics (being an academic himself) and proceeded to change the NIS's methodology to be more academic. While the NIS would not have an operational arm to the same degree that BOSS did (this function was more-or-less taken over by the Security Branch's sections),[13] it did deploy active agents outside the bounds of the Republic; it was forbidden from operating within the Republic (once again, a function left to – almost exclusively – Security Branch).

The strategic intelligence brief would not, however, be given to this new agency but would be placed with DMI: in Botha's thinking, as DMI was to be at the centre of the new security architecture, it was logical that it be given responsibility for providing the SSC with strategic intelligence. This was to be both the basis for the events of the 1980s, due partly to the thought rationalisation process that emanated from "Total National Strategy" in terms of combating opponents and the ability of DMI to act operationally upon intelligence gathered, and the willingness (already spreading to a Security Branch reintroduced to counter-insurgency operations after returning from Rhodesia to Namibia) to confront terrorist activity in a war-fighting (albeit largely unconventional) manner rather than through policing processes. This attitudinal shift in 1978–1979 led directly to the systemisation of the use of covert action, including especially assassination, against the perceived opponents of the Republic, whether they were members of an armed group or not. The reason for this was, as Major Craig Williamson (a long-term SAP intelligence officer and the eventual head of the Security Branch's A/G (Foreign) Sections) stated in 1982, "when survival is important it is often necessary for a service to resort to secret action which does not comply with the laws, morality, norms or values which control the public actions of the state".[14]

It is ironic that, in many senses, Botha's placing of the strategic intelligence brief with DMI – an agency entirely invested in the "Total Strategy" paradigm and the entire posture of South Africa as a security state – rather than with the new NIS, especially given its analytic function, may very well have been the single greatest factor contributing ultimately to the conditions that led to the collapse of apartheid and the negotiated settlement. As noted previously, DMI promoted a *Weltanschaaung* ("world view") that saw everything through the lens of counter-revolutionary warfare; this lens would – throughout the 1980s, as will be discussed – promote the notion that South Africa faced a "total revolutionary onslaught" from an ANC/SACP foe successfully building the structures and capabilities of a full-blown insurgency within South Africa itself. While the 1976 Soweto Uprising had stirred-up internal, violent dissent inside South Africa in a manner not seen since 1964, in reality nothing could be further from the truth, as will be discussed. In this sense, DMI was guilty of "gathering information because it is there and not because there is a consumer who wants it" – contributing to an intelligence picture which drove policy, rather than a policy which dictated the intelligence requirements.[15] This folly was reflected in numerous operations conducted by the state's intelligence components which resulted not in the garnering of a high level of useful information to the government, but rather in destructive and destabilising covert actions which did more to harm the state's strategy than enhance it. Indeed, DMI's belief in this "total onslaught" paradigm led directly to, first, the development of a counter-revolutionary strategy that placed front and centre an extremely oppressive national policy which left virtually no room for negotiating with the state's enemies; and, second, the creation of a covert counter-revolutionary warfare capability inside its structures, as well as those of the Special Forces and Security Branch, that would see South Africa's intelligence processes barbarised to the point of gross human rights violations and crimes against humanity.

Therefore, rather than seeking an outlet for a negotiated settlement at an earlier stage, DMI's strategic view – which this study clearly questions as having been "intelligence-led" – was directly responsible for the formation of Botha's extremely heavy-handed approach to dealing with opposition to the state in the 1980s. Indeed, it may be said that the apartheid government often reacted to failures by the secret services to provide proper intelligence to the decision-makers by reacting with even more drastic measures designed to combat the perceived threat. This conclusion may be most applied to the government's reaction to the upswing in township violence during the mid-1980s. Draconian states-of-emergency were declared, hand-in-glove with the use of covert action against the state's opponents, rather than attempt to deal with the problem more directly through a thorough and deliberate programme aimed at stabilising the situation through socially supportive and more democratically equitable activities which would have enhanced the livelihoods of South Africa's people and given the government an effective political solution to offer to its opponents – what should be the driving-force of any COIN programme. However, the prism of the "communist threat" against South Africa and the perception of an apocalyptical future for white South Africans should the liberation movements have triumphed in their struggle, did not allow for such a possibility to be considered.

Ironically, however, it has to be acknowledged that – by the end of the 1980s as is discussed in subsequent chapters – it was this very heavy-handed, counter-revolutionary push that may very well have created the conditions for a negotiated settlement with the ANC and PAC that future president F.W. de Klerk pursued. By that point, it would be almost impossible to tell whether – in a through-the-looking-glass manner – the blow and counter-blow of violence in the 1980s caused the upswing in domestic violence and insurgency which the state moved, by 1985, to crush and subsequently created the conditions for both sides to ultimately negotiate a way out of the conflict, or whether such society-wide violence could have been avoided in the early 1980s through an attempt to find an equitable settlement with apartheid's opponents had an intelligence-led vision of the state's and liberation movements' options been assessed accurately. As Johnson has noted, during this period, South Africa suffered from the "sins of strategic intelligence": the failure to provide policy-makers with objective, uninhibited intelligence; the disregard of objective intelligence by the policy-makers; the indiscriminate collection of intelligence; the indiscriminate use of covert action; and inadequate accountability in the intelligence chain of command.[16] This failure would have cataclysmic consequences for South African society through the 1980s and well into the 1990s, as will be discussed.

DMI now dominated everything to do with South Africa's national security strategy: it advised the prime minister (later president) on all aspects of national policy and strategy, ran the "Total National Strategy" and the National Security Management System, and even oversaw intelligence operations based outside of South Africa (including in South-West Africa). Partly as a result of this, the position of Chief of Staff, Intelligence (CSI) – a basic staff job prior to Botha's rise and DMI's ascendancy – became highly politicised. As Ellis notes, the position,

> previously relatively obscure, became a very powerful one since it became divorced from the usual line function and devoted increasing attention to executing covert operations rather than simply gathering or coordinating intelligence ... [its members] had political protection at the highest level in a chain of command which by-passed the conventional line of management.[17]

Its incumbents, Lt-Gen P.W. van der Westhuizen (1978–1985), Vice-Adm Dries Putter (1985–1989), and Lt-Gen R. "Witkop" Badenhorst (1989–1991), were all extremely powerful individuals politically and within the security establishment; Van der Westhuizen later served as secretary of the SSC until 1988.[18] Once BOSS had been removed from influence (and, thus, from power), Botha began to use DMI to provide the support for the co-option of the South African intelligence community as a whole into the "Total National Strategy" project. As a consequence, DMI ballooned in size and budget – growing to several thousand, many of whom had no background in the military.[19]

The new division of labour was not, however, seamless in its application nor in its coherence between agencies: fearing the NIS was attempting to encroach on its mandate to provide the strategic intelligence brief, DMI did everything it could to undermine NIS's status within the national system. Barnard himself, in interviews conducted more than a decade after taking responsibility for the NIS, stated that

> There is no doubt that in the first two years after my arrival in the NIS, a concerted effort was made to destroy the NIS. The underlying reason was a difference in interpretation of security intelligence between the NIS and SADF. The NIS had already stated in those years that the kernel of the security problem in South Africa lay in the domestic political arena ... Military Intelligence's point of departure was that the kernel of the problem was the communist threat that was being mounted outside the country. By bringing the neighbouring states under control and securing the expulsion of the communists through one or other way, the country's problems would then be sorted out.[20]

The reason for the NIS's survival was the fact that it was created by Botha to both offset the former power of BOSS and to act as a separate strategic analysis body to DMI; thus, it was Botha's patronage that saw it through these initial years. As will be seen, although the NIS was intricately involved initially in national security functions, it always remained a much more enlightened agency (generally speaking and compared with DMI and the Security Branch) and later became the government's principal clandestine conduit for negotiations with the ANC in the mid-1980s.

DMI was to become Botha's dominant intelligence force and fill much the same role that BOSS had under Vorster, as both guide and "policy talk-shop". This also produced its own problems, however. Because the position of CSI had been elevated to a key advisory position to the premier (later president) by both Botha and Defence Minister Malan, the position was coveted by officers on their way up the ladder. The CSI had previously, according to Ellis, been a relatively obscure position dedicated towards intelligence-gathering and -analysis; now, it had become one of the two focal-points (the other being the head of the Security Branch) for covert operations. Both of these factors "polluted the quality of intelligence since the politicisation of the office created pressures for intelligence estimates to be slanted for political reasons rather than in conformity with the intelligence officer's ideal of impartiality".[21] They also meant that – as happened with each political leader championing an intelligence service and its leadership – the intelligence officers' and operatives' "immense power was both derived from and dependent on senior politicians, and who were charged with the responsibility of protecting the state at all costs, even if this included unlawful action".[22] This would have devastating results in the period from the 1970s until the mid-1990s – and would reflect on a continued intelligence culture in the post-apartheid era in which the new political leadership would be accused of similar efforts to encourage illegality and corruption (in every sense) of the intelligence dispensation in the interests of politics (see Chapter 9).

To eliminate in-fighting within the intelligence brief, on 14 November 1980, Botha issued instructions to rationalise the intelligence structures in order to ensure better co-ordination. A Rationalisation Committee was set up that met secretly from 14–19 January 1981 in Simonstown; the agreements which resulted from these meetings, known as the *Simonstown Beraad* (Accords), delineated functions between the fledgling NIS (political and economic intelligence, counter-espionage, evaluation), DMI (military intelligence and contra-mobilisation) and the Security Branch (counter-subversion domestically and internationally against the state's opponents). Another result was Botha's approval, on 30 January 1981, of both the National Intelligence Interpretation Branch (NIIB) under the SSC Secretariat, which officially came into being on 1 January 1982; and the all-important Co-ordinating Intelligence Committee (*Koördineer Inligting Komitee* or "K" Committee, known generally by its Afrikaans acronym KIK), chaired by Barnard, also under the SSC Secretariat.

The KIK ensured closer co-ordination of activities and intelligence between all three intelligence services, as well as the non-security agencies (such as Foreign Affairs, Constitutional Development or Prisons) that contributed intelligence to the national picture. Activities of the KIK were supported by a system of sub-committees; these included the Covert Information Gathering, Open Information Gathering, Technical, Evaluation (this would later become the NIIB of the SSC), Counter-Espionage, and Security Intelligence sub-committees.[23] The most important of these, however, was the Counter-revolutionary Information Task Team (*Teen Rewolusionêre Inligting Taakspan* or *Trewits*), established under the Sub-committee for Covert Collection in late 1986 (see Chapter 7).[24] This co-ordination, however, did not always go well: due to the antagonism between the three principal agencies, both Security Branch and DMI refused to share any intelligence below a strategic level with NIS; neither would they share with each other. Problems of this nature would lead, in the mid-1980s, to the establishment of a number of new "co-ordinating bodies" tasked specifically with co-ordinating intelligence for targeting purposes.[25] Unlike the other Interdepartmental Committees of the SSC secretariat, this committee did not reside under the general activities of the SSC Working Group but rather reported directly to the SSC Secretariat (see Figure 4.2).

In the *Simonstown Beraad*, it was also determined that the NIS would provide the national intelligence brief, co-ordinating strategic intelligence assessment with both DMI's Directorate Intelligence Operations and the NIIB (for which the NIS provided all of its analysts). In addition, the SAP's intelligence operations would include running agents within South Africa and Swaziland, while the SADF would be responsible for the same within other Frontline States, including Lesotho; both would run agents abroad.

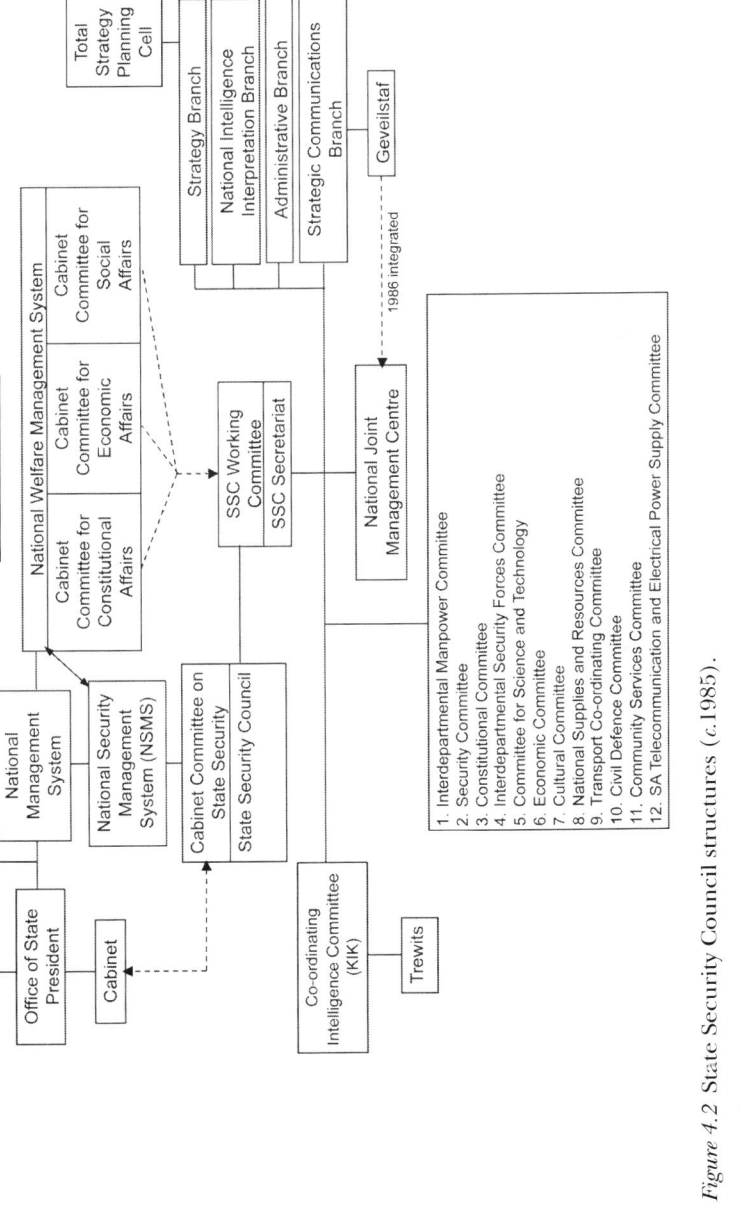

Figure 4.2 State Security Council structures (c.1985).

The NIS would have no offensive capability. Finally, in the "interests of countering revolution", the Simonstown deliberations decided that "abnormal" procedures were to be used in gathering intelligence and conducting cross-border operations against the liberation movements; this would include the establishment of a targeting capability within the NSMS which would identify "targets involved in the armed struggle" – this was *Trewits*. Finally, the security establishment was told at Simonstown to "take the gloves off in the fight against the revolutionary enemy". The result of these agreements were, as Seegers notes, "armed groups, hit squads, vigilantes and warlords ... they disrupted the work of Civic Associations, attacked or intimidated activists, office-holders and supporters, and destroyed and damaged property".[26]

South Africa's security: a changing paradigm

The legal basis for intelligence and counter-revolutionary activities

While the South African state used many covert methods to implement counter-revolutionary strategy, it also used overt, legal methods as part of its attempts to defeat the liberation movements. Legislation such as the "90-Day Act" (*General Law Amendment Act* No. 37 of 1963), the "180-Day Act" (*Criminal Procedure Amendment Act* No. 96 of 1965), the *Sabotage Act* (1962), the *Internal Security Act* (1972, amended 1976 and 1982), the *Public Safety Act* (1953, amended 1986), and the *Terrorism Act* (1967) were used to support detention without trial, banning and restriction to certain areas, the banning of public gatherings and organisations, the procedure of arrest and trial leading to capital punishment, and even torture. The intelligence services of the country – including of its four "independent homelands" – were supported in the 1972 *Security Intelligence and State Security Council Act*, the *Bureau for State Security Act*, 1978 (Act No. 104 of 1978); Bophuthatswana's *Internal Intelligence Service Act*, 1982 (Act No. 25 of 1982) and *National Security Council Act*, 1981 (Act No. 27 of 1981); the *Intelligence Service and State Security Council Act*, 1987 (Act No. 67 of 1987) of Transkei; and the *National Intelligence Service Act*, 1988 (Act No. 31 of 1988) of Venda. Often the legality of counter-revolutionary actions was justified as being simply "in the interests of the state"; as one observer noted,

> To protect the process of democratic development any security measure could be justified on the basis of the belief that the security, preservation and welfare of the state were the "highest law", which should be accorded precedence when weighed against other interests.[27]

In this sense, in the face of this conflict, individual rights were less important in the face of the needs of the state.[28] These legal provisions also appeared to grant further acquiescence to illegal or extralegal acts carried on under apartheid, particularly the selective killing of individual opponents of the state. Additionally, section 6 of the *Terrorism Act* granted the security forces the right to detain anyone for questioning to gain "information on planned and purposed activities of this nature". Critics of this allowance held that section 6 actually allowed the security forces to interrogate and torture individuals at will for the purpose of "obtaining information rather than for prosecuting the persons concerned in the courts". This was subsequently replaced by section 29 of the *Internal Security Act* which allowed for "detention for the purpose of interrogation".[29] Finally, the use of deadly force was also authorised under South African law, particularly to protect the person or property of individuals, or in the "arresting of a recalcitrant suspect", under the *Criminal Procedure Act* (1977); in a sense, this was interpreted to apply to counter-insurgent operations, where the killing of insurgents was a justifiable defence of the community.[30]

South Africa's security: changing regional and international dimensions

At the same time as the national intelligence dispensation underwent these colossal upheavals, South Africa's military engagement in South-West Africa, where the SAP has been sidelined with the SADF/DMI dominant, spread across the border into Angola, following the 1974 Portuguese coup – a country where the SADF and SAP would spend the next 15 years in counter-insurgency and conventional war-fighting – and, to a lesser degree, Mozambique. This would have three strong and immediate impacts. First, on the development of "operational intelligence" units for counter-insurgency, within both the SADF and SAP – including both the South-West African Territorial Force (SWATF) and the South-West Africa Police (SWAPOL), both administratively distinct security forces from the SADF and SAP respectively. These units would grow – most particularly within DMI's Directorate Special Tasks (which developed and ran units to undertake covert operations both external and internal to South Africa) and within the SADF's Special Forces structures (which would later include the elements supporting South Africa's chemical and biological warfare efforts in the 7th Medical Battalion and its affiliated Special Task Force) over the 1980s.

The second impact was on the Frontline States – those countries which surrounded South Africa. Prior to 1974 and 1979, Portuguese Angola and Mozambique, alongside Rhodesia, provided a geographic buffer-zone to South Africa – the ANC and PAC guerrillas operating against South Africa had to so do from far afield in Southern Africa (excepting those limited operations they were able to support from Botswana, Lesotho and Swaziland). After the loss of this buffer-zone, South Africa's guerrilla opponents were on the republic's doorstep, forging alliances with like-minded liberation movements across the Frontline States. Coupled with the 1976 Soweto Uprising – which saw a massive upswing in violent internal opposition to apartheid – Pretoria was, by 1980, faced with a significant war on all fronts, both foreign and domestic.

Finally, South Africa's intelligence and security relationships with the United States and United Kingdom particularly, along with other countries (such as Israel, West Germany, France, Algeria and Indonesia), became ever more important, especially regarding the Cold War context within which South Africa perceived itself to operate in Southern Africa (vis-à-vis Angola and the Cuban/Soviet intervention, the influence of Marxist-Communist regimes and liberation-movements on the ANC/SACP efforts, and other such elements). Throughout the 1970s and into the 1980s, Washington and London provided South Africa – sometimes directly, sometimes via proxies such as Mobutu Sese Seko in Zaire – with significant covert support, which only tailed-off in the mid-1980s, as President Reagan was forced by the US Congress to curtail all foreign covert actions (including, under the 1987 *Intelligence Authorization Act*, explicitly those with South African intelligence) and Prime Minister Thatcher was pushed finally to offer limited support to sanctions against Pretoria under pressure from the Commonwealth, who had introduced comprehensive sanctions by this time. These changes did not – it is worth noting – change significantly Pretoria's covert relationship with Tel Aviv, across a wide-range of co-operative ventures (the most significant of which being the development of South Africa's nuclear capability).

Overall, these three events had a direct impact on the massive enhancement of South Africa's intelligence and security capabilities – in every regard. Alongside the national reorganisation noted above, one other significant change occurred at the turn of the 1970s which would affect dramatically South Africa's intelligence and security dispensation throughout the 1980s and into the 1990s: the re-emergence of the SAP Security Branch as a dominant player in countering South Africa's opponents. Since losing its COIN role in South-West Africa and Rhodesia in the late 1960s, along with its security policing and intelligence role to BOSS in the 1970s, the Security Branch had languished – this changed significantly at the end of the decade, as the South African government decided to escalate its anti-opponent operations to counter-revolutionary warfare.

ANC intelligence in exile

It is useful to understand the ANC's approach to intelligence[31] as a function of both their "Revolutionary Strategy" (as outlined in Chapter 2) and – especially coming into the negotiated transition from apartheid (see Chapter 8) – their outlook on both the conflict and South Africa itself. Throughout its lifetime, the ANC/SACP's armed wing *Umkhonto weSizwe* (MK) had espoused a revolutionary war philosophy – seeking to overthrow the apartheid state by force, and bring about black-majority rule (with universal suffrage) in South Africa. The ANC's Department of National Intelligence and Security (known generally as NAT) had supported this, and as a consequence, undergone considerable changes over the years from its founding in April 1969 until its transformation at the end of apartheid (see Chapter 8).

As the ANC noted,

> Security and intelligence structures of the ANC were established within the context of its adoption of underground forms of struggle. Any underground movement requires relevant mechanisms to protect those involved in it [from infiltration] ... by agents of the regime [and] to minimise the damage that such infiltration would wreak ... to acquire information from the repressive state about its intentions and strategies; to carry out reconnaissance work for operations, and so on.[32]

In the 1960s, MK established a fledgling military intelligence unit focused on "undertaking reconnaissance missions to find routes for the infiltration of trained MK cadres; the establishment of reception areas inside the country for these cadres; and the selection of inanimate targets for armed propaganda attacks".[33] While this provided an offensive focus, the ANC and MK were left without a defensive – counter-intelligence – capability, which the apartheid intelligence apparatus exploited ruthlessly, and would continue to so do over the following decades. Therefore, a twinned focus on both penetrating South Africa's security intelligence structures and counter-intelligence aimed at preventing the same being done to the ANC by the apartheid state would be the lasting legacy of NAT;[34] while NAT's counter-intelligence and security cadres would have some successes in countering the apartheid state's penetration operations – most significantly, in a 1981 roll-up of huge infiltration-network "linked not only to Pretoria, but also to the intelligence services of some Western powers" in an operation known as "Shishita"[35] – the scale of the state's penetration of the ANC (most particularly, by Security Branch and the National Intelligence Service) would only come to light in the late 1990s long after the transition from apartheid to democracy (see Chapter 9).

Given these challenges, the ANC executive determined – in the Morogoro Conference of 1969 – to establish NAT and task it with "the protection of human and material resources of the ANC"; Moses Mabhida, then head of the MK Training and Personnel Section, was appointed as its first head. At the outset – and until 1981, effectively – the NAT had no formal structures, but concentrated on security and counter-intelligence particularly, with some external intelligence work being done, drawing all its personnel from MK (whose intelligence unit pursued offensive operations). These capabilities – and the staffing of them – were all created in "a relatively ad hoc fashion", at least until formalised intelligence training for ANC cadres – provided by the Soviet Union, East Germany, Libya, and (after 1980) allegedly Zimbabwe – was commenced.

For MK, its Special Operations unit was established formally in 1979, and its military intelligence capacity was formalised in the late 1970s, both under the direction of the MK Central Operations headquarters in Angola. Within the ANC/MK's Revolutionary Council (RC) structures – as it evolved – individual regional organs (sometimes referred to as "machineries") were responsible for security and intelligence operations, as well as military intelligence, in their region. Amongst these, Angola was treated differently, given not only its prominence in the direct conflict between the apartheid state and MK (who fought the SADF and SAP alongside the FAPLA forces) but also the presence of the infamous NAT "rehabilitation" Camp 32 (aka the Morris Seabelo Rehabilitation Centre or *Quatro*, established in 1979) there, resulting in the most extensive NAT security and counter-intelligence capability being implemented there.[36]

In 1976, Simon Makana replaced Mabhida as director of NAT, and was in turn replaced by Mzwandile (Mzwai) Piliso in 1980. Subsequently, in 1981, NAT was created as a National Directorate within the ANC's National Executive Council, and reorganised into three main sectors: Intelligence, Security, and Processing of Information. Combined with the training now being received overseas, NAT began to take on a professional structure and officers, many of whom – such as Joseph Nhlanhla, NEC secretary from 1978, secretary of the ANC's new Politico-Military Council (PMC, replacing the RC) after 1983, and head of NAT after 1987; Sizakele Sigxashe, senior NAT executive from 1985; Jacob Zuma, head of NAT Intelligence from 1985; and Ronnie Kasrils, chief of Military Intelligence from 1983 – became the backbone of the NAT and MK Intelligence (and, later, the post-apartheid) structures from this point forward.

Over the following years, NAT developed Intelligence, Counter-intelligence, Security and Correctional Services (*Mbokodo* – a Xhosa word for the stone used to grind maize, used as a derogatory reference to the "harshness with which the department treated its victims"[37] – which was responsible for the ANC's detention camps such as Camp 32), VIP Protection, and Central Intelligence Evaluation departments. By the early 1980s, it had also developed a strategic intelligence capability "capable of forewarning the leadership of enemy moves, rather than merely being on the defensive"[38] (see Figure 4.3). This intelligence and security apparatus would continue to evolve over the 1980s as the state's counter-revolutionary onslaught against the ANC/SACP/MK structures was, slowly and quietly, complimented by a clandestine initiative by the National Intelligence Service to begin secret negotiations with the NAT in exile (see Chapter 8).

"Total Strategy" and the National Security Management System

The creation of the apartheid state's national intelligence and security structures (for police and civilian intelligence) in 1978–1979 became the

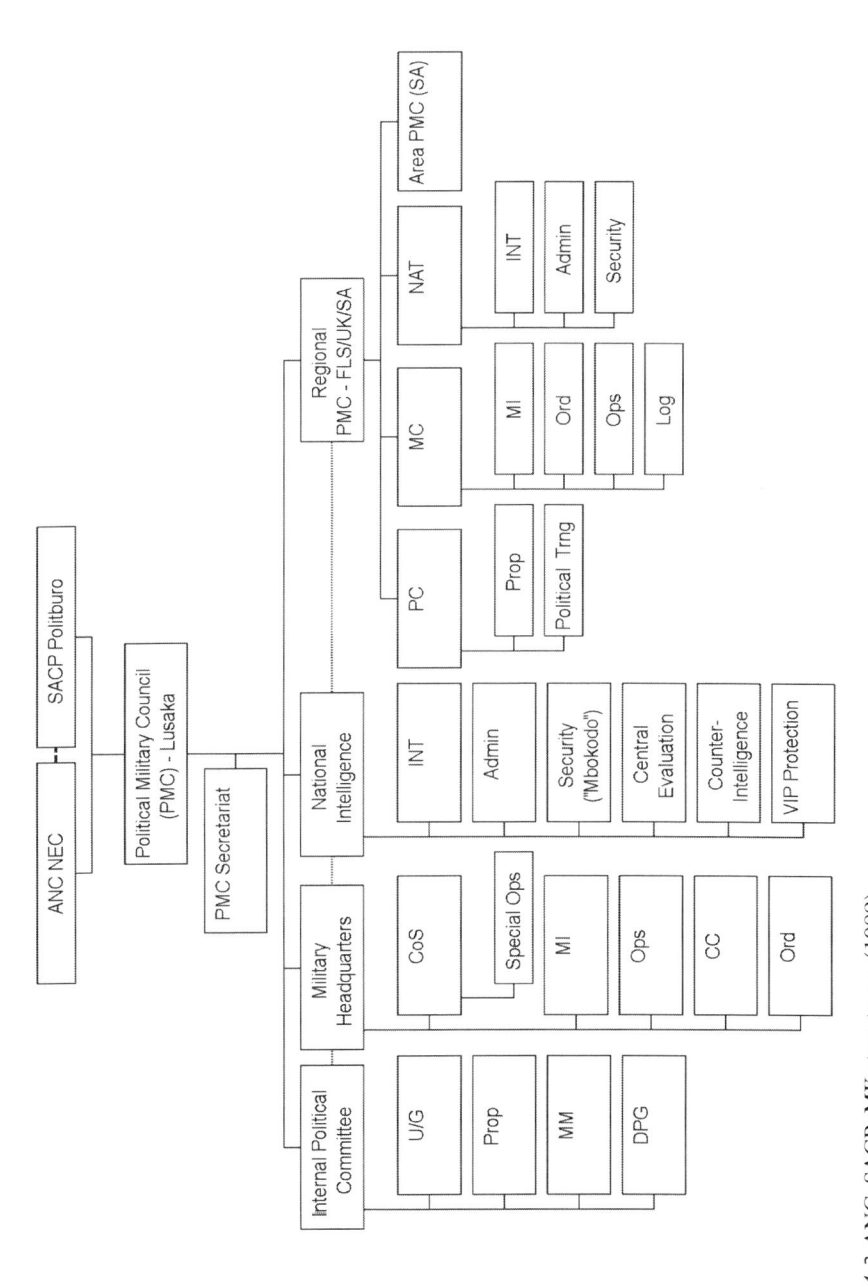

Figure 4.3 ANC–SACP–MK structures (1982).

framework for the implementation of "Total National Strategy"; this framework was the National Security Management System. The NSMS and its architecture was to have a radical effect on not only the implementation of the war-fighting capacities of the SADF in Southern Africa, but as well on the abilities of the state to mechanically and methodically eliminate its opponents through a highly developed targeting system which came to lie within the structures of the NSMS. What this ultimately led to was the "militarisation" of South African politics and society. DMI, and the SADF as a whole, became the dominant factor in South African policy-making and societal structures, followed closely by the SAP with their Security Branch providing similar control at local levels. These twin security structures, in the post-1978 period, replaced many of the more "traditional" decision-making elements in civil society and, by 1985/1986, had led to the militarisation of society. DMI further extended its influence throughout this political level by lessening even further (through personal networks, inter-service committees, and the national security system generally) the formal power of the individual services (army, navy, air force, medical service), transferring real power to its intelligence networks (including army intelligence).

This real-power influence was manifested continually for a number of reasons. First, Botha was an executive ruler, rather than a Parliamentary one. In the 1983 Constitution, this was formalised through the merging of the state presidency and the premiership. Thus, Botha believed that both Parliament and the National Party caucus could only "deliberate on matters of principle and not policy"; this realm would be reserved for the securocrats. Second, DMI controlled regional operations and policies through their strategic threat assessments. Finally, the "real fear that the Frontline States would seriously challenge, and end, South African hegemony within the region" meant the constant reliance on the SADF to defend against this threat.[39] Thus, DMI was at the centre of the militarisation of South African politics and society throughout the late 1970s and 1980s; this militarisation was accomplished through the SSC's network to control strategy and operations, the National Security Management System.

The implementation of the NSMS

The NSMS became the whole basis for carrying-out the "Total National Strategy" campaign throughout South Africa and the region. Based largely on the French national security system and the national war council system Britain used in Malaya, it was a response to the 1975 *Report on the National Security Situation* which outlined the need for an "active security management system to link national, interdepartmental, departmental and sub-departmental levels of operations". Furthermore, rather than relying on ad hoc meetings within the SSC, a permanent security staff was required to support the workings of such a system, as well as area and regional committees which would facilitate co-ordination at the regional and local levels.[40]

As Seegers has pointed out, "[the] origins of the perceptions [surrounding the NSMS] lie between 1961, when South Africa's departure from the Commonwealth severed the link with the United Kingdom's security institutions and interests, and the creation in 1972 of the State Security Council".[41] These origins have already been explored above in the discussions regarding the establishment of an independent South African intelligence dispensation following the withdrawal from the Commonwealth; however, what Seegers does point towards is that, with this same event, the *perception* of the value of what would become the NSMS (centred on the SSC) by both the public and the leadership of South Africa was similarly drawn from the feeling of isolation. Due to the rivalries inherent within this new dispensation in the 1960s, it was determined that only one national agency should have the ability to co-ordinate intelligence from these different bodies for the national intelligence brief; thus, the SSC was formed. The irony of this perception was that, in the 1960s and the early 1970s, politicians (including Prime Ministers Verwoerd and Vorster) and other leaders were trumpeting the safety and stability of South Africa, safe from assault or direct threat following the "crushing" of the insurgent liberation movements in the mid-1960s.[42] It was only within the small circle of Military Intelligence that the coming threat was being warned of after 1970.

This was all to change by the mid-1970s: as the violence grew in the post-1976 period, the state began to believe that they were not facing just a number of insurgent groups based outside the country and contributing to not much more than an annoyance level of concern; they began to believe, as the citizenry began to mobilise against the state, that they were facing a revolutionary war. In the face of this new level of onslaught, the securocrats revealed their new doctrine of counter-revolutionary strategy, which had grown out of the counter-insurgency doctrines of the 1960s and 1970s into an operational philosophy for the 1980s. This doctrine would require the activation of a national structure for implementation at every level, from the key decision-making body of the SSC down to the grassroots of every local police station and social support office, in order to succeed.

It was because the military had been warning about this coming onslaught that, when the threat emerged fully, "comparisons of departmental responsibilities for national security led to the view that the SADF was efficient and prepared, with serious wrongs being attributed to civilians".[43] Thus, Botha's securocrats (particularly DMI, who would be the spider at the centre of the web) activated the NSMS to oversee this doctrine. Overall, according to Major-General Charles Lloyd (secretary in the late 1980s), the NSMS was concerned with three areas: the government (for self-criticism and the correction of short-comings), the enemy (to "command, coerce and eliminate"), and the masses (whose support had to be won through communication and education).[44] Pretoria's overall aims were four-fold:

> To eliminate the radical black opposition...; to upgrade the physical and social infrastructures of selected townships; to reintroduce and legitimate community and town councils; and to gain the participation of "moderate" (some would use the term "collaborationist") black leaders in the National Statutory Council through which a new political/constitutional dispensation would emerge.[45]

The success of the first was obviously a prerequisite for the success of the other three. Thus, the NSMS was a true counter-revolutionary structure, aiming to meet most of the theoretical challenges with practical solutions. Its failings would be largely due to the fact that, *while it was successful at the national level as a strategic system*, the failure of a consistent strategy at the lowest level would pre-empt its possible success, and lead to its corruption and degeneration into a system of repression, societal destabilisation, and killing. The NSMS would become the framework within which systematised assassination was developed and implemented.

Such structures were not unique to the South African example but had been used throughout the post-1945 period by many powers engaged in counter insurgencies and indigenous wars of national self-determination. For this reason, the principal counter-insurgency theorists promote the implementation of such a system as part of their doctrine: Beaufre, Thompson and McCuen advocate the use of such structures, based on experience during the French Indochina and Algerian campaigns, the British Malayan Emergency, and the American Vietnam experience, in which such management structures were developed to implement and oversee the counter-insurgency strategies that confronted the liberation movements. The NSMS was organised primarily – around McCuen's theories on organising for counter-revolutionary warfare – as a means of co-ordinating the activities of the various security forces to confront the onslaught. Taking the teachings of these theorists to heart, the South African securocrats also looked to the significant examples of both Rhodesia and their own experiences in Namibia.[46] The latter served as both the testing-ground for the SADF's initial attempts at counter-revolutionary warfare and the securocrats "broader programme of economic, social and political reforms", and was thus central to later counter-revolutionary activities inside South Africa.[47]

The NSMS developed a new attitude, as well, in the security force members who controlled and ran it, from the highest level down; these members bureaucratised the security process – hence securocrats – believing that the grass-roots violence and the state's response to it could be managed effectively enough to defeat the revolutionary onslaught. As Williams has pointed out,

The seeds of this new identity and the emergence of this category of soldier were created in the 1960s. During the 1970s and the 1980s, they were to be consolidated via the institution of the State Security Council and the National Security Management System. In the early 1990s, it was from this category of soldier that the most pronounced praetorian tendencies were to emerge as the dominant factions of the Army struggled to adjust to the South African transition.[48]

The NSMS, as discussed above, was more-or-less premised on the belief that South Africa would soon have an executive presidency; indeed, from virtually the moment he became prime minister, Botha transformed the premiership into an executive position, relying heavily on the State Security Council as his main decision-making body and by-passing the Cabinet in every way except as a rubber-stamp for SSC policies and decisions. To meet the socio-political needs and underpin the security strategy, in August 1979, Botha introduced his "Twelve-Point Plan" for reform. Amongst other points, this included:

- The recognition and acceptance of the existence of multinationalism and of minorities in South Africa.
- The establishment of constitutional structures that provide for the full independence of the various Black nations in the republic, meaningful consolidation of the Black states and areas, and an acceptance of a socio-economic programme aimed at the development of such Black states and areas.
- The division of power among White South Africans, the Coloureds and the South African Indians within a system of consultation and joint responsibility where common interests are at issue.
- The maintenance of effective decision-making by the state, founded on a strong defence force and police force to ensure orderly government as well as a sound and efficient administration.
- The maintenance of free enterprise as the basis of economic policy.
- The recognition of economic interdependence of the population groups of the republic as well as the acceptance of the properly planned utilisation of manpower.
- The goal of a peaceful constellation of Southern African states respecting one another's cultural heritage, traditions and ideals.
- As far as possible, South Africa must follow a policy of neutrality in the confrontation between the superpowers and give priority to her own interests.
- South Africa's determination to defend itself against outside intervention in every practical way possible.[49]

Additionally, a rationalisation of the government was undertaken by Botha who, as a first-rate administrator, "aimed to impose some order on the government machine".⁵⁰ Differing radically from Vorster's more ad hoc decision-making process, Botha believed in a strong bureaucracy to develop and control policy. A Cabinet secretariat was established in the office of the prime minister by 1982; this was run by the shadowy Dr J.P. "Jannie" Roux. The existing 20 Cabinet committees which had existed under Vorster were rationalised to four: National Security, Constitutional, Economic, and Social Affairs; the first would eventually become part of the SSC, while the other three later formed the basis for the National Welfare Management System (see below). All four committees became far more powerful under Botha than they had been under Vorster.⁵¹ In August 1980, the Cabinet approved the first national strategy, entitled *Boek 1: Die RSA se Belange en die RSA-Regering se Doel, Doelstellings en Belied vir Ordelike Regering* [Book 1: The RSA's Interests and the RSA-Government's Goals, Aims and Policy for Orderly Government]; the same month, it created the South-West African Territorial Force (SWATF) and placed it under command of the Namibian Administrator-General, the general intention being to "Namibianise" the conflict.⁵²

The structure of the NSMS

The National Security Management System (see Figure 4.4) was instituted as an adjunct to the SSC, and was activated by the South African Cabinet on 16 August 1979; significantly, the 1979 *White Paper on Defence* had warned of "increased political, economic and military pressure on South Africa", also warning that "the military threat against the RSA is intensifying at an alarming rate".⁵³ According to Seegers' analysis (which is almost without comparison), the institutional evolution of the NSMS followed three clear phases. The first was during the period from the withdrawal from the Commonwealth in 1961 to the Potgieter Commission's recommendations in 1972 that led to the establishment of the SSC.⁵⁴ The second was from the rise of the SSC to the activation of the NSMS in 1979; this was due to "the recognition that the SSC, in its existing form, was inadequate". Finally, the third was the post-1980 developments, including the two states of emergency.⁵⁵ Heavily influenced by Military Intelligence, DMI would remain integral to the SSC and NSMS structures until the end of Botha's presidency in September 1989 and his replacement by De Klerk, who reduced DMI's influence, revamped the NSMS to a new National Co-ordinating Mechanism, marginalised the SSC in favour of a newly created Cabinet Committee on Security Affairs (thereby raising the position of the Cabinet once again), and enhanced the role of the NIS, in relation to the secret negotiations which had begun with the ANC.⁵⁶

The NSMS was by-and-large modelled on the security management system that General Jannie Geldenhuys had implemented in Namibia in 1977, and which subsequently began to develop inside South Africa. Comprising a Planning Committee at the executive level which had working groups responsible for security, socio-economic issues, and communica-

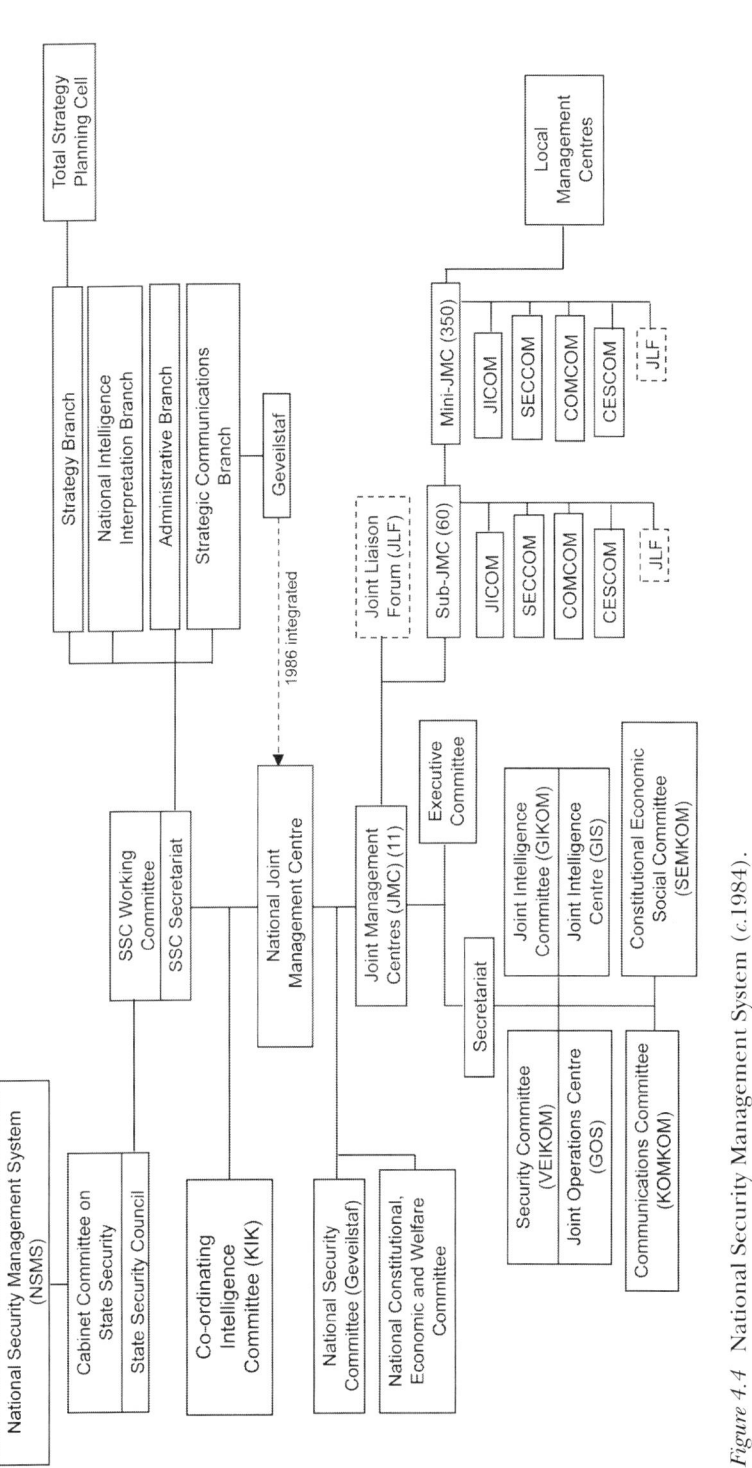

Figure 4.4 National Security Management System (c.1984).

tions, the Namibian system's work was replicated at the regional level throughout the SADF's various commands in the Operational Area.[57] Of particular interest were the *Gesamentlike Teeninsurgensie-komitees* (GTK or Joint Counter-insurgency Committees) which aimed at co-ordinating activities between the Security Branch (who were dominant in the Operational Zone in Namibia) and the SADF, who were called-in increasingly to assist the SAP as the violence escalated (the Security Branch did not have a fully developed counter-insurgency capability at this time).[58]

The NSMS was run primarily through the SSC secretariat, which was dominated (over 82 per cent) by the security agencies, in particular the National Intelligence Service; many of the *Veikoms* (security committees) attached to the system's Joint Management Centres (JMCs) were dominated by personnel from the SAP. With Botha's accession to the premiership, the reduction in influence of the Security Branch (and, in its turn, BOSS) and the rise of DMI meant that at the higher levels of the system, personnel from Military Intelligence dominated the proceedings, while NIS and Security Branch personnel filled-out many work-groups across the system.

Having already discussed the rise of the SSC in Seegers' first phase and the reasons behind its establishment in 1972, Seegers' second phase is of more immediate interest. The first part of enhancing the SSC process was to establish a framework structure for building the security needs of the embattled state. This was done, initially, with the establishment of the Working Committee of the SSC consisting of the heads of each government department and other Cabinet staff; its work was further sub-divided into 15 separate governmental areas, for each of which an inter-departmental committee (IDC or *Gesamentlike Veiligheidskomitee* – GVK) was established.[59] This became the heart of the system, functioning through a National Co-ordinating Committee to oversee the structures of the NSMS. In the mid-1970s, in response to unrest in Natal, the first Counter-insurgency Committee (*Teeninsurgensie Komitee* – TIK) was established in Durban under local SADF commander General Koos Lloyd.[60] As the NSMS was established throughout South Africa, it took on a similar character in terms of its complete dominance by members of the Security Branch or Military Intelligence.

The Joint Management Centres (JMCs)

The NSMS was structured along more-or-less the same lines as the Namibian security architecture: the SSC would comprise the executive-level co-ordinating structure with its secretariat and Working Group, and 12 Joint Management Centres (JMCs or *Gesamentlike Bestuurssentrums* – GBSs) were established at each SADF regional headquarters throughout the country (based on each province and the capital). In addition, five external JMCs were established to oversee Walvis Bay; Namibia Command; Southern Command for the TBVC states[61]; Northern Command for all Frontline States; and Angola. Finally, in response to the crisis in Rhodesia at the end of the 1970s, on 26 March 1979, the SSC established a JMC for Rhodesia to operate from the South African diplomatic mission in Salisbury, to complement the SSC's strategy of clandestine support for Rhodesia; six weeks later, on 27 August, the SSC also approved the establishment of a Mozambique JMC to co-ordinate further actions against Mozambique and in support of Rhodesia.[62] In February 1980, these two structures were folded.

The JMCs were the so-called "building-blocks" of the NSMS. Designed to "serve as a source of intelligence on the status of local conditions", they provided recommendations – at every level up the chain – on everything from local security concerns to infrastructural needs, facilitating the implementation of executive policy on socio-economic, political and security affairs.[63] Comprised of seven components, each JMC, established at the regional and command levels, replicated the national structures under the SSC. These components included:

1. *Daily Management Committee* or *Executive Committee* (*Uitvoerende Komitee*), which included the Chairmen of each of the four central committees below.
2. *Secretariat.*
3. *Security Committee* (SECCOM/VEIKOM), consisting of SAP, SADF, NIS, Security Branch, Railway Police, Civil Defence/Commando, and representatives of the state or provincial structures. Responsible for planning, monitoring and co-ordinating all regional security force actions, its functions (operational) were run through a Joint Operations Centre (*Gesamentlike Operasionele Sentrum* – GOS) which was run by the local SAP commander.
4. *Joint Intelligence Committee* (JICOM/GIKOM), which was composed of representatives from DMI, NIS, Security Branch, Department of Prisons, *Kitskonstabels*, and even private security companies operating in support of or co-operation with the security forces, as well as government officials on whatever level (provincial, regional or local). Headed by the local Army Intelligence commander, the GIKOM was run through a Joint Intelligence Centre (GIS). The function of the GIKOM was to provide day-to-day intelligence essential for the functioning of the JMC; this was done in co-ordination (through the GOS) with each of the security forces and other elements represented.[64]
5. *Communications Committee* (COMCOM/KOMKOM), that included representatives from SADF Combined Operations, the SAP and the Bureau of Information, was responsible for the compilation and dissemination of propaganda within its designated area.
6. *Constitutional/Economic/Welfare Committee* (CESCOM/SEMKOM), that included representatives from the various (Housing, Finance, Constitutional Affairs, Pensions, etc) government departments concerned with social welfare and reform.
7. *Liaison Committee* for dealing with the public sector.[65]

The break-down of the JMCs at each level followed geopolitical lines. At the top, directly under the National Co-ordinating Committee (NCC), resided the 12 internal JMCs. Below them, at the more local level, there were 60 Sub-JMCs corresponding to the SAP district divisions; finally, roughly 450 Mini-JMCs oversaw the counter-revolutionary strategy within each magisterial district. Each Sub-JMC and Mini-JMC reflected the same basic structure as the JMC, including its committee system.[66] With the later establishment of the Joint Security Staff (*Geveilstaf*) in 1986, the NCC was discontinued on 11 August 1986.

The command of each of these units corresponded to their level of responsibility; thus, the regional JMCs were commanded by the SADF regional commander, the Sub-JMCs by the District SAP commander, and the Mini-JMCs by the local SAP commander. At the lowest level, Local Management Centres (LMC) oversaw each city and designated town.[67] Thus, LMCs would report to Mini-JMCs, who would in turn report to Sub-JMCs, whose reporting would be done via the JMCs to the National Co-ordinating Committee (later the National JMC) and thus to the SSC itself (see Figure 4.5). An example of this is the Witwatersrand JMC: coinciding with the SADF Witwatersrand Command, four Sub-JMCS reported to it: East Rand, Johannesburg, Soweto and West Rand; the Mini-JMC of Alexandra Township, in turn, reported to the Johannesburg Sub-JMC. This whole system was "intended to identify and neutralise activists in the black townships, but also to win hearts and minds".[68]

While this was the ideal set-up according to the overall strategic picture (particularly given that DMI was the lead agency on implementing the counter-revolutionary strategy), at the regional and local levels, it was not always the best or most productive breakdown of command. The Intelligence Committees, for example, saw tensions between the Security Branch commanders, who coveted its leadership, and the Army Intelligence commanders who were statutorily in charge of the committee; this sometimes led to tensions between the two. Second, as the army had intervened on the ground in support of the SAP, another problem arose whereby Security Branch operatives – who had well-developed networks and contacts in place throughout the different communities (where the SADF were usually temporarily deployed in areas and, thus, had never developed this same kind of appreciation of their region or individuals) – were forced to operate under Army Intelligence personnel with little or no experience of a given situation and its finer points. This definitely detracted from the effectiveness of the counter-revolutionary strategy in various regions as well as the cross-agency co-operation and co-ordination.

Third, the army was attempting – with little experience, unlike the SAP in Rhodesia and Namibia, subsequently developed inside South Africa's borders – to implement a counter-insurgency strategy using literally textbook guidelines with considerably less regard for local issues; most interestingly, the JMCs were given the task of formulating local counter-revolutionary

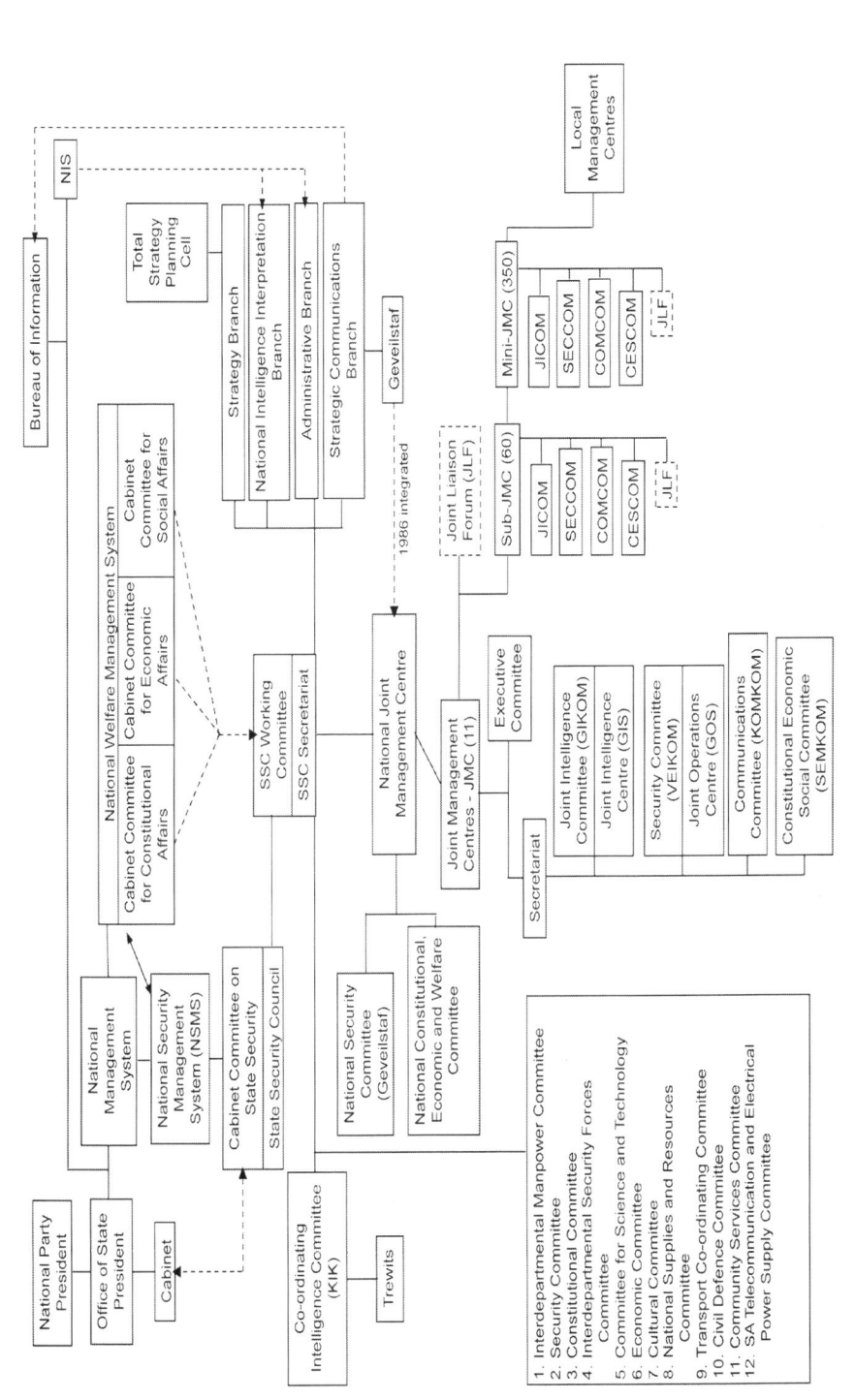

Figure 4.5 SSC and NSMS structures.

strategies to off-set the activities of the opposition movements.[69] The Security Branch officers operating within the area of an individual JMC would often refuse to reveal sources or even (occasionally) intelligence to Army members of the GIKOM because of this antagonism and the belief that SADF actions on this intelligence could jeopardise these sources; there would even occasionally be clashes between Army Intelligence and DMI in this regard. This often detracted from the effectiveness of the counter-revolutionary strategy. While DMI and Army Intelligence exerted key influence over the GIKOMs, the Security Branch controlled the VEIKOMs (the most important committee at Sub- and Mini-levels), as well as commanding overall the JMC at those levels. As Williams states, the "emphasis on the primacy of the SAP in the maintenance of 'law and order' continued to be adhered to".[70] Thus, while DMI and the SADF did exercise considerable control and influence over the strategy of the state and its intelligence requirements/operations, its total influence should not be overestimated. In 1982, most of the 12 JMCs were chaired by SADF Brigadiers, the officer commanding the provincial SADF command (except for the Western Cape and Witwatersrand JMCs which were commanded by the SAP Divisional Commander from 1984–1988);[71] this was largely due to the political alliance between the SADF (DMI) commanders and the political leadership under Botha.

Furthermore, the principal domain of intelligence continued to be within the individual Security Branch, DMI or NIS components within each area, rather than inside the GIKOM. What the GIKOM did contribute quite effectively towards, however, was the bringing together of "previously wary intelligence agencies" and the "contribution to a partial reduction in the duplication and parallelisation of their intelligence-gathering tasks".[72] It also ensured that intelligence was passed effectively up the chain-of-command within the NSMS, through each level of JMC, until reaching the National JMC and the SSC Secretariat (particularly the NIIB); this was meant to ensure an overall co-ordination of intelligence within the system, rather than intelligence being processed through individual agencies until being inserted through their command links with the SSC as an un-coordinated component at the top.

While a great deal of lip-service was paid towards the welfare component of the JMCs, the securocrats controlled the JMCs and saw that their overall dedication was towards the counter-revolutionary campaign.[73] This was particularly the case in terms of the JMCs' security-related committees (Intelligence, Security and Communications) where real authority lay; these committees oversaw, especially after 1985, the operational implementation of the counter-revolutionary strategy within the townships and regions, including the targeting of opponents for assassination or otherwise silencing (detention without trial, co-opting as *askaris*, etc) and the tasking for each operation.

This was "the heart of the whore" as it was once described: the region of figurative darkness where general guidelines brought down from the top (from the SSC secretariat, *Trewits* and the *Geveilstaf* through to Security Branch or DMI commanders) to deal with opponents of the state were interpreted as authorising their elimination and other acts, some criminal (such as domestic bombings and the extra-legal killings of opponents), as a legitimate tool of the state. This was partly due to the approximated ideology that exemplified both the individual political leaders (at whatever level) and the security force commanders. A similar *Weltanschauung* of both the world and South Africa's (and the Afrikaner's) place in it facilitated the interpretation of these orders, policies and guidelines. This is one of the principal starting-points for assigning responsibility to the political leadership, as well as the securocrats (both security force and civilian), for the implementation of an assassination programme as part of South Africa's counter-revolutionary strategy.

While this was designed to solve many problems of co-ordinating action within the counter-revolutionary strategy, as Seegers states, "efficiency required more than co-ordination, however, and the specified hierarchical relationships were intended to shorten and simplify the chain-of-command".[74] The reality was to be found in the third, post-1980 phase, in which the development of the NSMS was influenced by bureaucratic factors deriving from the relative newness of the NSMS structures (these new "civil servants" from the security forces had to be instructed in the ways of bureaucracies), as well as from the new "Revolutionary Oslaught"[75] assailing the state from without and within. What this was to result in was the excessive bureaucratisation of executive functions at every level: as Seegers states, "from its humble beginnings as providing advice to the Cabinet, the SSC ended astride a hierarchy of institutions intended to lead the whole state to efficiency".[76] As it was largely the SADF and SAP overseeing this bureaucratisation (with the NIS filling the administrative posts), the result was what has simply been referred to as the "militarisation of society".

Contrary to the original intentions of, first, the establishment in 1972 of the SSC and, later, the establishment of the NSMS itself – all designed to enhance co-ordination and eliminate overlap across the security forces – these new structures actually "perpetuated battles among security agencies over how best to manage South Africa's problems".[77] The different interests of each entity, agency or force begged budgetary support for their activities; thus, a constant pull existed between, for example, the weighting to be given to international, regional or domestic security concerns and the security force that would be responsible for seeing through the action. There was one area, though, in which the NSMS was to excel.

The Mini-JMCs were, according to Williams, the most important component of the whole NSMS and the counter-revolutionary strategy. Through the provision of the welfare needs of the population, alongside an effective counter-insurgency campaign in the townships and cities, the Mini-JMCs would "both neutralise and contain the near-insurrectionary mood that was sweeping the country".[78] The Mini-JMCs would also serve as the co-planning and co-ordinating bodies in the attempts (such as Operation KATZEN) to develop alternative structures to the ANC/UDF alliance. After the first declaration of a state of emergency, the welfare components of the Mini-JMCs began to gather greater importance; however, the domination of the securocrats continued all the same.

The JMCs were at the centre of the urban and domestic counter-insurgency campaign. What these structures served to facilitate was the targeting process of the state against its opponents. As the names of troublesome activists, UDF organisers and others generally perceived to be opponents of the state were processed through the JMCs for decisions on what action to take against them, the co-ordination of targeting across both the security forces and up the chain-of-command (sometimes, as will be seen, to the SSC and Cabinet levels) was completely facilitated by the NSMS-JMC structure. Instituted prior to the change-over from counter-insurgency to counter-revolutionary strategy, the JMCs were implemented to undertake four clear and progressive missions. First, they would see the return to military control and stability in the townships. Second, in so doing, they would restore the authority of the state and its functions. Third, they would legitimise the presence of the state through these restored functions. Finally, they would "develop and implement a long-term strategy capable of anticipating and containing future resistance via a compound of political, economic and military measures".[79] Thus, these missions reflected a sustained regaining of the initiative against the liberation forces and their allies within the urban areas of South Africa, the heart (because of the populations of the townships which fed the urban centres for labour) of the confrontation within South Africa. The success of these missions was not uniform, as conditions varied across townships and regions; local issues would often eclipse national (or even regional) ones in importance to the population. Thus, a blanket approach – all guided by the military securocrats from on high – was doomed to failure from the beginning, it could be argued.

The National Welfare Management System and the NSMS

This was, to some degree, anticipated and accounted for by these same securocrats; to both compensate for this danger and to provide for the political needs of the population (under standard counter-insurgency doctrine), the securocrats developed the National Welfare Management System as the twin-pillar of the state's strategy to the NSMS. In many senses, this represented the schizophrenia of the apartheid state. As observed by one senior security force commander, there was a "dual state": one part was the "government based on the Parliamentary process", while the other part was a "militarised stated based in the security establishment".[80]

Security was not, however, the sole focus of the NSMS; welfare and socio-economic issues were also of concern. This was to be reflected in the development – alongside and, in theory, of equal importance to the NSMS – of the National Welfare Management System (NWMS). While the NSMS was responsible to – and the responsibility of – the SSC, the NWMS was directly controlled by the OSP. This seeming split between direct chains-of-command at the national level was not reflected at the regional and local level, where both resided under the banner of the JMCs.

The NWMS was established under an 18 July 1985 executive order. With the changing nature of the conflict from one of counter-insurgency to one of counter-revolutionary warfare, it had become obvious that one of the primary methods to defeat the now-"Revolutionary Onslaught" was to "win the hearts and minds" of the population; the best way to do this, in the government's view, was to look to the welfare of the people. Thus, counter-revolutionary warfare (as counter-insurgency changed to in 1985) would be premised on the two leads of domestic (national) counter-insurgency in the townships, savannah and cities, and presenting the government as the provider for the people through their welfare needs – the classic twinning of "hearts and minds" with cross-the-board counter-insurgency operations.

The townships would become the specific target of the NWMS; the revolutionary violence that had broken-out in these population-centres had also become the centre of the uprising against the centre's power (and thus, in the perception of the securocrats, the "Revolutionary Onslaught" moving inwards from South Africa's borders) and therefore the primary security concern for the NSMS. This system centred around the three non-military Cabinet committees: Economic Affairs, Social Affairs and Constitutional Affairs, all of which would institute Working Committees (similar to the NSMS structures) to contribute to the whole of the NWMS; its overall management was the responsibility of the Welfare secretariat chaired by the state president. By integrating the NWMS into the OSP and building its structures alongside the NSMS at the national level and through the JMCs at the regional level, this would "ensure that welfare concerns were integrated into the conduct of counter-revolutionary warfare on an ongoing basis".[81]

Conclusions

With the implementation of the NSMS and the "Total National Strategy" on the ground – both overtly and through the development and deployment of covert units such as these – the political leadership in Pretoria assessed the situation as requiring a more even-handed approach to finding a political solution to the conflict, while maintaining pressure on the state's internal and external opponents through direct actions against them. As such, in the early 1980s, Botha's government instituted what could be called a twin-track approach – matching attempts at "reforming" the apartheid system to direct, intelligence-led targeting of the state's opponents; in this sense, the carrot and stick of apartheid's security paradigm.

5 Carrot and stick
The domestic COIN paradigm, 1980–1985

> We would just kill and that's how we got our kicks. We were adrenaline junkies, basically. The killings … obviously I have deep remorse now. But at the time, that's what we had to do. And we did it well. We were the best.
>
> Former Security Branch Commander

Revolutionary war – from Soweto to the Vaal Triangle

As the security situation deteriorated – and some in the apartheid government and securocracy began to develop a sense that a political solution, an accommodation of sorts, with the state's opponents had to be found while the security situation was stabilised – the Botha government introduced a twin-track approach of reform and direct, intelligence-led targeting. This approach was not, however, to succeed – and, as will be discussed here as well as in Chapters 6 and 7, an even more direct approach to countering the state's opponents would be chosen.

The failure of reform

In 1983, the National Party government proposed a series of reforms aimed at appeasing the internal resistance to its government. These included the establishment of a tricameral Parliamentary system with representation for Indians and Coloureds; a strengthened executive presidency which would allow the regime to control the pace of change; and "full African representation" in the political arena through the Homelands system and councils for "an elite of urban Africans".[1] In Botha's eyes, this would provide an answer (or at least as much of one as the National Party government was willing to support) to the political aspirations of the majority of the population, thereby fulfilling the political aims of counter-revolutionary warfare. In the eyes of the black majority, however, the fact that the tricameral system had no representation for Blacks doomed its acceptance from the start.

These proposals were roundly rejected, so much so that they sparked not only an internal revolt much stronger than the 1976 Uprising, but also the establishment of an internal protest movement that was more unified and purposeful in its aims than anything the ANC/SACP had been able to establish in more than 20 years of armed struggle. Following the failure of the National Party's reform strategies contained in the Constitutional reform proposals of 1983, Botha's government determined that any future reform initiatives should be made away from the glare of publicity; instead of top-down attempts to introduce reform (as the Constitutional package had been, based largely on the 1979 "Twelve Point Plan"), reforms would be introduced at the grass-roots "by improving living conditions in the townships and reforming local government".[2] This, it was hoped, would contribute sufficiently to the reform element of counter-revolutionary strategy; however, Botha and the securocrats would not loosen the security reins. Instead, the securocrats intensified and heightened the security initiatives – particularly the counter-revolutionary elements – against both the liberation movements and internal unrest, unleashing what would be the most all-encompassing counter-revolutionary strategy yet seen anywhere.

The UDF as an internal revolutionary threat

In January 1983, Allan Boesak, a radical Coloured cleric, proposed a broad-based coalition of resistance movements which would fight the National Party's proposals on constitutional reforms (including the *Black Local Authorities Act* and the implementation of Coloured and Indian Parliaments). This was to become the United Democratic Front (UDF). For all intents and purposes, it was – in the National Party's eyes – the internal wing of the ANC, allied closely to the Congress of South African Trade Unions (COSATU). In the UDF's eyes – as much as in the eyes of the leadership of the imprisoned ANC inside South Africa (as compared to the exiled ANC overseas) – it represented the ANC in only certain ways, but was its own movement in many others.

In 1982, facing-up to the upheaval after the 1976 Soweto Uprising and the near-marginalisation of the ANC to contemporary black youths in the townships, the ANC embarked on a new strategy – which involved a significant restructuring of the ANC/MK's governance model both in the Frontline States and in exile, including the establishment of the Political-Military Council structure (as noted in Chapter 4). This was to be better positioned to take-on the apartheid state in the aftermath of the Soweto Uprising, the changes in the apartheid state's own counter-insurgency capabilities, and the impact that the on-going raids and attacks by apartheid security forces were having on the ANC's Frontline structures. The new structure was also designed to provide maximum support to MK Special Operations – responsible for the "spectacular" attacks inside South African, including the South African Coal, Oil and Gas Corporation (SASOL) coal-oil refinery (1 June 1980), the Koeberg nuclear facility (20

December 1982), the rocket attack on the SADF's Voortrekkerhoogte headquarters in August 1981, and the car-bomb outside SAAF headquarters in May 1983. The last of these – with its high civilian and military casualties – was to be the trigger for the belief of the securocrats that they had to "abandon the Queensbury rules" (paraphrasing one of the leading counter-revolutionary operatives, Eugene De Kock, later) in order to strike hard at the ANC's capabilities and structures.

The UDF was seen by the government as central to the "revolutionary onslaught" and "mass offensive" orchestrated by the ANC/SACP; consequently, little distinction was made between the external and internal threat. The UDF, and its off-shoot the Mass Democratic Movement (MDM), was a loose conglomeration of church groups, human rights organisations, regional and local development bodies, and others; it also included the powerful but hated End Conscription Campaign, which was eventually banned in 1988. Interestingly, the UDF was never banned, although this was considered in mid-1984; the government decided that due to the high international profile of the UDF, a strategy of "containment whereby leadership would be removed and tensions within the organisations exploited to neutralise their effect" would be pursued.[3]

The UDF was launched nation-wide in August 1983; because of its support for the Freedom Charter and other principles of the ANC, the UDF and its activists were immediately targets for counter-revolutionary actions. Of some 24,000 people detained in 1986, for example, more than 80 per cent were UDF supporters.[4] This is evident from SSC documents under which the UDF was declared to be an organisation that was "dangerous to the state which had to be neutralised". The UDF was further accused of fomenting unrest and "directly and indirectly promoting the aims of the SACP/ANC" through actions it was involved in.[5] According to other documents circulated to all SSC members at a meeting in April 1986, the UDF was singled out as the most important body in the "internal revolutionary onslaught": "Although the UDF publicly distances itself from violence, the violence that flowed from UDF arranged actions was so intertwined with ANC terrorist actions that it was difficult to differentiate between them."[6] Thus, the UDF was seen as being completely involved in the internal revolutionary onslaught, either independently or on behalf of the ANC/SACP. This seemed to be all the more pertinent following the September 1984 Vaal Triangle Uprising; while the government tried to prove this resulted from co-ordinated UDF action, this uprising was the most serious and spontaneous the country had seen since 1976. As a result, the UDF had "to tread a fine tightrope between openly calling for the overthrow of the government, which would guarantee arrest, and articulating the feelings of angry township youth".[7]

As part of its alliance with the ANC, in 1985–1986, the UDF organised itself into similar revolutionary structures which would oversee and co-ordinate activities across the country, from the highest level to the streets;

these were seen as the alternative sources of governance for the townships, following the rejection of the government's imposed Black Councils. These structures coalesced around "street committees", which were established within the townships, so that literally every street had a committee. These committees would, in turn, report to an "area committee", which would be run by an "area co-ordinating committee" (ACC); these oversaw the townships area-by-area. Alongside the ACC was a "Forum" for the co-ordination of cultural and other popular organisations in the area. Finally, these were all responsible to the Regional UDF Executive which were ultimately answerable to the UDF National Executive. Within these structures, the infamous "People's Courts" were established to provide a form of law and order in the absence of any policing authority; originally designed to deal with petty crimes, the "Courts" soon became the forum for political trials of suspected informers and any who did not see eye-to-eye with the "young comrades".[8]

For the ANC, this organising for revolution by the UDF was all a godsend. Now, it seemed, the era of "people's war" had finally arrived. The cry to "make South Africa ungovernable" became the rallying-cry for the ANC and UDF supporters inside the country. "Young Comrades" in the townships began a reign of terror against the residents, forcing collaborators and informers out into the open where they could be judged by "People's Tribunals", often resulting in the "necklacing" of the accused. This, of course, resulted in the drying-up of the Security Police's intelligence networks and, thus, a serious reduction in the amount of intelligence reaching the counter-revolutionary structures.

The uprising also presented what was considered the ideal environment for the establishment, finally, of an internal MK structure to institute revolutionary warfare inside South Africa. As a result, MK officers and UDF politicos encouraged prospective recruits to stay inside the country and organise, as well as acting as reception committees for returning guerrillas, rather than leaving the country – as had been encouraged following the Soweto Uprising – to receive training abroad. This would, ultimately it was hoped, link the ANC/MK outside the country with the UDF and its "Street Committees" inside the country, and lead to full revolutionary war; unfortunately – for the ANC and MK – this would not be the case.[9]

The growth of the state's counter-revolutionary warfare capabilities

By the early 1980s, Pretoria's intelligence leaders faced a precarious and dangerous picture. The conventional war in Angola was not succeeding against either PLAN or FAPLA to the extent that had been hoped; special forces operations throughout the Frontline States were not achieving the debilitation or, preferably, elimination of the ANC and its supporters; and Rhodesia, South Africa's closest ally, had just fallen. The counter-insurgency campaign in Namibia was also not achieving the results desired, either military (against PLAN) or political (against SWAPO and in support of continued South African administration of the territory). And – most pertinently and immediately – following the 1976 Soweto Uprising and the growing activities by MK Special Operations units inside South Africa itself, the domestic security scene was deteriorating rapidly, with the securocrats feeling that the initiative was beginning to slip from their grasp. From Pretoria's perspective, this was no illusion. By 1983, the securocrats' views that they were faced with the threat of "armed Soviet clients attempting to prosecute a war of national liberation against the Republic" or even the "Algerian model ... wherein the metropolitan power ... was besieged by an insurgency" were changing. Looking up the continent, it was "externally backed African militaries" that threatened, supported by either neighbouring Marxist newly liberated governments (such as in Angola) or by continuing Soviet/Chinese support. This threat was primarily against the economic assets and well-being of the republic (recalling the economic down-turn following the Soweto Uprising and workers' strikes), which possessed the "continent's greatest conjunction of vital assets". Internal violence in South Africa was due to socio-political instability, which could be confronted; externally, those who presented a military (whether this was in conventional, revolutionary, guerrilla or terrorist form) threat to the republic would be crushed by military means.[10] This would, throughout the 1980s, come in the form of military destabilisation of the Frontline States by means of raids, bombings, the fomenting of internal guerrilla movements, and attacks on economic assets throughout the Frontline States.

This fed directly into the counter-revolutionary vision of the securocrats, who believed that violence could be destroyed by the threat and use of counter-violence, and that the political aspects of counter-revolutionary warfare would see to the socio-economic and politico-constitutional needs of the population. This violence began to spread alarmingly in September 1984 following the Vaal Triangle Uprising and the outbreak of violence in Sebokeng, Evaton and Sharpeville (the last quite significantly, given that it was the "Mecca" of the liberation movements following the 1960 Sharpeville Massacre which many chart as having begun the war for liberating South Africa). The security forces needed to restore law and order immediately lest it spread to other parts of the country. This was also significant as the "geography" of resistance began to shift from the major metropolitan townships to the ghettoised urban centres. Between the outbreak of violence and June 1986, 851 people were killed by the police; over the next nine years, according to the South African Institute for Race Relations, 18,997 people were to die from the renewed violence, many of them in the civil war between the ANC and *Inkatha* in ZwaZulu, Natal and the Witwatersrand.[11] At the same time, MK launched a number of infiltration operations against the state in Johannesburg and elsewhere. The SSC, in light of the inability of the SAP to contain the violence, ordered the deployment of 7,000 SADF personnel into the townships as a response to the violence on 19 October 1984; by 1986, this number had risen to more than 10,000 SADF personnel, roughly ten per cent of the SADF's total strength.[12] This deployment – in at least 96 townships – was part of what the securocrats called an "urban counter-insurgency role"; in reality, it was both the use of the SADF to contain the violence through aggressive patrolling, "hearts and minds" civic actions and *KomOps*, and (more relevantly) the positioning of the SADF both on the ground and in operational-planning discussions to assist in neutralisation and assassination operations through the regional and local JMCs. While it was at the local and regional level that the most important counter-insurgency work was carried out, in many respects, at the national level, a different approach to countering this growing revolutionary onslaught was clearly required.

Forming a counter-revolutionary warfare intelligence capability

Yet, by the early 1980s, concerns were beginning to emerge within the National Party's constituency regarding the "militarisation of South African society". This "creeping coup" by the SADF generally, and DMI particularly, was – by the early 1980s – the result of Botha's activation of the NSMS. As Williams points out,

> It was only when the reality of this militarization was to strike white society, the prime constituency of the SADF, that voices were raised in protest. In the pre-1984 period the militarization of the executive reaches of the state ensemble had been something "up there" removed from the concerns of the average white citizen. The SADF's various regional forays had been something "out there", removed from the domestic concerns of white society ... The post-1984 period brought the reality of militarization and the low-scale civil war home to many white South Africans.[13]

To combat this perception, in DMI's thinking, the fight had to be taken to the enemy by more covert and direct means. This would result in the development of a series of specialist units from within DMI, the Special Forces and the SA Army over the course of the 1980s for clandestine and covert operations within South Africa; it would only be in the early 1990s, after it became publicly apparent that these "specialist units started abrogating unlimited powers to themselves", that they would be reined in.[14]

The origins of the state's capability to conduct counter-revolutionary warfare lay at the end of the 1970s. By the end of the decade – a period in which the special forces were used almost entirely to support field-level COIN activities, alongside either the SADF's conventional forces or 32 Battalion – the South African securocrats were only starting to envisage the type of special forces structure that would be required to conduct effective counter-revolutionary warfare (as opposed to purely COIN). Following a 1979 meeting at Fort Klapperdorp of senior security force commanders and securocrats, it was decided to enhance the Special Forces into a unit more capable of disrupting the ANC's establishment of bases in neighbouring countries, as well as disrupting internal opponents and their structures.[15] This was clear from a February 1981 speech to Parliament by Malan, in which he stated that "we shall, by means of our security forces, locate and destroy hostile terrorist bases, wherever they may be established,"[16] which formed the basis for special operations strategy for most of the 1980s. Subsequently, a reorganisation of Special Forces took place on 1 January 1981, when Special Forces was transformed into an independent formation, directly under the command of the CSI; at the same time, the various Reconnaissance Commandos attained the status of Regiments.[17]

Yet the apartheid state required a far greater capability in counter-revolutionary warfare than either the Special Forces or the SAP's COIN units could provide to this point. In a document titled "Institutions and Functions of the Special Forces", the SSC determined that both SADF and SAP special operations units needed to be established which would "not need to answer to Parliament, but only to the SSC"; these would be funded from secret funds, develop autonomous intelligence-gathering capabilities, and recruit their operatives from all ranks of the government.[18] These units were the tools for implementing the government's counter-revolutionary strategy throughout the 1980s – including its formalised development of assassination as a tool of state policy and a technique within that counter-revolutionary strategy – and, ultimately, of the re-ordering of the security establishment into a rogue force blighted by power and unwilling to see through the reform process.

The origins of these specialist units – not only in DMI, but also in the Security Branch and across the national intelligence structures – lay not with the flood of Rhodesian special operators south after 1980, although this was the catalyst: the skills brought to South Africa by these experts in anti-terrorist, covert and counter-guerrilla operations would offer DMI the same hands-on skills that the SAP Security Branch had gained in their operations to support the Rhodesians during the 1960s and 1970s, as well as in their counter-insurgency operations in Namibia. However, the real basis for the development of these units lay with Botha's "empowerment of the SADF intelligence community".[19]

As a direct result, in January 1979, the Security Branch counter-insurgency unit *Koevoet* was formed in South-West Africa for operations against SWAPO (see below); a combination of SWAPOL and SADF Special Forces elements, it was to be South Africa's equivalent to the Rhodesian Selous Scouts to "act as the eyes and ears of, and to collect

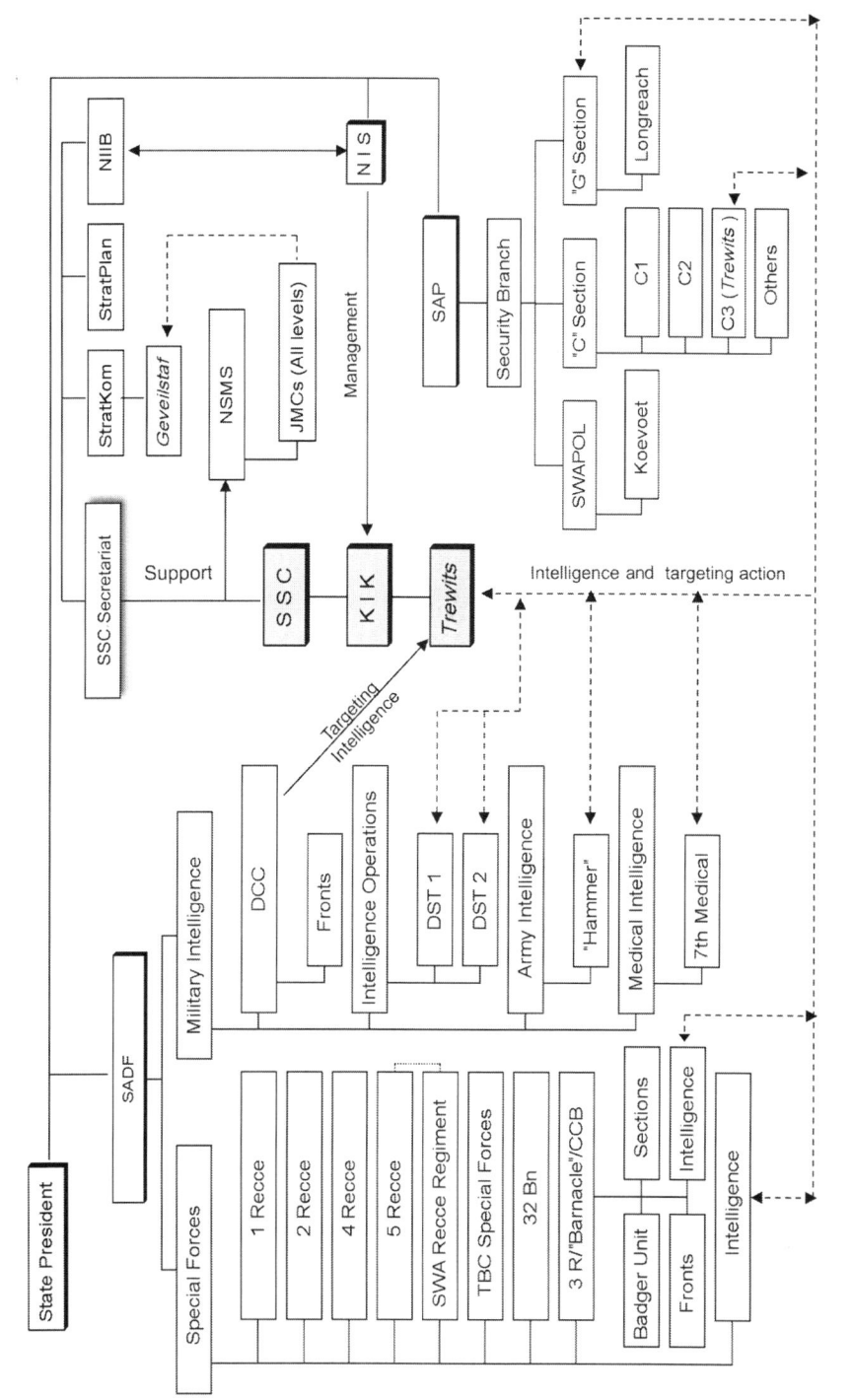

Figure 5.1 South Africa's covert structures (*c.*1986).

intelligence for, the military".[20] In 1983, elements of *Koevoet* were integrated with the Security Branch counter-insurgency unit C1 to support internal SAP counter-revolutionary operations. This unit, formed for the expressed purpose of "turning" then using captured ANC, SWAPO and PAC guerrillas to operate against their former comrades (in a practice known as "pseudo-operations"), was established in 1979 at the Vlakplaas police farm; similar units were established at other locations (see below).[21] Known as *askaris* (Swahili for "fighters"), the "turning" of such guerrillas was a practice instituted by the British in Kenya and the Rhodesians during their bush-war. Security Branch also accelerated its operations against the ANC/SACP internationally – particularly in London and across the Frontline States – where C1 and its partner in G Section of Security Branch (led by the infamous Craig Williamson) operated at will.[22] Finally, DMI also reorganised the former BOSS "Z-Squads" into "Delta-40" (or "D40") in 1979, tasked specifically with "monitoring certain external opponents of the regime with a view to their possible extinction" – in other words, an assassination unit.[23] By 1986, this unit had become the Civil Co-operation Bureau (CCB), responsible for conducting covert counter-revolutionary warfare within South Africa, as well as abroad, as the unit with primary responsibility for establishing the deepest-cover destabilisation programmes within South Africa, *regardless* of whatever political dispensation the future was to bring. As will be noted in Chapter 6, all of these were supported and co-ordinated centrally by the "K" Committee and *Trewits*, in whose monthly meetings "intelligence would be exchanged and targets identified" by Security Branch, DMI, Special Forces and NIS representatives. Established in 1986, *Trewits* – alongside the Joint Security Staff (*Geveilstaf*) of the SSC (see Chapter 7 further) – co-ordinated intelligence across the SSC and security force structures for the targeting of opponents, with the NIS providing "targeting databases" for each country concerned.[24] These developments were seen as a means of meeting the need for turning the counter-insurgency activities of the state security apparatus into a counter-revolutionary programme (see Figure 5.1).

Security Branch resurgent: SAP counter-intelligence capabilities

The capabilities developed by DMI to support counter-revolutionary warfare activities were by no means alone. While the NIS maintained its status as an analytic and co-ordinating actor within the national intelligence dispensation, the SAP Security Branch moved – by the end of the 1970s and throughout the 1980s – to redevelop the COIN capabilities that it has lost earlier in the decade; at the same time, it also began to develop some of the most brutal, horrific counter-intelligence capabilities within its structures which – on the one hand – leveraged those captured guerrillas who had been "turned" against their organisations, while – on the other hand – instituting an on-the-ground operational capacity inside South Africa which reflected its earlier COIN activities in Rhodesia and South-West Africa. The two units central to these capabilities were the COIN unit *Koevoet*, deployed in South-West Africa, and the C1 counter-intelligence unit deployed at the Vlakplaas police-farm near Pretoria (see Figure 5.2).

Koevoet *emerges*

One of the results of the "fall" of Rhodesia was the flood southwards of thousands of Rhodesian special forces and intelligence personnel. In 1978, SADF Chief Magnus Malan instructed the SAP to establish in Namibia a unit similar to Rhodesia's Selous Scouts to "act as the eyes and ears of, and to collect intelligence for, the military".[25] The unit – formed under Operation "K" by Brigadier Hans "Stirk" Dreyer (former head of the Security Police in Natal) – became known as *Koevoet* (its formal title was the South African Police Counter-insurgency Unit). Translated as "Crowbar" (*Koevoet* literally meant 'cow's foot', matching the cloven hoof shape of a crowbar), this name was encouraged by Law and Order Minister Louis Le Grange who spoke of the "crowbar which prises terrorists out of the bushveld like nails from rotten wood".[26] Based in Oshakati (Ovambo) and Rundu (Kavango), it gradually expanded its base-of-operations throughout the whole Operational Zone and into Angola.

Koevoet captured its first insurgents in May 1979, and became part of the South-West African Police (SWAPOL) – created in 1981 to provide law enforcement and counter-insurgency policing outside the Operational Zone – in 1985; it worked alongside both the SWAPOL Special Task Force (created in 1977 for riot control, anti-terrorism and counter-insurgency operations also outside the Operational Zone) and SADF Special Forces units (including most particularly 5 Recce and 32 Battalion).[27] Although originally founded as a policing unit with support from the Recces, by early 1980 *Koevoet* had developed operational capabilities similar to the Selous Scouts and the Portuguese *Flechas*;[28] this was to increase operational-effectiveness, using information retrieved from an informant or an interrogation, when the SADF was unable to react fast enough due to environmental conditions in the Operational Zone.

The original intention was to have two elements in *Koevoet*: one which operated similar to RENAMO, using local people to fight PLAN, while another element would use captured and "turned" PLAN guerrillas to conduct pseudo-operations against SWAPO.[29] For the first task, *Koevoet* had been established originally as a result of earlier failed attempts to create a Namibian surrogate force similar to RENAMO. A small group of "turned" ex-SWAPO fighters (known locally as *makakunyanas* which literally meant

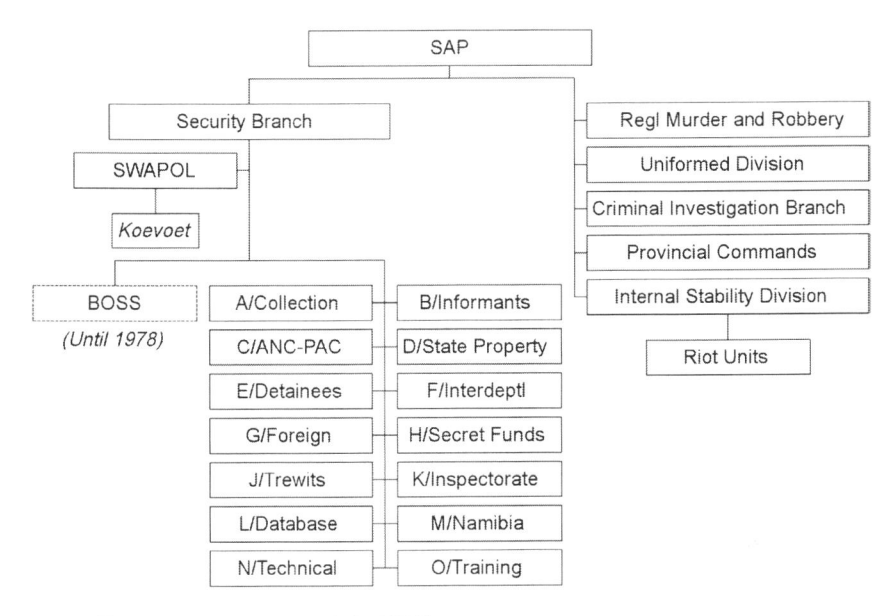

```
                              SAP
         ┌─────────────────────┴──────────────────────┐
   Security Branch                              Regl Murder and Robbery
   SWAPOL                                       Uniformed Division
     Koevoet                                    Criminal Investigation Branch
                                                Provincial Commands
   BOSS    A/Collection    B/Informants        Internal Stability Division
  (Until 1978) C/ANC-PAC   D/State Property     Riot Units
           E/Detainees     F/Interdeptl
           G/Foreign       H/Secret Funds
           J/Trewits       K/Inspectorate
           L/Database      M/Namibia
           N/Technical     O/Training
```

Figure 5.2 SAP Security Branch (*c.*1983).

"blood suckers") and former FNLA members were selected and trained as the nucleus of *Koevoet*. These groups grew over time until, at its largest, *Koevoet* comprised around 250 white officers and 2,750 black indigenous recruits, 90 per cent of whom were recruited locally in the Ovambo and Kavango peoples. The lot of these locally recruited "constables" was not good as they were immediately targeted by SWAPO for "collaboration": between 1978 and 1982, 198 "constables" were executed by SWAPO while off-duty in their homes.[30]

For the second task, *Koevoet* co-operated with 5 Recce across the Operational Zone.[31] Learning from the Selous experience – most of *Koevoet*'s officers and NCOs had experience from Rhodesia – *Koevoet* soon developed an autonomous combat capability, engaging in search-and-destroy missions against PLAN and FAPLA insurgents, as well as (occasionally) providing intelligence and other support to Jonas Savimbi's UNITA guerrilla group in Angola. Although numbering only some 10 per cent of the total security force capacity in Namibia, *Koevoet* accounted for upwards of 80 per cent of the insurgents killed;[32] on some missions, its success was absolute: in one contact in 1984, it killed 34 out of 34 PLAN guerrillas.[33] Its combat capability became so paramount that Dreyer virtually abandoned the intelligence-gathering mission of *Koevoet* in favour of search-and-destroy missions by 1984.[34] This often conflicted directly with the SADF's "hearts and minds" campaign in Namibia; *Koevoet* were time and again accused of being an assassination unit, and were indicted in

Namibian courts after independence in 1990 with gross human rights violations, including the killing of the elderly, women and children in the villages where the unit searched for intelligence on PLAN activities. One of the more distasteful aspects of *Koevoet*'s operations was that the Ovambo and Kavango "constables" who filled out the unit's ranks were paid *kopgeld* ("head money") for each guerrilla captured or killed; this amount ranged from R200 to R20,000 and served often "as an incentive for the extra-judicial murder of captives".[35]

The most significant element of *Koevoet*'s operations was its use of these *askaris*, mirroring the Selous experience; this would be particularly for the conduct of counter-guerrilla (in their parlance, "pseudo-terrorist operations" which formed part of anti-terrorist operations) operations developed by the Selous in Rhodesia. With approximately 300 white officers and NCOs, in 1988 *Koevoet* admitted to having approximately 40–50 "turned" guerrillas in its ranks.[36] These men had little, if any, reason to refuse to work with *Koevoet*: captured in a guerrilla conflict, they would otherwise be executed (strictly against the Geneva Conventions); additionally, once they started working for the South African security forces, they had little chance of being accepted back into their families or circles of friends. Thus, as Ellis points out, "battle-hardened, psychologically and socially divorced from their communities of origin and compromised by their treachery, *askaris* were well-suited to the grisliest acts of war".[37]

Koevoet was accused by opponents of South Africa's trusteeship of Namibia of being an assassination unit, with some saying the "K" in its code-name stood for "Kill". This suspicion was furthered when, in 1980, a list of 50 opponents of the South Africans was found on the body of an Ovambo official who had died in a traffic accident; the first two names on the list (businessmen David Sheehama and Mateus Elago) had already been killed by "suspected terrorists", and a third narrowly escaped a landmine planted under his car by *Koevoet* members. SWAPO immediately publicised this as an "assassination list".[38]

While *Koevoet* quickly gained a reputation as a most brutal unit, geared towards hard bush fighting and the assassination of PLAN/SWAPO leaders, even within such a fraternity, certain individuals stood out. One of the most ruthless and effective of *Koevoet*'s commanders was Captain Eugene de Kock. Considered later to be apartheid's "greatest assassin", De Kock had served in Rhodesia on 11 tours of duty between 1968 and 1973, training with the Rhodesian SAS and Rhodesian African Rifles, two of the most effective Rhodesian units. In the late 1970s, De Kock served with the Oshakati (Namibia) Security Branch prior to being transferred to *Koevoet*. After more than four years in that unit, De Kock requested a transfer to the internal counter-terrorism branch of the SAP.[39] He would feature prominently over the following decades as a central figure in apartheid's covert war against the liberation movements.

The domestic COIN paradigm 107

By the early 1980s, and with the strategic and structural changes occurring across the national intelligence dispensation, the Security Branch also reorganised itself to be a full player in the coming counter-revolutionary warfare effort. Indeed, by 1987, some 13 per cent of the SAP (of a total strength of 92,000 including reservists) worked for the Security Branch.[40] Generally speaking, the Security Branch was divided into 14 sections ("A" through "O" – see Table 5.1); while these would change occasionally, in the mid-1980s, these included:

As the most immediately relevant to the implementation of the state's "Total Counter-revolutionary Strategy" (see Chapter 7), "C" and "G" Sections are examined starting on p. 108.

Table 5.1 SAP Security Branch sections (*c.*1985)

Section A	Responsible for information collection, it was run in the early-1980s by Colonel Jac Buchner. By 1992, "A" dealt with "Revolutionary/Radical" groups.
Section B	Worked with a network of black activist informants in the townships, who provided information about the movements, activities and strategies of the ANC/UDF activists. This included non-mainline groups such as the Detainees Parents Support Committee, SA Council on Sport, etc. By 1992, "B" dealt with "Reactionary Groups".
Section C	An operative unit responsible for "anti-terrorism" activities, in reality counter-terrorism and counter-intelligence; also originally housed the *Trewits* within Security Branch.
Section D	Dealt with state property, border posts, airports, etc.
Section E	Dealt with detainees.
Section F	Covered inter-departmental committees, library, research, and (by 1992) legal advice.
Section G	Generally responsible for the long-term penetration of the ANC abroad.
Section H	Secret Funds (until 1992); reformed to cover Constitutional Services and connected into returning exiles and releases.
Section J	Connected to the SSC and the JMCs. By 1992, it had become the *Trewits* section within Security Branch.
Section K	Inspectorate. By 1992, Special Accounts/Secret Funds.
Section L	Database and Information Centre.
Section M	Namibia. By 1992, the Technical Division.
Section N	Technical Division. By 1992, the Administrative section.
Section O	Training.[a]

Note
a Security Branch information drawn from Pauw, *Heart of Darkness*, 194; and TRC2:3, Appendix 13.

Koevoet *enters South Africa: the Vlakplaas "C" Section*

In May 1983, elements of *Koevoet*, including now-Major De Kock, were withdrawn from Namibia by the Security Branch and relocated at a police farm outside of Pretoria called Vlakplaas. These elements were to expand the compliment of a unit designated C1 ("ANC/PAC Desk"), a Security Branch counter-intelligence unit formed for "the identification and tracking of ANC and PAC infiltrators and also their rehabilitation"; in practice this meant the expressed purpose of "turning" ANC and PAC guerrillas to operate against their former comrades.[41]

The Vlakplaas farm was originally established in 1979 when Colonel Jan Viktor and Brigadier Johan Coetzee, head of Security Branch, saw the need for turning the counter-insurgency activities of the state security apparatus into a counter-revolutionary programme, using members of the revolutionary forces that confronted the state against these same organisations; it was not originally envisaged as a "death squad". C1 sections, although headquartered at Vlakplaas, were deployed throughout the country; other such provincial "farms" were established at many other locations, including at Camperdown and Elandskop, and the *askari* unit in Natal run by Colonel Andy Taylor. At the same time, section C2 was established, responsible for monitoring the movement of activists leaving South Africa and the interrogation of arrested guerrillas, who would then – if willing – be passed on to C1; it was run throughout the 1980s by Major Martin Naudé, and developed an extensive collection of photographs, which was regularly updated and was given to *askaris* to identify individuals.

As a large part of its operations, C1 – in many respects Security Branch's equivalent of the SADF Special Forces – conducted covert operations on behalf of Security Branch and the central targeting intelligence unit *Trewits*, with which it liaised extensively; indeed, in the first half of the 1980s, "C" Section housed *Trewits*, rarely making any determination of targets on its own, but rather being directed by the commanders of Security Branch acting in co-operation with the SSC, its branches and *Trewits*. While C2 was a prime participant in *Trewits*' intelligence collection for target development process, it is also notable that a *Trewits* sub-unit – designated C3 – was established subsequently at Vlakplaas, run by Colonel Tom Louw, to gather intelligence to "specifically target opponents of the government".[42] Such targeting would then involve cross-border raids and clandestine operations where guerrillas would be tracked throughout South Africa and the Frontline States and snatched; in many cases, this involved targeting identified members of the ANC and PAC for assassination. Ostensibly, the primary *raison d'être* of C1 was for the *askaris* to "identify their former comrades and arrest them"; over the course of C1's existence, however, no more than two activists a year were ever arrested, pointing to Vlakplaas' more sinister goal.[43] *Askaris* would also be "loaned-out" to other SAP units or, at times, units of the Special Forces and DMI.

During its existence, "C" had a variety of heads: after overseeing its establishment, Colonel Viktor was replaced by Brigadier Willem Schoon, who commanded from 1980 to 1989. He was replaced, at the end of the 1980s, by Brigadier Nick van Rensburg, and, finally, Major-General I.J. Engelbrecht into the 1990s. When C1 was established, it was placed under the command of Captain Dirk Coetzee, a police counter-insurgency soldier who had fought in Rhodesia, in August 1980; initially it was quite small, composed of only five white policemen and 15 *askaris*, with the odd former ZAPU or RENAMO member occasionally involved.[44] In September 1981, when the unit officially became operational, it began to expand into four squads; by 1990, there would be nine. In December 1981, Coetzee was moved to other duties within the SAP and replaced by Captain Jan Carel Coetzee, who served throughout 1982, eventually being replaced by Lieutenant-Colonel Jac Cronje; ten years later, in 1989, Dirk Coetzee and former *askari* Almond Nofemala were the first to go public regarding the existence of "death squads" in the South African security forces.[45] Cronje left in 1985 to head the Northern Transvaal Security Branch, where he established another death squad with Warrant Officer Joe Mamsela, Captain Jacques Hechter and Warrant Officer Paul van Vuuren between 1985 and 1988.[46]

Over the course of the 1980s, Vlakplaas (as C1 came to be known) instituted a programme of interrogation, torture and murder against members of the ANC or PAC and their supporters in the country. It became known within the establishment as the "security arm of the National Party". Perceived equally as "the hyena" or "vultures" of Security Branch, Vlakplaas was often responsible for "cleaning-up" the problems created by other elements of the security forces. This happened time and again, for example when other members of the Security Branch had to dispose of individuals who had been killed or very badly maimed during interrogations; a favourite tactic for such activities was folding the body over a wad of explosives, binding it with ropes into a rotund package called a "Buddha", and detonating the explosives, demolishing both the victim and the evidence.[47] Other times, in order to eliminate the evidence, C1 personnel blew up bodies time and again until there were no identifiable fragments left.

In 1985, De Kock assumed command of Vlakplaas and accelerated the assassination programme, also introducing paramilitary training to the police members; along with De Kock came Warrant Officer Willie Nortje, described as the "second most effective assassin of the unit".[48] De Kock brought to Vlakplaas the brutal counter-insurgency experiences of *Koevoet*; under his command, C1 became a

> General-purpose death-squad which would be handed instructions to kill specific individuals who had been identified by the Security Branch in various parts of the country, as well as acting on the initiative of its commander, who had an effective power of life and death.[49]

De Kock would later admit that at least 24 people had been killed by Vlakplaas from the time he took command of it; however, other accounts put the number at 65.[51] It was during this time that De Kock, nicknamed "the Lion" during his time in Namibia, became known as "Prime Evil"; one of his colleagues would later remark. "I think we must understand from the start that Eugene was a warrior ... never a policeman".[51]

Maintaining that C1 was but "the last in line when it came to cold-blooded and sick murders", De Kock called Vlakplaas the *slaanarm* ("strike arm") of the SAP.[52] De Kock himself was once described by his former chief, General Engelbrecht, as "a hunter without mercy, single-minded, and nothing distracted him from the job at hand. He frightens members of the ANC/PAC/SACP alliance".[53] The attitude of De Kock towards the enemies of the state is instructive in understanding why the security forces appeared to take such a casual attitude towards the death that they were inflicting on their opponents: "I would have neglected my duty if I allowed a terrorist to cross the border into South Africa. The public could not defend itself".[54] This attitude was a common one amongst security force members; in this way, these individuals perceived those who were attempting to violently overthrow the state as "terrorists" who had to be stopped by any means possible.

C1 was one of the key means by which this practice was implemented. While BOSS had its "Z-Squad", responsible for assassinating those opponents of apartheid who were out of reach of the South African juridical system, the Security Branch developed similar capabilities in the 1980s, centring on C1 and other Security Branch units.[55] As noted, it is estimated that between 1980 and 1991, at least 24 political activists were assassinated by elements operating out of Vlakplaas (see Table 5.2); this does not include an unknown number of ANC/UDF or PAC supporters that were killed by Vlakplaas in co-operation with other elements of the security establishment, such as the CCB, Special Forces or DMI.[56] While this may represent a seemingly small number (roughly two killed per year), it is significant both for the fact that two murders a year within the context of a state-at-war is extremely low, and for the parallel fact that much greater numbers were not simply gunned-down within South Africa the way *Koevoet*, in many ways the prototype for C1, did in Namibia. In total, more than 65 people were killed by Vlakplaas up to 1993.[57]

While Vlakplaas focused their efforts inside South Africa, the nature of the "total onslaught" meant that many operations also involved cross-border raids to either kidnap or murder identified and targeted individuals suspected of being or known to be ANC personnel; Swaziland was a favourite "playground" for C1. The overall aim of C1 operations inside Swaziland through the 1980s was the termination of the ANC/MK structures inside that country; thus, individual commanders and other key personnel were targeted for abduction or elimination by Security Branch. It is estimated that throughout the 1980s, at least 22 alleged ANC members were assassinated in Swaziland. In more than a decade of conducting cross-border operations into Swaziland, C1 was never challenged once by the Swazi authorities; they were also powerless to halt MK infiltrations from Mozambique to South Africa across Swaziland.[58]

It was highly unusual for Vlakplaas to ever be ordered to assassinate someone; instead, euphemisms were used by senior commanders. To *maak 'n plan* (make a plan with someone) was the most common; more direct terms such as "eliminate", "remove", and the direction "so that they don't bother us again" were used to avoid a situation where a senior figure could be said to have given a direct order to kill someone. In the vitriolic statements of the politicians and the directives to "eliminate" the opponents of the state, it was clear to security force commanders that they were being directed to kill. As one security force commander observed about De Kock, "his superiors knew what he was and what he was good at ... when the enemy was no longer on the Angolan border but at home, they called him home. They knew..".[59] Indeed, as De Kock himself once stated, "statements by high-ranking officers and politicians about the elimination of people and the total onslaught left no doubt in the minds of people like me about what was expected of us".[60]

Their activities, however, slowly ranged out-of-control: from what began as "the white man's war to preserve his status in Africa", it rapidly decayed into "a rampage of murder, mayhem and sabotage, continuing long past the twilight of white rule".[61] This degradation will be examined in Chapter 7. Vlakplaas and its network of counter-intelligence units were not alone within the Security Branch in taking the fight directly to the apartheid state's enemies; within its headquarters intelligence elements, Security Branch had also developed a capability to take the war directly to the ANC and its supporters far outside of South Africa's borders, while engaging in directed counter-intelligence against the ANC's structures.

"G" Section: foreign counter-intelligence

With the reorganisation of the Department of National Security (the short-lived successor to BOSS prior to its evolution into the NIS) in 1980, "G" Section – which had existed within the Security Branch ever since the formation of BOSS – was resurrected. Generally responsible for the "long-term penetration of the ANC abroad", its responsibilities were divided between Foreign Intelligence (G1), Strategic Communication (G2), and Counter-Espionage (G3). In reality, under the command of Brigadier Piet Goosen (who in 1977 had been in charge of the interrogation and death of Steve Biko) and Major Craig Williamson – one of apartheid's most notorious counter-intelligence operatives, nicknamed "South Africa's Super-spy" – "G" Section carried out a number of assassinations outside of South Africa, and co-operated with other elements of the SAP to assist in similar operations. By 1992, "G" was also responsible for "interdepartmental linkages"

Table 5.2 C1 Assassinations and killings (examples)

Date	Victim	Location	Alleged/reported responsible
20 November 1981	Griffiths Mxenge, ANC lawyer	Umlazi	Joe Mamasela, David Tshikalange, Brian Mgqulunga, Nofomela, Dirk Coetzee[a]
22 November 1983	Zwelibanzi Nyanda, MK Operations Commander in Swaziland	NA	De Kock, Cronje, General Frans Steenkamp[b]
26 June 1985	Eight Congress of South African Students (COSAS) members	East Rand ("Zero Zero Incident")	De Kock, Van der Merwe, Cronje, Mamasela[c]
August 1985	Victoria Mxenge, UDF campaigner	NA	Unknown[d]
September 1985	Jappie Maponya	Krugersdorp	De Kock, Willie Nortje, Colonel Johan le Roux[e]
20 June 1986	Phillip Nwanematsu, senior MK Commander	Swaziland	C1, Eastern Transvaal Security Branch, Soweto Intelligence Unit[f]
July 1986	Piet Ntuli, KwaNdebele Minister of Internal Affairs	NA	Cronje, Mamasela, Nortje[g]
March/April 1989	Three unknown ANC members	Botswana	Brigadier Flip Loots, C1, Special Forces[h]
April 1990	Sam and Hajira Khan (aka Chand), and two sons, PAC organisers	Botswana	General Krappies Engelbrecht, Van Rensburg, De Kock[i]
May 1990–February 1991	Bheki Mlangeni (attempt to kill Dirk Coetzee)	Soweto	De Kock, Van Rensburg, Colonel Hermanus du Plessis[j]
20 July 1990	Brian Ngqulunga, (*askari*)	Vlakplaas	De Kock[k]
January 1991	Goodwill Sikhakhane (*askari*)	Vlakplaas	Colonel Andy Taylor, General Steyn, De Kock[l]

Notes

a "Ex-Security Policeman Coetzee Not Interested in Amnesty", SAPA, 30 January 1996; Patrick Laurence, *Death Squads: Apartheid's Secret Weapon*, (London: Penguin Books, 1990), 41.
b Pauw, *Heart of Darkness*, 46; Eugene De Kock, *A Long Night's Damage: Working for the Apartheid State* (Saxonwold (South Africa): Contra Press, 1998):107–110; "De Kock Tells how he Killed Nyanda's Brother in Swaziland", SAPA, 16 September 1996.
c "De Kock gave COSAS Booby-Trapped Grenades: Witness", SAPA, 22 January 1996; *Armed Forces Hearing – SAP*, 77; Pauw, *Heart of Darkness*, 47–48; *TRC*2.3, 391.
d Laurence, *Death Squads*, 6.
e "De Kock Tells Court he Regrets Killing Victims", SAPA, 19 September 1996; De Kock, op. cit., 122–126, 257, 265; "De Kock Not Guilty of Trying to Kill Dirk Coetzee: Counsel", SAPA, 6 August 1996; "Two Life Sentences, 212 Years' Imprisonment for De Kock", SAPA, 30 October 1996; Pauw, *Heart of Darkness*, 49–54.
f De Kock, op. cit., 135–136; *TRC*2.2, 261–263.
g "Vlakplaas Men to Appear in Supreme Court", SAPA 18 October 1996; Pauw, *Heart of Darkness*, 237.
h De Kock, op. cit., 168–169; *TRC*2.2, 321–322.
i "De Kock Tells Court he Regrets Killing Victims", SAPA, 19 September 1996; De Kock, op. cit., 191–193; Pauw, *Heart of Darkness*, 87–89.
j Pauw, *Heart of the Whore*, 250; "De Kock Wanted to Kill 'Traitor' Coetzee, Court Hears", SAPA, 31 January 1996; De Kock, op. cit., 203–210.
k De Kock, op. cit., 164–168, 186, 193–195, 257; "Counsel for De Kock Admits Client is Guilty of Five Murders", SAPA, 5 August 1996; "De Kock Tells Court he Regrets Killing Victims", SAPA, 19 September 1996.
l De Kock, op. cit., 211–214; "De Kock Not Guilty of Trying To Kill Dirk Coetzee: Counsel", SAPA, 6 August 1996; "Woman Tells of Missing ANC Boyfriend Allegedly Killed by Police", SAPA, 20 November 1995.

and included links/secondments to Venda, Bophutatswana, and Swaziland.[62]

In 1972, Williamson, along with Craig Edwards, had infiltrated the ANC's structures via the International University Exchange Fund (IUEF) based in Geneva, of which Williamson eventually became deputy-director. Upon his exposure in January 1980, he returned to South Africa to continue with foreign operations against the ANC. During their time inside the ANC, Williamson and Edwards became aware of a planned meeting between Black Consciousness Movement (BCM) leader Steve Biko and Oliver Tambo of the ANC, which would set the ground for close co-operation between the BCM and ANC inside South Africa; it is believed that it was because of this information that Biko was arrested in September 1977 and murdered in jail.[63] Williamson served in "G" Section until December 1985, when he was elected as a National Party member of the President's Council.

Equally significant was the assassination of Ruth First, the wife of Joe Slovo (one of the founders of MK and later the head of the SACP), who was killed by a letter-bomb in Maputo on 17 August 1982 sent by Williamson's unit; Dirk Stoffberg, the head of an organisation called "Z-Squad Incorporated", claimed responsibility in First's death, although Williamson was alleged to have admitted complicity to First's daughter during a 1997 interview.[64] The intention in First's death, it was believed, was to kill her husband, Joe Slovo, whom the securocrats believed (rightly) to be the leading strategist behind the ANC and MK's plans and operations. "G" Section was also involved in the assassination of activist Jeanette Schoon in Lubango, Angola; Schoon, along with her six-year-old daughter Katryn, was killed on 28 June 1984 by a letter-bomb manufactured by the SAP Technical Division.[65]

Another significant "G" Section operation was the 1982 blowing-up of the ANC's London offices in response to the ANC rocket attack on Voortrekkerhoogte in 1981. Ordered to carry-out the attack by General Coetzee, who was instructed by Police Minister Le Grange – Coetzee later maintained that Botha ultimately had ordered the attack – Williamson, who planned the operation with Goosen, visited *Koevoet* to recruit De Kock and Captain John Adam for the mission in early 1982. Another attack on the SACP offices in London was abandoned because of "too many lives would be at risk".[66]

As part of his activities, Williamson also established Longreach Pty Ltd in April 1986, originally a front company for Security Branch operations, but also used for co-ordinating operations with Military Intelligence and Special Forces. Longreach was used as Williamson's vehicle for carrying out intelligence activities abroad, including sanctions-busting operations, and was implicated – for a time – in the assassination of Swedish Prime Minister Olaf Palme in Stockholm in February 1986.[67] One of the most explosive of allegations against the Security Police, it was De Kock who first pointed the finger at Williamson, who denied the charge. According to a number of reports,

Williamson had been running an intelligence operation in Stockholm to steal money from anti-apartheid funders, under the cover of Longreach, at the time of Palme's death; also involved in this operation was Phillip Powell, later of *Inkatha*.[68] Determining the truth of the matter became more complicated when Dirk Coetzee named Anthony White, a former Selous Scout, as the assassin; although White was connected to Longreach, his involvement in Palme's assassination was later disputed by C1 members, including De Kock.[69] White had previously been involved in numerous attempts to kill ZAPU leader Joshua Nkomo during the late 1970s.[70] Although investigations since that time have not been able to prove Williamson's involvement in this operation, both Williamson and De Kock have themselves named Palme's killers; his death has still not been attributed conclusively to any individual, although a former Swede by the name of Bertil Wedin, hiding in Turkish North-Cyprus, has been named as implicated.[71]

Conclusions

While the Security Branch and its intelligence units were able to offer the apartheid state a fairly overt form of active counter-intelligence and counter-insurgency measures, by the early 1980s, it was clear that another – far more covert – tool was required to confront the onslaught. As the "home" of counter-revolutionary warfare theory and thinking during the apartheid era, DMI was also one of the centres of the effort to eliminate the liberation movements' politico-administrative and military structures, initially driving and later supporting the SSC's centralised intelligence targeting structures. As such, and alongside the SAP's counter-insurgency units *Koevoet* and C1, from the late 1970s onwards, DMI as a whole developed four separate specially tasked units for various functions, none of which were overt and all of which would form the core of DMI's counter-revolutionary operations (including assassination) over the coming decade. These included the Reconnaissance Commandos (which had been developed in the 1970s but were placed under the Chief of Staff, Intelligence, at this time) largely for clandestine operations externally (although they later undertook covert operations both internally and abroad); the Directorate Special Tasks (DST), which provided covert support to contra-mobilisation and guerrilla groups regionally and internally; the Directorate Covert Collection, which would act against opponents of the state through both counter-intelligence operations and pro-active intelligence-gathering operations (meaning the use of political violence, including planning assassinations, to obtain and implement intelligence); and the Civil Co-operation Bureau, which would be the basis for DMI's covert counter-revolutionary activities in the second half of the 1980s and into the 1990s. Alongside the special chemical/biological weapons programme (Project COAST), all were to contribute directly to the state's intelligence-led targeting efforts.

6 The assassins' web
The growth of counter-revolutionary warfare intelligence, 1979–1985

> The Security Police and the country could not afford a Nelson Mandela again.
>
> Major Sarel du Plessis "Sakkie" Crafford, Vlakplaas

From Special Forces to Special Tasks: DMI's covert capabilities

For DMI, this move into counter-revolutionary warfare hailed its new era of expansion, influence and power – as well as the ability to implement sustained, covert operations on the ground both within South Africa and internationally against South Africa's enemies. As DMI developed throughout the 1970s and into the 1980s, it began to function as a force unto itself, both gathering intelligence and acting on it, eliminating the transparency inherent in divided security functions. Between 1978 and 1986, DMI was expanded to include new intelligence directorates and a separate covert action wing (distinct from the generally clandestine activity of the Recces) to both enhance intelligence collection (through the Directorate Covert Collection) and to expand its ability to act on that intelligence (through the Civil Co-operation Bureau).[1] This allowed DMI to expand its powerbase and capabilities, eventually including all manner of operational capacity far beyond "traditional" intelligence collection – with its capabilities growing, throughout this period, to include covert intelligence gathering, clandestine operations, covert operations, contra-mobilisation and the training of surrogate forces, assassination, disruption and destabilisation functions, and counter-intelligence (including counter-espionage).

As DMI gained control over the Special Forces during the reorganisation of the SADF in 1979, this granted them the same integrated intelligence–special forces capability that the Security Branch had with *Koevoet* in Namibia and was developing in "C" Section domestically. This relationship under one command would allow for the exchange of intelligence and operational information between the intelligence-gathering half of the house (Sub-Division Military Intelligence and Sub-Division Intelligence

Operations) and the operational side of the house (Special Forces). In the middle of these would rest the three operational elements that, while nominally part of each side, in reality were covert wings of each: the Directorate Covert Collection, the Directorate Special Tasks and the Civil Co-operation Bureau, respectively.

The SADF enters on the ground: the Directorate Covert Collection

Established in the darkest of shadows, the Directorate Covert Collection (*Direktoraat van Koverte Insameling*) was perhaps the most dangerous of DMI's sub-units and definitely its most "operational" – in many senses, DMI's equivalent of the Special Forces' Civil Co-operation Bureau. The DCC was run overall by Brig J.P. Tolletjie Botha, who reported directly to the Chief of Staff, Intelligence. It is unclear as to when this unit was established; it was only in 1992, however, that its existence was discovered by chance during an investigation by a government commission into hit-squad activities (see Chapter 8). A unit which may have been its forerunner, the Directorate of Covert Information (DCI), was definitely operational in Namibia by 1982.

The DCC established six "fronts": the Eastern Front (Mozambique and Swaziland), headed by Col At Nel; the Western Front (Angola and Namibia), headed by Brig Koos Louw with his deputy, former Rhodesian CIO operative Major Geoffrey Price, commanding the Namibia "arena"; the Terrorism or *Tuis* (home) Front, later renamed Internal Sub-Theatre and headed by Col J.G.C. "Gerrie" Bornman; the TBVC Front; the Frontline States (International) Front; and the Foreign Intelligence Services Front, basically a counter-intelligence group headed by a Brig Van Rensburg. Importantly, the Terrorism Front was responsible for collection in respect of the liberation movements externally, as well as internally during the 1980s. Each front was commanded generally by a colonel. During this period, DCC field offices were established in each Territorial Command.[2] What this meant was that serving officers with "legitimate jobs" during the day-time would work for the DCC at night against the liberation movements; additionally, numerous members of DMI "resigned" their posts and went to work full-time for one of the front organisations reporting to the DCC. The aim was to establish similar operations inside South Africa to those which had gone on in Namibia and Angola; this included intelligence collection, pseudo-operations, and the elimination of the opponent.[3] To this end, numerous front-companies were established, including the Pan Afrika Industrial Investment Consultants CC (PAIIC CC), established on 7 November 1986 (which would later became the directorate's Achilles heel after its discovery by the Goldstone Commission in November 1992 – see Chapter 8), Africa Risk Analysis Consultants (ARAC), the Adult Education Consultants (AEC – see below) in Ciskei, Eduguide, Dynamic Teaching, African Information Systems (PTY) Ltd, and Longreach Pty Ltd (linked to Craig Williamson of Security Branch).[4] Indeed, in pursuit of these goals, the DCC often operated with the Security Branch in targeting the leadership structures of the opposition movements.

In parallel, the DCI also developed networks of informers throughout Namibia's Operational Area during the conflict there, using former Rhodesian and Portuguese personnel, as well as blacks and members of various Frontline States' militaries. In addition to intelligence-gathering through these networks, it also conducted "pseudo-operations" against SWAPO, deploying in the Operational Area for up to two weeks at a time.[5] As Namibia moved towards independence at the end of the 1980s, it was clear to DMI that it had to "extract" its operations from Namibia; the concept for this became known as Operation MAYONNAISE. Its development and planning was influenced by the Rhodesian members of the DCC who had had to extricate themselves, their operations and networks from Rhodesia in 1980 with the transition to Zimbabwe; a similar situation now existed in Namibia. Started in 1983, the aim of MAYONNAISE would be to transplant these covert operators from Angola and Namibia (and elsewhere in Southern Africa) onto South African soil. As noted by Seegers, DMI previously had "some domestic presence, but Operation MAYONNAISE made a quantum leap forward".[6]

Contra-mobilisation: intelligence for destabilisation

As part of the core strategies, the securocrats knew that one of the greatest initial aims of the insurgent forces would be the establishment of bases from which to operate. While the security establishment was fairly certain (at least, initially) that it could prevent any such bases being established within South Africa, both through crushing the ANC/SACP/MK structures inside the country and the prevention of any successful infiltrations from outside, the Frontline States were more concerning. This was made clear by Prime Minister Botha in February 1983 when he told Parliament that "Every country which offers shelter to anti-South African terrorists will have to deal with the security forces of South Africa as far as those terrorists are concerned".[7]

The apartheid state had long relied on a buffer of allied governments throughout Southern Africa to prevent the South African liberation forces from coming anywhere close to South Africa; however, the rapid Portuguese decolonisation of Angola and Mozambique culminating in the full withdrawal of Portuguese forces on 11 November 1975 – and the impending fall of Rhodesia – forced the securocrats to rethink what possibilities now lay in this strategy by the ANC of "hacking the way home" through the now-open Frontline States. To this end, Pretoria implemented a mix of détente and destabilisation within Southern Africa.

The primary aim of these policies, which would require separate study in themselves,[8] was to prevent the liberation movements, now with greater freedom of manoeuvre in the Frontline States, from establishing bases in any of these countries; this included SWAPO as well as the ANC, SACP and MK. The method chosen to implement these policies was, as Ellis states, "a combination of incentive and dissuasion". Incentives included preferential trade agreements with Pretoria, customs agreements (in the form of the Southern African Customs Union), development aid, and political partnerships (in the form of the Constellation of Southern African States initiative, which failed following Zimbabwe's independence, and the establishment of the Frontline States' Southern Africa Development Co-ordination Conference in April 1980), all aimed at inducing the Frontline States to co-operate with Pretoria. When these did not work, Pretoria implemented sabotage, covert interventions and raids, counter-guerrilla and guerrilla movements, banditry and – ultimately, in the case of Angola and threatened against other states – invasion as forms of internal destabilisation against the Frontline States.[9] This would, as the military promised Botha, prevent any Frontline State from supporting external ANC bases leading to a war of the kind that eventually saw the fall of Rhodesia. The irony of this was that, as noted by Price, under such pressures from South Africa,

> With Pretoria posing a military threat to its neighbours, they are likely to turn for assistance to whom-so-ever will provide it, and that translates into an increased political and military role in southern Africa for the Soviets and their allies.[10]

This was obviously contrary to everything South Africa worked for in attempting to halt the "Total Onslaught".

The overall South African aim was to destabilise the Frontline States to such a degree that it would be against their national interests to (continue to) allow the ANC/MK to base itself within these countries; in other words, the penalty for allowing the ANC/MK to base itself within one of the Frontline States would be continued destabilisation by Pretoria. Destabilisation has been described as:

> A complex of political, economic and military activities, separately and combined, short of a formal declaration of war, used by South Africa against independent African states and ... Namibia ... a policy of war by another name; it is an act of state terrorism by the apartheid state against its neighbours.[11]

This would, in many cases, involve support to counter-guerrilla forces in these neighbouring states, as Defence Minister Malan made clear in a February 1983 speech:

> Whatever methods we may have to use to combat South Africa's enemies in those countries, even if it were to mean that we support

anti-Communist movements ... and allow them to operate from our territory against Swapo and the ANC, we shall have to do so.[12]

To Pretoria, the guerrilla movements throughout the Frontline States were either proxies of the Soviet Union, and thereby fit into Pretoria's *Weltanschauung* of Southern Africa (with the collapse of the Portuguese colonies and Rhodesia) being an ever-constricting circle of black Communist threats to South Africa's own survival directed from Moscow, or were tools which could be used to fight this Communist threat. Thus, the line-up of guerrilla movements in Southern Africa was seen from Pretoria as being an alliance of the MPLA, FRELIMO, ZANU, SWAPO and the ANC/SACP supported by Moscow/East Berlin/Havana arrayed against the alliance of UNITA and RENAMO supported by Pretoria and Washington; from Pretoria's (and, increasingly in the 1980s, from Washington's) point of view, therefore, UNITA could operate against both the MPLA, SWAPO and the ANC, while RENAMO destabilised both Mozambique and (to a lesser degree) Zimbabwe. This would provide one solid – and internal – aspect of the destabilisation strategy.

As part of this strategy, however, Pretoria attempted to maintain the fiction that these movements were wholly independent of support from South Africa. In their origins, they were; however, their continued existence throughout the 1970s and 1980s (indeed, into the 1990s in many ways) was due almost entirely to this support, so much so that one observer has commented that "UNITA and RENAMO were so subordinated to South Africa that they served in practice as its proxies".[13] South Africa attempted to conceal, or at least minimise, these connections, preferring attempts to enhance the legitimacy of the movements internationally as a means of downplaying accusations of aggression by South Africa against the Frontline States. This was easier to achieve with UNITA, which had existed independently long before South Africa began to support it and was firmly rooted in one of the ethnic groups in Angola; with FRELIMO, which had been spawned by the Rhodesians and then integrated into South Africa's strategy against Mozambique, this separation was much more difficult to maintain.

From Special Forces to Special Tasks

It was the Special Forces and the Special Tasks units which played the central role in Pretoria's regional and internal destabilisation strategies. From the late 1970s onwards, the Frontline States – and, later, South Africa internally – was destabilised through means such as raids, bombings, the fomenting of internal guerrilla movements, and attacks on economic assets throughout the Frontline States.

From 1971, many DMI operators were trained Special Forces personnel, knowledgeable in clandestine and covert operations. These *Spesmagte* (as they were known in Afrikaans) were active throughout the Operational Area, but should not be confused with the Reconnaissance Commandos (the much-vaunted "Recces" of the Special Forces): the *Spesmagte* were covert operators. In 1975, as Portugal's colonies became independent, the *Spesmagte* were converted to *Spestake* ("Special Tasks"); at the same time, the CSI absorbed the Special Forces function from the army, thereby integrating under one command the functions of special forces, special tasks, covert paramilitary operations and military intelligence.[14] These capabilities were further enhanced with the 1980 intake of many Rhodesian personnel into the SADF.

The Directorate Special Tasks (DST) was established in the mid-1970s by Colonel Jan Breytenbach, the founder of the Reconnaissance Commandos and 32 Battalion; its first functioning head was Col Cornelius van Niekerk, who would later manage the RENAMO project. DST began its life as a small office established in Rundu (Namibia) in 1976 following the South African withdrawal from Angola following SAVANNAH. Its first operation was DISA which provided covert support (both in terms of materiel and logistics, and in terms of co-ordinating special support operations – including 32 Battalion "pseudo-operations" and guerrilla warfare) to UNITA in its war against the MPLA. In December 1978, the DST Rundu office was taken over by Major Marius Oelschig, who was to run this operation until December 1982, returning to Pretoria in January 1983 as senior staff officer (with the rank of Colonel) on DST's operations for the next three years.[15]

During the late 1970s and throughout the 1980s, the DST was responsible for overseeing the contra-mobilisation and counter-revolutionary activities of DMI throughout southern Africa as the "senior structure responsible for co-ordinating the strategy of regional destabilisation". This policy of support to external anti-Marxist guerrillas was laid out in a number of SSC documents, including *Boek 1* of 1980 (discussed in the last section), the March 1984 "Recommendations by the SSC", the December 1986 "Strategy for Southern Africa", and the *Nasionale Strewes en Beleidsgrondslae van die Republiek van Suid-Afrika, 1987* ("National Endeavours and Policybase of the Republic of South Africa, 1987").[16]

Not an operations unit, DST provided operational support in the form of training, command and organisation. These operations were code-named DISA/SILWER (the support to UNITA in Angola); DRAMA (support to Zimbabwean dissidents Super-ZAPU); PIKI/PUNDA MILIA/ ALTAR (support to RENAMO/MNR in Mozambique); PLATHOND (support to a surrogate force for destabilising Zambia); and CAPSIZE/ LATSA (support for the Lesotho Liberation Army).[17] The first began immediately following the end of SAVANNAH in 1976, the second and third were products of the transfer of power in Salisbury/Harare in 1980, and the fifth a result of the mid-1980s. Only Swaziland, which in 1982 signed a secret non-aggression agreement with South Africa, was spared destabilisation. These operations would generally focus on the development of proxy forces in neighbouring countries to counter the unfriendly government as part of South Africa's destabilisation programme; additionally, similar forces were established internally to off-set the power, influence and capabilities of the ANC and the UDF. This second element was accomplished through the training of two proxy forces (under Operations MARION and KATZEN) in Natal and the Eastern Cape, and the support of vigilantes and organised gangs in other regions of the country. While external operations such as UNITA, RENAMO, the LLA, and Super-ZAPU were similar counter-revolutionary means of offsetting the revolutionary interests of the guerrilla movements in Angola, Zimbabwe, Namibia and Mozambique, they do not speak to the same counter-revolutionary ends as the internal operations, which served as a means of achieving the elimination of the insurgent politico-administrative infrastructure.

Regional contra-mobilisation

DST maintained an extensive logistical network and infrastructure throughout the sub-continent to support its operations;[18] funding for DST projects was provided via the Chief of Staff, Finance, in the SADF.[19] Its operations on the ground were largely carried out by Special Forces; the involvement of each particular unit was due to its particular composition. DISA was supported by-and-large by 1 Recce as well as 32 Battalion (and, to a lesser degree, 31 Battalion); DRAMA was supported by 3 Recce (and, between 1980 and 1981, 6 Recce) until its termination in the mid-1980s; and PIKI/PUNDU MILIA's support to RENAMO was provided by 5 Recce. In the late 1970s, many of those who would form 5 Recce trained with the Selous at Inkomo Barracks in Salisbury under an agreement arranged between Major Ron-Reid Daly (head of the Selous) and GOC-SF Loots.[20] For this reason, 5 Recce was principally responsible for implementing pseudo-operations with RENAMO and operating against FRELIMO in Mozambique. 5 Recce's support to RENAMO provided virtually all of its logistical, materiel, and financial support under Operation PUNDA MILIA controlled by DST. This support often involved operating inside Mozambique, rather than simply launching raids and other operations from Phalaborwa (Transvaal) where 5 Recce was based.[21] There is also some evidence that Israeli special forces assisted in providing covert training to RENAMO.[22] When RENAMO's headquarters were moved from Phalaborwa to Gorongosa in Mozambique, South African officers began to serve inside Mozambique; these were usually divided into five-man teams of two South Africans and three (one Mozambican, one Angolan, and one Zimbabwean) Africans providing training on intelligence gathering or support to specific operations. The South African presence was reported as late as 1989; there were also numerous white mercenaries who served with RENAMO, usually with South African support.[23] In the Operational Zone of Namibia, 5 Recce also operated, using the same tactics as the Selous Scouts in using captured and "turned" PLAN guerrillas to conduct pseudo-operations against SWAPO. Often times, it would operate in co-operation with the SAP counter-insurgency unit *Koevoet*; this sometimes led to confusion, as when *Koevoet* "captured" what it thought were SWAPO guerrillas, but were in reality 5 Recce *askaris*.[24]

There is no evidence that 4 Recce was deeply, if at all, involved in DST operations outside of South Africa; however, internally, 4 Recce played a role in MARION (see below). DST operations were divided into two sections: DST-1 was responsible for UNITA, RENAMO and Zimbabwe; DST-2 was responsible for the LLA, MARION and KATZEN. Commanders included Brig Daan Hamman, who headed DST in 1982; he was replaced for six months in 1983 by a Brig Botha; Brig C.J. "Neels" Van Tonder replaced him, remaining in the position until 1986 when he was replaced by Van Niekerk.[25] Separate DST operations were commanded by: DST-1 – Oelschig and, after 1985, Brig Thackwray; DST-2 – Col van Niekerk; DISA/SILWER – Oelschig; DRAMA – Col Frayne; LATSA/CAPSIZE – Col May and, later, Col Benade; and PUNDU MILIA/ALTAR – Van Niekerk.[26] In the mid-1980s, DST was incorporated into the Sub-Division Intelligence Operations, headed by General Niels van Tonder.

The deployment of the various forces involved in these operations depended on the individual circumstances. In Angola, UNITA operated throughout the war (1975–1989) with support from 32 Battalion, which was stationed both inside Angola and on the Namibian border at Rundu. For Angola, supporting UNITA meant that the whole of southern Angola along the Namibian border would become a dangerous area for SWAPO/PLAN fighters to train, house, and operate from: as SWAPO was closely supported by the MPLA government in Luanda, FAPLA forces operated often with PLAN guerrillas. Thus, in the SADF's view, making UNITA as powerful as possible against FAPLA (and, therefore, PLAN) would lessen greatly the abilities of PLAN to infiltrate in strength the Namibian border. By looking at UNITA's success between 1976, when it controlled a tiny part of the south-east of the country, to 1994, by which point it controlled almost 80 per cent of Angola, it is obvious the UNITA grew much more powerful with South African (and covert US) support. This was also the aim of the SADF's conventional operations in Angola, whose strategic importance to South Africa was evident: possessing a long common border with vulnerable Namibia and rich natural resources (diamonds, oil, coffee, agriculture, and other mineral holdings), Angola also contained two of the best ports in the Southern Atlantic (Luito and Luanda) and the strategic Benguela railway, the "economic lifeline" to both Zambia and Zaire, two countries who shared good relations with South Africa.[27] Pretoria wanted UNITA to take control of the whole of southern Angola militarily and administratively, perhaps even creating a separately administered region – this would ultimately lead to the take-over of the entire country. Operations such as REINDEER (1978), SAFRON (1979), SCEPTIC (1980), PROTEA and DAISY (1981), SUPER (1982), MEEBOS (1982), and ASKARI (1983–1984) were designed primarily to support UNITA in its operations against FAPLA, as well as to crush PLAN guerrilla bases and co-operative operations between PLAN and FAPLA. However, following the withdrawal of the South Africans entirely from Angola in 1989 under the UN linkage agreement, South Africa's covert support did not end and UNITA continued to grow.

RENAMO personnel were based in the North Eastern Transvaal and infiltrated into Mozambique through Kruger National Park on the border. "Super-ZAPU" fighters were based in the Northern Transvaal, while members of the LLA were lodged at SADF bases in the Orange Free State.[28] One difference in these operations that must be understood was the difference in the composition of UNITA, the Zimbabwean opposition and RENAMO. UNITA had been in existence for a number of years prior to SADF support beginning in 1976; it also derived from a largely homogenous tribal base developed from the Umbundu people of south-east Angola. RENAMO was a construct of the Portuguese and Rhodesian Special Forces and had almost no indigenous tribal affiliation in Mozambique. This factor was to have a noticeable effect on the success of RENAMO contra-mobilisation operations during the 1980s, but it was definitely RENAMO's brutal but effective operations inside Mozambique which led to the Maputo government signing the Nkomati Accord in 1984 which terminated ANC/MK basing inside Mozambique in return for South African economic and infrastructural aid and support to the Mozambican government. Similar pressure being brought to bear on Swaziland, Botswana, and Lesotho led to the same result.[29]

External operations were also in the DCC's purview: in the mid-1980s, Captain Henri van der Westhuizen was responsible for establishing targeting dossiers on activists in Swaziland and Mozambique.[31] Much of this intelligence was co-ordinated with *Trewits* and the KIK, as well as with the CCB's and Special Forces' intelligence sections.

Such operations were also undertaken in Namibia. Under Operation ETANGO, the DCC and other DMI units launched a contra-mobilisation project to "establish a tribally-based, conservative 'Ovambo Movement' to counter SWAPO"; a similar project, under the name Operation EZUVA, aimed to accomplish the same thing amongst the Kavango people. Counter-guerrilla groups were also formed amongst most of the Namibian ethnic tribes, including the Rehobothers, the Namas, the Ovambos, the Bushmen (San), the Kavango, the Kaoklanders, and the Caprivians; these were generally formed into units within SWATF (31 Battalion – Bushman, 33 – Caprivi, 34 – Kavango, 35 – Ovambo, and the fully integrated 41/911 Battalion) or, later, SWAPOL."[30]

The practical success of such DST destabilisation operations externally cannot be doubted. The primary aim of the South African government was to protect its borders from infiltration by terrorists based abroad (meaning ANC/MK, PLAN and APLA fighters); this was especially the case within the neighbouring states (including Angola). As such, the general aim of such destabilisation operations (in the guise of contra-mobilisation) was to terminate any support being provided to the ANC/MK by the Frontline States. The provision of such support externally, as was DST-1's responsibility, paid dividends in itself and benefited the SADF: in exchange for such support, not only would Pretoria ensure a continuing destabilisation of the region where required, but it would also be able to obtain valuable on-the-ground intelligence from those forces which it was supporting.

Internal contra-mobilisation

Many of the DCC/DMI personnel involved in these activities moved, around 1985–1986, into South Africa to institute similar contra-mobilisation projects against the ANC/UDF. Such contra-ANC/UDF operations aimed particularly – but by no means exclusively – to leverage the civil war between supporters of the ANC/UDF and the Zulu-based political movement *Inkatha*, and foment black-on-black violence. This included vigilantes trained specifically for internal operations against the ANC/UDF known as *Witdoeke* (Western Cape), *Uma Afrika* (Eastern Cape), and reportedly the Black Cats gang in Ermelo.[32] There was also Project VALLEX which aimed at "removing the UDF from communities by means of violence using the colour-against-colour principle". By mid-1986, at least 23 such "projects" were running in South Africa and Namibia.[33] Other contra-mobilisation projects were run by a combination of DCC and other DMI units, all supported by *StratKom*. These included Project ANCOR/KAMPONG, which established the DCC front Adult Education Consultants (AEC) as a means for the "physical running of peoples' organisations and movements ... which attempted to manipulate civil society on a wide range of fronts"; this project continued until April 1991, when it was taken over by the army, and only terminated in October 1992. In a similar manner to *StratKom* operations conducted in Namibia in an attempt to prevent SWAPO from achieving a two-thirds majority in the independence elections, former security force members have stated that the aim of all such contra-mobilisation operations after 1990 were to "reduce the ANC to just another political party by 1994", the date for the first all-party elections.[34]

By far the most effective of such programmes instituted by the security forces, however, was its establishment of *Inkatha* hit-squads, and their usage as proxies of the state security apparatus in breaking the power of the ANC/UDF in Natal (and elsewhere) and eliminating its leaders. From

1975, BOSS had been instrumental in building-up *Inkatha* as a viable political alternative to the ANC in Natal; this included establishing "dummy" rival political contenders to Chief Buthulezi – such as the group *Umkhonto kaShaka* – providing funds to *Inkatha*, and quietly helping develop an acceptable image for it in the West. This all drove Buthulezi and *Inkatha* directly into the government's arms as clandestine collaborators in apartheid.

These efforts did not, however, go far enough. In 1986, under Operation MARION[35] and authorised by the SSC, more than 200 *Inkatha* cadres underwent training at the Caprivi Strip in northern Namibia. Trained in protection duties (for senior *Inkatha* leaders), interrogation techniques, weapons training, and hit-squad activities – and using weapons provided by the Special Forces and Security Branch unit C1 – these "trainees" soon constituted the core of an *Inkatha* hit-squad. The overall guidelines for MARION were laid down in a February 1986 SSC meeting at which it was determined that the Department of Constitutional Development and Planning would have overall responsibility for the project, indicating its non-military emphasis on top of the security/paramilitary training *Inkatha* required. The DST, operating through an AEC branch in Natal, Creed Consultants, and the security front-company Swart Security, would provide the military training and some political contra-mobilisation work. This was largely seen by the SSC as the litmus test for future contra-mobilisation projects, such as KATZEN in the Eastern Cape. *Inkatha* was crucial to the state's ability to counter-organise the population against the ANC/UDF, as well as to "put Inkatha into a position to neutralise the onslaught from Umkhonto we Sizwe".[36] As such, these new units engaged in hit-squad activities against ANC and supporter targets in Natal; the worst of these was the 21 January 1987 killing of 13 people at the home of UDF leader Victor Ntuli in KwaMakutha (KZN).[37]

It was an aim of Operation MARION to provide *Inkatha* with a capacity of "self sufficiency" which would enable it to act independently of the SADF; as a result, many of these trainees were placed in the KwaZulu Police (KZP) during 1989, through which hit-squad activity continued. However, partly as a result of such fiascos, by November 1988, the SADF saw continued support "for the taking of offensive actions as an unacceptably high security risk": cover-ups by the Security Branch for offensive actions were no longer being authorised by SAP Commissioner Van der Merwe or his Deputy Lieutenant-General Basie Smit; at the same time, the SADF was attempting to distance itself from all previous support for surrogate guerrilla forces, such as RENAMO.[38] As a consequence, MARION was terminated in December 1990.

Outside of Natal, a similar contra-mobilisation enterprise was undertaken in July 1986 with Operation KATZEN, an attempt to mobilise anti-ANC/UDF Xhosa support, known as *Iliso Lomzi* (the "Xhosa Resistance Movement" or XWB), in the Eastern Cape to culminate in the establishment of Xhosaland (similar to Zululand). To achieve this, KATZEN – a sister operation to MARION – was aimed partly at the overthrow and death of Lennox Sebe, the leader of the Ciskei; it was the brain-child of Brigadier G.P. "Joffel" van der Westhuizen, the Eastern Cape Territorial Commander (and later head of DMI), who, in June 1986, wrote to the SSC stating that "this XWB must in nature – and even extent – be similar to Inkatha and must together with our security forces form a counter-revolutionary front".[39]

As part of KATZEN, the Army Intelligence unit "Hammer" was instrumental in undertaking "urban counter-insurgency" in the Eastern Cape, using Citizen Force units given additional counter-insurgency training. Trained in "low-level intelligence gathering", "Hammer" was known as an "SADF Reaction Unit", a term usually ascribed to covert operations in the SADF; it was also referred to as a "recce unit" by Van der Westhuizen for special operations throughout the Eastern Cape. Believed to have been founded in late 1983 by Van der Westhuizen (with the assistance of former Selous Scout commander Colonel Ron Reid-Daly), it was aimed at conducting "immediate follow-up operations after enemy infiltration", action against kidnapping, special protection duties, counter-mine measures, and intelligence operations and observation, all in co-operation with the SAP in the region. There were also indications that it operated with the CCB and Special Forces internally.[40]

This effort to develop contra-mobilised forces in the Eastern Cape backfired spectacularly and horribly when, in what became one of the most examined assassinations of the conflict, Cradock teacher and UDF organiser Matthew Goniwe and three other activists – Fort Calata, Sparrow Mkhonto, and Sicelo Mhlauli (who became known as the "Cradock Four") – were killed on 27 June 1985 by the local Security Police as part of KATZEN.[41] As part of the wider DCC Operation ORPHEUS – which aimed "to remove the leadership cadre of alternative structures down to the fourth level of organisation"[42] – "Hammer" provided support for the operation.[43] A similarly infamous killing – that of three members of the Port Elizabeth Civic Organisation (PEBCO) – Sipho Hashe, Qwaqwahuli Godolozi, and Champion Galela – by members of the Security Branch C1 unit operating with the Northern Transvaal Security Branch death squad occurred on 11 May 1985.[44] PEBCO was believed to be an ANC front, as well as an organiser of escalating violence in the Port Elizabeth townships. Some three weeks following the death of the Cradock Four – and on the day of their funeral – the first state of emergency was declared throughout the country; as a reflection of the attitude at the time to these assassinations, one senior member of the unit later stated that "pressure was exercised from the Government's side to act in a drastic way to neutralise activists and to help the security situation to normalise".[45]

DST terminated all operations in the early 1990s, ending its existence within DMI.[46] Its legacy was lasting, however, in not only the violence which has swept South Africa since the beginning of the 1990s, particularly in the politico-cultural conflict between the ANC and the *Inkatha Freedom Party* which ravaged parts of the Witwatersrand and Natal until 1997, but also in the continuing instability and economic shortcomings of many Southern African states to this day.

While the DST and the DCC represented a particular brand of counter-intelligence capability for South Africa's security forces – one focused heavily on undermining the apartheid state's opponents through destabilisation operations which would, to be certain, occasionally foray into direct targeting – other units were required to take the fight directly to the enemy. To accomplish this, the "Hammer" unit and similar ones established in other parts of the country – as well as the Security Branch C1 and units like it (see Chapter 7) – represented the most visible tip of the apartheid state's "dirty war" intelligence capabilities. Yet, another unit developed within the state security apparatus which would be far more covert and – in many sense – far more deadly and dangerous a counter-revolutionary warfare capability than represented by any other intelligence unit.

Killers in suits: DMI and the Civil Co-operation Bureau

The most secretive of all such covert units was the Civil Co-operation Bureau (CCB – sometimes referred to by its Afrikaans name *Burgerlike Samewerkingsburo* or BSB), which marked the zenith of the active pursuit of apartheid's opponents. One of the missions of the Special Forces throughout its existence, although rarely acknowledged, was the collection of intelligence internally; this was used primarily to support external operations, but was also sometimes in support of both SADF and SAP requirements in attempting to counter the unrest and violence in the country. Ultimately, it was determined that a civilian organisation, totally separate from the Special Forces and with its own financial and bureaucratic authority, would be the best vehicle to achieve these ends. To this end, DMI searched for a unit which had the potential to develop into such an organisation; it found it in 3 Recce, itself a result of continuing evolution. This would eventually form the CCB, the actual implementation of the "Joubert Plan" (see Chapter 7).

Origins and development of the CCB

The most secretive of all such covert units, the Civil Co-operation Bureau marked the zenith of the active pursuit of apartheid's opponents. Conceived in November 1985 and officially formed in 1986 by Special Forces, it originally developed out of the remnants of the Rhodesian special forces who went to South Africa following Rhodesia's transition to Zimbabwe in 1980.

With the re-organisation of DMI and the Special Forces, the one additional element that was added to this mix was the concomitant re-organisation of the Bureau of State Security into the National Intelligence Service. BOSS had possessed certain executive-action elements known as "Z-Squads": designed almost entirely for assassination as well as other covert actions, these units were nominally disbanded by P.W. Botha and re-established within DMI as a unit designated "Delta 40" (or "D-40", apparently because there were 40 members initially). Under the leadership of Rhodesian Garth Barrett, D-40 was specifically tasked, according to investigations in the early 1990s, with "monitoring certain external opponents of the regime with a view to their possible extinction"[47] – in other words, an assassination unit. D-40 operated only from 1979 to 1980, before the flood of Rhodesian SAS and Selous Scouts personnel moving south were reconstituted in the SADF as 3 Reconnaissance Regiment; D-40 was integrated with 3 Recce in 1980.[48]

During the period 3 Recce operated (between 1980 and 1981), it was once again determined by the CSI that a further defining of operational mandates was required. With its formation, 3 Recce was divided into a number of operational units composed of both former intelligence and special forces operators from Rhodesia; this combination would see through 3 Recce's operations and those of its successor organisations. During this period, 3 Recce carried out numerous operations against the new Zimbabwean state. The South African securocrats viewed this new government in Harare as a threat to not only South Africa's regional hegemonic interests in maintaining stability (or instability, depending on the requirement) throughout the Frontline States, but as well to South Africa directly through its support of the ANC and MK. Therefore, the securocrats matched interests with these former Rhodesian special forces personnel and re-deployed them back into Zimbabwe on clandestine and covert operations. It must be recalled that South Africa had already provided a great deal of covert and clandestine support to the Rhodesians in the last few years of its existence; this included support for the multiple assassination attempts against Joshua Nkomo and those against Robert Mugabe.[49] Therefore, this use of ex-Rhodesian personnel was nothing new: many of the South African Recces' personnel had operated with the Selous or Rhodesian SAS on numerous occasions in the late 1970s.

The unit's first operation against the new Zimbabwe was against the Inkomo barracks in August 1981; operatives from the unit planted a massive bomb which destroyed more than R45 million worth of munitions and weapons.[50] In July 1981, the unit assassinated the ANC representative in Harare; five months later, it planted a bomb in the roof above the Cabinet Room in Harare (the Cabinet did not meet there in the end). Its final operation – and one of its most spectacular – was the destruction of 13 aircraft at Harare's Thornhill Air Base in July 1982. 3 Recce personnel were also infiltrated into Zimbabwe to recce ANC targets prior to SADF raids by conventional (usually air) units or Special Forces; similar operations were carried out in Maseru, Maputo and Gaberone[51]

Following the decision in late 1981 to once again re-organise the Special Forces units, all those members of 3 Recce who wished to continue in clandestine military operations were transferred to 6 Recce; those who remained would form the basis for a covert operations capability within Special Forces which would enhance the state's assassination capability. In 1981, a unit was established between Special Forces and the 7th Medical Battalion (the unit responsible for South Africa's offensive chemical and biological weapons programme – see further); designated the Special Task Force, this unit commanded an operation known as Project "Barnacle". Part of "Barnacle's" work entailed recruiting former Rhodesians for "part-time special operations"; the unit eventually comprised some 30–40 individuals, mostly black ex-Rhodesians.[52] Commanded directly by GOC-SF Loots through an individual known only as "K" (allegedly a former Selous Scout), "Barnacle" included numerous members of the covert structures.

Initially pointed externally, by August 1982 the unit was operating internally, generally in "urban counter-insurgency" (as anti-terrorist operations were euphemistically known); these types of operations formed the core of "Barnacle's" internal operations.[53] In addition, the unit served to dispose of "unwanted individuals": involved in poisoning activists during or following interrogation and dumping their bodies into the sea, as well as assisting in other assassinations – most involving chem-bio weapons – "Barnacle" also killed hundreds of SWAPO prisoners-of-war and members of the South African security forces suspected of disloyalty in an operation designated DUAL.[54] Overall, "Barnacle" was deeply involved in South Africa's use of chem-bio weapons for assassinating opponents of the state.

Assassination was the primary aim of these "urban COIN ops"; as such, it was at this time that "Barnacle", alongside the Vlakplaas C1 unit which was formed at around the same time, began to form the core of the structured – but, significantly, informal – assassination capability within the NSMS structures. Between 1981 and 1986, many of these "Barnacle" cells operated in and around the principal townships in South Africa. Williams cites the example of the Port Elizabeth cell. This unit, composed of six white, black and Coloured Special Forces personnel, recced the townships constantly; all operatives were fluent in Xhosa which enabled them to operate in the townships with ease. Their primary task was "monitoring opponents of the regime – primarily from the civic organizations – with a view to their annihilation".[55] This unit, according to the account, was involved in at least two assassination attempts in and around Port Elizabeth (one against a Coloured community leader and the other against a white activist); both failed.[56] Assassination attempts were also planned against MK Special Operations Commander Ronnie Kasrils and ANC-NEC member Pallo Jordan, both of which were aborted.[57]

One of the primary aims in establishing "Barnacle" was the perceived need, at some point in the future, to have a fully independent covert operations unit available to the senior securocrats. This was not only in keeping with one of the aims of counter-revolutionary strategy (the establishment of independent CRW units) but also perceived by the leadership (including at least the defence minister and the minister of police, if not the prime minister himself) as a potential "ace-in-the-hole" should the political reform initiatives of the government grant the liberation movements too much power; this is what would become, by 1990, the "Third Force" in South Africa. Thus, while intelligence, as stated above, was shared amongst the other members of the intelligence community, the "Barnacle" units attempted to build up their own networks in order to reduce their reliance on other actors; "Barnacle" also began to establish front organisations as a prelude to the CCB's later activities. "Barnacle" units were not accountable to the local or regional NSMS structures, nor to the SADF commanders; they reported only to the GOC-SF; they were also given "considerable latitude" with regard to target-selection and operations.[58] All of these points are hallmarks of covert units designed to operate independent of oversight, accountability and – sometimes – even command.

This independence could, however, have extremely negative and unintended consequences. As Williams states, "it was a system that was to invite empire-building, financial mismanagement and personal abuse" during its later stages.[59] The CCB, as will be seen, became not only a rogue element within the South African security structures but a criminal one, involved in narcotics-trafficking and diamond-smuggling, prostitution, extortion and fraud, and weapons-trafficking by the early 1990s. While many Rhodesian members of "Barnacle" left the SADF after 1983, "Barnacle" continued to operate its networks – especially in Zimbabwe, where it is believed one cell continued to operate throughout the 1980s. "Barnacle" was, however, to undergo a structural change in the mid-1980s which would see it become finally a unit constructed and dedicated to purely covert operations.

In early 1986, retiring SADF Chief General Constand Viljoen decided to reorganise certain structures within the security system; Colonel P.J. "Joe" Verster, the former commander of 1 Recce, was tasked with accomplishing this. In 1981, Verster had been assigned to Special Forces headquarters as the senior staff officer for Special Operations; in 1986, a new post of senior staff officer for Covert Operations was created and assumed by Verster as part of Viljoen's reorganisation. Verster later described his task as "developing a covert force to counter the covert operations of the ANC".[60] This task – and its intelligence aims – was further clarified by Major-General Abraham "Joup" Joubert, the General Office Commanding Special Forces (GOC-SF) who stated that:

> In the mid- to late eighties, one of the major goals of national security policy and strategy was to bring the revolutionary organisation and mobilisation by the liberation movements, particularly the ANC, to a halt ... by this time it was also clear that the ANC was not going to be

stopped by normal conventional methods and that revolutionary methods would have to be used ... since the necessity for unconventional and revolutionary action was already clear, it was also clear that clandestine and covert operations would have to take place internally, for which Special Forces members would be used...

Joubert went on to state that

The revolutionary and covert nature of the plan, amongst other things, involved: that ANC leaders and people who substantially contributed to the struggle would be eliminated; that ANC facilities and support services would be destroyed; [and that] activists, sympathisers, fighters and people who supported them would also be eliminated.[61]

To fulfil this goal, in July 1986, "Barncale" was redesignated the "Civil Co-operation Bureau" (CCB) as a means of disguising the nature of its operations and disassociating it from all other Special Forces and DMI structures; it began to operate fully in this capacity by 1987.[62] As noted by the Harms Commission, "the plan was to establish a covert organisation divided in such a way that its operations could not be traced back to the SA Defence Force or the State".[63] Its formation by General Joubert, was undertaken with the knowledge and authorisation of Minister of Defence Magnus Malan (who later claimed no knowledge of the unit prior to November 1989) and General Jannie Geldenhuys, the chief of the SADF.[64] Its mandate to target the opponents of apartheid internally using unconventional methods was allegedly approved at a secret meeting on 28 Aril 1987 between senior members of the SADF, including Generals Joubert and Geldenhuys.[65] Up until at least 1988, the CCB only operated inside South Africa in support of the SAP; after 1988, whether or not this restriction continued to exist is unknown. During this time, in cooperation with SAP units, it was known to have killed at least 12 individuals.[66]

As a central means of conducting counter-revolutionary warfare, the CCB was a long-term project which required at least a ten-year gestation period in order to develop an effective covert capacity. In this sense, the CCB was the answer to Joubert's counter-revolutionary plan: the establishment of the CCB was seen as a necessary step by the securocrats to "disrupt maximally the enemies of the State in support of other parts of the Force"; its operations would be "directly ordered by the Chief, SADF".[67] As with many intelligence services the world over, the goal was to create a subterranean network of companies world-wide that would be both legitimate businesses and fronts for operational intelligence. The companies would be headed by businessmen who were well-integrated into their communities but remained skilled covert operatives able both to run successful firms and to collect intelligence and act on it where instructed. The overall intention was that the CCB would be fully functional sometime in the mid-1990s, partly because it was recognised that it would take that long for a soldier to transform himself into a career businessperson within his new working environment. The escalating nature of internal unrest in the late 1980s, the needs generated by the States of Emergency, and the desire to prevent a SWAPO victory in Namibia derailed this timetable, however, and the CCB was pulled into the counter-revolutionary effort before it was properly established.[68] There may have been an even more sinister reason for the CCB's existence, however: one source maintains that the CCB was designed to provide a covert counter-revolutionary capability to the existing government *following* the loss of power to a black majority government.[69] The veracity of this claim would lie in the existence of the "Third Force" following 1990.

The SADF later was to state that the CCB's formation was in direct relation to the ANC's change in tactics "by intensifying its underground and unconventional methods both externally and internally".[70] Webb outlined its mission as "to infiltrate enemy networks, collect information about them and to act against enemies who planned to overthrow the state"; in this sense, killing conducted by the CCB was not considered "murder" but rather "an attack on an individual enemy target with non standard issue weapons in an unconventional manner, ensuring that innocents are not hit".[71] This definition, composed by Geldenhuys and derived from an April 1987 report by Joubert, pointed to the concern amongst SADF personnel that such extralegal killings as the CCB (and other covert units) carrying out could be construed as "murder" and, therefore, subject the unit's members to criminal prosecution.

The CCB formed the third arm of the "Third Force" in South Africa, alongside Vlakplaas and DST's "projects". The establishment of the CCB was seen as a necessary step by the securocrats in the SSC to "disrupt maximally the enemies of the State in support of other parts of the Force"; its operations would be "directly ordered by the Chief, SADF".[72] It operated under the SADF Special Forces but in close co-operation with DMI and other covert units attached to the SAP Security Branch and other government structures; however, as had been the slow process since the formation of "Barnacle", it severed itself entirely from the family of the NIS, DMI and Security Branch. Based initially at Special Forces headquarters at Swartkop Park in Voortrekkerhoogte outside Pretoria, it soon moved its headquarters to Erasmia west of Pretoria, where its base became known as "Die Kop" ("the head/Summit of the Mountain"). The CCB itself, in the traditional parlance of the trade, became known as "the Organisation".[73]

The CCB's operational remit was further clarified by Major-General Jan Klopper, chief of the army, who stated that it "only undertook violent actions outside South Africa … its primary offensive function was to disrupt the activities of the ANC, the [SACP] and the [PAC]"; this was obviously not entirely accurate, as one of the prime missions of the CCB was internal operations, known as the "Red Plan": the monitoring, intimidation, harassment and elimination of apartheid's opponents through "projects".[74] For the CCB, the "enemy" were "people that threatened the security of the state but against whom the [SAP] could not take action ... these people were CCB targets"; it included "people merely suspected of involvement in enemy activities".[75] While the "enemy" was generally based abroad, either in the Frontline States or in Europe, as the ANC and its allies moved back inside South Africa in 1990 following their unbanning by De Klerk, this also meant that CCB projects on these individuals and structures would move internally. By 1990, the CCB considered 11 organisations, of which four were banned, and 25 individuals living in South Africa as "enemies".[76]

Structured along quasi-corporate lines, it was funded via the SADF Special Defence Fund, and comprised a "Chairman" (Joubert himself was the first from 1987–1990; by 1990, he had been replaced by Major-General Edward Webb, the new GOC-SF), a "Managing Director" as operational head (the first was Verster and six regional commands, each disguised as a commercial company.[77] CCB personnel almost entirely used *noms de guerres* for their operations and existence with the unit; often, "informal members" would be used, some completely unaware that they were working for the CCB. These often included criminals and former policemen. The CCB overall was divided into Regions; these were responsible for Europe, Zimbabwe, Swaziland, South-West Africa, Mozambique, Botswana, Lesotho, Malawi, Zaire, Zambia, and the internal regions. Each region was composed of individual "Cells", run by a "Co-ordinator", and operated with anywhere from five to 20 full-time operatives, with many more "informals". The overall size of the CCB never exceeded 250–300 full-time personnel.[78] Region 2, for example, was responsible for South-West Africa and became intricately involved in the DMI covert operation to destabilise the independence elections of Namibia in 1989, while Region 6 was responsible for internal operations and was run by Daniel "Staal" Burger and Wouter Basson (alias "Christo Brits"). Its operatives included Abraham "Slang" van Zyl, Ferdi Barnard, Calla Botha, and Chappie Maree, all former policemen or soldiers who had been indicted in various murders and other criminal activities.

Despite subsequent protestations to the contrary, certain senior members of the SADF (and, thus, the Defence Ministry) were aware of the existence of the CCB from its inception. The Chief of Staff, Finance, for example, approved CCB funds in co-operation with senior officials from the Treasury and Auditor-General's department (which differed from drawing funds from the Defence Special Account). The state purse would not always remain the CCB's source of funding; by the late 1980s, the CCB had established numerous front-companies and businesses, as well as becoming involved in criminal but extremely lucrative activities, as an adjunct of its operations. In 1989, the CCB received R28 million from the state; however, much larger amounts were obtained under "Plan Blue", the use of these front-companies for generating funds. As such, these fronts developed into truly lucrative pursuits for the soldiers, policemen and spies which ran them – proliferating to eventually form hundreds of companies carrying-out

> Covert activities in fields such as peddling political influence, trading weapons and disseminating propaganda.... A vast private sector arose, employing tens of thousands of people, consisting of either security companies or companies offering such mundane services as risk analysis, transport and so on, run by active soldiers working under cover, or by former security officers who, though no longer on the state payroll or subject to orders, retained contact with their old colleagues.[79]

This was all in keeping with the belief that a unit such as the CCB could only be truly successful if it was entirely independent from the state and dependent on its own resources.[80]

CCB operations

The CCB was established because DMI wanted a specialist unit that was capable of internal covert operations against the perceived opponents of the regime. This decision, as Williams points out, "reflected a shift in DMI's counter-insurgency emphasis".[81] By the early-to-mid-1980s, DMI officials did not believe that the pillar of reform (embodied in the constitutional reform programme and the National Welfare Management System, as discussed in Chapter 4) was succeeding; indeed, with the new "revolutionary onslaught" by the liberation movements and their internal allies beginning in 1985 and the shift from counter-insurgency to counter-revolutionary warfare (as DMI now believed the liberation movements were moving into the third stage of revolutionary warfare), a radical new approach was required. Security Branch had C1 as the "jackals" of the National Party government; DMI – and, its "eyes and ears", Special Forces – would have the CCB. As such, the "elimination of opponents was seen as necessary to ensure the success of the state's counter-revolutionary strategy".[82] And eliminate they did: a reflection of this was that the CCB's head, Verster, was arrested in March 1990 for the deaths of Anton Lubowski and David Webster (see below).[83] The CCB was also implicated in, among other things, the 1989 bombing of the Early Learning Centre in Athlone, the attempted murder of Gavin Evans, the attempted murder of then-ANC lawyer Dullah Omar (later minister of justice), and – their most bizarre operation – the planting of an ape foetus at the residence of Anglican Archbishop Desmond Tutu.

The approval and authorisation process for CCB operations was short and direct. The overly sensitive cases were considered by the Chief of the

SADF who would then determine where they required to be passed through to the SSC for authorisation; this was especially the case for those operations involving the assassination of a leading opponent (such as Dulcie September, Dullah Omar or Albie Sachs) of the regime. Other operations were approved by the Operations Committee of Special Forces or authorised individually by the director of the CCB. In theory, the Minister of Defence, in consultation with the Chief, SADF, had to authorise all Special Forces operations, including those by the CCB; should the operation be of extreme sensitivity, the State President was required to authorise the action.[84] Often times, the CCB's operatives would carry out "hits" without authorisation from either the SSC or even the director; as Williams has pointed out, "an astonishing abuse of power occurred within the unit itself and there were even indications that some of the targets had been chosen for purely personal and not political reasons".[85]

Between its formation and late 1987, the CCB by-and-large supported other Special Forces elements in their operations in the Frontline States by undertaking reconnaissance of ANC targets in these states prior to conventional or unconventional raids (much as its predecessor, 3 Recce, had done), as well as acting as "pathfinder" units during the actual raids. The CCB operated as well, at least in its early stages, as an integral part of the South African intelligence network. It received from and exchanged information with other elements in the community, including Special Branch, the NIS, and other elements within DMI (including Special Forces intelligence itself).[86] Part of this was reflected in their training: as a part of this, CCB operatives would be dropped into Soweto or another township for up to three days and left to survive. These "survival courses" were designed to both test the capabilities of the operative and to give them an idea of the type of operation that they would be expected to carry out in the future.[87] In many of these operations, first "Barnacle" and later CCB members would don civilian clothing and drive through the townships; white members of the units would use "black is beautiful" camouflage cream to disguise themselves (much as the Selous and other SADF Special Forces units often did during covert and clandestine operations) to the township's residents.

Given its rather Orwellian name, it is no surprise that the CCB was the total embodiment in South Africa of Ian Fleming's fictional SPECTRE (the "Special Executive for Counter-intelligence, Terrorism, Revenge and Extortion") organisation which featured in Fleming's Bond chronicles. An indication of this was demonstrated when Region 2, responsible for South-West Africa, was implicated deeply in the fiasco surrounding the attempted sabotage of the Namibian independence elections in 1989. This operation, as part of DMI's efforts, involved CCB personnel intimidating voters and candidates within Namibia, disrupting election meetings by SWAPO with grenade attacks and other methods, all in addition to providing support to the DMI propaganda campaign against SWAPO through "PRO

Communications Projects" in support of the Democratic Turnhalle Alliance.[88]

The most infamous cases which they have been indicted in, however, surround the assassinations of two prominent anti-apartheid figures and the attempted assassination of a third. On 1 May 1989, University of the Witwatersrand lecturer David Webster was gunned-down outside his home in Johannesburg;[89] this was followed on 12 September by the murder of SWAPO lawyer Anton Lubowski at his home in Windhoek. Evidence provided at the time and since, through testimony at the Truth and Reconciliation Commission, indicated that the CCB had planned and carried-out these two murders on the express orders of military commanders. Lubowski's alleged killer, Donald Acheson, worked for Ferdi Barnard in Region 6 of the CCB but was released during his trial in Windhoek due to a failure by the Namibian government to subpoena two key CCB operatives for evidence.[90]

Another assassination attempt was made on Albie Sachs, the ANC representative in Maputo, who was almost killed by a bomb which tore off his left arm. Other high-level targets that the CCB considered but did not kill included Archbishop Desmond Tutu, Reverend Frank Chikane (who was jointly targeted by the CCB and 7 Medical Battalion, the authors of Project COAST, the South African CBW programme) and Reverend Allan Boesack.[91] The CCB also conducted innumerable other assassinations of lower-level officials and cadres, both within South Africa and South-West Africa, and abroad. While the evidence for these assassinations and others carried-out by the various covert elements of the security forces in South Africa is still being examined through criminal investigations, it is clear that the CCB was a highly integral part of the most secretive elements of the apartheid security apparatus. At the time that it was exposed in 1989, newspapers reported that the CCB (and other organisations that it had assisted) had carried-out more than 75 assassinations since 1977.[92]

Conclusions

With the development and deployment of covert units such as these – alongside the failure of domestic political reform to check the liberation movements' strength – the belief grew in the securocracy that the insurgency was moving into its "third stage" (open conventional warfare). This led Botha to "take the gloves off", and authorise the intelligence services to take all necessary steps to crush the liberation movement once and for all.

7 Crossing the Rubicon
"The gloves come off" for a total counter-revolutionary strategy, 1985–1990

> What did they think we were collecting all this information about addresses, cars, movements for? To send Christmas cards?
>
> *Trewits* participant

The states of emergency and counter-revolutionary strategy

The assassination of the "Cradock Four" on 27 June 1985 was to prove, in retrospect, a kind of turning-point; three weeks later, on 21 July 1985, the same day as their funeral, protest reached such a pitch that Botha declared the first state of emergency in 36 magisterial districts of South Africa, approximately one-third of the country. This marked one of the turning-points of the 1980s: while instituting nominal political reforms domestically, most of these were regarded as window-dressing – at the same time as South Africa's domestic opposition increased dramatically its violent actions against the apartheid regime, resulting in the securocrats' – mistaken – belief that the ANC (and its domestic ally the UDF) had entered "third-stage revolutionary warfare". As a result, Botha and his security leaders declared "the gloves off" in their counter-revolutionary strategy against the liberation movements, both domestically and across the Frontline States and abroad. Botha authorised the intelligence services to take all necessary steps to crush the insurgency (i.e. the liberation movement) once and for all. With the increased deployment of SAP and SADF personnel into the Western Cape, the Eastern Cape, and large sectors of the Witwatersrand, their powers also increased dramatically, signalling the first stage of the "gloves coming off" which would determine the counter-revolutionary direction from this point onwards for the highest levels of the decision-making.

The "revolutionary onslaught"

On 18 March 1985, the SSC approved a document delineating the revolutionary climate – based upon strikes, protests, guerrilla attacks, arson and murder – which gripped South Africa. Calling for the selective arrest of key anti-government leaders, Botha – ever more recalcitrant and defiant in his defence of South Africa's position, both domestically and internationally – backed this move at a 15 April SSC meeting with senior security force officers with demands on the security force leaders to "fight the revolutionary climate";[1] according to one senior commander, "PW gave us hell ... he told us we must take the gloves off".[2]

The origins of this new counter-revolutionary warfare stance can be traced to this meeting. The effect was noticeable immediately: on 14 June 1985, 5 Recce raided Gaborone and killed 12 people, injured six, and destroyed five houses. Claiming that this was a "major ANC control centre" for the "Western Front" – based on intelligence gathered by agents of the Soweto Intelligence Unit, who had identified four primary targets as those "responsible for planning and execution of terror onslaught" – the SADF succeeded in intimidating the ANC Chief Representative to leave the country following the raid; only four of the dead were ANC and none of these were the four targeted. The Botswana raid had been preceded by a June 1985 finding that "36 acts of terror" had originated from Botswana over the previous ten months; the "trigger for the raid" had been the attack on the Cape Town house of a deputy minister. It was therefore seen as being of major importance to the SSC; this was signified by the presence of Colonel Albertus Steyn, who co-ordinated planning and intelligence-collection, for the raid, as co-ordinator of the Western Transvaal Security Branch; Brigadier Wickus Loots and Commandant Charl Naudé; and Generals Johan Coetzee (SAP Commissioner), 'Kat' Liebenberg (GOC Special Forces) and Constand Viljoen (Chief, SADF) in the planning meetings. The Soweto Security Branch under Colonel Lodewyk de Jager provided intelligence and supported planning for the raid at Special Forces headquarters, at which the Johannesburg and Western Transvaal Security Branches, the NIS, DMI, and Special Forces were all present.[3]

This was not to limit, however, in any way the overall counter-revolutionary strategy of the state. With such a robust and visible statement

Table 7.1 Statistical analysis of terrorist incidents (July 1976–April 1990)

Target	Number	% of total
Police	485	31.3
Military	63	4.1
Juridical	36	2.3
State	242	15.6
Economic	339	21.9
Civilian	369	23.8
Other	15	1.0
	1,549	

Source: Malan Submission.

of Pretoria's intentions, the securocrats pushed ahead with further counter-revolutionary measures. At an SSC meeting held on 18 July, the SSC tabled a report titled "Principles for the Combating of the Revolutionary Onslaught" which laid out a number of counter-revolutionary principles, all of which coincided with "lessons" and principles set out by writers such as Fraser and McCuen; these were subsequently adopted by the SSC.[4] At the same meeting, a state of emergency was determined for 20 July 1985.

On 26 August 1985, the SSC approved an intelligence assessment finding that South Africa "was now in a state of revolutionary war"; it had already been determined at an SSC meeting two weeks previous that "the unrest has developed into a revolutionary struggle". Such views were not to be made public until 1986.[5] This amounted, as Ellis points out, to a formal finding that "the revolutionary onslaught had now reached the phase of guerrilla war inside South Africa ... the appropriate step was to fight fire with fire, organising guerrilla forces of their own for deployment inside South Africa".[6] In addition, the government outlined a three-stage counter-revolutionary strategy: first, re-establish law and order; second, institute socio-economic upgrading of the townships; third, institute constitutional reform. These would form the guiding principles against the "Revolutionary Onslaught".[7]

As a practical indication of the aims of the SSC in targeting directly the sources of opposition, Minister of Law and Order Adriaan Vlok stated in October 1987 that the "government would pay particular attention to dismantling alternative governmental structures – including people's courts, protest education, street committees and para-police groups. These governments within the government ... posed the most serious threat to law and order". Under emergency regulations adopted in December 1986, the organisation of such structures was considered treason by the state, and was treated as such.[8] Thus, the SSC would target "people's power" as a means of preventing "people's war". This, too, was in line with McCuen's teachings: as the "street committees" and "people's courts" were removed from the townships, either through detention or intimidation (involving both the security and surrogate forces), the government moved in to replicate these structures with their own, designed to "fill the vacuum with their own reinstated administrative structures".[9] Thus, the endeavours of the ANC and UDF to organise the population for "people's war" would be targeted and defeated by the intelligence-led counter-organisation tactics of the government.

At the Second Federal Congress of the National Party, Defence Minister Malan stated, in a warning to both the Frontline States and internal opposition, "We have not even started using our muscle and capabilities"; he stated further that South Africa had "no intention of negotiating with terrorists" and should not be toyed with.[10] Botha further instructed his military commanders to clamp down on unrest, giving them the order that the situation country-wide "be normalised by the end of December 1986".[11] This marked the turning point from countering the "Total Onslaught" to countering the "Revolutionary Onslaught": the emergence of South Africa's counter-revolutionary strategy and the fruition of the NSMS web of securocrat control of South African society. This strategy would not be aimed at retrenching white-minority rule in South Africa but rather at "managing" the process of reform over the long-term; thus, reform remained very much a part of the Nats' strategy – only at their pace and not that of the liberation movements or international community. This reform was placed in the hands of the military and national intelligence securocrats, as well as those other members of the bureaucracy who had a stake in the process (Constitutional Development, for example).

What this meant was that, ultimately, with the refocusing of the threat away from Communist-inspired subversion and onto South Africa's developmental problems, "being part of the 'Third World's poverty and instability' legitimated state violence and rationalised the white electorate's fears of 'lowered standards' ... Chaotic and incapable of natural order, a third-world society permanently needed vigorous management".[12] Thus, the conclusion that can be drawn from this is that putting this view forward as a legitimisation of the state's violence (including assassination and other killings as part of counter-revolutionary war within South Africa's borders) followed from this re-interpretation of South Africa's problems to its public by the securocrats of the NSMS: it was "the nature of the problem" in the Third World for this kind of state action to be needed. Assassination would not, however, become simply a mass tool to counter the revolution; as General Johan Coetzee, the head of Security Branch and later Commissioner of the SAP, stated in a 1994 interview, there was an

> Unresolved debate in the upper reaches of government about the merits of the "Argentinian route" ... [but] if you want an Argentina, fine. Take two weeks and kill everybody in the ANC. No problem. And then what? Might give you another ten years.[13]

Thus, an intelligence-led, targeted mass-killing – similar to the US PHOENIX programme devised in Vietnam for decapitation of the Viet-Cong Infrastructure – was not to be the practice in South Africa; rather, a selective removal – where the judicial system was inadequate or insufficient – of opponents would be the key. In this sense, the securocrats chose selective assassination for the most troublesome (or unreachable) leaders of the liberation movements, in tandem with mass round-ups and other legal instruments, to confront the "Revolutionary Onslaught"; this appears to have been a conscious choice by the securocrats rather than a method arrived at by happenstance.

This restructuring of the threat perception had a direct impact on the attitudes of the securocrats and security force members tasked with

Table 7.2 MK incidents (1976–1987)

1976	4
1977	20
1978	13
1979	12
1980	19
1981	55
1982	39
1983	55
1984	44
1985	136
1986	231
1987	235

carrying-out the counter-revolutionary strategy. As Seegers has noted, these attitudes included "promoting the value of uncritically submitting to authority, of being aggressive against those violating conventional norms, of de-emphasising concern for individual human beings, and of encouraging thinking in rigid conventional terms".[14] Therefore, human life had less perceived value, and blind obedience and loyalty to the ideal of the counter-revolutionary strategy was key. Extralegal killings and assassinations were shunted aside in light of stipulations within the *Defence Act* and *Police Act* that indemnified personnel from prosecution from all such acts in the course of duty: the *Defence Act* granted absolute immunity to members of the security forces for murder, assault and other criminal behaviour "if done *bona fide* for the purpose of or in connection with the prevention or suppression of terrorism in any operational area".[15] Thus, such legal stipulations appeared implicitly to authorise the security forces to use any means necessary to combat the "Onslaught", without regard for the law. These attitudes were also impacted on by the Afrikaner's natural abhorrence (due to fears over the dangers of division amongst the community in the face of a threat, an attitude which goes back to the early settler days and the Boer Wars) of disunity, including ideologically.

"Total counter-revolutionary strategy"

The first state of emergency was lifted on 7 March 1986 in an attempt to defuse the crisis; however, by that point, events had already progressed to the point that only the total collapse of the National Party government would satisfy the liberation movements and their allies. The lifting of the state of emergency proved to be a "costly mistake": there was an immediate resurgence of violence in the black communities, increased violence in and around "white" areas, and a new wave of limpet-mine attacks.[16] As the townships continued to erupt, it became apparent to Botha's securocrats that only the elimination of the opposition, by violent or political means, would succeed in maintaining the Nats' hold on power. In the months between the introduction of the tri-cameral Parliament in September 1984 and June 1986, more than 2,500 people died in "unrest incidents" within South Africa, approximately 10,000 had been "detained", and more than 3,500 resided in the country's jails.[17] Intelligence indicated that, on 16 June, country-wide demonstrations were to be held to commemorate the tenth anniversary of the Soweto Uprising. To prevent this, on 12 June, barely three months after the lifting of the first state of emergency, the government declared a second one nation-wide following an emergency meeting of the SSC. The goals of this state of emergency would be to "secure stability" (the "restoration of law and order"), then bring the situation back to one of "normality", finally creating circumstances for constitutional, economic and social "development" to occur;[18] partly as an indicator of the first step, during the first year of this nation-wide state of emergency, between 25,000 and 40,000 personnel were detained by the security forces.[19]

This had followed the failure of the visit by the Commonwealth Eminent Persons' Group (EPG) to South Africa in an attempt to negotiate a settlement to the conflict; the EPG, led by Australia's Malcolm Fraser and Nigeria's Olusegun Obasanjo, stated that the ANC was willing to negotiate with the National Party on the condition that Mandela was released. The response was immediate and obvious: on 19 May 1986, 11 members of 1 Recce were dropped into Bulawayo and ferried into Harare, where they (supported by three former Rhodesians who had been working in Zimbabwe for the SADF since 1981) attacked two buildings in downtown Harare, alleged to contain the ANC's regional offices. This raid – along with a similar attack on a suspected ANC transit facility in Gaborone and an airstrike on a Lusaka ANC office – signalled a hardening of resolve amongst the National Party government: many political observers felt Botha was demonstrating domestically and internationally that the South African government was not going to bow to any pressure and would always have the capability, no matter what the circumstances, to counter its enemies; each capital had been visited by the EPG during their mission, thus the choice of these targets was unmistakable.[20] Condemned internationally, the raids brought about the immediate end of the EPG mission; significantly, Foreign Minister Pik Botha, who had been responsible for dealing with the EPG, was not informed of these raids and was livid.

President Botha had been making increasingly vitriolic statements since his infamous 15 August 1985 "Rubicon speech" in Natal warning the international community against attempting to "interfere" in South Africa's "internal affairs". This moment would mark, many observers felt, the "dominance of the civilian and military 'hawks' within the state and the National Party for the next five years".[21] It is noteworthy that, according to Pik Botha, the original intention of the "Rubicon" speech had been to announce the release of Mandela (on the condition that he renounced violence) and the dismantling of apartheid; however, at the last moment, the President removed these sections from the speech. The result was "a bucket of iced water in the face".[22]

The decision to scuttle the EPG meeting and take the "hard repression" option was not, however, just the result of Botha's own bluster but also the result of a schism within the securocrats: while one group (centred around SAP Commissioner Coetzee) believed that "soft repression strategies" emphasising limited coercion to control the low-intensity conflict facing the state would be the best way forward, another group (centring on SSC Secretary Lloyd, Security Branch Head Major-General Johan van der Merwe, and SAP counter-insurgency Head Major-General Bert Wandrag) simply "redefined the problem" by translating the tactics of counter-insurgency, until now pursued through the "Total National Strategy", into the tactics of counter-revolutionary warfare. This latter group, which won the day with Botha, had been faced with the decision prior to the EPG mission, following schisms with the Department of Constitutional Development and Planning (DCDP) over the shape of reforms, of "releasing Nelson Mandela and negotiating a transfer of power from a position of weakness" or re-establishing control over the country by "crushing resistance in civil society" and promoting "new black leaders".[23] Botha chose the latter, pushing aside the political reformists in the DCDP; significantly, Minister of DCDP Chris Heunis, had in 1984 been permanently co-opted onto the SSC by Botha specifically for the reason of finding constitutional solutions to the gathering crisis.

To meet the goals of the state of emergency, a counter-strategy was designed by the securocrats: this included an assessment of the "type of war in which South Africa was involved", a determination of "who the instigators of unrest were and what their strategy was", an assessment of "how the implementation of their strategy differed from the normal democratic process", and, finally, an evaluation of an effective counter-strategy.[24] Thus the "Total Counter-revolutionary Strategy" was born; its origins generally lay in the 12 May 1986 SSC meeting at which a number of counter-revolutionary strategies were laid out. As a strategy, it already had the tools taking shape, in the form of the covert operations units, to see through this new phase of the conflict. For this reason, counter-revolutionary warfare theory became dominant amongst the securocrats; this can be witnessed in such statements as that by General Wandrag regarding the political objective of "Total Counter-revolutionary Strategy".

> Drastic action must be taken to eliminate the underlying social and economic factors which have caused unhappiness in the population. The only way to render the enemy powerless is to nip revolution in the bud by ensuring there is no fertile soil in which the seeds of revolution can germinate.[25]

This would involve three key actions: the "countering of planned subversion on all fronts", the "elimination of the revolutionaries", and the "reform of the environment". Vlok further outlined the aims of "Total Counter-revolutionary Strategy" as being "security actions ... against all those who took part in the revolutionary onslaught and who hindered the successful implementation of the other two components": "good government for all South Africans", and "the finding of a constitutional dispensation which would be acceptable for the majority of South Africans by means of effective and imaginative negotiations". "Security actions" were seen as being "holding action", to allow progress to be made in the other two areas. The change in attitude within the security establishment was reflected in the statement that "where once there could be no security without reform, now there can be no reform without security".[26]

The overall aim would be to bring the country back under control. To achieve this, the government instituted a number of key socio-economic and political actions in an attempt to "reform the environment" of South Africa while establishing security throughout the country; the logic behind this was that, as the success of the revolutionaries was based on the exploitation of local grievances, the elimination of both these grievances and the revolutionaries themselves would answer the bigger political questions (i.e. opposition to apartheid itself). The "oil spot" technique was used internally for the first time: identifying 34 key target areas and 200 townships for "upgrading projects", the DCDP instituted a R16 billion programme aimed at socio-economic upgrading which would see more than 1,800 projects implemented; these included housing developments, electricity and water supplies, community beautification, road-works, and other similar initiatives, in such areas as the Vaal Triangle, Atteridegeville, the Uitenhage and Port Elizabeth townships, and Crossroads. On the political front, local government reform, the scrapping of influx controls, and the legitimation of state structures were all aimed at promoting support for the black local councils and "moderate" black leaders.[27] These continued to be, however, couched within the terms of the same "reform apartheid" proposals which Botha's government had been promoting since before the failure of the 1983 Constitutional proposals; what did change, however, was a "bottom-up" approach, rather than the previous "top-down" one, to finding reform solutions. Security initiatives, as outlined throughout, were seen to by the use of vigilantes, *kitskonstabels* and the army deployed into the townships; one year after the declaration of the second state of emergency, 97 townships were under military occupation.[28]

In addition to the socio-economic and political actions were security ones. The aim of these operations was the elimination of the enemy leaders and the counter-organisation of the population. This was clearly laid out in a 14 April 1986 SSC document which stated that, to "stem the deteriorating security situation", the security forces must "neutralise/eliminate enemy leaders and the influence which they exercise". This was to be achieved through a variety of practices, including "exploiting differences among the enemy; harassment actions; smash and grab actions; turn actions; identifying the weak points and vulnerabilities of enemy leaders"; in addition, legal methods such as arrests, prosecution, banning and detention without trial were to be used.[29] It would be extremely rare for a politician or securocrat to authorise an assassination; instead, they were "sanctioned" by the system.[30] This type of action was usually only sanctioned once all other legal options had been exhausted.

In discussing the authorisations given for operations with the intention to "neutralise/eliminate enemy leaders", terms such as *elimineer* ("eliminate"), *neutraliseer* ("neutralise"), *uitwis* ("obliterate or wipe out"), *vernietig* ("destroy"), *opspoor en vernietig* ("track down and destroy"), *hou vas breek* ("break their grip"), *maak 'n plan* ("make a plan"), and *permanent ui die saamelewing verwyder* ("permanently remove from society") were common in directives and guidelines issued by the SSC and by individual politicians and ministers. While politicians and other senior figures would later state that, to them, this meant using every legal method possible to bring about the "neutralisation/elimination" of the enemy leadership, it appeared obvious to the security forces that the use of the terms such as "eliminate" and even such euphemisms as "permanently remove from society" meant "to kill". As Ellis notes,

> Members of special units interpreted the concept of total war quite differently from the more cerebral of the securocrats, for whom it was all about sublimating military activity and indeed every other branch of state activity to strategic political goals. For the rank and file of the special units, total war meant simply war without rules. None of the operatives seems ever to have imagined that one day they might be held to account for their actions.[31]

In retrospect, some senior members of the security establishment felt that this language was kept "intentionally vague or all-encompassing" by the securocrats who wrote the orders up, so as to allow for interpretation by the security forces.[32] It was clear that this language was chosen for a reason: as others were to state, "if they wanted to give any other meaning to the word 'elimination' they would have used another word ... 'elimination' in this context means 'to kill'".[33] However, there were senior commanders who, when confronted with the usage of these terms, stated clearly that "it means just what it says, to kill ... there was never any lack of clarity about 'take out' or 'eliminate', it meant that the person had to be killed"; thus, interpretation could be said to play a role in this question.[34] The result of this was "a blurring in the minds of the security forces between people who posed a real danger to public safety, on the one hand, and people who merely opposed the government's policies, on the other": all were lumped together as one target for elimination.[35]

From countering insurgency to countering revolution: intelligence-led targeting

The formation and co-ordination of the apartheid state's overt and covert counter-revolutionary warfare intelligence capabilities in the mid-1980s is clearly demonstrated in the marked increase in targeted-eliminations after 1985, which coincides with the shift in strategy to counter-revolutionary warfare. In the face of increasing militancy and unrest throughout the country, the threat to South Africa was no longer seen principally as external (in the form of armed MK insurgents infiltrating from neighbouring states), but increasingly as internal. Therefore, covert means of eliminating the state's opponents internally had to be found – and while the units to conduct counter-revolutionary warfare had been established, much of the required co-operation and co-ordination between units would only be provided in the mid-1980s.

Specialist action and the "Joubert Plan"

At an SSC meeting in August 1986, the SSC adopted a document entitled "*Strategie ter bekamping van die ANC*" ("Strategy for the Combating of the ANC"), which recommended "*om die ANC leierskap te neutraliseer*" ("to neutralise the ANC leadership"); and "*om die magte en invloed van sleutelpersone van die ANC en hulle meelopers te neutraliseer*" ("to neutralise the power and influence of key persons in the ANC, and their fellow-travellers"). This was further clarified at a 1 December 1986 meeting in which the SSC adopted a document entitled "*Konsep Nasionale Strategie teen die Rewolusionêre Oorlog teen die RSA: NR 44*" ("National Strategy Concept against the "Revolutionary Onslaught" against the RSA: NR 44"); this document, which can be regarded as the definitive strategy document for the counter-revolutionary strategy of the South African state, stressed earlier goals and introduced a new dimension where it is stated that "*Intimiteerders moet dmv formele en informele polisiëring geneutraliseer word*" ("intimidators must be neutralised by way of formal and informal policing"). As a follow-up to *Konsep NR 44*, a strategy document dated 24 January 1987 suggested that the strategy should be to "*identifiseer en elimineer die rewolusionêre leiers en veral dié, met charisma*" ("identify and eliminate the revolutionary leaders, especially those with charisma").[36] As part of this, Defence Minister Malan, sometime in 1983, ordered the end of the use of the term "total onslaught", as it was felt that this presented an "exaggerated and fearful assessment of the challenges to the apartheid regime".[37]

On 12 June 1986 – the day the second state of emergency was declared – and following an SAP request, Major-General Abraham "Joup" Joubert (the General Office Commanding Special Forces after 1 November 1985) was requested by SADF Chief General Jannie Geldenhuys to draw-up a plan by which Special Forces could support SAP operations inside the country. In his report, Joubert proposed that the Special Forces be allowed to "engage in unconventional and revolutionary methods in order to combat the revolutionary onslaught against South Africa". As a result of this proposal, the internal mission of the Special Forces was expanded to include conducting covert operations internally; this was referred to as *verskerpte optrede* ("intensified action") by Joubert.[38] His overall plan focused on the "problem areas of South Africa" for the SADF and SAP, namely the Northern Transvaal, Witwatersrand and Eastern Cape Territorial Commands. As a result, Special Forces liaison personnel were sent to these commands, as well as the regional heads of the Security Branch, to co-ordinate targets for action in which the Special Forces would support the SAP; this included assigning, through the "Barnacle" unit, Charl Naudé to the Northern Transvaal and Colonel Joe Verster to the Witwatersrand, two individuals who would feature prominently in the CCB.

These actions would be aimed at "totally destabilising and stopping" the ANC and its allies in these regions. Therefore, the "revolutionary and covert aspects" of the plan held that "ANC members and people who contributed to the struggle [as well as the] ANC's activists hangers-on and people who supported them had to be eliminated"; in addition, the "ANC facilities and supporting structure had to be destroyed".[39] Because internal security was the responsibility of the SAP, Special Forces operatives were to act in support of the Security Branch; this meant that each operation needed to be authorised by the Security Branch before Special Forces operatives could participate. Their function was to meet with the Security Branch in the assigned areas and decide on joint operations. Such operations included killing, usually after targets had been identified at joint meetings attended by other high-ranking SADF officials.

This plan, however, was never implemented fully, as the requirement to support the SAP faded away by early 1987. Thus, the Special Forces teams which had been seconded to the various Territorial Commands were recalled and the "Joubert Plan" was shelved. The concept for covert internal operations had not, however, similarly faded away: months before, the Civil Co-operation Bureau was founded as the prime result of this restructuring of the Special Forces' mission (see Chapter 6), and would be responsible for taking this plan forward for DMI.

The national intelligence structures and targeting: *Geveilstaf* and *Trewits*

Other structures slowly took shape to co-ordinate the activities of these units. Central to these was a key and extremely secretive committee, based in *Stratkom* and established sometime in 1985–1986. Formerly the Interdepartmental Committee on Intelligence, "in the face of rising resistance and apparent inability of the security forces to contain it", it was upgraded to become the Joint Security Staff (*Gesamentlike Veiligheidstaf*, referred to as

Geveilstaf or GVS), described as the "operational executive co-ordinator of the security community". The Deputy Minister of Law and Order was relieved of all duties in order to manage it; however, following the imposition of the second state of emergency in June 1986, the *Geveilstaf* was integrated into a National JMC (NJMC) in February 1987. While very little is known about the functions and interests of the *Geveilstaf*, far more significant to the counter-revolutionary efforts was the establishment in 1986 of the *Teen Rewolusionêre Inligting Taakspan* (Counter-revolutionary Intelligence Task Team or *Trewits*), in whose monthly meetings "intelligence would be exchanged and targets identified" by Security Branch, DMI, Special Forces and NIS representatives.[40]

Both of these committees were responsible for selecting the operational priorities of the security forces to counter the liberation movements (*Geveilstaf*) and for gathering intelligence on and selecting individuals in the liberation movements and other opponents of apartheid to be "neutralised" (*Trewits*). The latter, in fact, was established to co-ordinate intelligence across the SSC and security force structures for the targeting of opponents; it is believed that the NIS was instrumental in providing "targeting databases" for each country concerned.[41]

Trewits

In 1985, the security forces established *Trewits* whose primary task was to identify targets for action, including elimination. This followed similar but less co-ordinated efforts by various elements of the security forces prior to *Trewits*' establishment; indeed, before this, identification of targets was done by the different security force components separately and often on an event basis. An example of this is the "Z-Squad" being involved, as early as 1974, in identifying installations in neighbouring countries.[42]

As conflict escalated in the mid-1980s, the SADF established a target identification workgroup; authorisation for this came from Brigadier Chris Thirion (Chief Director, Military Intelligence), Major-General Joubert, and Major-General Dirk Hamman (Chief of Army Intelligence). One of this group's sub-branches, established in the Eastern Transvaal in late 1986 under Captain Henri van der Westhuizen of the DCC, co-ordinated targeting information from the NIS, Security Branch and DMI under the overall leadership of Security Branch divisional commander Brigadier Schalk Visser. The Eastern Transvaal was the primary infiltration route for MK personnel from Mozambique and Swaziland; similar groups were later established in Ladybrand (covering Lesotho) under Security Branch commander Frik Fouche, Zeerust (Western Transvaal) covering Botswana, and in the Northern Transvaal covering Zimbabwe and Angola.[43]

As the Eastern Transvaal workgroup was established, the decision to set up *Trewits* was made in September 1986. As one of its members noted,

The fact that MK and eventually APLA members started using neighbouring frontline states as a springboard for launching their armed attacks against the Republic led directly to the establishment of a cross-border capability aimed at eliminating or neutralising this very real threat. It was [its] task to properly evaluate and co-ordinate all intelligence regarding the revolutionary threat facing the RSA and especially with regard to identifying and prioritising political targets which posed such a threat. These threats could be in the form of an individual, a group, an organisation, an accommodation or logistical facility and were prioritised in terms of the level of political destabilisation each target posed.[44]

Trewits was established following recommendations by Brigadiers Jac Buchner (head of the Pietermaritzburg Security Branch at the time) and C.P. van der Westhuizen (head of the Eastern Cape Territorial Command) to deal with "the hardest cases" internally. Its operational imperative is clear from its location and membership: located operationally within "C" Section of the Security Branch, it co-ordinated targeting intelligence activities across the security forces. Thus, while *Trewits* fell under the command of Security Branch, it was nonetheless a sub-structure of the Covert Collection Sub-committee of KIK, chaired by Brigadier J. "Tolletjie" Botha, head of the DCC.[45] It became fully operational on 12 January 1987. From the beginning, it identified targets throughout the Frontline States, later extending its scope inside South Africa. Under the chairmanship of Buchner (who was replaced in 1987 by Brigadier Bob Beukes and, finally, Brigadier C.J.A. Victor), *Trewits* was described as "a new, joint effort by the relevant members of the IG to bring about a solid information base for meaningful counter-revolutionary operational action".[46] The responsibility to develop ANC and PAC targets had been placed, by March 1986, with Commandant Callie Steijn of DMI, who had been involved in target development from at least 1981 through 1985/1986; others, such as Commandant Jan Anton Nieuwoudt (DCC) and Major Craig Williamson (Security Branch), were also involved in target designation, many of which resulted in cross-border raids (such as Maseru) and assassinations. Other security force units assisted with target recce and designation: the Security Branch C1 unit's involvement in both killings and abductions in neighbouring countries from the early 1980s onwards meant that its operatives were involved in the process of gathering intelligence on key ANC/MK personnel in the Frontline States.

Involvement in killings (primarily cross-border) precedes both the establishment of target groups and *Trewits*; it is notable that members of *Trewits'* committees had previously played a significant role at both an intelligence-gathering and operational level, including a number of Security Branch members who had significant border duty both in Namibia and Rhodesia, showing the continuity between counter-insurgency warfare in the region and Security Branch work inside South Africa. It would appear that those chosen for service in the regions were chosen precisely for their counter-insurgency experience.[47] With representatives seconded from NIS, Security Branch, DMI and Special Forces, *Trewits* pooled and discussed the records of activists, their activities, location, and "problem" status, as well as training-camps, infiltrations and planned operations. Its purpose was described as being "to co-ordinate tactical information with regard to the former liberation movements in neighbouring countries".[48] More exactly, its function was "to consolidate, evaluate, interpret and distribute all relevant information with a view to operational actions to realise the RSA's counter-revolutionary strategic aim".[49]

Trewits functioned generally at the national level, with regional meetings being held between concerned parties on an ad hoc basis with representation from the Security Branch regional officer commanding, a mid-level NIS officer, and a senior Special Forces or DCC person to represent the SADF. In addition to formal *Trewits* meetings, those who attended regional meetings enjoyed on-going and regular liaison with those involved in the target workgroups of Special Forces. For example, in 1989, a Security Branch document indicated that the "actual development of target studies" was still being performed by a project group of Special Forces; this was because "the group has the necessary experience, expertise and equipment at its disposal" to carry-out such tasks.[50] Thus, there may have been a separation between tasks within *Trewits*: in 1987, DMI's target section was transferred to Special Forces where it was placed under the command of Colonel Mielie Prinsloo, the head of Special Forces Intelligence; however, individual DMI members continued to serve on the workgroups, but were based at Special Forces. Further links were maintained, particularly with the DCC.

Therefore, the purpose of *Trewits* was not simply to gather intelligence (as members of the security and intelligence communities have argued recently), but rather that intelligence was gathered for specific operational purposes, and that the location and personnel chosen were selected precisely for their operational capacity. To help with this, the SADF targeting groups were drawn into *Trewits* in February 1987 – at the same time roughly as the "Joubert Plan" was being discussed and other covert counter-revolutionary activities were being established within the security establishment.

Targeting processes and authorities

Within the apartheid intelligence structures from the national level downwards, generally speaking, there were four levels of "authorisation" for direct targeting and assassination:

- the SSC level ("the highest", as it was termed) for the biggest cases
- securocrat level (military, political or intelligence commanders)

- mid-level commanders (majors and colonels, often involving personal reasons)
- the lowest (hit-squads and township political violence)

Prior to roughly 1986, this authorisation was informal: targets were chosen on a case-by-case basis at any of these levels. The "mechanised" or institutionalised (systemised) targeting of opponents did not come into being until 1986 when *Trewits* was established; it did, however, have its forerunners in the regional and local KIKs and *Veikoms* from roughly 1981 onwards. As such, *Trewits* functioned in close co-operation with the *Veikoms* in each JMC. Once targeting was agreed, it was communicated down through the structures of the NSMS to the relevant authorities (i.e. the commander of the SAP Security Branch or the Chief of Staff, Intelligence, for DMI) for action. This followed similar but less co-ordinated efforts by various elements of the security forces prior to *Trewits'* establishment. Over the course of the 1980s, *Trewits* came to be closely integrated with the SAP counter-insurgency function, to such a degree that – as already noted – *Trewits* was established directly within Security Branch to facilitate targeting.

There can be no doubt that the prime function of *Trewits* was target identification: once an individual's name appeared on a *Trewits* target list, he/she was seen as a legitimate target. In the words of a participant, "what did they think we were collecting all this information about addresses, cars, movements for? To send Christmas cards?"[51] The target development process worked in the following way. First a structure would be identified – for example, the ANC RPMC in Mozambique; then all its components/sub-structures and various positions assigned and names placed next to positions. Following this, dossiers around each individual in the structure would be developed, including personal and political information. This would lead to a set of new names and so the process would continue. When a target was complete, action could then be taken against it. Political considerations played a role in determining operations and when a target could be attacked; at other times, however, political considerations would also dictate carrying-out operations based on old or incomplete intelligence. For this reason, the wrong target could often be hit because of such poor or faulty intelligence.

It should be noted that targets included ANC personnel and not just those associated with MK: the 20 members of the ANC-NEC were considered targets, against which specific authorisation for any action was not required. In Mozambique, for example, Jacob Zuma, Sue Rabkin, Mohamed Timol, Bobby Pillay, Keith Mokoape and Indres Naidoo were all targeted for collection and possible elimination.[52] Each target would then be considered at the SADF General Staff level, followed by a briefing by the CSI to the minister; if targets were agreed upon, they would be handed over to the tactical planning level, usually involving Special Forces

Intelligence and the DCC. Targets were also discussed at *Trewits* regional meetings, where the NIS and Security Branch would also provide input. The project group also liaised extensively with the Security Branch, both at a regional level and with units C1 and C2.

Information for targeting was obtained from a number of sources, including *askaris*, intercepted communications, the infiltration of opposition networks, and other means. The detention of virtually the entire Western Cape MK machinery occurred, for example, when Special Forces intercepted a phone call from a Cape Town MK operative to their Lesotho office; as this illustration demonstrates, targeting did not always lead to killing. In the words of one operative, emphasis for these operations was placed on "disruption by ... indirect means of getting the enemy to kill itself, to detain itself and to disrupt itself. And physically killing them was placed more or less ... as a last resort".[53] Seemingly in contradiction, former SAP Commissioner General van der Merwe stated that, in relation to the elimination of targets by *Trewits*, "in the country, no, but overseas, yes".[54]

For this reason, the heaviest toll of such killings – carried out by DMI, Special Forces and the Security Branch structures – occurred outside the country, concentrated in areas adjacent to South Africa's borders with its immediate neighbours. These killings were the "end result of a process of operationally directed intelligence collection on targeted individuals". All three intelligence services (NIS, DMI and Security Branch – specifically C2) undertook such activities and co-ordinated their information through these mechanisms whose primary role was *inter alia* to target individuals for killing externally.[55] Overall, assassinations were targeted primarily at high-profile activists, whether politico-administrative or military, both inside and outside South Africa in the opposition structures, as well as at those activists whose conviction could not be secured through the judicial process.

Internal targeting

Although it professed to have a wider focus, it would appear *Trewits* focused almost exclusively on the ANC. While the initial work focused entirely on external targets, a decision was taken later to develop internal targets; this was because, as one senior commander put it,

> The Botswana machinery may be in Gaborone today but tomorrow they are somewhere in the Western Transvaal. So should we stop our operation at the border or should we follow the pipelines through to their courier systems and their safe houses inside the country?[56]

From early on, target identification and development was to be one of *Trewits*' responsibilities. This was clear from May 1987 KIK documents

154 *Crossing the Rubicon*

which stated that "Trewits *ook as die sentrale invoerpunt vir teikeninligting vanaf die Intelliegensiegemeenskap moet dien*" ("*Trewits* must also serve as the central inputer of target intelligence from the Intelligence Community").[57] This emphasis on "*teikenontwikkeling*" ("target development") for intelligence collection is important, as one of *Trewits*' functions was "*die insameling van alle inligting tov ANC-teikens in die buiteland ... en die byhou van sodanige inligting met die oog op optrede teen ANC-teikens*" ("the collection of all intelligence on ANC targets in a foreign country ... and the verification of such intelligence with the source to take up action against ANC targets").

While *Trewits* continued to function through the end of the conflict and into the negotiating phase, its functioning declined after 1988 as a result of internal conflicts and political developments; however, the networks that had been established continued to function in the manner necessary. In 1991, *Trewits* was redesignated "C4" with "C" Section, taking over a number of previous *StratKom* operations under the new De Klerk dispensation.[58] *Trewits* was closed down in early 1992 and its documentation destroyed.[59]

The JMCs and counter-revolutionary strategy

In March 1986, just two months prior to the first public schisms within the NSMS, Defence Minister Malan was criticised by Parliament for allowing the SADF to "militarise society" through the JMCs. Malan denied these accusations, saying that normal civilian functions of government were still controlled and implemented by their normal government departments; the JMCs simply "co-ordinated" security force activities.[60] To illustrate his point, Malan briefed Parliament by stating that individual JMCs would be presented with a problem or issue to deal with; once it was determined that this presented a threat to South Africa's security, it would be passed up the structure until a decision could be reached on dealing with it. Particularly dangerous or sensitive threats were considered by the SSC. This would often, according to Malan, take the form of a housing or health initiative, rather than a security force response.

This was not the truth. The JMCs were very highly militarised structures by 1986, with almost all their efforts devoted towards security force activities; it must also be recalled that the Joint Operations Centre of each *Veikom* was the operations wing within each JMC, giving lie to the statement that the JMCs engaged solely in "co-ordination". The SADF – through the prominent roles played by, first, the Army Intelligence commander of the GIKOMs, second, the dominant presence of DMI representatives within the JMC, and third, the position of SADF commanders on the JMC secretariat and committee – exerted extensive influence within and control over the JMCs; to maintain that they were not "militarised" (as Malan did) was pure fantasy.

The 1983 tricameral Parliamentary election and the new 1983 Constitution resulted, in part, in the redesignation of the boundaries of the South African state, which – in turn – resulted in the redesignation of JMC boundaries.[61] As the JMC and Sub-JMC structures were based around political boundaries throughout the country, including those which took responsibility for most of the black areas, this redrawing of boundaries created further confusion amongst the NSMS structures. Partly to alleviate this, in 1985, the Angolan, Southern Command and Northern Command JMCs were amalgamated into an External Working Group under the National Joint Management Centre.[62]

The NSMS was overseen by a new National Co-ordinating Committee, established on 31 July 1985 under the SSC. In 1986, with the state of emergency and country-wide activation (coincidental with the deployment of the SADF into the townships) of the NSMS, this was redesignated the National Joint Management Centre (NJMC) (see Figure 7.1). Chaired by Deputy Minister of Law and Order Roelf Meyer,[63] the NJMC centred around two committees: the *Geveilstaf* (now designated the National Security Committee) and the National Constitutional, Economic and Welfare Committee;[64] the KIK and *StratKom* also fed directly into the NJMC's processes, while the Directors General of each government department and the SSC Secretary composed the Working Committee of the NJMC. With this reimposition of a state of emergency in June 1986, the NSMS was activated for the first time at the district and local Mini-JMC levels; while the NSMS had been slowly activating regional JMCs since 1984, it was only in 1986 that these lowest levels became functional. This served to ensure that dialogue was kept going between the NSMS structures and the developing National Welfare Management System committees, as the socio-economic counterpart to the politico-security pillar of the NSMS.

The NJMC devised a multi-layer counter-revolutionary plan for the country under the new state of emergency, which included:

- Establishing short-term stability by neutralising those actions taken by the revolutionaries which could not be classified as actions of a democratic nature – including (generally as short-term reactive measures):
  - to limit intimidation by isolating those members of the "People's Army" who were responsible for deeds of intimidation, including through detention without trial
  - limiting armed propaganda by restricting the publication of visual images of violence and destruction, including through media regulation
  - restricting the political activities of organisations furthering the aims of the ANC/SACP (as a result, 34 organisations had restrictions placed upon them).
- Developing a long-term plan to eliminate the causes of unrest,

including both the personal (i.e. liberation organisations) and socio-economic.
- Finally, once stability had been created and the socio-economic needs of the people were being satisfied, the political aspirations had to receive high priority.[65]

The securocrats believed that this would suffice to attack the causes of the revolution at its roots.

Under the NSMS, the *Veikoms* (security committees) dominated the process: although technically having equal standing to the other principal committees (JIKOMs, KOMKOMs, and SEMKOMs) within the JMCs, the "activities of [the *Veikoms*] often surpassed those of the *Komkoms* and *Semkoms* ... [with] information only on a need-to-know or too-late basis, and generally flowing vertically upwards to the NJMC and SSC".[66] This was because, under the conditions of the state of emergency, the NSMS structures had become more and more reliant on the actions of the security forces supporting the *Veikoms*, at the expense or exclusion of other actions. This was particularly the case with the targeting of opponents for elimination: within the agreements established between the Security Branch, DMI and Special Forces, the Security Branch member in the specific *Veikom* would identify targets, based largely on intelligence derived from its own sources as well as Special Forces internal operations (largely conducted by the CCB) and DMI sources. Next, a joint plan would be drawn-up between the various security force elements within the *Veikom*, which would then be passed up the chain-of-command for approval. Once this was received, these targets would then be passed to, in terms of kills, either operational Security Branch units (such as "C" Section) or the CCB for action, or, in terms of the judicial processes, to the uniformed SAP or Security Branch for arrest and detention.[67] This same procedure was used for targeting installations; overall, it represented the mechanics of eliminating the opponent politico-administrative structures within the country (see Figure 7.1).

Throughout the state of emergency, the JMCs conducted a "holding-action against the mounting tide of resistance in the townships".[68] This was largely due to the fact that the state was entirely unprepared for the extent and intensity of the uprisings which were, in turn, fuelled by the States of Emergency; thus, while the NSMS with all of its components was intact and activated, its commanders were temporarily dazed and unable to react effectively. Thus, there was no immediate co-ordinated response to the uprisings but rather a fragmented and disjointed one based around the interests of each individual agency; the NSMS never truly recovered from this initial disjointedness: "the initial unity of purpose exhibited by the different apparatuses and branches of the state was to fragment from the late 1986 period onwards as different apparatuses sought to define their own micro-strategies in response to the crises".[69] The Frontline States raids con-

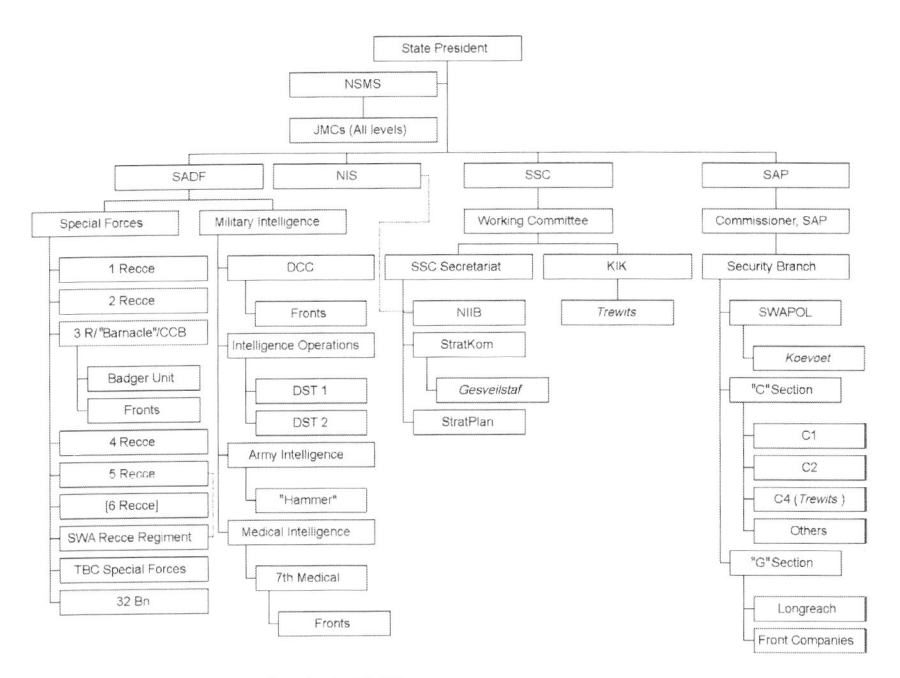

Figure 7.1 The assassins' web (*c.*1986).

ducted during the May 1986 Eminent Persons' Group visit (noted above) were exemplary of this fragmentation of purpose even to the very top where the diplomatic efforts of Pik Botha's Foreign Ministry were scuppered by Defence Minister Malan's hard-line approach to dealing with cross-border incursions.

From 1986 onwards, however, the reality of a varying lack of unity was not to deter the securocrats in their purpose of utilising the NSMS as the means of overseeing the counter-revolutionary strategy. With the NSMS fully functional across the country, the SSC would now be able to utilise a fully co-ordinated, intelligence-led response to the challenge of removing "non-constructive" opposition to the government and its reform programme. The impression should not be gained that there was no unity of purpose between the various elements that comprised the NSMS: in reality, much as within the JMCs themselves, the security forces got along well and contributed to a co-ordinated effort at dealing with the security situation. It was between those elements involved in the NWMS and the security forces (the two camps within the political–military dichotomy of counter-insurgency theory) that the disunity existed primarily. The activation of the JMCs did succeed greatly in enhancing co-operation and co-ordination between the security forces; but it did little to ensure the matching of military and security objectives with welfare, political and social ones.

The SADF's influence on both the JMCs themselves and, thus, on the operations of the security forces (including in their covert and clandestine operations both within and originating in South Africa) should not be underestimated. It is not so simple as to say (as we have seen thus far) that since DMI controlled the SADF and the SADF controlled the JMCs, DMI controlled the JMCs; the answer is far more complicated than this and should be appreciated as such. What must be kept in mind at the beginning of the revolutionary period (from 1985 onwards) was that, in enacting a state of emergency, the executive not only granted the SADF extensive emergency powers entailing the (at least partial) suspension of civilian law but also subordinated Parliament to the executive's own dictates. Given Botha's patronage of DMI particularly, and the SADF generally, this allowed the SADF much greater influence within the reaches of power (especially given the SADF/DMI's influence and role within the workings of the SSC) than would normally have been its want. This included access to the Special Defence Account for covert and clandestine operations, the fact that most of Botha's personal advisors were former or serving SADF personnel, and the simple fact that this was declared as a "war" that South Africa had originally been fighting outside its borders (the Frontline States and the "border wars") but which had now, as the "Revolutionary Onslaught", come within its borders, thus immediately giving the military dominance over the police.[70]

This entire approach to a "Total Counter-revolutionary Strategy", which the securocrats and their intelligence services implemented from the early 1980s onwards, flowed from the original development of "Total National Strategy" that Botha had championed in the early 1970s as defence minister: the SADF had wanted to exercise its full counter-insurgency capabilities – Botha had granted its wish. Williams has called the NSMS "a military manager's dream replete with sub-committees on a national basis";[71] the fact that the SADF controlled the state's strategy (through the SSC Strategy Branch) and oversaw all training in the JMCs further reinforced this total control over the strategic doctrine and direction of the state. The circumstances which had led to DMI's desires in the late 1960s, however, had changed radically by 1986 from the counter-insurgency campaign that the SADF had envisaged into one of full counter-revolutionary warfare, something the SADF – or the Security Branch or NIS – was neither equipped or trained for, nor prepared psychologically for.

The "academic exercise" that this had started out as in the early 1970s had evolved through numerous and ever-more-perilous shifts in South Africa's strategic landscape – including Botha's accession to power, and the power and control he immediately handed to DMI and the SADF – to reach a critical point in 1986 when the SADF lost sight of the political and "let slip the dogs of war" on all fronts, foreign and domestic. The fact that the SAP Security Branch was so far into doing the same thing at this time – with DMI, Special Forces and Security Branch units all supported by the

NIS and its central role in the national intelligence-led counter-revolutionary structures and processes – only made matters much worse.

Containing and countering the revolution

Following the reorganisation of the security forces in 1979–1980 and the subsequent introduction of counter-revolutionary doctrine within the security forces, it was determined that the security forces required a more "integrated" approach to counter-revolutionary warfare; this was largely because, following evaluations in 1985–1986 with the advent of revolutionary war, the security forces were deemed to have developed "infrastructures for conventional and not revolutionary war".[72] Specifically, this "integrated" approach entailed the establishment – or, indeed, consolidation from existing assets – of a new capability which would encompass all of the security forces' counter-revolutionary capabilities. This was to be known as the "third force", resting between the SAP and SADF.

Establishing a "third force"

The term "third force" was first suggested to President Botha by Deputy Defence Minister Vlok on 4 November 1985, who envisioned it as a "special capability unit existing independently of the police and the Defence Force" – hence, a "third" force.[73] Its potential use increased in importance after the 1986 declaration of a nation-wide state of emergency, in which the policy of "Total Strategy" was changed to "Total Counter-revolutionary Strategy". At an SSC meeting on 12 May 1986, the Ministers of Defence and Law and Order were told to examine the creation of a "third force"; this was not to be simply another statutory unit but a unit designed specifically for conducting counter-revolutionary warfare:

> The third force must be mobile and have the capacity to wipe out terrorists effectively ... it must be prepared to be unpopular and even feared, without marring the image of the Defence Force or Police. The security forces must work together in the setting up of the third force in order that those who undermine the state are countered with their own methods.[74]

The SSC document stating this capability has proven to be *the* most contentious of all: all members of the SSC at the time maintain that this referred to a third paramilitary unit to take up station in the security forces halfway between the army and the police, primarily for riot control; they maintain that the Internal Stability Unit (ISU) of the SAP became this force (see below), and that it was *not* referring to the development of a covert capability across the security forces. Malan later stated that he was opposed to the idea of establishing a "third force" because "the SAP and

160   *Crossing the Rubicon*

local commandos of the SADF needed no help in their counter-insurgency tasks".[75]

The reality of it was that this "third force" – with its real focus on direct action, intelligence-led, counter-revolutionary activities, as opposed to "riot control" and internal stability – was formed from a conglomeration of covert units. As noted by the Truth and Reconciliation Commission in 2003 in reference to the fomenting of violence which occurred after 1990 and appeared to be far more directed than random,

> While little evidence exists of a centrally directed, coherent or formally constituted "Third Force", a network of security and ex-security force operatives, frequently acting in conjunction with right-wing elements and/or sectors of the [Inkatha Freedom Party], was involved in actions that could be construed as fomenting violence and which resulted in gross human rights violations, including random and target killings.[76]

The units that were active under the "third force" banner – developed in the mid-1980s and active long after the transition began in 1990 – were to be "cut off from their sources of intelligence and oversight, and were told they must identify and act against political targets;"[77] thus, they would become not only autonomous but would also be able to operate outside of oversight and without transparency, the two greatest "restrictions" on covert operations. The actual composition of the "third force" was debated between the SAP and SADF, with the SAP arguing for the strengthening of the existing riot units, and the SADF arguing that such an enhanced "special capability" already existed within its counter-insurgency structures.[78] Further confirming that the "third force" was – in reality – for direct action counter-revolutionary purposes – the SADF demonstrated, in a document entitled "The Creation of a 'Third Force' to Combat the Revolutionary Onslaught", that this "third force" already existed within the following security force units:

- SADF's counter-insurgency forces (including territorial, Army Intelligence, and *Hammer* units)
- SADF's Special Forces (including 7th Medical Battalion and the Special Task Force)
- SADF's Special Tasks
- SAP's Security Branch
- SAP's counter-insurgency forces ("C" Section of the Security Branch and *Koevoet*)
- SAP's Special Task Force elements (including the technical section of the Security Branch)[79]

Upon reporting back, Vlok's sub-committee investigating the feasibility of a "third force" recommended that the establishment of a "third force" was not necessary, given existing capabilities in the SAP and SADF (primarily as outlined above). It concluded that the anti-riot capabilities of the SAP be enhanced instead; the result was the Internal Stability Unit (ISU) of the SAP, rather than the establishment of a dedicated counter-revolutionary warfare unit. Given the internal situation faced by South Africa at this time, it can be accepted that the ISU was the most pressing requirement, as neither the SAP nor the SADF possessed a riot unit capable of dealing with the demonstrations wracking the country. While the issue of a "third force" was revisited by the Secretary of the SSC on 2 June 1988 and again on 5 April 1989,[80] it was never established in statute; however, even though a counter-revolutionary warfare unit was never *formally* established within the security forces, its equivalent capability existed throughout the security structures.

A covert capability for counter-revolutionary warfare

What must therefore be debated is whether the SSC or individual elements/personnel within the security structures, through a combination of explicit directives or implied agreements, determined that such a capability should be developed against the regime's opponents. Given the direction of strategy and decisions outlined here, this appears to be a much more likely explanation: that, rather than establishing formally a counter-revolutionary unit in the full glare of public knowledge, the securocrats decided to capitalise on the capabilities which already existed within the security forces and direct them implicitly – through a combination of personal contacts, SSC directives, secret meetings, and the very existence of units which were structured to carry on such activities – to launch the most effective counter-revolutionary tactics they could without regard for the process of political reform, public transparency or (in many cases) domestic and international law.

This interpretation becomes even clearer when it is taken into account that, following the debate on the establishment of a "third force", Vlok (soon to become Minister of Law and Order) was selected to chair the new *Geveilstaf*, created at the same 12 May 1986 meeting in which the SSC debated the formation of a "third force": stating that "a situation-room under the direct command of the chief of counter-revolutionary forces" was required, the SSC further determined that "this directorate must co-ordinate all counter-revolutionary strategies".[81] This would form the heart of a joint operations approach to counter-revolutionary strategy. In pursuance of this plan, the cadres and structures of the ANC, UDF and allied organisations were to be targeted for elimination.

As noted in previous chapters, at the centre of this web was *Trewits*: its formation was followed immediately by the acceleration of all counter-revolutionary units within the South African security forces. As evidence of this, in July 1985, Eugene de Kock took command of the Vlakplaas C1 death-squad; in May 1986, the SADF Special Forces founded the Civil

162   *Crossing the Rubicon*

Co-operation Bureau; in mid-1986, DMI began training contra-mobilisation forces in KwaZulu under Operation MARION, while similar moves were made in Ciskei and Transkei under Operation KATZEN – both involved the elimination of opponents using a "middle group". Agreements (such as that between C1 and the CCB, and between C1 and the DCC) were implemented to facilitate interaction in pursuit of the counter-revolutionary goal of the "maximum disruption of the enemies of the state".[82]

This, then, was the counter-revolutionary capability of the South African security establishment, as it began to take form at the very end of the 1970s when the ANC/MK was still considered to be not much more than a negligible threat to South Africa. In many respects, the securocrats took McCuen's guidance literally, as was meant from his text-book approach to counter-revolutionary warfare; Lloyd would even state that "it was McCuen's account which fit our case best".[83] Where McCuen talked of using locally recruited militia units, quickly trained special constables, and counter-revolutionary guerrilla bands, the South Africans recruited *kitskonstabels* from the ranks of the unemployed who were given a six-week crash course in political repression, developed vigilante bands who opposed the ANC's "comrades" in the townships, and exploited rivalries within the African community by establishing contra-mobilisation groups amongst *Inkatha* for assassination-style operations against the ANC and UDF cadres. In April 1986, the SSC further endorsed the application of "anti-revolutionary groups", such as *Inkatha* and vigilantes, to fight the counter-revolutionary war; as Ellis points out, this was "perhaps the most effective counter-revolutionary tactic of all since vigilantes could fight the comrades of the ANC in their own communities".[84] As a notable result of this, between 17 May and 12 June 1986, for example, the *Witdoeke* vigilante group ranged through Crossroads township, driving more than 70,000 people from their homes and literally eliminating four settler camps while killing hundreds; the security forces sealed the township and watched.[85] This was a literal implementation of McCuen's dictums.

Overall, what makes this explanation for the "third force" appear most plausible is the existence of units and structures (specifically, the CCB, *Trewits, Geveilstaf*, the DCC, C1, and the DST) whose only capability matched this need to carry the counter-revolutionary war to the enemy using the most covert means possible. This covert capability, however, had to be matched to the overall aims of the "Total Counter-revolutionary Strategy"; therefore, SSC direction was still required to match capabilities to strategies, at all levels. This would result in everything from individual cases being considered in the SSC's structures (such as assassinations considered by *Trewits*) to commanders on the ground (at the level of the Sub- and Mini-JMC) determining the elimination of "troublesome" members of the opposition. As a further means of inculcating the security commanders, on 10 September 1986, Botha authorised the circulation of an Afrikaans translation of Fraser's "Lessons Learnt from Past Revolutionary Wars" (*Rewolusionere Oorlogvoering: Grondbeginsels van Teeninsurgensie* or "Declaration of Revolutionary War: Basic Principles of Counter-insurgency"), which was considered "the Bible" for counter-revolutionary training in the SADF, to all those involved in the counter-revolutionary struggle.[86] Fraser specifically related the use of force to acts of terrorism, which was referred to as a "particularly appropriate weapon since it aims directly at the inhabitant". After cautioning against the indiscriminate use of terror, he stated that "the use of terrorism by government forces must be decided upon at the highest level, and it must be so applied as to avoid it boomeranging";[87] Fraser would later change this view of terrorism, stating that it would be "self-defeating, giving rise to social disorder which was the opposite of the counter-revolutionary's aim". The Fraser document also advocated the creation of guerrilla forces as "an important adjunct to a government's strategic force".[88] With Operation MARION and others, the government adopted this strategy: the political and military support supplied to *Inkatha* (and other anti-revolutionary groups within and outside South Africa) fell squarely within this strategy.

The beginning of the end: a failing counter-revolutionary strategy?

The ANC designated 1986 as "The Year of *Umkhonto we* Sizwe", an overly ambitious propaganda attempt which generally failed to ignite further uprisings within the country as, during 1986, "liberation mania began to dissipate".[89] As 1986 turned to 1987, schisms began to appear within the establishment's support for the counter-revolutionary strategy. One of the most significant of these was the 1987 proposal put forward by the Department of Constitutional Development and Planning (DCDP), the arm of the government responsible for seeing to the welfare component of the "Total National Strategy". Arguing that only "a minority of radicals or other political leaderships were exploiting socioeconomic problems", this document (entitled *Ons Srik Vir Niks* – "We Are Not Afraid of Anything") put forward the proposal that it was counter-productive that nearly every independent (black) political leader in the country was being removed or otherwise incapacitated by the security forces; this left only substitute leaders who were more radical. Therefore, it was better to leave the opposition in place, to unban political organisations, and to remove some laws (such as the *Group Areas Act*) which had become unenforceable.[90]

This document was greeted with disgust in the SSC and President's Office; as far as the securocrats were concerned, the only way to confront the "Revolutionary Onslaught" was through the methods already being used, namely the removal of political opposition and its replacement with "moderate" leaders who would support the government's reform programme. This was not necessarily reflected, however, in actions from the

SSC. Many of its members were recognising the importance of political change as the way forward; in this sense, the "constitutional-political was in the forefront of state actions" from 1987–1988 onwards.[91] Similarly, by 1987, the NIS had withdrawn from involvement in the Local JMCs, citing a shortage of manpower; in reality, it was refocusing its interests on the strategic implications of alternative futures, and was about to begin secret negotiations with ANC leaders in exile. This was not surprising as, since the early 1980s, NIS intelligence evaluations had consistently emphasised that all of South Africa's security problems were "political of nature and could only be solved through a constitutional negotiated process".[92] From the NIS's point-of-view, the security forces should maintain order and stability in order to provide the basis for a political solution.[93]

Much of this was in conflict with the SADF's and SAP's view of the future; for these more conservative elements of the security forces, the black Communist threat embodied in the "Revolutionary Onslaught" still presented an intolerable threat to their future. The SADF was, however, caught in a bind of its own making: having always argued that counter-revolutionary warfare was 80 per cent political, it was now faced with the situation where it would have to either accept this or refute almost two decades of theoretical construct; in a manner of speaking, it chose the latter. Thus, while the NIS and many of the securocrats on the SSC began to move toward finding a constitutional-political solution to the conflict, the SADF and SAP remained entrenched in the old security paradigm.[94]

In reality, by 1987, the SADF and SAP had "crushed the rebellion in the townships", breaking the back of the violent protests that shook South Africa during the States of Emergency; this had been accomplished largely through "superb intelligence and decisive action ... [which] foreclosed insurrection and revolution as pathways to a new dispensation".[95] This success was reflected in the fact that, in comparison with 1985–1986 when more than 40 town and community councils had collapsed under intimidation and popular resistance, in 1987 only five were dissolved.[96] Rather than continue to attempt overt control over the situation, the securocrats left the violence to control itself through the presence of vigilantes and hit-squads on both sides. This pointed to one of the biggest problems that the security forces had: separating the criminal and hard-core element within the resistance (the "young comrades") – which, it was believed, intimidated the vast majority of the population into supporting the resistance – from those protesters who were more interested in socio-economic upliftment than political change or criminal opportunism.[97] At the same time, the various covert units of the security forces increased their activities over the period from 1986–1992; this, too, reflected the desire by the securocrats to have the conflict manage itself while, on the strategic level, negotiations would be used by the National Party to continue with attempts at managed reform.

In a September 1987 speech to Parliament, Defence Minister Malan laid out six conditions for lifting the state of emergency: law, order and stability must prevail; third-level structures (town councils) must function effectively and "alternative" structures be eliminated; prompt satisfaction of the need for urban housing and land ownership; education and training for all population groups must be advanced and "normalised"; a joint private/public sector plan must be put in place to prevent the country from being undermined by strikes; and, finally, the creation of job opportunities was essential.[98] These were couched in clear counter-revolutionary terms. The unlikelihood of such changes occurring was evident; this simply represented another move as part of South Africa's "urban counter-insurgency strategy", tying political action closely to security/military initiatives. These views were reflected in the composition of the SADF's command at the time of the second state of emergency: SADF Chief Jannie Geldenhuys, Deputy Chief Lieutenant-General Jack Gleeson, and Army Commander Lieutenant-General André Liebenberg all firmly believed in the "hearts and minds" technique of counter-insurgency, rather than solely military or security action to effect compliance.[99] This was made quite apparent when the SADF lodged complaints against SAP "heavy-handedness" in dealing with the uprising in the townships, considering such actions as counter-productive to long-term political solutions.[100]

The government had not, however, succeeded in its major objective, to end "resistance and win black majority support for its reform programme".[101] While the government had succeeded in disrupting – in some places, destroying – the ANC/UDF politico-administrative structures for organising the population, the popularity of and support for the liberation movements had not disappeared from the population; on the contrary, it continued to grow. Nor did black "moderates" rush to the government's support in attempting to find a constitutional reform package acceptable to both the majority population and the National Party (the latter being unwilling to surrender its rule). Thus, while the security situation may have been stabilised, the political aspirations – and, therefore, that 80 per cent of counter-insurgency which is socio-political – of the population remained unsatisfied. The socio-economic reform programme of the DCDP had not succeeded in enticing the population to the government's side, any more than the use of the "oil spot" technique in the townships had succeeded in "reclaiming" any of these to the government's side; instead, the security forces continued with their heavy-handed methods of eliminating the guerrillas and their structures from within the population, while the political reform programme continued to fall short of the population's demands: the release of all political prisoners (especially Mandela); the unbanning of the ANC, SACP and PAC; the end of the state of emergency and the removal of all troops from the townships; the return of all political exiles; and the scrapping of all laws which supported apartheid.[102] From all of this, it can be argued that, by 1987, the

166 *Crossing the Rubicon*

SADF and SAP had lost sight of the political nature of the state's counter-insurgency strategy and were embarked on a military endeavour to see through counter-revolutionary strategy to its bitter end. This is what Seegers has referred to as "frontier warfare", differing from counter-insurgency. "Frontier warfare" looked for "military solutions to political problems", as opposed to the central theme of counter-insurgency which supported the notion that all security and military endeavours were in pursuit of the grander political objective.[103]

International events and the collapsing security equation

In one other significant forum, however, events over which neither the ANC nor the National Party had any control were moving ahead swiftly, with an impact that would be felt around the world. With the coming to power in 1985 of Mikhail Gorbachev, the Soviet Union began to move towards a more "accommodationist" stance with the West; for the developing world, this meant a winding-down of support for proxies in regional conflicts, and the introduction of the concept of "linkage": using a united East–West approach to find solutions to the many Developing World conflicts. For this reason, the withdrawal of Soviet forces from their disastrous war in Afghanistan was linked to the withdrawal of South African and Cuban forces from Angola, and, ultimately, the independence of Namibia, both under negotiated peace agreements. By the late 1980s, for the ANC this led to both the reduction in material and financial support it received from the Communist bloc and the beginnings of pressure to find a diplomatic solution to the liberation struggle; as early as 1986, the Soviet Ministry of Foreign Affairs had been suggesting to the ANC the possibility of a "negotiated settlement", an option the ANC was unwilling to consider at that time.[104] Finally, following the disaster (politically, if not militarily) of the battle of Cuito Cunavale in early 1988, the influence of Pretoria's military strategists – in shock and at a metaphorical loss to find yet another military-oriented "solution" forward which would re-secure South Africa's geographic hegemony in southern Africa – began to wane. The international negotiations which would bring about an agreed withdrawal of all military forces from Angola – Cuban, Soviet, South African and ANC – alongside Namibian independence from South Africa, would also mean that the ANC would now be based further away than ever from South African soil (being forced to move out of its Angolan camps and bases for Tanzania and Uganda). For the National Party government, this would also increase dramatically the pressure – now stiffened by sanctions imposed not only by the United Nations but also the United States – to negotiate a settlement with the liberation movements.[105]

Thus, overall, Gorbachev's rapprochement with the West affected greatly the third arena – the international – where both the National Party and ANC had long fought to gain legitimacy, the former to portray itself as a vital part of the Cold War containment network against Communism, and the latter as the representatives of the majority of the South African population. Inside the South African security establishment, the pressure was increased massively to find a politico-constitutional solution to the conflict as the events in Eastern Europe and the Soviet Union itself "removed the major strategic concern that had dominated the thinking of successive governments for decades".[106] At the same time, the security establishment was forced to watch the withdrawal of its forces from Namibia and a triumphant SWAPO entering the political process in Windhoek; the securocrats would not, however, allow SWAPO a free hand in determining the future of Namibia and interfered deeply – through psychological warfare *KomOps* programmes – with the 1989 election process.[107]

Throughout the 1980s, South Africa's intelligence and security relationships with British and American intelligence – in particular – had become ever more important, especially with regard to the Cold War context within which South Africa perceived itself to operate in Southern Africa (for example, in Angola with the Cuban/Soviet intervention, through the influence of Marxist-Communist regimes and liberation-movements on the ANC/SACP efforts, etc.). With this growing international isolation, however, even these intelligence relationships became strained – even with the Reagan administration's attempts to retain clandestine links to Pretoria, and Thatcher's insistence that terminating relationships with South Africa would be counter-productive to the Cold War efforts of the West. Indeed, it was only in its intelligence relationship with Israel that Pretoria was able to maintain a semblance of the links that it had developed earlier. As such, South Africa's international isolation became virtually total, with even the Reaganites forced ultimately – by Congress – to terminate their clandestine relationship with South Africa.[108]

Inside South Africa, however, by the end of the 1980s, the military's infiltration into almost every sector of society (excepting, perhaps, the churches) was apparent; the popular dissatisfaction with this was even more apparent. As a result, Botha had little support left for his rather slow and very unpopular "reform" programme that was looking more and more like retrenchment rather than reform. According to Williams, "Total Counter-revolutionary Strategy" had run its course and had not succeeded in defeating the enemy, only in holding it. This may not be an entirely accurate assessment, however: by the end of the 1980s, "the security situation in Southern Africa had ... achieved a level of overall stability such as the government had not experienced" since 1984. South Africa had withdrawn from Angola and was soon to leave Namibia; internally, while the state of emergency had "effectively crippled the anti-apartheid movement within a few short months of its imposition", domestic dissatisfaction and revolt remained high. Finally, in addition to all this was South Africa's almost total isolation internationally.[109] By 1989, it was clear that the counter-revolutionary strategy had failed to achieve its ends – political acceptance by the majority of the population – but had, contrary to some analysts' views (including Williams), succeeded in crushing the revolutionary drive of the ANC.

For the future, then, it now seemed only a matter of time before the ANC would be entering into its own negotiations with the National Party government on the future of South Africa. NIS Director Barnard had, in 1987, produced a report stating that the "ANC was unbeatable" so long as it remained in exile; however, a "legalised ANC" could be weakened through a "protracted negotiations process" and forced into a coalition government. In this way, the National Party would not sign over its power entirely to a new black-majority government.[110] Based on conclusions such as these, by the end of the 1980s and with secret discussions between the ANC and the government – facilitated by the NIS (see Chapter 8) – the way forward seemed clear. Partly in anticipation of these events, in its 1988/1989 reorganisation, the NIS created new planning units for politics, the economy and related matters; these paralleled those existent in the Department of Political Development.[111] Even as the NIS prepared for negotiations, however, events in Namibia did not give cause to the soldiers and policemen of South Africa to trust the ANC: SWAPO's betrayal of the UN-brokered election process with its 1 April 1989 attack and attempt to seize power (which was, ironically, fought off by the SAP counter-insurgency unit *Koevoet*, one of the most vilified of any South African unit) meant for many South Africans that liberation movements could not be trusted and that "the ANC could turn out to be another SWAPO" following a negotiated settlement.[112] Therefore, the security force commanders had every intention of not only staying vigilant against such a move by MK during the lead-up to negotiations but also continued to target it right through the negotiations phase. That the security forces did, in fact, uncover an attempt by MK and the SACP to install underground revolutionary structures inside South Africa during the negotiating phase appeared to justify this fear (see Chapter 8).

This was not to be, however. The National Party government had succeeded – through its destabilisation of the Frontline States and thereby the ANC's bases; through its infiltration of the ANC and MK structures; through its institution of a draconian counter-revolutionary strategy against the ANC and its internal allies; through its marshalling of both internal and external resources to fight the insurgency, even in the face of international sanctions and embargo – in defeating the ANC/SACP's strategy, in place since the 1960s, of a guerrilla struggle against the National Party government.

Botha's fall and the new political landscape

The process by which the South African security establishment developed was quite a lengthy one. By the time P.W. Botha took the premiership in September 1978, all of the elements necessary to implement "Total National Strategy" were in place within the security establishment and were forming in society. Botha pushed DMI to oversee the implementation of this policy and to be the lead agency in enforcing its presence throughout both South Africa and its regional wars. The reaction within South Africa to these measures was predictably fierce, resulting in the successive states of emergency from 1985 onwards and the implementation from 1986 onwards of the "Total Counter-revolutionary Strategy" – which, paradoxically, created even more violent opposition to the state, which the strategy and its operational precepts was attempting to counter, than may have been the case had a more socio-political solution been sought at this stage. DMI's total dominance of the politico-intelligence scene and strategy meant that there could be almost no room for finding an effective political solution throughout most of the 1980s. In this sense, it is arguable that the development of the "Total Counter-revolutionary Strategy" – and its feeding by an intelligence apparatus which both misconstrued the quality of the ANC's revolutionary warfare pursuits, and ultimately reacted to the resonating results of its own operations – represented the overall failure of this strategy of confrontation. Its failure brought about the demise of Botha, of his patronage of DMI, and the rise of the "radical reformers" under F.W. de Klerk, Pik Botha and Roelf Meyer.

Negotiating a settlement?

The combination of the most destructive covert attacks – involving extensive assassinations of leading ANC/SACP figures and virtual non-stop "raids" and similar attacks against ANC/SACP offices and individuals in the Frontline States – combined with the development of "third force" capabilities in the Zulu and other communities (such as in the Eastern Cape), brought the ANC/SACP "revolutionary onslaught" to a virtual halt, and pushed it to consider a negotiated settlement with the apartheid government. By the late 1980s, it was becoming clear that a stalemate existed between the ANC and the National Party; the costs of the struggle were far out-weighed by any benefits to be derived and, as such, both sides began to consider negotiation – or, at least, discussing negotiations.

To this end, several secret meetings were held, beginning in 1985, between government officials and representatives of the ANC, including the imprisoned Mandela. While it is not part of this study to discuss the mechanics of these negotiations,[113] it is necessary to note their initiation as an indication that *at least* certain elements within the state structures (as well as, most interestingly, the *Broederbond*) felt the counter-revolutionary strategy was not achieving its goals and that a different tack had to be taken – namely, looking for a political settlement. This was to reflect one of the most frustrating and damaging characteristics of events from the mid-1980s (significantly, at the same time as Botha "took the gloves off") to the April 1994 multiracial elections, namely that while one part of the government attempted to find a political solution through negotiating a settlement, another part was accelerating the covert aspects of counter-revolutionary strategy against the liberation movements; during this period, the assassination of opponents, as well as acts of violence perpetrated by the state, accelerated. While some securocrats advocated inclusion and negotiation for the ANC – NIS Director Barnard stated after the 1988 New York Accords that the government "had to strike a deal with the ANC before our backs are against the wall"[114] – others were not, however, going to let it end that way. The covert security structures continued to implement the counter-revolutionary strategy for at least another three years, until F.W. de Klerk – the new leader of the National Party following Botha's stroke in February 1989 and, by September of that year, the new State President – attempted once and for all to shut them down in 1992. This would be, by no means, an easy or simple process:

> Botha's departure from the National Party, however, did not presage the total decline of military influence within both state and society. The armed forces had penetrated virtually all levels of state and society, and their removal from these regions was to prove a complicated and difficult task.[115]

Conclusions

With the loss of its patron and the winds of change blowing into Pretoria, DMI's power began to wane as various key political actors – not least of these De Klerk – committed themselves to negotiating a settlement with the ANC by the end of 1989. By this point, Botha and the securocrats of the SSC were confronted by a mighty array of forces supporting radical reform; composed of elements from within the liberation movements, the international community, the trade unions, and the business and academic communities, this force demanded Botha's removal from the Office of State President following his stroke. Botha stepped down from the presidency in September 1989, terminating DMI's influence over South African politics in the apartheid-era once and for all, concomitantly sidelining Security Branch from the NSMS structures and the pursuit of its "dirty war" against its opponents, and presaging the rise of the NIS as the dominant intelligence service for and in the new era.[116] These forces – and the securocrats who drove and used them – would not, however, all go quietly into the night; equally, while it had been defeated on the revolutionary battlefield and forced to accept a negotiated settlement, the ANC was not ready to give-up on its aspirations to overthrow apartheid through revolutionary means – a decision which would have dire consequences for the process of negotiating a way out of apartheid and the security and intelligence paradigm which gripped both sides.

8 Negotiating a settlement
Reform and retrenchment for all, 1990–1994

> We concede the fact that we never broke the back of the South African Defence Force and South African Police, but you must concede that you never broke the spirit of the liberation movement.
>
> Chris Hani, 1990

The way forward and the end of "armed struggle"

With the recognition that neither side could win the war – and with Namibia's independence being ushered in the year before – De Klerk's new government and the ANC began to negotiate a settlement. On 7 August 1990, the ANC suspended its armed struggle, following its unbanning – alongside that of the SACP and the PAC – by De Klerk on 2 February 1990, and the release of Nelson Mandela and all other political prisoners nine days later.[1] The end of apartheid would – in many senses – be brought about by the intelligence services of both sides.

Restructuring ANC intelligence and security

As discussed in Chapter 4, the ANC's NAT – and particularly its security arm "*Mbokodo*" – had come increasingly into disrepute during the 1980s, significantly for its Stalinist approach to internal security and its stifling of dissent (under the guise of counter-intelligence) within its camps and against suspected apartheid spies. Some of this was, as Ellis notes, due far more to the political imperative of the struggle dragging-on rather than, in every case, real evidence of apartheid infiltrators:

> If the armed struggle made less progress than was desired, and than the rank and file called for, then an explanation had to be found. And it was found in the agitation of spies. Where spies did not exist, they must be invented ... the longer the ANC's armed struggle lasted, and the more it became apparent that its success was far from certain, the more pressing became the need to find scapegoats, real or imagined.[2]

Following the reports of severe human rights abuses by "*Mbokodo*" at the detention camps[3] – due not in a small way to the alleged "ideological and political aspects" to the ways in which security and counter-intelligence were generally approached by "*Mbokodo*"[4] – at its May 1985 Kabwe Conference, the ANC decided to restructure NAT yet again, including significant new oversight by the NEC and its president's office,

> to halt the abuses that had occurred by members of the security department of NAT, to reorganise and improve the functioning of the Department, to improve conditions under which prisoners were held, and to ensure that investigations and sentences were carried out fairly, with the accused entitled to proper legal representation.[5]

Piliso was removed as head, and Alfred Nzo – along with Nhlanhla, Zuma, and Sigxashe – was given the responsibility for the restructuring. By July 1987, Nhlanhla had become the new permanent director of the revamped NAT – now including Intelligence, Counter-Intelligence and Security, and Processing and Analysis (the Central Intelligence Evaluation Sector or CIES) sub-sectors – with Zuma, Sigxashe and others as his deputies.

As secret negotiations between the NAT and the NIS got truly underway (see below), the NAT was restructured yet another time – to structure itself for its post-unbanning, to prepare itself for these negotiations, and for the eventual transition to the post-apartheid security and intelligence structures. The NAT – based out of Lusaka – was reorganised to form a new Department of Intelligence and Security (ANC-DIS); still headed by Nhlanhla, with Zuma as deputy, it included six main sub-sectors: Intelligence, Counter-Intelligence, Central Information Evaluation Section, Security, Technical, and Administration.

While the DIS continued with clandestine – and, later, open – negotiations with the NIS, this was all occurring at a time that the ANC had launched two major intelligence operations inside South Africa – Operation BIBLE, the NAT's reportedly highly successful development of moles and double-agents within the apartheid security structures; and Operation "VULA", launched by Joe Slovo, Ronnie Kasrils, Mac Maharaj and Siphiwe Nyanda of MK Intelligence – both the first real success that the ANC/MK had in establishing underground structures inside South Africa. The DIS and MK leadership would subsequently note that this capability also allowed them to mitigate against a failure in the negotiated settlement.[6] That such intelligence operations were occurring at a time when the NAT/DIS was involved in secret talks with the NIS to reach a negotiated settlement would have severe repercussions – not the least of which due to the perception that the ANC had been negotiating with one hand while covertly preparing for a return to conflict, albeit this time with an internal network developed under the cover of the negotiations.

Too little, too late – Operation "VULA"

While secret negotiations between the United States, the Soviet Union, Pretoria, Luanda and Havana to end the Cold War paradigm in Southern Africa were playing out in London in May 1988, the chance of a revolutionary take-over of South Africa was rapidly slipping away. The ANC/SACP were not, however, about to give up trying: Operation VULINDLELA (Zulu for "to penetrate", generally shortened to "VULA") was an attempt to find the solution to the central problem of an underground network, never established inside South Africa. Aimed at establishing leadership inside South Africa which would, in turn, spawn the underground networks necessary for mobilising the masses to a "people's war", "VULA" began in August 1988 (although planning had begun with Oliver Tambo and senior SACP leaders as far back as 1986) – the same month South Africa, Angola and Cuba signed a withdrawal agreement for Angola – with the infiltration by Maharaj, Nyanda and other ANC/SACP leaders into South Africa.[7] Over the course of two years, "VULA" established cells, arms dumps, informer networks and other underground structures within South Africa – more, in fact, than had been accomplished throughout the past 30 years of struggle. One of the reasons for its success, according to O'Malley, was the ANC's Operation BIBLE – effectively the "VULA" intelligence and security apparatus, under the leadership of Yunus and Moe Shaik (two leading MK Intelligence brother operatives working for Zuma in Mozambique) – which succeeded in developing a significant number of "turned" sources of its own within South Africa's intelligence apparatus. This intelligence not only gave them insights into the Security Force's apparatus, operations and decision-making, but also – crucially – the Security Branch's records on its moles within the ANC's ranks. BIBLE became sophisticated enough to even "recruit" false agents to improve the record of its Security Branch moles.[8]

This was finally the realisation of Phase One of guerrilla warfare: the establishment of a military and politico-administrative structure within the country. All this was occurring at a time when the December 1988 New York Accords had cemented the South Africa withdrawal from Angola and the independence of Namibia; the New York Accords also committed the ANC to withdrawing from Angola, placing them even further away than ever before in Zambia, Tanzania and Uganda. Even though "VULA" was in place and operating, the future appeared bleak as the ANC was pushed further and further away from South Africa. It was obvious now that Pretoria would want to renegotiate its relations with the South African liberation movements. Having witnessed SWAPO's betrayal of the negotiated settlement in Namibia in 1989, throughout these new negotiations with the ANC, the security force commanders had every intention of not only staying vigilant against such a move by MK during the lead-up to negotiations but also continued to target it right through the negotiations phase.

When the security forces did uncover this attempt ("VULA") by MK and the SACP to install underground revolutionary structures inside South Africa during the negotiating phase, these fears appeared to be realised.

With the unbanning of the ANC, SACP and PAC, and the release of Mandela and other ANC leaders, "VULA" was thrown into uncertainty: as negotiations were to begin with the National Party government, was it necessary to continue implementing an underground network? Most "VULA" leaders felt it was, as "it was too difficult to trust a regime that had always acted with such duplicity; this was just another trick".[9] Thus, although "VULA" had begun as an effort to establish an underground network, as the negotiations moved ahead – and more leaders and arms were infiltrated into the country without end, increasing in fact during the initial stages of negotiation between the ANC and National Party – "VULA" came to represent the ANC's backstop "against the possibility that negotiations with the government ultimately would break down".[10] Similarly, with its unbanning, the ANC/SACP did not simply terminate the revolutionary struggle; indeed, they continued to send members abroad for military and intelligence training (although this had become more difficult with the fall of East Germany – one of the largest providers of these services – and other Eastern bloc states in the autumn/winter of 1989–1990) after 1990.

It was not easy for the ANC – "straining to adjust to the world of freedom", as Waldmeir notes[11] – to deal rapidly or easily with its unbanning; for months, it went through the process of consolidating its presence inside South Africa, bringing more than 20,000 exiles home from abroad (a huge number of which were woefully under-trained MK cadres that the ANC expected to form the nucleus of a new defence force in post-apartheid South Africa);[12] integrating a scattered leadership, and – finally – building an internal organisation inside the country. To switch from being a liberation-movement-in-exile to a political party negotiating a future did not prove easy – and, to this day, has still not proven so. Particularly difficult was learning to co-operate and integrate with the UDF, an organisation based on grass-roots support and organisation while the ANC, in exile for 30 years and out of touch with its constituents, was based on a top-down approach of decision-making and directive.[13]

This was all to have a strong impact on the negotiating climate when, in July 1990, a large number of the "VULA" network was arrested by the Security Branch, having been tipped to "VULA" by one of its former operatives; had it not been for these arrests, "VULA" would have continued right through the negotiations phase.[14] This immediately caused much of the good climate which had begun to develop in the negotiations with the National Party to dissipate, as the ANC were accused by the National Party of establishing a "terrorist network" and of "negotiating in bad faith". This was, in a manner, the nightmare scenario which Pretoria had envisioned: the development of Phase Three revolutionary war inside South Africa. It also meant that, in the minds of the mid-level security force commanders, they were right to continue with the covert undertaking of a counter-revolutionary strategy, as the ANC continued to drive its revolutionary strategy forward.[15]

On 7 August 1990, however, the ANC suspended its armed struggle; while this meant that negotiations could move into high gear, even then, "VULA" continued to operate until February 1991 when it was determined by the ANC/SACP leadership that the National Party was negotiating in good faith: as Jenkin has pointed out, "so long as the regime maintained its arrogant attitude and the situation could not be said to be irreversible there was a need to maintain structures that could be aroused to carry on the struggle".[16] Into the 1990s, those who supported the counter-revolutionary strategy of the 1980s, in the words of one observer, "remained victims of their own ideology and were prisoners of a counter-revolutionary theory that did not, and could not, accommodate broader political participation in its framework".[17] Ultimately, as with many counter-revolutionary practitioners before them, the securocrats would lose the objective of political reform within the rubric of security initiatives to counter the "Revolutionary Onslaught". The reaction to these failings would result in not only a renewed political reform drive that would eventually bring about the end of apartheid, but would also result – more immediately – in the restructuring and, in some cases, demise of the state security structures that had supported the counter-revolutionary strategy. These included the SSC, the NSMS, the Office of State President itself, and the dominance of the military and police intelligence structures within the intelligence hierarchy. As political reform became the primary interest of the state from 1990, however, the Department of Constitutional Planning led the way, supported by the National Intelligence Service in its alliance with the ANC's Department of Intelligence and Security. The civilian spies would see the new era in.

Searching for the new dawn, 1989–1993

Initial feelers – the spies' first contacts

Secret discussions between the ANC in exile and the government – facilitated and conducted generally by the NIS – may have begun as far back as 1984 when, in the wake of the Nkomati Accord, a similar such resolution was considered well worth exploring with the ANC;[18] these contacts continued throughout the late 1980s. The NIS – and Barnard specifically – took a strong interest in nurturing these contacts with the overseas ANC leaders as a means of opening yet another channel to the ANC. They were enhanced through the contacts developed between the ANC's Thabo Mbeki (head of the ANC's International Department), and Oliver Thambo (the ANC's president), and the *Broederbond* members and University of Stellenbosch academics Sampie Terreblanche and Willie Esterhuyse in the

United Kingdom from 1987–1990, building on earlier *Broederbond* contacts with the ANC the year previous. These ultimately led to the first face-to-face meetings between the NIS and the ANC at meetings in Switzerland, under what the NIS called Operation FLAIR; the NIS were represented initially by Maritz Spaarwater (Chief Director of Operations) and Mike Louw, (its Deputy Director), and were joined later by Barnard; while the ANC were led by National Executive Council members Mbeki and Zuma (also the deputy director of the ANC-NAT), joined later by Nhlanhla, the head of ANC-NAT. De Klerk authorised the meeting without really grasping its true nature – and was "nonplussed" subsequently when progress was reported back to him.[19]

At an earlier time – and with Botha's permission – Barnard, Justice Minister Coetsee, Louw, Johan Willemse (Commissioner of Prisons), and Fanus van der Merwe (the Director General of the Prisons Department) instituted the first of many meetings with Nelson Mandela in jail.[20] Seen as an opportunity to both judge Mandela's political (and – crucially – business and commerce) views and discuss under what terms and conditions he might be released, this secret committee under Barnard's direction would pursue these meetings for more than three years. Meeting Mandela – categorically seen as not only the strongest leader of the imprisoned ANC leadership inside South Africa but also, as Barnard himself noted already by 1989, as a future state president once a peaceful transition post-apartheid had been achieved[21] – separately from *both* his ANC colleagues in prison and any contacts with the ANC in exile had two clear reasons. First, it provided the NIS with an opportunity to potentially split the ANC between its domestic and overseas wings, while – second – an intelligence-gathering opportunity to both see what Mandela knew (or, indeed, learned contemporaneously) about the exiled ANC leadership and what splits might already exist in that leadership.

Nevertheless, this was the beginnings of the negotiated settlement – led by the spies of both sides – that would culminate in the new political dispensation that came from the CODESA negotiations, the Transitional Executive Council (TEC) and – following the April 1994 elections – the Government of National Unity (GNU).

The rise of the NIS and the fall of DMI

Under De Klerk, the NIS came into a position of prominence – finally eclipsing DMI and pushing the reactionary securocracy into the background. De Klerk reduced DMI's power and position severely, while Security Branch underwent a massive transformation into the Crime Combating and Investigation Service (later the National Crime Intelligence Service of the newly reformed South African Police Service). This, then, was truly the end of the apartheid security forces and their total dominance over South African politics and society.

178 *Negotiating a settlement*

It was not, however, to signal the immediate end to the NSMS and the approach to a national, intelligence-led internal security apparatus which it underpinned. In an attempt to consolidate his hold over the "securocracy", alongside other changes (see below), De Klerk moved both the NIS and the Bureau of Information (which was responsible for open government media activities) under his direct control within the Office of the State President; under Botha, the NIS had reported largely to the DMI-staffed SSC as well as to the President. He also instituted an internal review – led by the SSC Working Committee – of all SSC structures and efforts, in an attempt to "reduce unnecessary duplication of departmental activities by the NSMS, the hours wasted on NSMS meetings, and the international perception that the state under P. W. Botha was, de facto, a military state".[22] As a result of these moves, in 1991, De Klerk abolished the NSMS and created the National Co-ordinating Mechanism (NCM) to replace it. He also terminated the SSC and replaced its authority with a new National Security Committee (NSC) functioning under the new Cabinet Committee for Security Affairs (CCSA);[23] this restored Cabinet decision-making over the previous dominance the SSC had had since the mid-1970s. The NSC would eventually give way to a new Co-ordinating Intelligence Committee and later the National Intelligence Co-ordinating Committee (NICOC), while the CCSA would become the new Cabinet Committee on Security and Intelligence (CCSI), both after 1994 (see Chapter 9).

These moves placed the NIS firmly under De Klerk's control: as Henderson notes, the "NIS had become essential for … [furnishing] warnings of disruptive elements both within the government security forces and outside", while providing intelligence-led insights for the government in the Convention for a Democratic South Africa (CODESA) constitutional talks, which began in December 1991.[24] This control would also – first – ensure that an intelligence picture on the myriad challenges South Africa faced in the 1990–1994 period (see below) would flow continuously to the President; while also – second – ensuring that De Klerk had a clear picture of the impact that his reforming policies pushing South Africa's emerging transition were having on the attitudes of those countries internationally who had either supported the liberation movements in exile (such as the now-former Soviet bloc or China) or were pushing for the end of apartheid while looking for opportunities to support such reforms (such as the United States, Britain, Canada and others). Given the almost impossible position South Africa's international isolation had led to by 1990, it was essential to "know precisely which domestic reforms would be sufficient for each Western government, and its domestic constituencies to end its sanctions policy".[25] More quietly, it also aimed to ensure that De Klerk had an up-to-date intelligence picture of the ANC's negotiating positions and leadership during the settlement talks – not the least of which due to reports that "VULA" had succeeded, through its Operation BIBLE, in placing at least seven "moles" into the state's intelligence structures prior to 1990.[26]

While De Klerk and his lieutenants maintained that this was significantly part of the overall effort to "rein-in" the securocrats and DMI's influence within the state security dispensation, nevertheless these were criticised severely as simply being the NSMS and SSC in another form, given similar structures and control.[27] This represented one of the most difficult aspects of negotiating the settlement in the security environment which existed in the post-1990 period. While critics questioned the need for such mechanisms – and, most obviously, their association with the hated apartheid system, designed to confront the "total onslaught war of destabilisation against the apartheid regime" – the dramatic upswing in political violence domestically raised the pragmatic need for a capability aimed at co-ordinating the state's response to the violence (as discussed below).

Finally, reflecting on the upheavals and internecine conflict between the intelligence services over the last two decades – brought on significantly due to poorly defined and overlapping mandates and areas-of-responsibility since BOSS's establishment – De Klerk also imposed new functional limits on each service's activities and concerns, at the same time as many of their covert activities were being curtailed – both fundamentally, as noted above, and through the termination of both the NJMC and the *Veikoms*. He asserted the NIS's ultimate dominance through pointedly giving it the strategic intelligence brief responsible to the Office of State President and the CCSA; despite this pointed snub, DMI retained significant power both because of its original control over many of the covert units now suspected of comprising the "Third Force" involved in destabilising South Africa, and because of its relationship to the TBVC states' defence and intelligence services.[28] To oversee this brief, De Klerk appointed Roelf Meyer – formerly Deputy Minister of Law and Order under Botha – as Deputy Minister of Information Services in the Office of the State President, responsible for both the government's public image and leveraging NIS and SSC assessments in support of the President's intelligence needs. In this sense, a perception emerged that while Meyer pushed the development of intelligence "more appropriate to a negotiating president", the NIS under Barnard would continue to provide more mainstream intelligence reporting to the President – in effect, creating two leads on strategic intelligence within the governance structures.[29] De Klerk also – in a March 1990 directive to the SADF – moved to curtail the SADF's (and thereby, in theory, both DMI's and the Special Forces') activities inside South Africa to protecting the country's borders and supporting the SAP in controlling unrest, although this would not prove successful in the short-term. It was to this end that, as Williams has noted, De Klerk saw the NIS as a told to "help him identify and control the right-wing elements who run military intelligence and the security police", in addition to its other uses in both providing on-going intelligence on political violence, as well as on the ANC's negotiating positions.[30]

Alongside the numerous reviews into both covert funding and "third force" activities (as outlined below), the most tangible result of these scandals was the fall from grace – and from their portfolios of Defence Minister and Minister of Law and Order respectively – of Magnus Malan and Adriaan Vlok, two of Botha's security chiefs, in an August 1991 Cabinet reshuffle. Moved from Information Services, Meyer became the new Defence Minister – while Deputy Minister of Finance Theo Alant, became Deputy Minister for the National Intelligence Service, becoming in effect the "Cabinet watchdog over the funding of ongoing covert operations" until he was moved on in a February 1993 Cabinet reshuffle. At the same time, Hernus Kriel – a politician with "no previous links to the SSC/NSMS structures"[31] – was appointed minister of law and order. By 1992, with it clear that Meyer was not succeeding (or possibly capable) in controlling SADF covert activities (following a statement by the SADF's Chief of Staff, Finance, that SADF covert projects were now limited to those in its "scope of duty" which included counter-intelligence and military intelligence gathering), the defence portfolio was passed to former Justice Minister Kobie Coetsee.[32]

De Klerk faced a serious uphill struggle, it was clear – in reining-in the covert security apparatus and the securocrats (in terms of *both* their domestic and overseas activities, which continued into the early 1990s); in controlling the unrest that was sweeping the country and growing worse (especially as it became clear that it was, in part, being fomented by these same covert security force elements); in continuing to monitor the ANC/MK and PAC/APLA for possible efforts to sidestep the negotiations and reintroduce guerrilla-led attempts to overthrow the government (as in the "VULA" operation); in countering the growing clamour of disgruntlement from the white right-wing (both politically – in the form of the Conservative Party, the Afrikaner Volksfront, and the Freedom Front – and on-the-ground – in the form of the AWB and other violent, armed militias emerging into South Africa's communities) and from the Zulu *Inkatha* Freedom Party, from both of which a violent reaction to the negotiations would ultimately emerge; and in trying to stay ahead of – or at least on top of – investigative news reports on these covert forces from all sides. De Klerk was also becoming increasingly concerned that the security forces were – to some degree – starting to break apart, given the government's investigations into the forces' covert actions which succeeded in forcing many underground or into the "private" sector (as noted below), the fears that right-wing sympathisers within the intelligence structures were clandestinely feeding groups like the AWB (which proved largely unfounded as far as the national intelligence structures were concerned), and fears that those members of the intelligence structures who were opposed to the negotiated settlement were both the source of the many leaks witnessed during this period and of internal resistance to change within the services. The degree of these challenges meant that they could only –

ultimately – be met through a unified approach by both sides in the negotiations.

The shards of apartheid: reining-in the covert operators

At the end of the 1980s, the covert elements of the security forces were facing an uncertain future. With the change in government from Botha to De Klerk, the continued existence of many of these units was very much in doubt. In anticipation of this, the CCB allegedly was ordered to wrap-up all of its projects by 1 September 1989, regardless of the fact that its aim was to establish long-term covert existence.[33] This was none too soon: on 17 November 1989, former Vlakplaas commander Dirk Coetzee went public about the existence of death squads within the South African security forces. Stating "I was the commander of the South African Police's death squad … I was in the heart of the whore", Coetzee proceeded to reveal all, in a serious of interviews in *Vrye Weekblad* to journalist Jacques Pauw, about C1 and other death squads (such as the Brixton Murder and Robbery Squad) within the SAP, and in the security forces more widely.[34] Coetzee used the term *moordbende* ("murder gang") to describe C1's activities. Ironically, the previous night, Law and Order Minister Adriaan Vlok had denied the existence of police death squads during a television interview.[35]

Following these revelations, in 1990, De Klerk ordered investigations into the allegations – in particular the assassinations of David Webster, Anton Lubowski and Griffiths Mxenge. Chaired by Justice Louis Harms, the "Commission of Inquiry into Certain Alleged Murders" – struggling with a weak mandate[36] – based much of its initial evidence on the stories related by Coetzee, who defected to the ANC in 1989. Much of the evidence given to the Harms Commission – the first of *many* such commissions of inquiry into the shards of apartheid's covert security apparatus and its continuing involvement in covert activities within South Africa and Namibia – was later proven to be false or misleading, however, including evidence given by members of C1 and other such units under oath. And as political violence continued to grow in the early 1990s, accusations grew that a decision had been taken by three generals – including Basie Smit (former commander of the SAP Security Branch) and Johann ("Jannie") Roux (former head of the president's office and then Deputy Minister for National Intelligence) – who determined at the time of the National Peace Accord in September 1991 that it was necessary for covert elements such as C1 and the DCC to "disappear underground" into the "new" Vlakplaas structures within the SAP's revamped Crime Combating and Investigation Service – and even National Party structures – in order to continue their activities covertly.[37] Other senior politicians also clearly supported the continuation of covert efforts to undermine both the ANC/UDF and any post-apartheid transition: in mid-1990, Vlok told a meeting of senior Security

182 *Negotiating a settlement*

Branch officers that "I support you in these [covert activities], but you must know I would be committing political suicide if they ever came to light".[38]

As noted in Chapter 7, in its subsequent investigations, the Truth and Reconciliation Commission found that this was, indeed, the case,[39] and that the covert continuation of such units – at least, through the period of negotiations – was aimed at "levelling the playing field" between the ANC and De Klerk's government. Indeed, even when confronted with the size of such continued covert activities by the Steyn and Goldstone investigations (see below), De Klerk noted that such units would "continue to infiltrate or gather intelligence on organizations whose activities were aimed at endangering state security" – even in a time of negotiations with the ANC, an organisation which De Klerk noted was "not exempt from attention by the intelligence agencies" if its activities were "aimed at endangering state security".[40] In many senses, this was the flip-side to the ANC's implementation of "VULA" – maintaining covertly the capability to influence or otherwise affect the negotiations through the threat or actual use of overt violence, as well as be in a position of strength should the negotiations fail. Just as many ANC cadres reacted to the August 1990 suspension of the armed struggle "with dismay", the covert operators of the apartheid government saw the negotiated settlement and – notably – the Harms, Steyn, Kahn and Goldstone investigations as "public relations exercises rather than determined initiatives to root out 'dirty practices'".[41] Given both these factors, it is indeed a "miracle" – as Sparks called it – that the negotiated settlement succeeded at all.

Killing the hydra? The CCB and Vlakplaas in abeyance

Although the report of the Harms Commission suggested enough evidence of "problems" within the SAP Security Branch or DMI, due to the tainted nature of the evidence, it did not present De Klerk with sufficient evidence that hit-squad and assassination activities were being carried-out from within the government.[42] It did, however, lead to the uncovering of the CCB and – subsequently – the arrest of many of its members, including those suspected of involvement in Lubowski's murder in Namibia, beginning at the end of October 1989. Investigations by the SAP were to conclude that a "secret organisation" whose mission was to "terrorise left-wing radicals" existed within the SADF; this was the CCB.[43] At the time of its revelation, the CCB was said to be involved in more than 200 'projects'.[44] Upon its revelation, the Defence Minister, claiming no knowledge of its existence prior to November 1989, ordered its immediate "suspension"; the head of Military Intelligence, General Rudolph "Witkop" Badenhorst, also professed to have not known about the unit until November 1989, a curious claim given that the CCB worked closely with the Recces and DST directly under the CSI position, let alone the fact that he

Negotiating a settlement 183

and the Defence Minister had authorised the CCB's establishment.[45] While the CCB was technically "disbanded" on 31 July 1990, many of its members simply joined the DCC (see below), the Security Branch, the Special Forces or the private sector. In April 1991, Malan fired Joe Verster – the head of the CCB (see Chapter 6) – and 27 other operatives who refused retirement or transfer.[46]

It is now clear that the CCB was designed to provide a covert counter-revolutionary capability to the existing government *following* the loss of power to a black majority government; therefore, the fact that the unit ceased to operate as a cohesive whole after 1990 may not have had much impact on its individual members, who had been preparing – since 1986 – to go underground within other structures. Numerous CCB members either continued to run front-companies established under apartheid – the private military company Executive Outcomes is but the best example of this, GMR Pty Ltd being another good example – or established entirely new fronts to carry-on with either covert operations or illegal/criminal activity, such as Staal Burger's "Badger Unit", about which very little is known. Allegedly involving former CCB operatives Chappie Maree, Ferdi Barnard and Eugene Riley, it was established in a Hillbrow hotel owned by Burger. At the time of its discovery by reporters, it was suspected of being a co-ordinating hub between various elements of the "Third Force" active after 1990; officially, it was established in 1991 as an "anti-terrorist unit focused on combating illegal gun-running and explosives". Security Branch command approved its establishment and "sent out certain operatives to perform certain functions in the townships" as part of Badger's operations.[47] Other similarly barbarised groups – such as former CCB members who reportedly established a new organisation known as the "Binnekring", which "combines drug-trafficking and gun-smuggling for profit with activities designed to bolster opposition to the ANC"[48] – began to spring-up from the shards of these covert units.

Similarly, by the beginning of the 1990s, the Vlakplaas personnel were engaged in destabilisation operations within South Africa's borders. With the ANC's unbanning and the return of thousands of exiles into the townships and cities of South Africa, the conflict between *Inkatha* (now the newly formed *Inkatha* Freedom Party or IFP) – which had, of course, been stoked originally by DMI's covert contra-mobilisation projects in the 1980s – and the ANC/UDF/MDM supporters spilled-over into broad, community-wide violence. At the same time, many of those elements of South African society involving socio-economic deprivation, which the apartheid state – and the NSMS and NWMS – had attempted to keep the lid on, also contributed to a growing anger within both the township communities and the returning exiles that their socio-economic and educational positions would not be instantaneously improved by dint of the end of apartheid and the introduction of universal suffrage. This was noted by the government and ANC intelligence officials negotiating the settlement (see below), who recognised that whatever would come of attempts to control the political violence sweeping the country, criminal and economically motivated violence would remain a serious challenge for years to come:

> Massive socio-economic degradation, with poverty, hunger, homelessness and unemployment being the order of the day, [which] will render the political changes meaningless if they are not accompanied by a significant improvement in the quality of our people's lives. Whilst politically motivated violence is on the decline, there has been an increase in common criminal activities.[49]

With an estimated 55 per cent unemployment in parts of the townships, a shortfall in suitable housing of more than one million homes by 1994, and an estimated 5–8 million refugees crossing South Africa's borders between 1989 and 1994 – borders which the transitioning SADF recognised it could not control sufficiently – these problems would contribute dramatically to the political anger and internecine violence that South Africa experienced after 1990, and would not be remedied anytime in the near future. The 1994 *White Paper on Intelligence* also recognised the dramatic growth in external threats ("new global political, social and economic problems are filtering South Africa's borders"); at the same time, it expressed strong concerns about increased "foreign intelligence activities in South Africa", which had reportedly witnessed a hundred-fold increase in the numbers of *declared* – let alone undeclared – foreign intelligence officers in the country between 1990 and 1994, presenting a serious challenge for protective security and counter-espionage.[50] In addition, radical right-wing elements of the Afrikaner community – the most infamous being the *Afrikaner Weerstandsbeweging* (the Afrikaner Resistance Movement or AWB) – also sought to destabilise the negotiations through a campaign of targeted disruption and violence against ANC supporters across South Africa (including into the so-called "independent homelands" of Transkei, Bophutatswana, Venda and Ciskei).

As such, this potent mixture of political and socio-economic anger, which drove the dramatic upswing in violence and contributed to the danger of the very real threat of a multifaceted civil war within South Africa, was seen by De Klerk and his lieutenants as the greatest threat to South Africa's stability while the negotiations for the post-apartheid settlement were continuing. Yet the dying embers of the apartheid covert security operators would – in either directly disobeying their President or at the least misleading him – see this as an opportunity for disrupting the negotiated settlement and, in many ways, implementing the very "stay behind" capability that had been envisioned for the CCB and other DMI covert capabilities in the counter-revolutionary warfare climate of the 1980s.

The "Third Force" unleashed

This was one-part of the so-called "Third Force" capability that the securocrats had envisioned in the mid-1980s (see Chapter 7), although – with the transition from apartheid to democracy now progressing, the ANC/SACP and PAC unbanned, and violent clashes between ANC/UDF and *Inkatha* supporters sweeping the townships – the climate within which this "Force" operated had changed dramatically from that envisioned when it was first proposed. No longer – necessarily – a structured set of covert security force units operating under the command-and-control of the SSC, KIK and securocrats, it was now an

> Amorphous "mafia-like" network within South Africa ... [involving] serving security forces personnel, former securocrat officials and security personnel, individuals who had financially gained (or lost) as a result of regional upheaval, and criminal elements involved in clandestine activities ... parts of various black homeland security forces, extremist groupings (white and black), and some private business ... which was responsible for much of the indiscriminate political violence — whether by direct action, indirect manipulation or financial commission[51]

whose covert operators would "train, organize, arm, and deploy" both in support of the *Inkatha* forces arrayed against the ANC/UDF (recalling, continuing and building-on the contra-mobilisation activities of the 1980s) and, more generally, to stir-up black-on-black violence in the townships through "pseudo-operations" and related covert activities.[52] This was all – as Henderson has noted – largely down to the fact that many securocrats, National Party leaders and right-wing sympathisers within the security forces saw a need for "reform with security" which argued for a *kragdadigheid* ("use of force") to "ensure white security during and after the volatile political negotiations".[53] Perhaps more astutely, though, Ellis notes that – when considering the evidence for the formal development of such a "third counter-revolutionary warfare force" by the securocrats of the mid-1980s, the evidence of the political violence tied to this state-organised "third force" in the early 1990s may have been "organised from a very high level, certainly until 1989, after which its senior command and control system were gradually eroded until 1992. Thereafter it was effectively privatised".[54] In this sense, the "third force" may have been an effective tool – used either wittingly or unwittingly – for the senior National Party leadership in their negotiations against the ANC. Nevertheless, they could never have imagined the degree to which the whole enterprise – founded on the principles of a structured intelligence capability – spun out of control.

The violence which swept South Africa during the 1990–1994 transition claimed more than 14,000 lives, more than at any other comparable point in the conflict's history. While the majority view the violence was that it was – conspiratorially – fomented by this "third force", in reality the civil war between the ANC/UDF and *Inkatha* supporters which broke into the open in the townships of the East Rand, killing not only thousands of township residents but also hundreds of mainstream policemen, was a huge contributor to this violence in and of itself. Equally, the militias of the ANC/UDF, *Inkatha*, the AWB, and APLA – alongside the SAP Internal Stability Unit and the National Peacekeeping Force[55] – all contributed to, alongside the state's covert structures, the destabilisation of the country.[56] Despite this fact, with time, all political violence in South Africa came to be attributed to "third force" elements operating within society – becoming a convenient shorthand to excuse either specifically directed violence (i.e. because so-called "third force" violence was spoken of as being insidious, faceless and of almost phantom-like qualities) by any specific group, or for the now-dominant ANC to blame, sometimes with great justification and evidence, continued violence or domestic opposition in the post-transition era on lingering elements from the apartheid security forces. Indeed, Mandela himself first used it in September 1990 to refer to the train violence (in which masked gunmen armed with Eastern bloc weaponry shot-up carriages full of commuters around Soweto) which was besetting the areas around Soweto. In the longer-term, the label "third force" would linger as an epithet used by ANC leaders until as late as 1999 when condemning either opposition to its policies or corrupt or irregular activities from within the post-1994 security and intelligence establishment.

Specific security force units played large roles in this "force". Beginning in mid-1990, the outbreaks of train violence and taxi violence (in which rival taxi-stands were shot-up by similar masked gunmen) were initially due entirely to operations by Vlakplaas, acting individually or in tandem with other covert security force members (such as 5 Recce or members of 32 Battalion). The intention was to demonstrate to supporters of the ANC (as had been successfully demonstrated by RENAMO using the same tactics in Mozambique) that the organisation was unable to protect its supporters, and therefore it was not "healthy" to be one; this seriously disrupted the ANC's ability to organise throughout much of the early 1990s and, thus, had the intended counter-revolutionary effect.[57] After evidence of these atrocities began to come to light in the Harms Commission, De Klerk ordered the unit suspended; while this did not occur immediately, Vlakplaas was no longer treated as the "golden boys" of the Security Police. Too much information and the identities of too many people had been revealed to Harms (and, therefore, the public) during his inquiries, and too many senior commanders had been accused in the press and in public throughout the proceedings. Thus, C1 was shunned by those commanders and politicians who had previously entertained themselves (literally) at Vlakplaas "*braai* and booze festivals".[58] Following the Harms Commission, however, De Kock suggested to Brigadier Krappies Engelbrecht that Vlakplaas be closed down, as negotiations with the ANC were developing rapidly; Engelbrecht disagreed, telling De Kock "we don't know what the ANC is going to do, whether they'll honour agreements. We need to keep Vlakplaas alive".[59] In this sense, the security force commanders hedged their bets against a future war with the ANC inside South Africa – more cynically, however, they also attempted to maintain a grip on the revelations of covert security force activities which might (indeed, would) see them indicted later for crimes against the state and the people.

With the transition to independence in Namibia, Vlakplaas' ranks were swollen by former *Koevoet* members – including a significant number of ex-SWAPO *askaris*, so much so that by mid-1990, De Kock was in command of more than 300 *askaris*;[60] this formed a massive counter-revolutionary resource which could be deployed at the volition of either De Kock or the government. On 30 April 1993, however, De Kock was asked to resign from the SAP; at the same time, the government authorised a R17.5 million pay-off for 84 Vlakplaas policemen. "Prime Evil's" 25-year career as a covert operator had come to an end.[61] Vlakplaas itself was not finally disbanded until the eve of the 1994 elections, and its members continued their activities from within Security Branch. In 1991, the Security Branch was transferred to the Criminal Investigations Branch of the SAP, and redesignated the Crime Information Service (CIS), while C1 was redesignated "C10" and "officially reorganised" to investigate illegal weapons trafficking[62] – or, in co-operation with Military Intelligence, in fomenting black-on-black violence through bombings, train violence, killings, and the like. With the passing of both De Kock's rein and Vlakplaas' activities, the old order in South Africa could finally be said to be passing; what would come afterwards – in terms of the position and attitude of both the "old guard" security forces and the "new guard" ANC securocrats and security-force members following the negotiated settlement – remained to be seen.

The Goldstone and Steyn Commissions: getting to grips

While Vlakplaas had been the most visible of the apartheid state's counter-revolutionary warfare elements active in South Africa – even if its exact nature remained unknown until Coetzee's revelations and the Harms Commission – the CCB was not alone amongst those apartheid-era covert units exposed under De Klerk. The "sufficient evidence" that De Klerk had sought through the Harms Commission's investigations was not to come until a serving member of the C1/C10 unit testified anonymously to the Goldstone Commission (formally, the *Commission of Inquiry into Acts of Public Violence and Intimidation* (1991–1994) chaired by Justice Richard Goldstone and created under the National Peace Accord in September 1991 and the *Prevention of Violence and Intimidating Act* (No. 139 of 1991)) in 1994 that hit-squad activities, the training and arming of IFP hit-squads, illegal killings, fraud, forgery, bombings and other acts of public violence were being planned and/or carried-out at Vlakplaas and elsewhere. At the same time, a former senior officer in DMI – Gert Hugo – testified publicly to the existence of similar "Third Force" capabilities within the military, providing the "highest level of evidence" of the "Third Force".[63]

De Klerk sought assurances from both political and security force leadership that such the covert, illegal activities of such units were being terminated – and, alongside the investigations noted here, moved to terminate their funding (see below). However, it was clear very quickly that De Klerk neither had sufficient assurances from these leaders – particularly those with securocrat legacies – nor sufficient insight into the nature of such covert units. In November 1992, in one of the most shocking revelations by the Goldstone Commission, the very existence of the DCC was "uncovered" following a raid by Goldstone investigators on the headquarters of the PAIIC (one of its front-companies) outside of Johannesburg.[64] The DCC – one of the most covert intelligence units developed by the security forces (see Chapter 6) – had long run covert assassination and destabilisation operations against the ANC, SWAPO and other groups opposed to South Africa across the sub-continent. These operations continued in the transition phase, when – at the beginning of 1990 – the DCC's lead operator, Lieutenant-Colonel Jan Anton Nieuwoudt, organised an operation to topple the military ruler of the Transkei, Major-General Bantu Holomisa, who was to be overthrown because of his assistance to the ANC and PAC in the Transkei. C1 was used to support this operation, mostly through the supply of weapons (AK-47s, RPG7s, mortars, grenades and ammunition) which were delivered to Nieuwoudt in November 1990. The operation fell apart when the leader of the DCC team, Colonel Craig Duli, and 11 members of his team were killed during the coup attempt by members of Holomisa's security.[65] The coup was also assisted by the International Researchers-Ciskei Intelligence Service (IR-CIS) which was established by Nieuwoudt in Ciskei as a means of re-establishing a base in the Eastern Cape against Holomisa.[66]

At the time, it was believed that the DCC was "at the centre of third force activities" in South Africa, as the planning group for a military coup against the new dispensation.[67] This proved not to be the case, although the evidence uncovered by Goldstone proved that the DCC had taken-in CCB operatives after the CCB was "officially disbanded" in April 1990 – yet, despite its existence since at least the late 1970s (see Chapter 6), the DCC had never been avowed by the SADF leadership to De Klerk or other political leaders.[68] It was later concluded that PAIIC activities, contrary to denials, may have been "central to the strategy of the De Klerk regime during the negotiations phase", another indication that De Klerk continued to capitalise on DMI covert operations in the post-1990 period.[69]

The starkness of these findings forced De Klerk to act. With Goldstone's July 1992 report into both the involvement of SAP personnel in the Boipatong massacre of 45 people by IFP supporters on 17 June 1992 – and the SAP's own reaction to and investigation of the massacre[70] – De Klerk demanded the resignation of senior SAP officers; Minister of Law and Order Kriel would "purge" the SAP's senior ranks of 19 of its 55 generals, but was subsequently criticised for not removing any of those leaders "with the most notorious reputations".[71] To investigate the DCC's existence and role – as part of an attempt to get to the heart of the continued existence of covert DMI and Special Forces units – De Klerk subsequently appointed SA Air Force Chief of Staff Lt-Gen. Pierre Steyn (assisted by General Conradie of the SAP) to investigate "all the intelligence functions of the SA Defence Force" and specifically those within DMI. Leveraging the previous inquiries, Steyn's report to De Klerk – presented orally in December 1992[72] – noted the existence of these units (DCC, Army Intelligence, Special Forces, Vlakplaas and the 7th Medical Battalion, responsible for the apartheid state's CBW programme) and their involvement in "a wide range of illegal and/or unauthorised activity" such as establishing arms caches (in Portugal, South Africa and across the Frontline States in Kenya, Zambia, Mauritius and other unidentified countries), engaging in covert contra-mobilisation activities within South Africa (including both efforts to get PAC cadres to murder ANC supporters in the Transkei, and continued covert training and support to the Ciskei intelligence and defence forces, and the IFP after 1990), engaging in corrupt business practices (including around ivory, drugs and weapons smuggling), supporting the white right-wing (for example, that "senior officers in the SADF were involved in framing contingency plans for a right-wing coup"), and other such things. Steyn also noted that 1 Recce and 5 Recce were "probably" involved in train violence (under an operation code-named PASTOOR, which was alleged to govern all SADF covert "third force" activities under the management of former CCB members), and that there was "probably" a CBW programme in the Special Forces. Steyn noted that the qualifier "probably" had to be used due to the "extensive destruction of documents" and other evidence, alongside fears by investigators that "those implicated would resort to murder if they felt threatened".[73]

The Steyn Commission report – the full version of which was not released publicly until May 2006, 14 years after it was originally compiled – forced De Klerk to now act against the SADF. On 19 December, following advice from the SADF's leadership – including the SADF's Chief Directorate of Counter Intelligence, SADF chief General "Kat" Liebenberg, army chief General Georg Meiring and Chief of Staff, Intelligence, General C.P. van der Westhuizen – De Klerk announced that 23 senior commanders of the SADF military intelligence establishment (including the deputy Chief of Staff, Intelligence, and the chief of the DCC) had been dismissed for unauthorized clandestine activities linked to the countrywide political violence; by the end of the year, however, almost two-thirds had been investigated – by the Attorneys-General of the Transvaal and Witwatersrand, following Steyn's recommendations to De Klerk – and cleared of illegal activities or illicit links, with many citing "bureaucratic intrigues organised by the NIS" as the cause of their having been named and fired, a claim not impossible to believe given the history of enmity between the NIS and DMI.[74]

By late 1992, De Klerk had – finally – moved to control the "Third Force" and the securocrats who may have been orchestrating it, directly or indirectly. Even with such serious concerns about the security and intelligence forces being noted, however, De Klerk still emphasised in early 1993 that the government and its investigations had to be careful to ensure that it "dare not allow our security forces in general, and our intelligence services in particular, to be crippled in their capacity to work against the evil plans of those responsible for violence and unrest", that "the work of the intelligence community was not party-political, but genuinely security-oriented", and that "there's no witch-hunt" after individual members but that "they will, in fact, be strengthened and encouraged by effective action against the malpractices concerned which have cast a shadow over everyone".[75]

Steyn left further investigations to the Goldstone Commission, and took early retirement in October 1993, noting in his final report to De Klerk in April 1993 that "few, if any, of the suspects had been questioned and that there had been little progress in gathering evidence".[76] Between 1993 and 1994, however, Goldstone's investigations began to build a significant picture, heavily due to testimony received from serving security force members.[77] Off the back of such testimonies and investigations, Goldstone found a great deal of evidence to indicate that former and serving members of the police and the defence forces had become engaged in covert paramilitary activities aimed at destabilising the settlement process, as well as in attempts to seek revenge against former colleagues. While there were no indications of involvement in these activities by the NIS personnel, former and serving members of DMI, Security Branch and, in particular, the KwaZulu Police Force were deeply implicated in such activities. It was ultimately in Goldstone's final report of 18 March 1994 – which built on his earlier 1992 and 1993 reports, and detailed the testimonies and investigations that ensued from those[78] – that the existence of hit-squads in South Africa, operating with the complicity of the security forces, was proven: finally, the so-called "evidence of the existence of a Third Force" in South Africa.

While the Harms and Khan Commissions (see below) were seen to be weak and ineffective, the Goldstone Commission made significant headway in uncovering the nature of the "Third Force" and continuing covert activities and units. Before the transition had even started, a mere six weeks prior to the first universal elections in April 1994, De Klerk was forced – by Goldstone's March 1994 report – to move yet again against the security force commanders, and order "immediate leave from duties" for ten senior SAP officers, including SAP deputy commissioner Lt. Gen. Basie Smit, for "conspiring to foment violence and destabilize the country". He did so all the while pointing out that – even with both the Steyn and Goldstone reports detailing clearly the state of "Third Force" capabilities and involvement in political violence since 1990 – "at no stage did [the government] have evidence of an organized entity within the security force that could be described as a Third Force".[79] In the end, Goldstone was unable to prove that these activities were tied to or had been authorized by the political leadership in Pretoria – such evidence was not to come until the trial of Colonel Eugene de Kock finished in October 1996, alongside the trials of other former security force commanders such as Brigadier Jac Cronjé and Major-General Nick van Rensburg, as well as that of former Defence Minister Magnus Malan and his co-defendants (see Chapter 9).[80]

Covert accounts, "Inkathagate" and the Khan Commission

The fall-out from such "Third Force" activities were not limited to violent covert action by the security forces only – in a similar manner to the efforts made by DMI to skew Namibia's 1989 elections away from a outright SWAPO victory,[81] domestic efforts inside South Africa were instituted by DMI – under Project ECHOES – to undermine the ANC during the negotiations process through disinformation, provided by SABC and British journalists, alleging links between its armed wing MK, the Provisional Irish Republican Army and the Palestine Liberation Organisation.[82] Much like the *StratKom* operations of the 1980s, the ANC believed that ECHOES was not merely an attempt to discredit it, but rather that it was aimed at "subverting Self-Defence Units" (the armed militias of the ANC/UDF in the townships).[83] The project collapsed when two DMI agents – Leon Flores and Pamela du Randt – were arrested in London and deported, suspected more for planning the assassination of ex-Vlakplaas head Dirk Coetzee than of "probing links between the ANC and IRA".[84]

In July 1991, Security Branch documents leaked to the media noted the payment of state funds to the *Inkatha* Freedom Party to support their "development into a political movement" as an effective counter-pole to the ANC/UDF alliance inside South Africa;[85] in reality, the funds were alleged to have been used to support the IFP's violent confrontation with the ANC's supporters in the townships in Natal and around Johannesburg. The ensuing "Inkathagate" scandal also revealed the existence of at least six other government covert "special accounts" to provide such secret funding – to both contra-mobilisation and covert security forces – as well as the funding of anti-SWAPO parties in the Namibian elections. Finally, it also provided yet more evidence of covert internal destabilisation activities by the security forces – in particular by both 5 Recce and 32 Battalion.[86] Despite De Klerk's admission to the funding and his assurances that the funds were actually designed to "support black movements opposed to the economic sanctions imposed upon South Africa and which were part of the government's clandestine antisanctions efforts, begun in 1986", the scandal led to yet more investigations by De Klerk into secret accounts and covert political projects, and the termination of at least 41 of these immediately – especially those involved in "continued support for political organizations" – with all others being placed under a new Advisory Committee on Special Secret Projects. De Klerk also demanded the termination of "the role of all security services in special secret projects falling outside the normal area of their line functions".[87] As was seen in the other government investigations, however, the effectiveness of this termination and (re)newed oversight was questionable: these steps "apparently failed to uncover ongoing covert operations ... [and] considerably public doubt still existed about de Klerk's ability to make the various secret services accountable".[88]

Alongside the Harms and Goldstone Commissions, De Klerk also launched the Kahn Committee (under Professor Ellis Khan) to investigate all covert projects – crucially, only those brought to their attention by the security structures – with an eye to recommending their cancellation "wherever possible". Kahn – and the Ministers' Committee, chaired by Kobie Coetsee, which followed to implement Kahn's recommendations – worked for only four months, and noted a total of 44 projects (16 by the SADF, 11 by Foreign Affairs, nine by the SAP, seven by the NIS, and one by the Department of National Education).[89] All were funded covertly by the state, and all were subsequently subject to the new *Secret Services Account Amendment Act* (No. 142 of 1992) – which dictated that all further covert actions had to be funded by the Secret Services Account only, and overseen by a Secret Services Evaluation Committee – the reviews of which were ultimately folded into the Transitional Executive Committee (see below).[90] Somewhat astonishingly, when De Klerk was told about Project ECHOES – as part of Khan's investigations – he authorised its continuation, although it is not clear whether De Klerk was aware of its alleged true nature.[91]

De Klerk's weak grasp on covert operations

Such public efforts to (re)gain control over the funding of covert projects, ultimately, proved to be illusory for two reasons. First, despite these provisions surrounding the Secret Services Account, a separate Security Services Special Account was established which would fund NIS operations – a reflection on government efforts world-wide to muddy public accounting for funds spent on intelligence activities.[92] Second, as noted, many of the operators involved in illegal or illicit covert activities, following De Klerk's efforts to rein them in, simply invested in private enterprise, seeking and finding funding for their efforts through both licit and illegal activities.

Throughout these attempts to rein-in the security forces, De Klerk appeared to be caught in an ever-narrowing avenue where – on the one side – the "Third Force" formed in the 1980s continued to pursue covert actions against the ANC/UDF even after De Klerk's normalisation of relations with the ANC in February 1990, usually "without Cabinet authorisation or notification",[93] while – on the other side – efforts to gain both insights into and control over these units led them increasingly to move underground and into the private sector, thereby significantly hampering such efforts. While the Goldstone and Steyn Commissions did – eventually – get to grips with these issues to some degree (although it would take the investigations of the Truth and Reconciliation Commission in the mid-to-late 1990s to truly confirm many of the allegations), the Harms and Kahn Commissions were, as the TRC would later note, weak and seriously flawed. They were given insufficient political support by De Klerk to achieve results, their mandates were severely limited, they were reliant by mandate on the security forces themselves to bring illegal activities to their attention and to report irregularities, and they often involved inappropriate (i.e. involved) security force leaders in following-up allegations of illegal covert activities. Ultimately, they were "largely ineffectual in rooting-out the modus operandi and thinking that had developed during the previous period or, crucially, dismantling the associated 'informal official' networks" which continued the existence of the apartheid covert elements in the post-apartheid era.[94]

It remains unclear, though, whether De Klerk intentionally structured such weak and ineffectual commissions to investigate the alleged "third force" activities, or whether – with no significant security background himself upon assuming the presidency (he had been Minister of National Education previously), he was simply insufficiently knowledgeable and empowered to really confront the hydra that the apartheid security apparatus had become by the beginning of the 1990s. Henderson notes this dilemma in the face of the third influencing factor here – that

> De Klerk's control over his "inherited" intelligence and security community ... was intrinsically weak from the beginning as a result of ... the ongoing covert operations and network linkages managed by his inherited securocrats [which] continually threatened to undermine de Klerk's control over the white-dominated South African Parliament and occasionally derail the fragile negotiation process.[95]

While Williams notes that "far from coordinating the activities of a 'Third Force,' de Klerk lacks the executive and operational muscle to contain them" – highlighting the fact that the securocrats had vested interests in maintaining the covert security networks, capabilities and operations both against the ANC during the negotiations, and – crucially – to avoid being indicted for illegal acts by a new, ANC-dominated government.[96] Ellis, however, notes that – rather than being ill-suited to the task – De Klerk

Kept his distance from the details of such covert operations, and he probably did not wish to know exactly what measures some of these entailed ... while he was determined to restore the authority of the Cabinet, he also fully intended that the security forces should maintain their grip over the country.[97]

Ultimately, as Henderson notes, De Klerk was forced, time and again, to choose between maintaining his intelligence capacity and reining-in his security commanders, and the shards of the covert counter-revolutionary warfare machine that successive South African leaders back to Vorster had instituted over the last three decades.[98]

De Klerk would also maintain that he was only made aware of the "dirty tricks" units in DMI, Vlakplaas and the Special Forces – most particularly the CCB – months after taking office, and only of the DCC after the Steyn investigation uncovered it in 1992. He reportedly shut-down the SSC's covert structures – around *StratKom*, the KIK, *Trewits* and *Geveilstaf* – in light of both the restructuring of the SSC (as noted above) and the Harms, Goldstone and Steyn reports, yet this was not the whole picture, as has been discussed; it remains unclear – to this day – just which covert operations he was aware of (both during his presidency and previously as a co-opted member of the SSC), and how much he knew about those operations. In taking account of both the findings of the commissions of inquiry noted above, and the statements De Klerk made concerning the utility of the intelligence services in supporting the government's position during the negotiations phase, the National Party leadership "found clandestine operations an essential instrument for their reform strategy, while their control over those who managed the operations was weak".[99]

At the same time, the indictment of so many former and serving members of the apartheid-era security forces in these commissions and inquiries called into question the whole approach to amnesty and indemnification that De Klerk introduced. Under the provisions of the *Indemnity Act* (Act 35 of 1990), the *Indemnity Amendment Act* (Act 124 of 1992), and the *Further Indemnity Act* (Act 151 of 1992), De Klerk had granted indemnity from prosecution to any individual who had conducted illegal activities committed for political purposes. The cut-off date for this blanket amnesty was to have been 8 October 1990, but was later moved to 8 October 1992, and then to December 1993. In addition, in an effort to avoid fears amongst the security forces of a Nuremberg-style tribunal being established after the accession of a black-majority government, the third act extended the amnesty to "persons who had advised, directed, commanded, ordered, or performed offences with a political objective".[100] Sections 48(1–3) of the *Promotion of National Unity and Reconciliation Act* (Act 34 of 1995) – which established the Truth and Reconciliation Commission in the post-apartheid era – repealed these bills, as the ANC had warned it would do at the time (as the *Further Indemnity Act* had been pushed through by De Klerk using the executive President's Council and not Parliament)[101] but not the indemnity which they granted. Under the rubric of these acts, more than 3,500 security forces personnel were offered indemnity from prosecution. However, it remained unclear as to whether these amnesties were, in fact, ever granted by the De Klerk government: the new ANC government declared all applications invalid for "not being properly completed" prior to the 1994 elections. Indeed, many individuals subsequently put on-trial for alleged crimes committed during apartheid – including former Defence Minister Magnus Malan and other senior security force leaders – fell under that amnesty ruling.[102] Equally, De Klerk's rush to introduce amnesty and indemnity for the security forces was criticised for the appearance of attempting to brush under the carpet – whilst the negotiated settlement was being hammered out in the Transitional Executive Council (TEC – see below) – the human rights violations and other crimes committed by members of the security forces, subsequently exposed by the Harms, Steyn and Goldstone Commissions.

Apartheid's intelligence failures

Ultimately, it is clear that the long-term corruption of the intelligence process and the individuals overseeing it – as noted in Chapters 4–7 – also contributed to the National Party's failure to uphold apartheid, in whatever form. While politico-constitutional intelligence was gathered by the National Intelligence Service to, ultimately, support constitutional efforts to achieve a settlement of the conflict and bring about a new political dispensation in South Africa, Botha's government relied on DMI's operational intelligence focus and capabilities – especially those covert ones – to not only halt the "Revolutionary Onslaught" of the liberation movements, but to eliminate them as a viable political and revolutionary force. Both of these efforts failed. As Ellis notes, DMI's dramatic rise, the politicisation of the Chief of Staff, Intelligence, position, and Botha's willingness to accept whatever DMI proposed to him as a course-of-action to confront the wrongly perceived and incorrectly assessed "revolutionary onslaught" meant that virtually all intelligence reaching the political leadership from DMI was "polluted". This was not only by DMI's own fixation on counter-revolutionary strategies but – in a reflection of other countries' intelligence failures which were predicated on an erroneous reading of the results of their own intelligence actions, referred to as "resonance" (or sometimes "blow-back") in the intelligence world – also by the politicisation of the intelligence stream (as noted in Chapter 4) which "created pressures for intelligence estimates to be slanted for political reasons rather than in conformity with the intelligence officer's ideal of impartiality".[103]

Therefore, by relying far more heavily on the covert operational intelligence capabilities of the state, the apartheid government brought about its own downfall. This much was clear when secret negotiations were

196 Negotiating a settlement

begun by the NIS with the ANC in exile during the late 1980s;[104] had such a process, excluding the covert operators, begun earlier, the National Party may have been able to retain greater control over the post-conflict negotiating process. Indeed, the NIS reportedly produced an assessment for Botha in 1987 which concluded that the ANC was "unbeatable" as long as it remained in exile, but a "legalized ANC" could be weakened through a protracted negotiations process and drawn into a future coalition government – this aim appeared to drive much of the intelligence-led efforts of the SSC in the late 1980s and, if assessing Barnard's intentions cynically, the NIS's clandestine engagement with the ANC in exile.[105] While this may have been the result of a "twin-track" approach to ending the conflict – secret negotiations conducted by the most "enlightened" elements of the security forces, at the same time as the most pervasive covert intelligence actions by the most regressive elements – it was to prove an ultimate failure to the National Party's strategy. Instead, the National Party was rebuffed by a much more powerful ANC time and again during the negotiations towards a settlement. The ANC was also instrumental in providing an "out" for the security force commanders to empower them to rein-in the covert operators – first, through offering

> Constitutional terms which were broadly acceptable to the [leadership of the SADF, as the only force in the country capable of opposing the transition through force], as Afrikaner nationalists, and thus to tempt them into peace, as well as by its political handling of the generals themselves;

and, second, in persuading the National Party negotiators to keep many of the more "questionable" members of the apartheid dirty tricks units within the security forces for the time being, rather than unleash them into society where there was far less chance of keeping some degree of control over their actions, and thereby preventing them from making common cause with the white right-wing and elements of the "Third Force".[106]

Building the new intelligence dispensation

The meetings in Switzerland were the initial phase of the negotiations – topics concerning the unbanning of the ANC/SACP, the re-entry of their leaderships and cadres back into South Africa (past – as Sparks put it – "security forces trained to shoot them on sight" and a "white population indoctrinated against them for generations"), the defining and release of political prisoners, "greater discipline" by the ANC of the violent protest campaign sweeping South Africa, and a plan to end the ANC's armed struggle. In the last meeting in March 1990, a steering-committee was established by the spies to lay the foundation for the overt negotiations that would follow – once the ANC and SACP leaders in exile had returned to South Africa.[107] Indeed, the NIS reorganised itself at this time to be better able to deal with these negotiations, creating – in an internal restructuring in 1988 – its own planning units on politics, the economy and related matters, to parallel those in the Department of Political Development (later Constitutional Affairs).[108]

The TEC and intelligence

Most of the new policies and legislation emerged out of discussions between the NIS and the ANC-DIS between March and July 1993. In the negotiations towards a political settlement between Pretoria and the liberation groups, many NIS officials were transferred to the Department of Constitutional Affairs in order to "provide intelligence/policy support for [the] government negotiating team. Their intelligence experience and linkages allowed them to be utilised as key planning assets;"[109] indeed, NIS chief Barnard was himself appointed as Director General of that department in 1992, and was replaced by his deputy Louw. At the same time, NIS Deputy Director-General Mauritz Spaarwater was transferred from the NIS in March 1991 to run a new directorate, responsible for analyzing the political situation and the key players and for supporting the government's negotiators.[110]

The conclusions from these initial negotiations – both directly and through unilateral declarations by both sides which laid-out publicly their intended positions on various points arising in the negotiations – were incorporated more officially into the discussions and negotiations of the Sub-Council on Intelligence (SCI) of the TEC, formed in November of 1993 to oversee the period up to the elections and the transfer of power, as well as negotiations on the Interim Constitution.[111] Participants in these discussions included the NIS, ANC-DIS, the Transkei Intelligence Service, the Bophutatswana Internal Intelligence Service, the Venda National Intelligence Service, and – later – the Pan-Africanist Security Service (Ciskei did not officially have an intelligence service).[112] The SCI became, crucially, the forum through which discussions on the future structure of the intelligence community were carried out prior to the establishment of the GNU. This was especially important because the future scope and focus of South Africa's intelligence community was not covered in the Interim Constitution (unlike the military and police which were) and, therefore, was not subject to the Constitutional negotiations during the settlement process.[113] This was largely due to the fact that the negotiators on intelligence were not prepared to have their particulars placed in the Interim Constitution when similar sections on the police and national defence forces were required.

The SCI also became responsible – under the TEC's mandate – for the operations of the security and intelligence services (as was the case with parallel Sub-Committees on Law and Order, and Defence). While this had as its primary focus concerns for running the evolving security dispensation, it also served as an attempt to further bring into the spotlight – and

198 *Negotiating a settlement*

under control – the "Third Force" elements which continued to destabilise South Africa right up to, and even past, the election of April 1994. At the same time, a Joint Co-ordinating Intelligence Committee (JCIC) was established within the TEC. Initially, the ANC had asked for managerial control through this body over the day-to-day functions of the intelligence community; the NIS opposed this. The compromise, written into the mandate of the *Transitional Executive Council Act*, stated that the TEC would oversee the intelligence services' operations while day-to-day control would be left to the individual department heads, much as with the military and the police.[114] The JCIC was authorised to oversee the co-ordination of the intelligence services, to investigate the activities of any service which appeared to contravene its mandate, and to provide intelligence information to the TEC and its other sub-councils.

These were, however, almost completely derailed by two key events in this period: first, the discovery of MK's continued operational planning – under "VULA" – to overthrow the republic; and, second, the assassination of charismatic SACP leader Chris Hani by white right-wingers in 1993. The fact that neither of these events – alongside a number of other clashes and atrocities in this period (including massacres perpetrated by all sides, the political violence in the townships, the assault on the CODESA negotiations by the AWB, the Bisho and Boipatong massacres, and other such events)[115] – precipitated a civil war in South Africa was due to both the strength of leadership on both sides – Mandela and De Klerk – and to the bonds that had developed between each sides' spies in the on-going negotiations.

As was noted in the previous chapters, in the past, South Africa's governance and intelligence picture betrayed a failure to appreciate strategically the nature of the conflict in South Africa and, consequently, support earlier moves towards finding a negotiated settlement. It proved to be almost impossible for the DMI-driven intelligence picture to appreciate – through the prism of the "communist threat" against South Africa – anything other than an apocalyptical future for white South Africans should the liberation movements have triumphed in their struggle. For the new intelligence dispensation, therefore, the requirement to develop a comprehensive and accurate strategic intelligence picture to support policy-making was noted at an early stage – alongside the need to ensure that not only would the new dispensation be able to fulfil the government's (the consumer) needs and requirements for information on issues of concern, but as well that they would be able to clearly delineate – for themselves – the usefulness and limits of the information which they are gathering. While these failures and intelligence "bear-traps" appear to have been closely reflected on by those who undertook the negotiations for the new intelligence dispensation, as will be discussed in Chapter 9, events surrounding the new intelligence dispensation appeared to indicate that these dangers were not taken to heart ultimately within both the new structures and the new government.

The JCIC eventually gave way to the Heads of Combined Services (HOCS) Committee, which became the basis for the future, post-apartheid National Intelligence Co-ordinating Committee (NICOC) (see Chapter 9). The reason behind the changes in the intelligence and security structures were partly a result of the general government restructuring following the transition, but as well to allow for the integration of ANC intelligence, along with all other intelligence services in the country, into the new national intelligence structures. This restructuring was also an attempt to reflect on the general re-examination of intelligence functions and structures that took place in the immediate post-Cold War environment globally. This was not only the case in the West – especially in the United States (with the Brown Commission and other bodies examining the future of US intelligence), in the United Kingdom (where the first public acknowledgments of the existence of the security and intelligence services were occurring at this time), and in the newly reunified Federal Republic of Germany (where the task of dealing with the fall-out from the former East German state security and intelligence structures – both in terms of their domestic oppression and their penetration of the former West German government – was also just beginning) – but also in the former Soviet bloc, where the newly emerging democracies of Central and Eastern Europe (such as Czechoslovakia, Poland, Hungary and Romania particularly) were also confronting former state security apparatuses which had been dedicated to internal repression and external targeting. Indeed, in the post-Soviet space, Russia and other former Soviet republics were also undergoing significant changes to their intelligence dispensations. The SCI was starkly aware of the debates underpinning these changes globally, and sought to reflect these in both its discussions and the new intelligence framework resulting from this. As Nhlanhla indicated in 1992,

> The current situation presents all intelligence actors with an opportunity unique in our history – to redefine the political principles, organisational culture and morality in terms of which intelligence in future shall be practised. In discussing the future of intelligence in our country, we cannot negate the fact that we, as intelligence actors, constitute a tragic legacy: a legacy of opposition to one another – some of us struggling against apartheid, others defending it – actions that were dictated by the very nature of our highly politicised roles respectively. Today, a new mission must be determined for the South African intelligence community – a mission which is in line with the desired goal of a non-racial democratic order.[116]

A new national security paradigm and the "philosophy of intelligence"

In order to not only reflect the changes that occurred in the transition, but as well to attempt to place the secret services of South Africa in a more conventional and useful position to serve the government's needs, the new South African Constitution redefined national security to reflect "the resolve of all South Africans, as individuals and as a nation, to live as equals, to live in peace and harmony, to be free from fear and want, and to seek a better life".[117] National security as it was narrowly defined in the past was expanded to encompass a great many more issues and concerns than previously; within the South African context, these included the growing importance of non-military security, threats to stability and development, and the reality of international interdependence. This last point is the most important for the purposes of this discussion: as the 1994 *White Paper on Intelligence* indicated,

> The intermingling and transnational character of modern-day security issues furthermore indicates that solutions to the problems of insecurity are beyond the direct control of any single country and cannot be rectified by purely military means. The international security agenda is shifting to the full range of political, economic, military, social, religious, technological, ethnic and ethical factors that shape security issues around the world. The main threat to the well-being of individuals and the interests of nations across the world does not primarily come from a neighbouring army, but from other internal and external challenges such as economic collapse, overpopulation, mass-migration, ethnic rivalry, political oppression, terrorism, crime and disease, to mention but a few.[118]

South Africa's new national security policy would, therefore, encompass as its objectives not only the "absence of war" but as well the pursuit of democracy, of sustainable economic development, and social justice. Regionally, it aimed to advance the principles of collective security, non-aggression, and peaceful settlement of disputes.[119] National security would increasingly be defined as threats to the *people* rather than threats to the *state*. Nhlanhla, subsequently the Deputy Minister (and then Minister) for Intelligence, stated in 1992 that

> The redefinition of South Africa's security needs and the inter-relationship between the security of the state and that of the people must be seen in arriving at a new definition of national security. The security of the state depends on its ability to maintain its political independence, sovereignty and territorial integrity ... The security of the people depends on the satisfaction of their political, economic, cultural and social needs ... The security of the state depends on the security of the people, and the security of the people depends on the security of the state.[120]

The *White Paper on Intelligence* expanded on this theme by stating that

> National security should be understood in comprehensive terms to include the military, political, economic, social, technological and environmental dimensions. National security should therefore besides its traditional concern with defence, violence and subversion, encompass the basic principles and core values associated with and essential to the quality of life, freedom, justice, prosperity and development.[121]

Given the history of South African intelligence interference in society, it is not surprising that the approach outlined in the SCI and introduced into new dispensation outlined a new "philosophy of intelligence" as its foundation for change. Noting that

> Prior to the election of a democratic government, security policy was formulated by a minority government. Its ability to detail what was in the national interest, was therefore flawed. More-over, since the minority government was faced with a struggle for liberation, this issue dominated the question of security and, consequently, the activities of the statuary instruments that served it ... the role of the state's security apparatus was over-accentuated with virtually no institutional checks and balances,

the new government believed that

> Reshaping and transforming intelligence in South Africa is not only a matter of organisational restructuring. It should start with clarifying the philosophy and redefining the mission, focus and priorities of intelligence in order to establish a new culture of intelligence.[122]

The Sub-Council on Intelligence agreed that as part of the continued approach to the new intelligence dispensation proposed, new principles and practical requirements – including allegiance to the Constitution, subordination to the rule of law, a clearly defined legal mandate, budgetary control and external auditing, an integrated national intelligence capability, political neutrality and the separation of intelligence from policy-making, a balance between secrecy and transparency, and the absence of law-enforcement powers – were included in the mandates of the services for purposes of control and accountability.[123] These were in addition to the four principal mechanisms for oversight and control of the intelligence services built into the new structures: the appointment by the President of Inspectors-General to oversee the services, the establishment of a Parliamentary committee on intelligence (subsequently the Joint Standing Committee on Intelligence), the implementation of a code of conduct for the intelligence services, and a strict limit in definition of the briefs of each service.

In order to ensure that those agencies tasked with carrying-out the intelligence and security work of South Africa would be able to execute their tasks with minimal interference and question, three final guidelines were established within the government. First, the services had to accept as primary the authority of the government and other democratic institutions of society, as well as those bodies constitutionally mandated to participate in and monitor the determination of intelligence priorities. Second, the services had to be assured that no changes to their operational doctrines, structures and procedures would occur unless approved by the government and the people. Finally, the services would bind themselves to the new agreements through a mutually agreed set of norms and a code of conduct.[124]

Many of these principles – including especially those of political neutrality, the separation of intelligence from policy-making, and achieving a balance between secrecy and transparency – would be called into question as the 1990s turned to the twenty-first century, and the ANC achieved overwhelming political control over the government (see Chapter 9). The politicisation of the intelligence process, in many respects, coupled with the continuing lack of national reconciliation – even by 2005, a decade after the end of apartheid – has meant that the intelligence processes in the country, including the agencies, command and control, oversight and accountability, have been stunted and – indeed, in some cases – still-born in their abilities to truly serve the national interest. Despite these questions which would arise in the future, the initial efforts at achieving an equitable – indeed, very enlightened – approach to intelligence and national security, as it was negotiated through the TEC, were laudable, and reflective of a professed desire by all sides to create "another country", as Sparks had called it.

Conclusions

In hindsight, it was supremely ironic that, in the 1990–1994 period, the elements within the security forces and white right-wing who saw themselves as fighting legitimately in defence of *Afrikanerdom* – a battle joined in the nineteenth century against the British, triumphally hoisted by the National Party victory of 1948, and subsequently fought through increasingly barbaric means after the 1976 Soweto Uprising and the effective loss of the Frontline States buffer in the late 1970s – became another insurgency inside South Africa. In the CODESA negotiations – restarted after the near-misses of the Bisho massacre, the Hani assassination, and the AWB's Bophutatswana "battle" – it was the ANC which recognised the need to provide a political solution to end *this* insurgency. This was – most notably – far less about the political leadership of the apartheid government, and far more to do with the rank-and-file of the security forces, most particularly those who had been brutalised by (and who, in turn, had been barbarous in) fighting the state's dirty wars. As Ellis has noted,

Middle-ranking officers like Colonel Eugene De Kock and Colonel Joe Verster, the managing director of the CCB, saw themselves as warriors, professionals who had been trained to attack the enemy until unambiguously ordered to stop. They had been brought up to believe that to fight for *volk* and *vaderland* was their highest duty.[125]

Abandoning this hard-fought, in-the-blood attitude would be nigh on impossible for many of these "warriors"; equally, as is noted in Chapter 9, turning from an authoritarian liberation movement into a representative, transparent and democratic political party would also prove challenging for the ANC and SACP.

At its heart, though, the most important aspects of this transition – for the intelligence and security services specifically, as reflective of the wider angst inherent in South African society in the transition to this new future – remained the resolution of past grievances, tensions and conflicts, and the development of a new, unified intelligence community which would support the new political establishment. In that sense, and throughout the negotiations, it was hoped that eventually – as Mike Louw (by then Director General of the NIS) stated – South Africa could have "an intelligence service at peace with itself".[126] In order to accomplish this, Louw went on to say, "the watchwords must be control, accountability and supervision. Too many people equate us with other secret organisations. We need to establish our own identity".[127]

9 Progress and problems
South Africa's new intelligence dispensation, 1994–2005

> The security of the state depends on the security of the people, and the security of the people depends on the security of the state
>
> Joe Nhlanhla, 1992

First steps: the new South African intelligence environment, 1994–1995

When change did come, it ultimately reflected this negotiated-settlement and its inherent compromises – a solution that could never solve all the problems found in both the old and new dispensations. The new intelligence dispensation that was established in 1994 was – first – crucial to the furthering of a peaceful settlement between the former apartheid government and the former liberation groups, while – second – aiming to develop solutions for many of the problems cited in other intelligence and security services.

On 26 April 1994, South Africans of all backgrounds began to vote in the first truly democratic election that the country had ever seen. As Waldmeir noted, the days before the election witnessed "carnage, as right-wing car bombs left dismembered bodies strewn across the streets of Johannesburg and the television screens of the nation". Yet the election day itself dawned calm, clear and ordered – and, by the end of the election process, De Klerk had conceded the presidency to Nelson Mandela, and the ANC had won 62.7 per cent of the popular vote, against the National Party's 20.4 per cent. Crucially, the IFP was also satisfied with the vote – and so, as with the rest of the negotiated settlement in ignoring the evidence of significant voting fraud, South Africans moved into a new future under an ANC-led Government of National Unity (GNU).[1]

In many ways – and as agreed by almost every analyst of the results – the real loser was De Klerk and the National Party who, as was discussed in Chapter 8, could have pressed harder for a more favourable deal with themselves and their myriad constituencies (including their links to the white – heavily Afrikaner – right-wing) at earlier points in the negotiating process when the ANC's position was weak(er).[2] It seemed clear – however coincidental or conspiratorial – that once De Klerk moved effectively against the "Third Force"-supporting elements within the security forces and securocrats in 1992, he and the National Party negotiating the transition began, inexorably, to lose power and position to the ANC. It is highly noteworthy – in this sense – that this time also reflected the change in control over the intelligence services from the Office of the State President under De Klerk to the TEC's Sub-Committee on Intelligence, its Joint Co-ordinating Intelligence Committee, and (later) its Heads of Combined Services Committee. Once he had lost control over the NIS – and, as noted in Chapter 8, notably also "lost" Niel Barnard to the Department of Constitutional Affairs – De Klerk lost the initiative, and the upper hand, to the ANC.

Mandela moved quickly to consolidate his hold on the intelligence and security dispensation. Appointing new ministers and managers to oversee the dispensation, immediate tensions over equality within this "GNU" emerged with the National Party and the IFP, as all ministerial positions relating to security were given to ANC personnel: Defence to MK commander Joe Modise; Safety and Security to Sidney Mufamadi (an SACP leader and trade unionist); Justice to Dullah Omar; and Foreign Affairs to ANC Executive Alfred Nzo. The Intelligence portfolio was created under a Deputy Minister of Intelligence Services reporting jointly to the Minister of Justice and the Office of the State President.[3] The only security-related portfolios to be given to non-ANC personnel were those of Home Affairs (to Mangosuthu Buthelezi, head of the IFP) and the chair of the Cabinet Committee on Security and Intelligence (to De Klerk, now Deputy President and leader of the National Party). While the appointments inevitably raised comparisons to the reign of the former securocrats during the apartheid regime, it was clear that – at least during the time of the GNU and, at least on paper – a far more robust oversight and accountability mechanism existed in the post-apartheid era than had existed during it. Nevertheless, issues would emerge – significantly, around the ANC leadership of the security and intelligence portfolios, as well as with the new intelligence services created in 1995 – that would demonstrate continued problems with a politicised and polluted intelligence environment.

The constitution and the intelligence dispensation

This change was first acknowledged on 21 October 1994 when Minister of Justice Dullah Omar announced the intended new structure of South Africa's secret services. This was in conjunction with the release of a government *White Paper on Intelligence* the same month outlining future policy considerations, and was followed in December 1994 by three new Acts restructuring the intelligence and security services, as well as the mechanisms for control, co-ordination, oversight and accountability. The principal pieces of legislation that concerned the new structures were the *National*

Strategic Intelligence Act, the *Intelligence Services Act*, the *Intelligence Services Control Act* (originally introduced as the *Committee of Members of Parliament on an Inspectors-General of Intelligence Act*), and the 1994 *White Paper on Intelligence* (see below). In addition, aspects of the 1995 *South African Police Services Act*, the 1996 *National Crime Prevention Strategy*,[4] and the 1995 *White Paper on Defence: Defence in a Democracy* are relevant to any examination of the new national security structures.

Although the original intention of the Parliamentarians who wrote this legislation – and who participated in the TEC's and Constitutional Assembly's debates on the new Constitution – was to have the mandates, areas of responsibilities, and a code of conduct for the intelligence services written into the new Constitution (similar to sections on the National Defence Force and the Police Service), it was decided that the Constitution would support the existence only of intelligence services, and defer to the legislation governing these services in this area only (as had been the case under chapter 14 of the Interim Constitution which laid-out the mandates for both the National Defence Forces and the Police Service, with no mention of the intelligence services). Under the new Constitution, the role of the intelligence and security services in South Africa was made clear. Section 185 of the Constitution indicated that the intelligence services must be monitored, co-ordinated and controlled largely in conjunction with those principles laid out in the *National Strategic Intelligence Act*, the *Intelligence Services Act*, and the *Intelligence Services Control Act*, including multi-party Parliamentary oversight of the services, civilian oversight through an Inspector-General, and co-ordination of all intelligence (including defence and police) activities in South Africa. Furthermore, the security services were prohibited, under section 187(7), from attempting to influence, positively or negatively, the political process.[5]

Ultimately, it was determined that the new mission of the South African intelligence community would be to safeguard the Constitution, uphold individual rights enunciated as Fundamental Rights in the Constitution, promote the interrelated elements of security, stability, co-operation and development, both within South Africa and in the region of Southern Africa, assist in the achievement of national prosperity whilst making an active contribution to global peace and other globally defined priorities for the well-being of humankind, and promote South Africa's ability to face foreign threats and to enhance its competitiveness in a dynamic world.[6]

Needless to say, these represented a tall – but highly commendable – aspirational order for an intelligence community having been wrenched through a difficult rebirth, and still hurting from the process, which was reflected in the new "philosophy of intelligence" outlined in the 1994 *White Paper on Intelligence* (as discussed in Chapter 8). In many ways – like other aspects of the policy programme of the new GNU, such as the much-touted Reconstruction and Development Programme (RDP) – such high aspirations would, almost inevitably, fail to be met. Criticised by many[7] for falling far short of the "new dawn" vision outlined in the *White Paper on Intelligence*, one of the principal reasons for this was this failure to enshrine the mandates, areas of responsibilities, and a code of conduct for the intelligence services in the new Constitution – leading to, amongst other very serious shortfalls, a dramatic weakening over the subsequent 15 years in the role played by Parliamentary oversight of the new intelligence dispensation.

Restructuring: integration vs. destruction

In order to fulfil the missions laid out for the new South African intelligence community, a finite definition of national intelligence was first devised in order to provide parameters for both the restructuring of the community and the new (or continued) operational mandates of these agencies. National intelligence functions would, therefore, include counter-intelligence, foreign intelligence, crime intelligence, military intelligence, and domestic intelligence. In addition, the President was authorised further to approve "special activities" by the South African intelligence community. In order to avoid the problems which occurred under the apartheid regime, the *National Strategic Intelligence Act* clearly defined these new briefs and what they meant for each agency.[8] Specific services were made responsible for each of these functions within their own area of operations.

The end of national intelligence (and the NIS)?

The National Intelligence Service, which had led the push for a negotiated settlement with the ANC (alongside leading many of the negotiations themselves, as was discussed in Chapter 8), was not – in the end – simply disbanded and a completely new national intelligence structure created from scratch to replace it. Much as had been the case in the transition from BOSS to the NIS in the late 1970s – although obviously in a markedly different political climate, within a completely different ethical construct in the post-apartheid state that South Africa was evolving into – the previous structures were redesigned to meet the new political requirements of the state. As such, the NIS was terminated in fact on 1 January 1995, and – in its place, under sections 3(1) and 3(2) respectively of the *Intelligence Services Act* – a new National Intelligence Agency (NIA) was established, building on the NIS's previous domestic security intelligence focus, alongside a new South African Secret Service (SASS) focusing on the NIS's previous foreign intelligence focus (with its mandate defined in section 2(2) of the *National Strategic Intelligence Act*).

The new structures integrated those former members of the NIS, the ANC-DIS, the Pan-Africanist Security Service, the Transkei Intelligence Service, the Bophutatswana Internal Intelligence Service, the Venda

National Intelligence Service, and any other members of any intelligence service either attached to a political organisation or operating in the independent homelands or self-governing territories.[9] Although the new agencies included members from all of these services, a percentage of these former members instead became members of the new South African Police Service (SAPS) rather than intelligence.[10] Of the approximately 4,000 personnel included in the new civilian structures (NIA and SASS only), 2,130 came from the NIS, 910 from the ANC-DIS, 304 from Bophutatswana, 233 from Transkei, 76 from Venda, and the remainder from the PASS (see Table 9.1).

By dividing the operational mandates of the old National Intelligence Service between its foreign and domestic roles, it was hoped that this would "promote greater focusing, effectiveness, professionalism, and expertise in the specialised fields of domestic and foreign intelligence".[11] There were still cohesive ties between the two services in that the Directors General of the NIA and SASS were required to consult with each other on all decisions regarding operations and plans for the services. Foreign intelligence responsibilities would also remain with the Foreign Intelligence Bureau of the Department of Foreign Affairs, through its interaction with both agencies (NIA and SASS) for sourcing and co-ordination of foreign intelligence.[12]

Table 9.1 South African intelligence personnel (1994–1995)

Intelligence agencies pre-integration (as of 31 December 1994)		
National Intelligence Service (NIS)	4,000	
SADF Military Intelligence Division (SADF-DMI)	7,000	
SAP Crime Combating and Investigation Division (SAP-CCID)	3,500	
ANC Department of Intelligence and Security (ANC-DIS)	800	
MK Military Intelligence	500	
TBV Intelligence Services	850	
Inkatha Freedom Party (IFP) Intelligence and Security	Unknown	
Pan-Africanist Security Services (PASS)	Unknown	16,650 Total
National Intelligence structures post-integration (as of 1 January 1995)		
National Intelligence Agency (NIA)	2,500	
South African Secret Service (SASS)	1,500	
SANDF Intelligence Division (SANDF-ID)	2,000	
SAPS National Crime Investigation Service (SAPS-NCIS)	500	
Others (including political organisations)	Unknown	6,500 Total

Source: Author interviews, Pretoria, 1995

Note
All figures are estimates.

Seegers notes that – while the existence and nature of the SASS, concerned with foreign intelligence and external dangers, is as to be expected in any modern state – the fact that, in the NIA, a domestic security intelligence service was created is "remarkable" and "ironic", given the tainted legacy of security intelligence work in South Africa's twentieth century history (the "subject of sustained and substantial criticism"). Seegers continues in noting that, given this history, the need for such an agency was never explained – especially alongside the 1996 National Crime Prevention Strategy which gave the new South African Police Service (SAPS) responsibilities for, amongst other things, domestic security and stability (through its Record of Understanding signed with the NIA, SASS and the SANDF Intelligence Division).[13] Therefore, was a civilian security intelligence service required? Conversely, given the police service's own deeply troubling history with security work under apartheid, should the SAPS have been given sole responsibility for security intelligence? It was this paradox which required the ANC-led government to be very careful in developing this tainted portfolio into the coming years; as would be seen over the following decade, however, this was not to be the case.

Generally, within the civilian services, Deputy Minister of Intelligence Joe Nhlanhla, the former head of the ANC-DIS, reported in late 1994 that the integration of these former enemies has gone ahead smoothly with little or no problems internally. This is partly due to the fact that included in the *Intelligence Services Act* was an invitation to all those who formerly worked for the above organisations to voluntarily *not join* the new agency; many took this option, either resigning or being asked to leave.[14] While many would have thought that the NIS should have been disbanded due to its links with the old order, many in the ANC argued for its retention due to a number of factors – the most important being the NIS's contribution to the compromises which led to the settlement between the government and the ANC, which evidenced a far more enlightened attitude than was the case in DMI or Security Branch. As well, the NIS possessed assets and capabilities that the ANC would not want to lose, including sources, information on both the white right-wing and extremists in parties such as the IFP, technological capabilities, and greater professional training than those in the ANC (see below).

The first head of the NIA was the former deputy head of the ANC Department of Intelligence and Security, Sizakele Sigxashe; while the first head of SASS was the former Director General of the NIS, M.J.M. (Mike) Louw.[15] Many of the former NIS department heads retained their positions, with the addition of the DIS and PASS personnel. The NIS's old structures – now divided between the two new agencies – were largely left intact through a mutual agreement reached between the NIS and ANC-DIS prior to the elections so that the "constant flow of intelligence should not be disrupted" in order to ensure "a balance between continuity and change".[16] This retention of senior personnel (not including those who voluntarily resigned) was mandated in section 2(b) of the *Intelligence Services Act*. Similarly, the principle of "effective management" was established to ensure that those serving at the upper management positions would be competent and not simply political appointees – it was, equally, intended that this would also prevent the disruption of the intelligence process by affirmative action programmes.[17] Subsequent events – up to and past 2005 – would call into question this principle, with the leadership of the NIA (particularly) increasingly politicised and pulled into the ANC's in-fighting over Mbeki's presidency and Zuma's succession in 2009.

The end of Security Branch and DMI

The former Crime Combating and Investigation Division of the South African Police, established in April 1991 with the merger of the SAP Security Branch and the Crime Investigation Division, was disbanded in July 1994. In its stead was created the South African Police Service National Crime Investigation Service (NCIS), solely concerned with crime intelligence and no longer with issues of national security. Further support for the institution of a democratic culture within SAPS started with the demilitarisation of its command structure, which began in July 1995, as well as the appointment of a civilian Ministerial Secretariat similar to the Defence Secretariat in the new SANDF structures. Finally, an Independent Complaints Directorate was established in late 1995 under civilian control independent from the SAPS and reporting directly to the Minister of Safety and Security and the Parliamentary Joint Standing Committee on Police Services, in consultation with the Secretary for Safety and Security and the National Police Commissioner.[18]

Within the new South African National Defence Force (SANDF), formed in April 1994 following the first universal election, the Intelligence Division was greatly downsized and brought under civilian oversight, remaining under the purview of the Defence Secretary (initially Pierre Steyn, responsible for the Steyn Commission under De Klerk). It included former members of DMI, MK intelligence, APLA intelligence, and the intelligence components of the defence forces of the Transkei, Bophutatswana, Venda, and Ciskei. Its role would be to provide advance-warning of potential military threats and instability through its collection of strategic military intelligence, thereby contributing not only towards defence planning and the conduct of operations, but as well to the concept of force multiplication, supporting generally low force levels normally. The *National Strategic Intelligence Act* also provided that, where the SANDF is deployed internally, the Intelligence Division could gather domestic intelligence in a covert manner only with the authorisation of the Chairperson of the National Intelligence Co-ordinating Committee (NICOC), acting with the concurrence of NICOC and Cabinet. Such covert collection would be limited to the geographical area and time-scale specified in the authorisation.[19] Ultimately, though, Defence Intelligence – like all other intelligence agencies – would be subject to accountability and oversight in the forms of the Parliamentary Joint Standing Committees on Defence and Intelligence, the Inspectors-General of the SANDF and Intelligence, and other mechanisms provided for in the new intelligence dispensation such as NICOC.

Oversight and accountability in the new dispensation

Executive/Cabinet responsibility for and co-ordination of intelligence

For accountability purposes, the civilian services were made directly responsible to the Office of the State President, originally through the Deputy Minister who reported to the Minister of Justice (although this was subsequently replaced by a Minister of Intelligence Services). In the case of Defence Intelligence and the NCIS, responsibility flows respectively through the SANDF Chief of Staff, Intelligence and the Defence Secretary in consultation with Minister of Defence, and the SAPS National Commissioner in consultation with the Minister of Safety and Security, and Secretary for Safety and Security to the President.

One of the legacies from apartheid for the national intelligence function was the retention of a national co-ordinating mechanism for intelligence and security. Rather than fully disband – and reject – the old SSC and NSMS structures (which had already undergone transformation under De Klerk, as noted in Chapter 8), the GNU decided to keep and reform the national co-ordinating structures, at both the national and provincial levels. While questions remained as to the need for such a system, it soon became apparent that the country's level of violent crime – including criminal violence, the "taxi wars" of the mid-1990s, and increasing politico-religious-criminal activities such as Muslim vigilantes in the Western Cape Province – and external infiltration (from illegal aliens mostly) meant that the GNU were concerned to retain the ability to share intelligence quickly across the national and provincial structures. A more cynical view would also say that once the ANC came into control of much of the apartheid national security apparatus, it was loathe to give it up – perceptively stuck in a similar world-view mind-set which had beset the securocrats at the time of the establishment of BOSS in the early 1970s. This was disputed by a senior ANC intelligence official involved in the transition, and characterised more as reflecting the former point within the need to avoid destabilising the intelligence dispensation unnecessarily through the transition, while – at the same time – garnering best practices from many countries globally, a pursuit which the TEC-SCI members certainly did.[20] In whichever case, the reforms to the old structures meant that a newly formed Cabinet Committee on Security and Intelligence (CCSI), in co-operation with other Cabinet committees, would direct security policy; within this structure (see Figure 9.1), it was plain from the transition of power that the securocrats had been removed and new individuals appointed at all managerial and ministerial levels by the GNU. Such a strong national security system was required to ensure co-ordination, accountability and the continuous flow of essential intelligence to the executive.

During the transition, as noted in Chapter 8, the Joint Co-ordinating Intelligence Committee of the TEC eventually gave way to the Heads of Combined Services (HOCS) Committee, which became the basis for the National Intelligence Co-ordinating Committee (NICOC). The JCIC had been authorised to oversee the co-ordination of the intelligence services, to investigate the activities of any service which appeared to contravene its mandate, and to provide intelligence information to the TEC and its other sub-councils; NICOC took on this same role – reporting to the President through the CCSI (which was chaired initially – during the GNU – by Executive Deputy President de Klerk)[21] and comprising the National Intelligence Co-ordinator, the Director General of each service (including the NCIS and Defence Intelligence) and, on an ad hoc basis, the Inspectors-General, the Deputy Directors of each services, and Parliamentary representatives.[22] NICOC was also responsible for periodic intelligence assessments including the National Intelligence Estimates and the National Intelligence Priorities; in addition, it now operates the National Early Warning Centre to anticipate threats, with growing links to Regional and Continental Early Warning Centres in Gabarone and Addis Abba respectively.[23]

In addition to these formalised structures of co-ordination, a number of agreements were reached between the security services on sharing intelligence in pursuit of domestic security issues. The most important of these initially was a memorandum of understanding concluded between SAPS, the NIA, SASS and the SANDF on 10 May 1996, which aimed to ensure the sharing of information relating to combating organised crime. Included in the memorandum was a provision to establish a National Management Forum attached to NICOC, to co-ordinate the anti-crime strategy between the security agencies.[24]

Similar to NICOC, Provincial Intelligence Co-ordinating Committees (PICOCs) – chaired by provincial co-ordinators – were created at the provincial level. Used largely for policy and strategic co-ordination – as opposed to operations (as had been the case with the NSMS JMCs) – the PICOCs were terminated in 2004. Nevertheless, in conjunction with the position of the provincial Members of Executive Councils (MECs) for Safety and Security, and Provincial Secretariats for Safety and Security co-ordinating and overseeing SAPS activities at the provincial level, a clear security structure emerged. Therefore, while by 1996 it was clear that although the apartheid-era policies had obviously changed, in practice – and as agreed in the TEC-SCI debates – many of the legacy structures and national security management processes from the apartheid era were simply modified to fit

Figure 9.1 RSA Intelligence structures (1996).

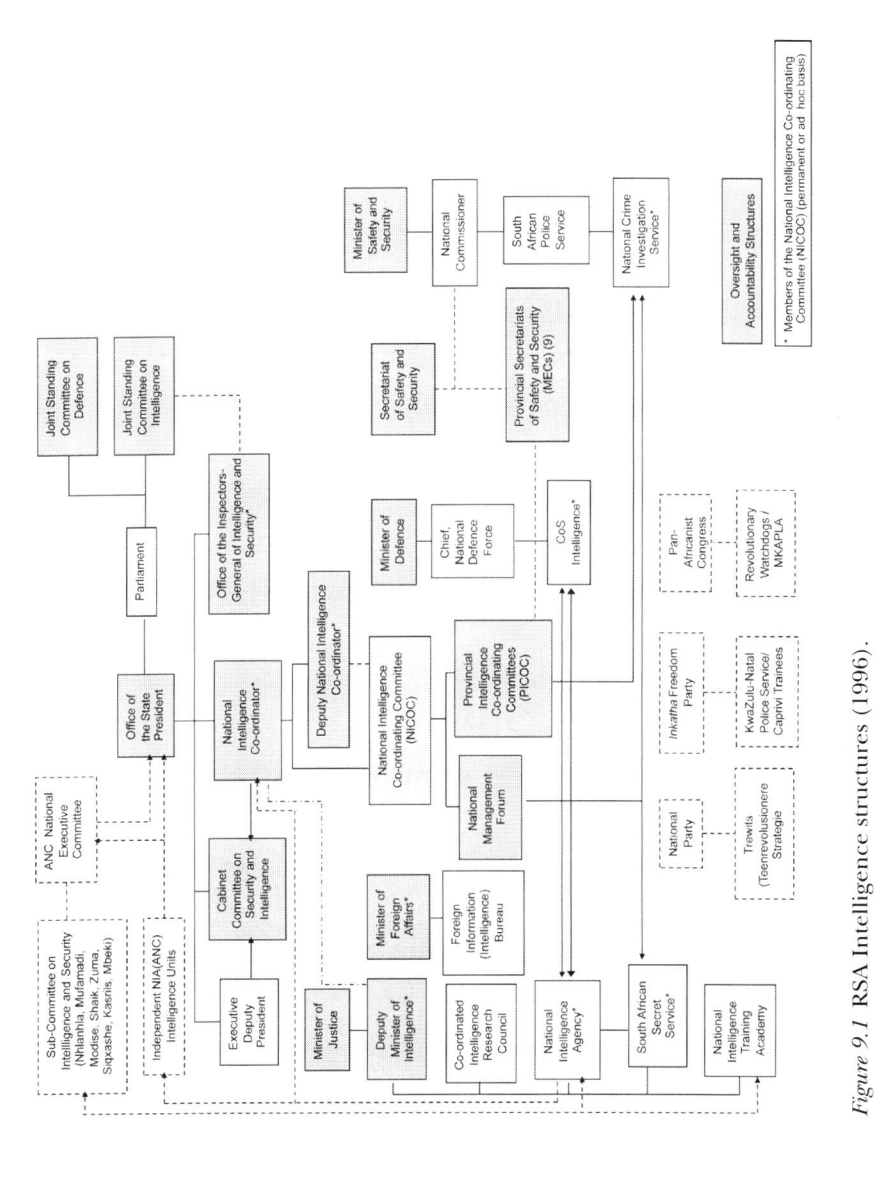

214 *Progress and problems*

the post-apartheid requirements of South Africa. This was most notable in, effectively, the continuation of an SSC-like capability in the CCSI and the NICOC structures – regardless of the dramatically different focus the apartheid-era SSC had (on countering dissent and liberation efforts while upholding apartheid) compared with the post-1994 structures (on stabilising the country against increasingly criminal violence and other sources of instability, themselves a type of insurgency against the government).

Finally, a further mechanism for such co-ordination, but outside of the formal chain of responsibility, was established through the appointment of an advisory aboard for the Directors General of both the NIA and SASS as mandated in section 31 of the *Intelligence Services Act*. The function of these bodies was noted as advising the Directors General on the use of their powers.[25]

Parliamentary oversight of intelligence

Within Parliament, an oversight committee was established in September 1995. Similar to the Canadian Security Intelligence Review Committee (SIRC) in its functions,[26] the role of the Joint Standing Committee on Intelligence (JSCI) is to receive reports of the services from both the auditors and other evaluators of the services, make recommendations on both legislation related to the services and the activities of the services themselves, and to order investigations and hold hearings on matters relating to intelligence and national security. It is also responsible for monitoring the activities of the services with a regard for human rights and other rights entrenched in the Constitution. Its jurisdiction covers not just the NIA and SASS, but also Defence Intelligence and the NCIS; it reports directly to the President, and through him to Parliament.[27]

This committee was seen as one of the most significant changes in Parliament following the 1994 elections. In the apartheid Parliament, committees were closed to the media and to the public – their proceedings were secret and their decisions were publicly disclosed only after they had been taken. In the democratic Parliament, however, all but the JSCI are held in the open, with journalists reporting on their proceedings and decisions, and the public, including advocacy and monitoring groups, are entitled to attend hearings.[28] While the JSCI hearings are not public, this overall move towards openness and transparency is remarkable nonetheless.

The committee's mandate is quite broad and intrusive. Although section 4 of the *Intelligence Services Control Act* authorises the committee access to any and all information that it may require in its investigations and duties,[29] the same section also authorises the services to withhold from the committee information on any person or body engaged in intelligence or counter-intelligence activities, information which could reveal the identity of a source, or any knowledge of intelligence or counter-intelligence methods carried out by any service if that information could also reveal a source.[30] This absolute protection of sources is one of the key political compromises that led to this point: as both sides prior to the 1994 elections engaged in espionage activities against the other, it is assumed that each side had (and may have continued to maintain) sources in the other camp. Thus, any revelations regarding the nature of sources at this point in time could have greatly damaged the negotiated compromise achieved within the services themselves.[31]

The committee was originally composed of 18 members appointed by the President, proportionally representative to the seating of the various parties in Parliament. Subsequent legislation led to a change in the numbers and composition of the committee to be more proportionally representative of Parliament,[32] while demanding that all members received security clearance from the NIA.[33] Questions were raised early on, however, on the sanctity of the committee's secrecy, given that a number of parties sitting on the committee were deeply implicated (to varying degrees) in allegations of links to "third-force" and other destabilising activities aimed at the new democratic process; this was especially the case with Deputy Minister of Safety and Security Joe Matthews, the *Inkatha Freedom Party* (IFP) representative on the JSCI, who was closely linked with IFP attempts at resurrecting their intelligence capacity.[34]

A welcome move was also the requirement for the committee to

> Within two months after 31 March in each year, table in Parliament a report on the activities of the Committee during the preceding year, together with the findings made by it and the recommendations it deems appropriate, and provide a copy thereof to the President and the Minister responsible for each Service.

It was furthermore required to "furnish Parliament, the President or such Minister with a special report concerning any matter relating to the performance of its functions".[35]

Inspectors-General of the intelligence services

At the same time, the *Intelligence Services Control Act* created the position of Inspectors-General for the services (NIA, SASS, Defence Intelligence, NCIS), to whom the Director General of each service is accountable. The functions of the Inspectors-General are to review the activities of the intelligence services and to monitor their compliance with policy guidelines and other established mandates and principles. They must be allowed full access to documents, budgets, reports, and all other classified information; each Director General is mandated to ensure that all matters of interest and concern having to do with the services is brought to the immediate attention of the Inspectors-General.[36]

The first Inspector-General to be appointed was Lewis Skweyiya, a former advocate and the commissioner who looked into corruption in the former homeland of Bophutatswana; however, upon reflection, he decided that the remuneration offered was too low.[37] In mid-2000, the JSCI confirmed Fazel Randera, a former Truth and Reconciliation commissioner, to be the IG; however, he only served for six months (he was appointed in May 2000 but was only officially sworn in June 2001) before being appointed as the health adviser of the Chamber of Mines.[38] In February 2004, a new IG – Zola Ngcakani – was appointed finally to the office by President Mbeki – a worrying sign overall, given that in the previous nine years of the new intelligence dispensation, the post had only been occupied twice briefly, with each incumbent resigning soon after taking office.[39] This, in addition to the continued "tinkering" with the mandate and role of the IG in the legislation (see below), would appear to indicate a serious concern over this one key – indeed, crucial – area of oversight.[40]

A code of conduct for the intelligence services

Further, a Code of Conduct was written into the *Intelligence Services Act* as an additional mechanism of oversight and accountability. This code emerged out of discussions between the NIS and ANC-DIS in which the ANC wanted detailed guidelines with real regulatory powers which spelled out the rights of operatives, how to handle sources, etc. The NIS argued that this would make intelligence work extremely difficult, possibly even endangering operations and agents; it wanted a code which would bind agents as little as possible.[41] The compromise, written into the purview of the minister responsible for the intelligence brief, became the Code of Conduct. It includes provisions that all members of the secret services shall adhere to the basic principles of their profession, as well as the policies, regulations and directives of their respective services; shall respect the norms, values, and principles of a democratic society including the basic human rights of individuals; shall strive to be responsible in the handling of information and intelligence, and shall at all costs prevent the wrongful disclosure of national security interests; shall commit themselves to the promotion of mutual trust between policy-makers and professional intelligence workers, as well as co-operation with all the members of the intelligence community; and will conduct themselves in their personal life in a manner which will not prejudice their organisation, their profession and fellow craftsmen, or the facilities entrusted to them.[42] Breaches of this code and other guidelines were laid out very specifically in the *Intelligence Services Act*;[43] should violations or misconduct occur, the Director General of each service is mandated with presidential authority to "charge any member with misconduct", to establish a board of enquiry following an unsatisfactory explanation from the individual in question, and to sentence that individual should they be found guilty; these powers could be used-extra-territorially should the offence occur outside of South Africa's borders but still fall under the purview of the *Intelligence Service Act*.[44] Finally, the Code had the function of authorising intelligence officers to disobey any orders which contravened either the Code or other statutes on operational capabilities.[45]

Finally, the Auditor-General and the Standing Committee on Public Accounts monitor the relevant intelligence budgets, while the Constitution provides for protection against state abuse through the public prosecutor and the Human Rights Commission.[46]

Integration issues

While the integration of the previous services proceeded, a number of key concerns began to emerge – some of them falling-out of the integration process itself, while others related to the legacy of both apartheid's counter-revolutionary war and the negotiations process of the early 1990s. Initially, there were concerns voiced by the now-President Mandela that the intelligence services had not been achieving their full capability with regard to their duties and functions; however, as Nhlanhla pointed out in October 1995, this was largely due to the fact that the vast majority of the services' energies and resources had been dedicated to ensuring a successful transformation through training and reorientation programmes run throughout 1995. Now that this process had been achieved, Nhlanhla maintained, the services would be able to direct their fullest attention to fulfilling their mandates.[47] This would prove optimistic.

Another major issue of concern – quite legitimately – was that, should the intelligence professionals who had served the apartheid state for many years be forced from their positions either through prosecution or restructuring processes, they might have turned on the new state; this was no ethereal threat but a stark one as evidenced by the suspected "Third Force" violence already noted. Equally, and directly related to this, was the dramatic growth in the private intelligence sector (as noted in Chapter 8), manned heavily by many of the former covert operators who were not only suspected of fomenting the "Third Force" violence but also retained ties into the new intelligence structures.

Another issue of concern was the fact that there were a number of individuals from the past included in the new intelligence structures who have caused concern by their position. The most obvious of these was Dirk Coetzee, the former commander of Vlakplaas who had defected to the ANC in 1989. Coetzee, who had confessed to numerous assassinations, murders, bombings and the direction of acts of political violence, was appointed as the director of Counter-Terrorism for the NIA through the mid-to-late 1990s. When confronted with this fact and questions regarding its ethical implications, Nhlanhla stated that "[the NIA] has no problem with people who had been involved in murders working for the NIA".[48] Other individuals who were similarly reported to be employed by the NIA include Chappies Klopper, Willie Nortje and Brood van Heerden, all of whom formerly worked for Eugene De Kock at Vlakplaas. There was also evidence that, as late as 1993, the ANC-DIS still employed personnel found guilty of human rights abuses and even murder in the ANC bases in Angola and elsewhere;[49] whether or not these individuals were taken into the new agencies is unclear, but it is hoped that through the bipartisan vetting process carried out between 1994 and 1995 they were prohibited from joining the new structures. This has raised further concerns that all may not be right with the new structures.

This was not, however, an issue germane to South Africa's transition alone – as Adams has pointed out, in discussing the post-Cold War evolution of intelligence structures internationally (as noted above),

> [Within the new intelligence structures internationally,] by and large the old institutions have simply evolved to absorb the new roles assigned to them. This is hardly surprising. No bureaucracy yields power willingly and few democratic countries have policy makers with sufficient courage and muscle to force through revolutionary change. What has been striking about the reform process [is that it] has largely been organised from within.[50]

In many senses, this points to the professional character of intelligence personnel – even in previously autocratic or totalitarian regimes – in following along with the changes in the political arena to serve the political dispensation of the day. This attitude was reflected generally in the decisions of the individuals tasked with co-ordinating the new intelligence dispensation in South Africa.

At the same time, a more insidious concern existed within the ANC which many believe prevented it from being too destructive of the old NIS structures and personnel, should it have wanted to. While not stated openly, the NIS also possessed information of great interest to the ANC: information on the ANC itself, its leaders and cadres, which it accrued through the placement of "moles" and other penetration exercises into the ANC and PAC ranks. An extremely contentious and heated issue, when this issue was tabled during the TEC negotiations, it was decided to leave the issue aside for the time being, as both sides had informers within each other's ranks, and the launching of mole-hunts could have been extremely detrimental to the success of the transition – indeed, by loosing this information, the NIS could have inflicted considerable damage on the Government of National Unity.[51] The issue would not, unsurprisingly, go away, and finally came to a head in 1997, when the ANC insisted that such individuals had to be revealed. There is evidence that President Mandela was informed in 1994 that up to five senior ANC officials had worked for the apartheid government as informers. However, initially, only one of these was revealed: a senior member of the ANC administration in KwaZulu-Natal province, who was summarily expelled from the party. Ultimately, the issue would remain an extremely contentious one – with continuing rumours and suspicions swirling around then-President Thabo Mbeki in 2000 and again in 2003 (including rumours of coup attempts against him), as well as growing tensions within the post-apartheid security apparatus and political leadership – ultimately resulting in Mbeki appointing the Hefer Commission to investigate these accusations. The fall-out from Hefer would see Mbeki resign from the presidency and corruption charges against Jacob Zuma quashed, clearing the way for him to become President.[52]

As noted above, training and professional standards – in a community resulting from the integration of personnel from different backgrounds – were also an issue considered by the TEC-SCI. It was clear that there were different professional standards and backgrounds to each side – NIS and ANC-DIS, primarily – within the newly integrated civilian services. While the NIS had been – at least, structurally and procedurally – developed and trained largely according to Western norms and practices, it was also a key player in the SSC, KIK and NSMS structures governing the counter-revolutionary warfare campaign against the liberation movements. As noted in previous chapters, it failed – perhaps not as badly as DMI, but nonetheless – to provide objective intelligence assessments, and suffered from an amateur's approach to intelligence in far too many instances. Nevertheless, its origins – in RI and BOSS, and their origins and links to the British and American intelligence services – did provide it with a Western-style intelligence outlook. The ANC-DIS (and PASS) was trained primarily by the KGB and GRU, the Cuban DGI, Libyan intelligence, and even the East German SSD (or *Stasi*) – inevitably, this training was suffused with an ideological fervour based on the socialist/communist politics of most members, which was reflected in the ANC's and SACP's numerous statements at its congresses, councils and other public outlets. While the NIS was instilled – somewhat – with a sense of evolutionary reform during the 1980s, which as this study has noted has to be treated with a degree of cynicism – the ANC-DIS were being taught methods of intelligence by the KGB and SSD, which other studies have long held were successful at operational tradecraft (which would prove most useful – for example – in Operations BIBLE and "VULA") but very poor at intelligence analysis and assessment.[53] Indeed, Trewhela – a former SACP and MK member who served prison-time in South Africa – has himself noted that "the training of the ANC security apparatus by [the KGB] and [the *Stasi*]" involved applying "the methods of East European Stalinism within the ANC's [security apparatus and camps in exile]"[54] – an influence which impacted not only on the approach to security and counter-intelligence by the ANC (as discussed in Chapter 4) but also on the political outlook and democratic tendencies of the ANC/SACP leaders, even long after the transition from apartheid.

This is not to say – to any degree – that the ANC-DIS did not develop new visions of intelligence: the new structures, the philosophy of intelligence and other statements and initiatives by the ANC-DIS leaders in the transition period of the SCI clearly demonstrated an evolutionary understanding of the changing nature of intelligence in the modern world, and its application to South Africa's unique problems. What is at question is that both of these roles often led to a complete intolerance for dissenting views from those held by the apartheid or ANC leadership respectively, and gave an ideological character to – for the former – the internal activities of the apartheid security services against white liberals, liberation groups, and other dissenters; and – for the latter – the periodic purges carried out within the ANC and SACP, alongside the oft-times totalitarian, brutal approaches to counter-espionage within their ranks and camps in exile.[55]

Therefore, it is not so much the coming together of these former enemies that is the issue, but a successful and effective synthesis of their operational and training backgrounds. As a former senior ANC-DIS and MK intelligence leader noted to the author in 2008, this issue had been noted early in the transition, but that the "slippage of time since 1994" meant that those integrated initially from different backgrounds would, over time, develop new common standards, reference-points and professional capabilities – especially as the older generation retired and newer members moved into the agencies.[56] Like any such situation – now almost a generation beyond the transition and integration point – time will tell whether this is, in fact, the case, or whether the continuing troubles faced by the modern intelligence dispensation (see below) are a symptom or a cause of such challenges in the integration process.

Still searching – the Truth and Reconciliation Commission

As the new intelligence dispensation was being developed, a series of politically charged processes were underway which would – culturally, if not legally – affect the process of both building a cohesive intelligence community in the post-apartheid era "at peace with itself", as Louw had noted previously, and test the commitment of the ANC-led Government of National Unity to transparency, accountability and anti-corruption in the public service. These processes included centrally several criminal prosecutions of former apartheid-era security force commanders and foot-soldiers – such as former Defence Minister Magnus Malan, former Vlakplaas commander Eugene de Kock, former CCB hitman Ferdi Barnard, and former police commanders Jac Cronjé and Nick van Rensburg – and the establishment of the Truth and Reconciliation Commission (TRC) by the GNU on 19 July 1995, under the rubric of section 2(1) of the *Promotion of National Unity and Reconciliation Act* (Act 34 of 1995). Originally mandated to look into the activities and alleged crimes of the security forces under the apartheid regime, pressure from now-Deputy President de Klerk on the commission to include the activities of ANC/SACP security forces in exile – MK and NAT – both within the ANC camps in the Frontline States, and in MK operations throughout Southern Africa, as well as those of the PAC's armed wing the Azanian Peoples Liberation Army (APLA) meant that these were added to the commission's purview.[57]

While these trials will not be noted here,[58] the TRC had a dramatic effect on both South Africa's approach to societal reconciliation, and attempts to build a "post-racial" security establishment where the successful integration of the security forces (both apartheid-era and liberation movement) hung heavily on a number of very sensitive topics, including the admission of guilt for gross human rights violations by both sides, the end of debates surrounding the "moles" that each side placed within the opposing security apparatus, and the acceptance that recognising such atrocities and violations by both the victims and the perpetrators would mean moving-ahead in building the new country. In this sense, the TRC was a "commission of inquiry" of a different shade to the others noted throughout this book (e.g. Potgieter, Koetsee, Harms, Goldstone) – while its mandate was to investigate the past, rather than assess the workings of the present intelligence dispensation, its deliberations and outcomes would inevitably have an effect on the present. In the end, its final reports recounted the story of the apartheid state's covert and murderous war against its liberation movements, predicated on thousands of amnesty applications and hearings into gross human rights violations.

The TRC would never achieve what was hoped of it – not the least of which due to, on the one hand, the extremely poor quality of the submissions by the apartheid-era political and security force leaders, which were criticised severely by the TRC; and, on the other hand, the ANC's oft-times antagonistic attitude towards the TRC. In terms of the former, while more than 7,700 lower-level security force members – as well as some very high-profile ones such as De Kock – applied for amnesty for a wide-range of acts (along with thousands from the township anti-apartheid United Democratic Front movement and the Zulu-based *Inkatha* movement),[59] almost no senior apartheid political or security force leader applied for amnesty or testified to the TRC's hearings, by-and-large refusing to accept full responsibility for the activities of their security forces during the apartheid era; instead, they blamed "transgressions" on the perpetrators and insisted that no orders were given, for example, to carry out assassinations of apartheid's opponents.[60]

In terms of the latter, many ANC officials said publicly that they viewed the TRC as a forum for apartheid perpetrators to come forward, not the least of which because the ANC had been fighting a "just war of liberation" which justified any and all activities which had been carried-out in this time period;[61] as such, very few of its members pressed to apply for amnesty individually, while the ANC leadership claimed "collective responsibility" for its actions in exile.[62] Many observers did not agree, and criticized the ANC for taking such a self-righteous stance on an issue that could prove so divisive to peace in South Africa.[63] At the same time, the ANC maintained that it had no need to participate in the process, as it had held its own internal "commissions of inquiry" (most recently, the 1990 Montsuenyane Commission) to deal with alleged human rights violations in its camps in Angola, Zambia, Tanzania and Uganda.[64] This initial refusal by the ANC was rejected and criticised severely by Archbishop Desmond Tutu, the chair of the TRC, which tainted severely the sense that the TRC was balanced between all sides in the anti-apartheid conflict; after much politicking, the ANC quietly agreed to send its members amnesty applications and requested that those who felt the need to do so should apply for amnesty.[65]

Generally, the TRC achieved a notable success: it brought South Africans, of all races and backgrounds generally, to accept that the past must be confronted in a manner in which the future could be built. However, in terms of the more direct success of the commission – such an achievement as being able to conclusively state that all the graves had been uncovered, all the ghosts confronted, and all the actions known – remained beyond its grasp, and probably always would so be. The downside of this process was also that, in its early days, it was heralded as the solution to the nation's problems, but as time passed, participants and observers alike realised that this was not the case: many South Africans, faced with the world's highest crime levels, began to ask why resources and attention were being spent on the past, when the challenges of the present were so significant. Ultimately, the TRC achieved what it could – a degree of truth and a degree of reconciliation – while forcing to the surface a much greater understanding of past atrocities and policies; no process, it would seem, would ever provide a complete picture.

Tinkering with the system: further steps 1998–2005

While the new dispensation introduced in 1994–1995 looked great on paper, its implementation proved somewhat more problematic. Inter- and intra-party politics, corruption, factionalism, the politicisation of the intelligence structures, and other factors – such as the failure to secure a permanent Inspector-General of the Intelligence Services – combined to show the new South African intelligence services, and their ministerial governance, in negative light.

A series of high-profile scandals did not improve the situation – which was further worsened by allegations that the two main services, the NIA and SASS, were virtually unable to fulfil their missions due to internal factionalism and incapable analysts and managers. By the turn of the century, the now-ANC-run South African government was forced to introduce a further raft of legislation to modify or enhance the 1994–1995 legislation to take into account these "growing pains".

In the regards noted above, it was hoped that – through combining constitutional entrenchment of the intelligence dispensation with a revised legislative mandate, newly rigorous oversight mechanisms in the JSCI and the Inspectors-General (at least, on paper), a ban on domestic covert actions to avoid a return to the horrors of the past, and the efforts of the TRC – progress on moving ahead smoothly with the new intelligence dispensation would be a cornerstone in building a new country. Unfortunately, and for a number of reasons, this was not to be.

Reshaping the intelligence dispensation

While the focus here is not on the day-to-day activities of South Africa's intelligence services, suffice it to say that between 1994 and 1996, the new dispensation encountered many serious problems – both externally and internally (see examples below).[66] To determine what adjustments were required in the system, Deputy Minister Nhlanhla established the Pikoli Review Commission in 1996, to review progress and make recommendations for changes. The commission reviewed the intelligence services and wider dispensation for its organisational form and content; functions and allocation and utilisation of resources; personnel, team-building and co-operation within the intelligence community; and capacity to fulfil functions. As a result, between 1998 and 2005, several amending Acts were passed by Parliament with a variety of aims, including structural reformation (see Figure 9.2).

The first, the *Intelligence Services Control Amendment Act* (Act 42 of 1999) updated the *Intelligence Services Control Act* to clarify the composition of the JSCI, and to change the number of Inspectors-General to one. This Act was followed in 2002 by a second *Intelligence Services Control Amendment Act* (Act 66 of 2002) which further solidified and tightened the roles of the JSCI, the Inspector-General and created the Minister of Intelligence Services; crucially, this new Act also mandated that each Service submit an annual report to the Minister and the Inspector-General which outlined the "activities of that Service during that period" as well as reporting on "any unlawful intelligence activity or significant intelligence failure of that Service and any corrective action that has been taken or is intended to be taken in connection with such activity or failure".[67] In the Act, the JSCI's oversight purview was expanded from "intelligence and counter-intelligence functions" to now include "the administration, financial management and expenditure of the Services".[68] In addition, the committee was also authorised to

> For the purposes of the performance of its functions, require Minister responsible for a Service, the Head of a Service, the CEO or the

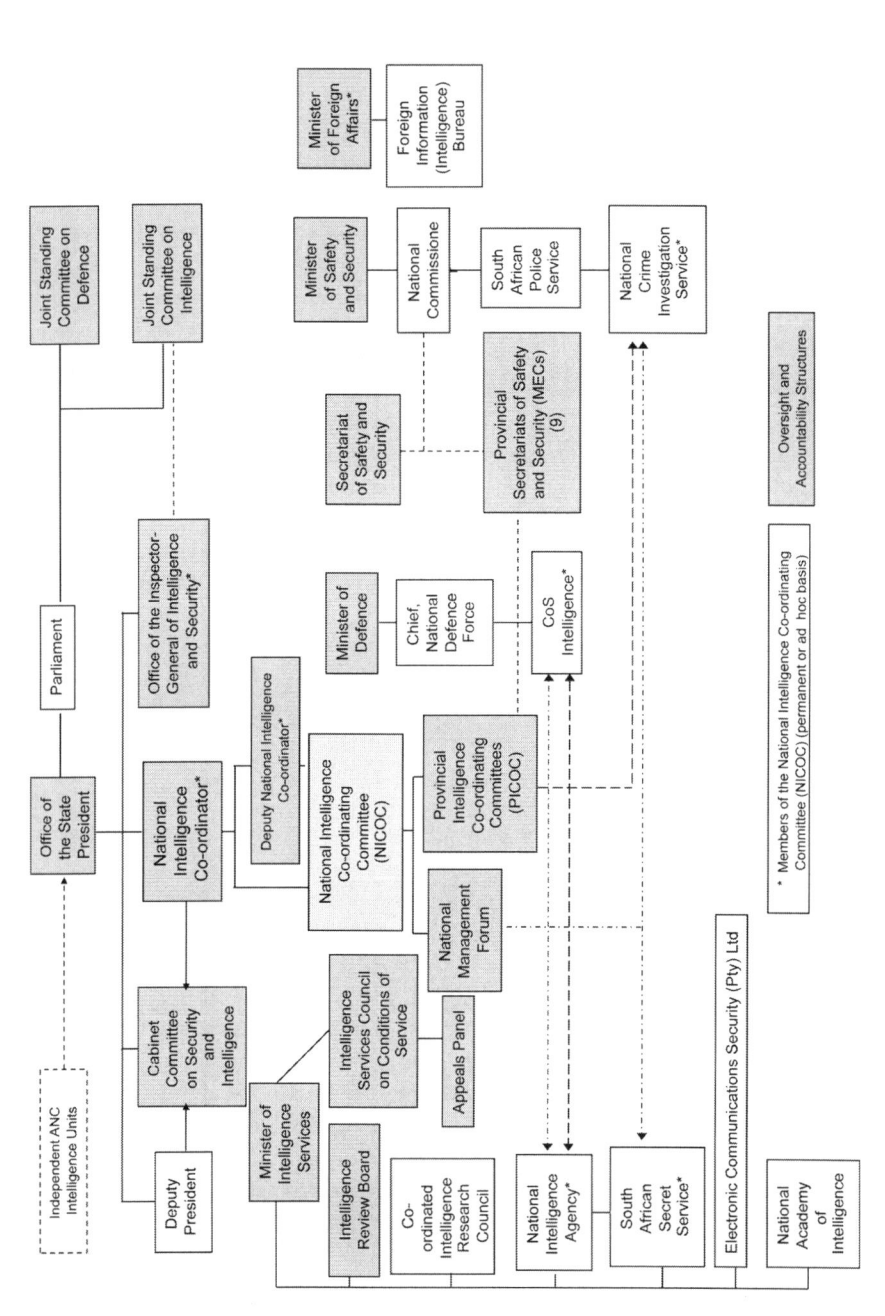

Figure 9.2 RSA Intelligence structures (2003).

Inspector-General, to appear before it to give evidence, to produce any document or thing and answer.[69]

The role of the IG changed further with subsequent legislation: first, in a serious change from the previous, the 1999 Act stated that there would now be "one or more Inspectors-General of Intelligence", rather than the previous dictate of "for each Service an Inspector-General".[70] It also stipulated that the IG could be approved by "at least two-thirds" of the members, rather than the previous "majority of at least 75 per cent" – relating clearly to the failures to appoint an IG successfully.[71] The IG's purview was also expanded in section 6 of the Act as being

> To receive and investigate complaints from members of the public and members of the Services on alleged maladministration, abuse of power, transgressions of the laws and policies referred to in paragraph *(a)*, corruption and the improper enrichment of any person through an act or omission of any member.[72]

In relation to this, it was stipulated that an IG

> Shall have access to any intelligence, information or premises under the control of the Service in respect of which he or she has been appointed ... No access to intelligence, information or premises ... may be withheld from an Inspector-General on any ground.[73]

These problems were thrown into an even starker light when the subsequent 2002 Act deemed that there should only be one Inspector-General of Intelligence – once again pointing to the difficulty in appointing even one, let alone multiple IGs. The IG's overall mandate was again expanded:

> *(a)* to monitor compliance by Service with the Constitution, applicable laws and relevant policies on intelligence and counter-intelligence; *(b)* to review the intelligence and counter-intelligence activities of any Service; *(c)* to perform all functions designated to him or her by the President or Minister responsible for a Service.[74]

In addition, the complaint mechanism from the public was strengthened and the IG's mandate was expanded to also include this capability.[75] Finally, the IG also now had submit "certificates ... [and] reports" to both the Minister and the committee pursuant to their functions; this was reflected, for the heads of services, in the requirement that they now must

> In respect of every period of 12 months or such lesser period as is specified by the Minister responsible for that Service, submit to that Minister a report on the activities of that Service during that period,

and shall cause a copy of such report to be submitted to the Inspector-General.[76]

Furthermore,

> Each Head of a Service shall report to the Inspector-General regarding any unlawful intelligence activity or significant intelligence failure of that Service and any corrective action that has been taken or is intended to be taken in connection with such activity or failure.[77]

Other new Acts passed included the *National Strategic Intelligence Amendment Act* (Act 67 of 2002), which further amended the 1994 *National Strategic Intelligence Act* so as to exclude the Minister as a member of NICOC; to redefine counter-intelligence; to provide for security-screening by the relevant members of the national intelligence structures; and to clarify the Minister's role in being responsible for "advis[ing] the President and the national executive on national strategic intelligence and co-ordination of intelligence". In addition, the *General Intelligence Law Amendment Act* (Act 66 of 2000) focused on labour relations, retirement and salary stipulations for employees, and established an Intelligence Review Board mandated to "consider and approve any application by a former member to disclose information or material" relating to their former employ, thus ensuring that a statutory body would be in-place to consider how former employees used their knowledge gained during their employ with the intelligence services.[78] A new *Intelligence Services Act* (Act 65 of 2002) revisited and rewrote significant parts of the 1994 *Intelligence Services Act* – establishing a National Academy of Intelligence[79] and an Intelligence Services Council on Conditions of Service.[80] It also established clearly the powers of the Minister of Intelligence Services,[81] and proposed "Offences" for all employees of the intelligence services.[82]

Signals intelligence and electronics security

The 2002 *Intelligence Services Control Amendment Act* also placed the Electronic Communications Security (Pty) Ltd – established under the *Electronic Communications Security (Pty) Ltd Act* (Act 68 of 2002), supporting the National Communications Centre and providing the government with a communications-security capability – on a statutory footing within the wider intelligence dispensation.[83] The creation of "Comsec" (as the ECS(P)L is referred to in the Act) was a significant step forward, as it both created a stand-alone body responsible for signals intelligence (previously the domain of DMI) and – somewhat oddly – created that body as a private company, subject to Parliamentary and ministerial oversight. It is governed – under ministerial direction – by a board and a CEO.[84] While its focus was mandated as being to "provide electronic communications security products and services to organs of state" – much like Britain's Communications-Electronics Security Group (CESG) – it also has a mandate to "perform any other function not inconsistent with this Act that is necessary for the effective functioning of Comsec".[85]

Finally, in 2003, an additional *General Intelligence Laws Amendment Act* (Act 52 of 2003) was tabled, which – amongst other things – regulates the interception and monitoring of communications (further to the *Regulation of Interception of Communications and Provision of Communication-related Information Act* – Act 70 of 2002, which itself saw an update tabled in 2006), in particular by the newly established National Communications Centre (NCC) and its Office for Interception Centres (OIC), responsible for signals intelligence and the interception of communications;[86] established an Appeals Panel process responsible to the Minister of Intelligence Services;[87] and – most importantly – further supports the Intelligence Services Council, answerable to the Minister and the President, "to promote measures and set standards to ensure the effective and efficient performance and implementation of policies on human resources within the Academy or the Intelligence Services, as the case may be, and to make recommendations to the minister".[88]

Postscript: Indeed, another country? The ANC's politicisation of intelligence

It is clear that these new intelligence structures were the product of great negotiation and discussion; yet – by the first decade of this century – the efforts at achieving a balanced, transparent, accountable and legitimate (in every sense) new intelligence dispensation appeared to be coming apart. Indeed, it is wholly questionable whether the intentions and aspirations laid-out in those negotiations can now – in hindsight and 15 years after the transformation began – have been met, or whether a new disease of corruption (once again, in every sense) has crept into the post-apartheid intelligence dispensation.

Over the course of the mid-to-late 1990s, South African intelligence suffered from numerous scandals – including accusations of different political parties "bugging" each other; the ANC using the NIA to spy not only on political opposition parties but also on the SAPS leadership – wholly illegal under the Constitution; spying on friendly governments' diplomatic missions; the unlawful and suspicious deaths of at least two leading intelligence figures; allegations of collusion with the so-called "third force" of former apartheid and former ANC intelligence and special forces operatives engaged in destabilising the country (making – as some referred to it – a "Fourth Force"); of collusion with the country's top bank-robbers, themselves alleged to be former members of an MK Special Operations unit; and other scandals.

While there are many pressing problems that must be addressed at the operational and management levels of the services, the outright politicisation of the leadership of the intelligence services – in terms of the appointments of tainted-but-loyal ANC officials parachuted into key positions in the upper-management of the intelligence services and architecture; of the un-Constitutional role that these leaders have then played in either supporting or undermining different political leaders within the ANC; and of the development of parallel (political) intelligence structures, a serious problem first identified at the time that the transformation of the intelligence dispensation was fully underway (the mid-to-late 1990s) – would appear to be the greatest of all on-going concerns.[89]

These serious concerns have continued well past 2005 and into Jacob Zuma's presidency; indeed, the role played by corrupt intelligence leaders in Zuma's rise and accession to both the ANC leadership and the state presidency is perhaps the worst indictment of these services' independence and accountability to the public yet.[90] To qualify this issue, however, it must be noted that this was driven – in part – by fears that there were far too many "old guard" members of the intelligence services actively pursuing a process of undermining and destabilising the ANC's push for transformation. This was exemplified starkly in the so-called "McBride Affair" of 1998 which surrounded allegations made by then-Chief of the SANDF Georg Meiring that a coup was being plotted against Mandela's presidency from within the ANC, allegations that proved to be so false as to lead to Meiring's resignation and further transformative measures for the Intelligence Division of the SANDF (believed to have been behind the disinformation campaign) in the form of a commission of inquiry into Transforming Defence Intelligence – which would follow the same direction as the 1997 Pikoli Commission (as noted) which investigated the civilian intelligence services in the same manner following a number of scandals.[91] Nevertheless, while elements such as these purported destabilisation efforts by the "old guard" contributed to the ANC's push for a loyal intelligence community, they were not the main ones.

As mandated in the 1994 *Intelligence Services Act*, the Directors General of each agency are responsible for ensuring not only that all national security intelligence, collection methods, sources and the identity of members are protected to the fullest extent from unauthorised disclosure, but as well to ensure that

> No action is carried out that could give rise to any reasonable suspicion that the Agency or Service ... is concerned in furthering, protecting or undermining the interests of any section of the population or any political party or organisation.[92]

Therefore, this clear politicisation is extremely troubling, coming as it does around a capability – intelligence and security – which remains highly sensitive in light of both the state's history and its very nature, and a highly powerful tool (or weapon) to wield against opponents should a political leader so choose to.

One of the reasons behind this continuing sickness within South Africa's intelligence services has been the on-going failure to secure all the instruments of oversight – in terms of ensuring proper public loyalty (via the Constitution and the laws of the country, as well as through an effective Parliamentary oversight body – the JSCI, by all accounts, not being that) while depoliticising the services' roles in society. In reflecting on the activities and attitudes of the ANC's former *Mbokodo* security unit, and the Stalinist counter-intelligence-led outlook which drove it, against the manner in which "intelligence" – as both institution and process – is used today as a political instrument, as noted here, an unfortunate line of continuity can be drawn. All of this means that South Africa's intelligence services are very much in crisis – and show little sign of recovery.

In recognition that things were going very badly wrong – and triggered specifically by yet another scandal, this time surrounding the then-head of the NIA, Billy Masethla, and his firing for criminal activities[93] – in 2006, then-Minister of Intelligence Ronnie Kasrils struck the Ministerial Review Commission on Intelligence under Joe Matthews. The Matthews Commission noted many of the concerns covered in this chapter, and concluded – starkly, in light of the concerns noted above about whether South Africa should even have a domestic security intelligence service, given the politicised past of such a function – that the NIA was "politicised" and maintained an "inappropriate focus on political activities", with the mixing of the NIA's covert intelligence capabilities and its role in "monitoring and reporting on transformation within government departments, on competition within and between political parties and on the impact of political policy decisions" considered to be "very troubling". This was significantly due to the fact that the NIA's mandate under the 1994 *National Strategic Intelligence Act* – and especially those elements encompassing its role in providing political intelligence, counter-intelligence (especially where "subversion, treason and sabotage" were concerned), and departmental intelligence (under its responsibilities for monitoring transformation across South Africa's government departments) – was "too broad and open to interpretation ... impractical and unnecessary".[94] While outside of this study's timeline, it is instructive to note that the commission's report provided many concrete and hard-hitting recommendations on cleaning-up and improving the intelligence dispensation – especially those elements concerning the elimination of corruption and misuse in the intelligence services, the primary *raison d'être* for the commission in the first place, including the transparency, oversight, non-politicisation and public accountability of the intelligence services. These do not however, appear to have been taken-up by the post-Mbeki intelligence leadership under now-President Zuma.[95] If anything, with the new intelligence leadership appointed in October 2009 (see below) – all of whom have questions about their pasts – there is now even more cause for concern in this regard. Equally, the (reportedly) disastrous internal collapse of the functions and capabilities of the NIA (particularly)[96] and SASS – which, it must be recognised, is also clearly due to the fractious nature of the integration process and its history in the apartheid anti-liberation war, and has resulted reportedly in external security consultants becoming deeply involved in the NIA's day-to-day activities – is but one symptom of this failure, and calls into question even further the degree to which the NIA is clearly accountable to the oversight function.

This is but one of the reasons for – in October 2009 – the decision to merge the NIA and the SASS into a new State Security Agency (SSA), a highly significant move, the success or otherwise of which it will be possible to judge only in the coming years. While the NIA and SASS will – under new "heads" reporting to an SSA Director General – continue to operate within their individual domestic and foreign spheres respectively, the SSA will also amalgamate the South African National Academy of Intelligence (SANAI), the National Communications Centre (NCC) and the Office for Interception Centres (OIC), the Electronic Communications Security (Pty) Ltd, and the Intelligence Services Council on Conditions of Employment (ISC). While State Security Minister Siyabonga Cwele – who replaced Kasrils in 2007, and himself appears to suffer from some of the same problems which have blighted some of his colleagues[97] – noted that this amalgamation would "centralise command and control of the intelligence structures [and] create greater efficiency and effectiveness, enhance cooperation between the various intelligence structures as well as effect savings", it is clear that, in reality, this would appear to represent not only a continuing failing in the institutions of the state concerning the intelligence dispensation, but would also be representative of a return to one of the themes of the apartheid era when the political leadership exerted the highest degree of control possible on the civilian intelligence service in order to bend it to their political interests and viewpoints – rather than allowing it to function as a truly independent provider of "truth to power".[98] As Nathan has mused, "the Zuma administration had learned a lesson from the Mbeki experience – 'ensure that your top spies are appointed above all on the basis of personal loyalty, never mind loyalty to the Constitution'".[99]

In assessing this politicisation over the course of the last 15 years – and reflecting on how a similar politicisation occurred, through the securocrats and the SSC/NSMS structures, as discussed over the previous chapters – it is notable in three key regards. First, in the political leadership of the government of the day – the ANC – aiming to match the current political climate, both through the placement of ANC loyalists into key positions within the intelligence services and from those within the services wishing to simply meet the anticipated expectations of the political leadership; in many ways, this is the least problematic of the three. Second, and somewhat following from the first, in ensuring factional integration within the intelligence services between old enemies. Early on in the integration process, there were strong concerns regarding not only the independence of the public service from ANC party policy, but as well to an increasing degree of dissatisfaction within the public service and an increasing level of resignations. Reports of "factionalism" within the NIA emerged, indicating that similar problems which existed within the ANC during exile had not been solved, but rather enhanced with the power such individuals and factions found in their new positions; this is in addition to the not-surprising division between the old and new guards. These problems would appear to still persist.[100] Third, and finally, the development of parallel intelligence structures for political purposes, due significantly to a total lack-of-trust in the national intelligence functions, has been notable not only in the National Party and the IFP – both during the transitionary period of the GNU – but also, most worrying of the three, within the ANC itself: in the mid-1990s, the existence of a sub-committee on intelligence and security attached to the ANC National Executive Committee was discovered (composed of Joe Nhlanhla, Joe Modise, Sidney Mufamadi, and Bantu Holimisa); additionally, an ANC document published in the mid-1990s analysing the success of the GNU, recommended that a number of small, mobile, professional intelligence units be set up to "detour deficiencies within the official ranks of the NIA and the information flow that runs through NICOC to the government"[101] – seen as providing a means to get around the lack-of-trust and suspicions that exist in the national structures. This trait would appear to have carried-on well into the twenty-first century.[102]

Overall, this raises serious questions regarding the separation of policy surrounding intelligence from that of ANC party policy itself: the two must remain separate and distinct for obvious reasons. As one government source stated to the author in the mid-1990s:

> No government can rule effectively without having the power to ensure that the leadership of the government departments will act according to the political will of the government. The old civil service was full of personnel who had no commitment to fulfil the will of the new government – should we have left them in an untransformed civil service?[103]

Ironically, this has led – it could be argued – to the re-emergence of the dominance of securocrats within the South African government, albeit this time ANC ones.

Conclusion

All-in-all, it is clear from the legislation tabled through the turn-of-the-century that the Parliamentarians were attempting to come to grips with not just some of the more serious problems that South African intelligence had faced during the 1990s but also with those aspects of the original Acts – passed immediately at the end of apartheid and subject to the influences of the time – which had proved lacking over the last decade. At the same time, as South Africa became involved increasingly in Sub-Saharan Africa as the region's heavyweight and peacekeeper, questions were raised over its ability to provide sufficient and accurate intelligence support to its wider geostrategic interests and external operations (witness its disastrous intervention in Lesotho in September 1998).[104] While its external focus raised questions about its ability to conduct effective tactical and strategic assessments, domestically an increasing number of political scandals rocked the government and society, many of these involving – directly or indirectly – the intelligence services. All of this is occurring at a time of heightened requirements for South Africa's intelligence services – whether in observing and combating domestic extremism (white right-wing, Islamist, and organised crime) or in adjusting to new challenges, such as the evolution of technology and South Africa's role as regional/continental super-power and peace-maker. Sadly, this has continued to call into question the abilities and future role of South Africa's new intelligence dispensation – still subject to much debate today.

10 Conclusion

Still fighting the war – the legacy of South Africa's intelligence history

> When the maintenance of political power is the prevailing preoccupation, the suppression of domestic political dissent frequently becomes a political priority.
>
> Lauren Hutton

South Africa represents one particular kind of case: that of a transitional state, moving (still, it can be argued) from white-minority rule to universal suffrage and multi-party democracy. In this sense, it retains a legacy from its past which has led to it both rejecting certain paths and options due to their (imagined or real) association with that past, while retaining other aspects of the past in the current dispensation. As Seegers notes, "in intelligence matters there may be more continuity with the past than we would like to admit".[1]

In this sense, the evolution of South Africa's intelligence dispensation since 1948 has been neither linear nor constant – the case both before and since the 1994 transition. Ultimately, the question must be asked: when is the "transition" actually over? Have we passed that point and, therefore, have to accept that South Africa's post-apartheid intelligence dispensation has reached a finite point from which the problems that occur are the results purely of "the new South Africa"? Or can South Africa's intelligence structures still be said to be – in 2010 – "in transition"?

Almost two decades now after this transition began – both in terms of the integration process of the security forces (which began before the 1994 elections and ended at the end of the twentieth century) and in terms of the completeness of those instruments (legislation, policies, structures, etc) which make-up and support the intelligence dispensation – it is clear that, in almost every aspect, the transition is over. The piece which remains "in transition" – and may forever be – is the development of a transparent, internally peaceful (as Louw put it), incorrupt (and incorruptible) and properly overseen intelligence dispensation that is answerable to the people of the land, and not the political leadership of the day, as was noted in Chapter 9. In this sense, South Africa's on-going problems in intelligence are due to the failings of the current leadership to assist in creating the "culture of intelligence" to which they so strongly committed themselves to two decades ago.

With these problems in stark relief, it is clear that the legacy of this transitionary phase has not only been its impact on the state and its institutions, but also the impact it has had on the state-of-mind of the individuals responsible for intelligence and security matters, derived not insignificantly from their personal and "struggle" histories. Apartheid – and the impact that it had on its people, its country, its state and its institutions, its region, and its enemies – was a crime against humanity, but one which developed for complex reasons historically that defy a simple explanation, with a symbiosis of brutalising and being brutalised – in many who were touched by it, including from the security forces as much as from the people it oppressed and the liberation movements which fought to overthrow it. It has created a type of post-traumatic stress disorder on those who fought in its name, those who suffered for it, and even in those who have attempted to build the new South Africa from its legacy – it may be generations still before this legacy and the brutalised nature of South Africa's society and people recover from it fully.

Yet, while the slippage of years beyond the transition has meant that many of the younger members of the intelligence community not only have no experience of working under apartheid but have also developed their professional skills in common (as opposed to those from the apartheid and liberation movements sides who were integrated in 1995), South Africa's intelligence dispensation today – tragically – continues to reflect much fall-out from this legacy, with many of the themes identified in this study continuing well into the post-apartheid period for the reasons outlined. As a result of these legacies, there is clearly – today, more than 15 years into the post-apartheid era, in South Africa and also more widely[2] – a lack of trust inherent in the new intelligence dispensation as it faces a continuing sense of fractiousness, factionalism, lack-of-trust and corruption in its structures and personnel. This lack of trust is notable between individuals – (not just "old guard" and "new guard" but also between the various individuals affiliated with one liberation group or party who now find themselves working together, or indeed the different factions involved in the ANC's fratricidal conflict since the late 1990s; in the institutions where serious concerns exist over the functions of the NIA, as noted above, as well as more broadly in the workings of the national oversight and accountability mechanisms (for instance, around the Jackie Selebi affair, alleged spying on journalists, or the appointment of tainted ANC officials to lead the intelligence services); in the intelligence itself – deriving from both of the other two points; and, perhaps worst of all, in what appears to be a total politicisation of the intelligence process, with both the intelligence product becoming politicised and the political leadership developing parallel-but-independent intelligence structures due to their own professed lack-of-trust in the state structures – with the role played by corrupt intelligence leaders in Jacob Zuma's rise and accession to both the ANC leadership and the state presidency perhaps the worst indictment of these services' independence and accountability to the public yet.

Is South Africa to be held to higher standards than other countries? A severe critique would say yes – and this is a severe critique – if for no other reason than that the architects of South Africa's new intelligence dispensation stated that they would hold themselves to far higher standards than not only the system which they looked to replace, but also international standards for the field. The professions of the ANC intelligence professionals in the period before and during the TEC process, as well as those sentiments enunciated in the *White Paper on Intelligence*, were towards the highest standard of quality, transparency, accountability, control and oversight; regrettably, any clear assessment of the current state of South Africa's intelligence dispensation would note failings (and worse) in each of these areas.

In assessing the South African experience and dispensation, failing a grade should be granted to South Africa in terms of the strength of its transparency, independence, accountability and oversight mechanisms for its twenty-first century intelligence dispensation. The intelligence services are barely independent from the executive – indeed, as noted above, in some senses they could be seen to be slaves to the executive's policies and interests. The oversight mechanisms remain fragile and bare; while Parliamentary oversight has strengthened over the last decade – in terms of its membership, staff, access and proactiveness – the continuing failure to appoint a lasting Inspector-General for the Intelligence Services is a glaring void in oversight. In this sense, while the institutions and mandates which underpin the intelligence function appear to be strong on the surface, upon further examination these can be found to be weak and problematic at best, despite significant moves – in the form of new legislation and the establishment of new oversight-and-accountability-related bodies – in the early twenty-first century to makeup for such serious shortfalls.

In all of these senses, therefore, South Africa's intelligence dispensation today is both a product of the decisions that were made concerning its transformation at the end of apartheid, and ironically in far better shape than many other intelligence communities which have undergone such a transformation at the end of such a divisive conflict. If a balance can now be found between the ANC domination of the government and public service – which bears with great importance on the absolute necessity for clear co-ordination and accountability within the security services – and the concerns of the professionals that serve in these agencies, a peaceful and stable environment will be developed for an equitable future within the country's intelligence community. As has already been seen from the decade of the new dispensation, clear problems exist in co-ordination between services and co-operation with not only each other but with the political leaders of the day. This problem must be solved in order to ensure a peaceful future both within the services and within South Africa itself.

Notes

1 Introduction: South African intelligence in revolution and counter-revolution 1948–2005

1 This anecdote is included in Allister Sparks, *Tomorrow Is Another Country: The Insider Story of South Africa's Negotiated Revolution* (London: William Heinemann Ltd, 1995): 113.
2 Apartheid was recognised as illegal and a crime against humanity by the United Nations – and, as such, the South African Truth and Reconciliation Commission of the post-apartheid era recognised the "just war" of the liberation movements of South Africa in opposing the apartheid government (see Truth and Reconciliation Commission, *Final Report – Findings and Recommendations*, volume 6, section 5, chapter 1, paragraphs 19–24, 28–62; and volume 6, section 5, chapter 5, paragraph 41. Online, available at: www.justice.gov.za/trc/report/finalreport/vol6_s5.pdf (downloaded 9 April 2010). Without being facetious, however, this finding paints far too black and white a picture of the complexities which underpinned South Africa's history over the last 200 years. For an excellent examination of this complex history – including an appreciation as to how and why apartheid came into being, why it was defended so vigorously (often, brutally) against these liberation movements during the period this study covers, and why in almost every way South Africa's "liberation" was different to any other post-colonial state – see Allister Sparks, *The Mind of South Africa: The Story of the Rise and Fall of Apartheid* (London: Heinemann, 1990), an exceptional study of South Africa from its beginnings.
3 James Sanders, *Apartheid's Friends: The Rise and Fall of South Africa's Secret Service* (London: John Murray, 2006): 1–2, 7.
4 This book results in part from interviews conducted with official and private sources in South Africa, Canada, Britain, Australia and the United States during 1994–2008. As most of these interviews were confidential in nature, I have tried to find corroborating open-sources for such information throughout this book; where this has not been possible, the confidential interview will be referenced or, if this is not possible, no reference will be cited. In addition, while some of the information in this study is drawn from previous work by the author – including all those noted in the bibliography – every attempt will be made to include the original source citation in this study.
5 This is largely due to English (British) policies towards the Afrikaners after Britain took the Cape Colony in the nineteenth century, after the British expanded into the "independent republics" of the Transvaal and Orange Free State in pursuit of the newly discovered deposits of gold and diamonds, and later due to their use of concentration camps during the Second Boer War

(1899–1902) in which more than 20,000 Afrikaner women and children died, mostly of disease: Sparks, *The Mind of South Africa*, pp. 111, 128.
6 Annette Seegers, *The Military in the Making of Modern South Africa* (London: Tauris Academic Books, 1996): 126–132.
7 Bill Keller, "Trial offers glimpse of apartheid's dying sting", *New York Times*, 19 February 1995.
8 It is also worth pointing out – and keeping in perspective – the numbers involved: while those killed through direct-targeting by the state for elimination numbered fewer than 100 (averaging around five per annum between 1977–1989), tens-of-thousands were killed in the ANC–Inkatha civil war in Natal, itself partly – and a very strong part, at that – the result of the contra-mobilisation tactics of the SADF during the 1980s, and a direct subscription to counter-revolutionary theory. Therefore, the different "levels" of killing must also be kept in mind.
9 Despite the evident "for" in its title, the Bureau for State Security became acronym-ised as "BOSS", largely – as Sanders points out – as it both produced a popularised/able nickname for a sinister organisation, and became pejorative in so doing: Sanders, 36.
10 For the purposes of this study, "intelligence" shall be used to mean, in all its aspects, a *process*, an *institution* (as seen through the lens of a Western formalised and bureaucratised approach), an *activity*, and a *product* (as taken from Sherman Kent, *Strategic Intelligence for American World Policy*, revised ed. (Princeton, NJ: Princeton University Press, 1966); Allen Dulles, *The Craft of Intelligence* (New York: Harper & Row, 1963); and Harry Howe Ransom, *Central Intelligence and National Security* (Cambridge: Harvard University Press, 1958)). References throughout this study to an intelligence "dispensation" or "enterprise" should be considered to reference all four aspects collectively as an aspect of national power.

2 The birth of South Africa's intelligence capability and the rise of the "securocracy", 1948–1972

1 Douglas Blackburn and W. Waithman Caddel, *Secret Service in South Africa*. Reprinted from the 1911 edition (Honolulu: University Press of the Pacific, 2001): 1–25; and P.C. Swanepoel, *Really Inside BOSS: A Tale of South Africa's Late Intelligence Service (And Something about the CIA)*, Revised edition (Derdepoortpark (Pretoria), 2008): 3–4. Blackburn's and Caddel's book makes a fascinating reading of the role of secret services and intelligence in the period around the Second Anglo-Boer War and the establishment of the Union of South Africa, where the primary tensions and enemies were the British and the Boers, with the "natives" playing a secondary role. Swanepoel's book makes equally fascinating reading, as he is allegedly a former South African intelligence officer of some years service and has self-published his book to try and "set the record straight" concerning South Africa's intelligence history. These are two of the only five books known to have been written on this topic specifically – the other three being Gordon Winter's *Inside BOSS: South Africa's Secret Police* (London: Penguin Books, 1981), James Sanders' *Apartheid's Friends: The Rise and Fall of South Africa's Secret Services* (London: John Murray, 2006), and Riaan Labuschagne's *On South Africa's Secret Service: An Undercover Agent's Story* (Alberton (South Africa): Galago Books, 2002). These latter three modern sources all present an equal mixing of interesting facts and anecdotes with contentious perspectives (for example, see Christopher Andrew, *Defend The Realm: The Authorized History of MI5* (New York: Alfred A. Knopf, 2009): 636, 636n7 on Winter). The problem for this study is that there are so few

published sources on the alleged or reported covert activities (as opposed to the structures, policies and strategies) of South Africa's intelligence services in detail – certainly up until the publication of the South African Truth and Reconciliation Commission's multiple reports at the end of the twentieth century – that such sources must be taken into account. Nevertheless, this study has been circumspect in its use of such sources, preferring the TRC's reports as the definitive public record of such activities from 1960–1994, as well as interviews with former and serving South African, British, American and Canadian intelligence and security personnel, to corroborate or extend specific (and often contentious points).

2 For a comprehensive examination of this relationship, see Jonathan S. Chavkin, *British Intelligence and the Zionist, South African, and Australian Intelligence Communities during and after the Second World War* (Unpublished PhD Thesis – Faculty of History, University of Cambridge, 2009), *passim*. The author is grateful for Dr Chavkin's thoughts and discussions on the early period of South Africa's intelligence development which provide excellent context for many of the later developments in South Africa's intelligence dispensation.
3 Kent Fedorowich, "German Espionage and British Counter-Intelligence in South Africa and Mozambique, 1939–1944", *The Historical Journal*, 48:1 (2005): 218. This – alongside Chavkin – provides an excellent analysis of the role played by intelligence in South Africa's war-time activities domestically and in South West Africa.
4 Fedorowich, 218–219.
5 Fedorowich, 212.
6 Fedorowich, 212.
7 Seegers, *The Military*, 60–61, 76–77. Swanepoel notes that this concern over "native agitators" was identified by the SAP intelligence arm in 1931 – see Swanepoel, 5–8.
8 Fedorowich, 213.
9 Seegers, *The Military*, 63.
10 Fedorowich, 215–216; Chavkin, 191–192, 198.
11 Seegers, *The Military*, 63.
12 Chavkin, 223.
13 Chavkin, 187.
14 Chavkin, 231–235; Sanders, 11.
15 Andrew, 444; Chavkin, 229, 235. Britain's intelligence lead in its relationship with South Africa after 1961 would pass to MI6, with its responsibilities for foreign intelligence (as South Africa – no longer a dominion – was now): Sanders, 15.
16 Seegers, *The Military*, 77.
17 Seegers, *The Military*, 125.
18 Chavkin, 241.
19 Sillitoe, as quoted in Chavkin, 236–237.
20 Sillitoe, as quoted in Chavkin, 236–237 and 243.
21 Seegers, *The Military*, 94.
22 Seegers, *The Military*, 96–97.
23 Chavkin, 266.
24 Sanders, 16, 30–33, 43–44.
25 Several excellent histories of the ANC exist, including S. Ellis and T. Sechaba, *Comrades Against Apartheid: The ANC and South African Communist Party in Exile* (London: James Currey, 1992); F. Meli, *South Africa Belongs to Us* (London: James Currey, 1989); H. Holland, *The Struggle: A History of the African National Congress* (New York: George Braziller, 1990); and P. Walshe, *The Rise of African*

Nationalism in South Africa: The African National Congress 1912–1952 (Berkley: University of California Press, 1971). Other histories include M. Benson, *South Africa: The Struggle for a Birthright* (London: James Currey, 1966); N. Manganyi and A. Du Toit, *Political Violence and the Struggle in South Africa* (London: Macmillan, 1990); D. O'Meara and S. Dlamini, *The Struggle for South Africa* (London: Zed Books, 1988); and E. Feit, *South Africa: The Dynamics of the African National Congress* (London: Oxford University Press, 1962). Finally, T. Lodge's *Black Politics in South Africa Since 1945* (London: Longman, 1985) is excellent.

26 For a detailed discussion of the PAC's evolution – alongside its armed wing the Azanian People's Liberation Army (APLA) – see Tom Lodge, "Soldiers of the Storm: A Profile of the Azanian People's Liberation Army", Jakkie Cilliers and Markus Riechardt (eds), *About-Turn: The Transformation of the South African Military and Intelligence* (London: Croom Helm, 1985): 105–117. APLA had a small Intelligence and Security Department, about which – while little else is known about it (including just how structured it actually was) – it is known that its internal security arm was found guilty by the TRC of "extra-judicial killings" of several of its members, both in camps in exile and inside South Africa, alongside assault and torture being "used as mechanisms to deal with suspected dissidents or infiltrators", both of which actions were "largely the result of divisions within the PAC leadership, military command structures and APLA members" rather than necessarily actual counter-intelligence cases (which would not – of course – excuse such killings): see TRC, *Findings and Recommendations: Holding the Pan Africanist Congress Accountable* – volume 6, section 5, chapter 5, paragraphs 19–22. Online, available at: www.justice.gov.za/trc/report/finalreport/vol6_s5.pdf.

27 Founded in 1960, the ARM was closely tied to the National Union of South African Students. Its history is significant only in that it was involved in approximately 11 bombings and sabotage operations against the state between August 1962 and July 1964, when its leadership was arrested and tried; it was revealed, however, following its most spectacular attack (on a Johannesburg train station on 24 July 1964) that the Security Branch had intelligence on its operations long beforehand. In reaction, the government and Parliamentary opposition demanded greater co-operation and co-ordination between the intelligence services; it was out of these actions that the national security structures of South Africa were born. See Seegers, 129–131.

28 ANC, *Strategy and Tactics of the ANC* (May 1969). Online, available at: www.anc.org.za/ancdocs/history/stratact.html (downloaded 2 March 2000).

29 ANC, *Strategy and Tactics*.

30 ANC, *Strategy and Tactics*.

31 ANC, *Strategy and Tactics*.

32 While this study will not provide a detailed discussion of the ANC's revolutionary warfare strategy, the author's "A Blunted Spear: The Failure of the ANC/SACP Revolutionary War Strategy 1961–1990", *Small Wars and Insurgencies* 14:2 (Autumn 2003): 27–70 provides a detailed assessment of this. For earlier studies of the ANC's guerrilla tactics and their failures, see S. Johns, "Obstacles to Guerrilla Warfare – a South African Case Study", *Journal of Modern African Studies* 11:2 (1973): 267–303, as an excellent primer on the ANC's strategy and failures; J. Bowyer Bell, *The Myth of the Guerrilla: Revolutionary Theory and Malpractice* (New York, 1971); Bell, "The Future of Guerrilla Revolution in Southern Africa", *Africa Today* 19 (Winter 1972), pp. 7–15; K.W. Grundy, *Guerrilla Struggle in Africa: An Analysis and Preview* (New York: Grossman, 1971); and M. Morris, *Terrorism: The First Full Account in Detail of Terrorism and Insurgency in Southern Africa* (Cape Town: H. Timmins, 1971). For later

accounts, see H. Barrell, *MK: The ANC's Armed Struggle* (London: Penguin Books, 1990); and S. Ellis and T. Sechaba, *Comrades Against Apartheid*.
33 Seegers, *The Military*, 126.
34 Ellis and Sechaba, 127; ANC Submission, 6.2.2.
35 Gavin Cawthra, *Brutal Force: The Apartheid War Machine* (London: International Defence and Aid Fund, 1986): 217–218.
36 This quick summary can be investigated in more depth through Kevin A. O'Brien, "A Blunted Spear: The Failure of the ANC/SACP Revolutionary War Strategy 1961–1990", *Small Wars and Insurgencies* 14:2 (Autumn 2003): 27–70.
37 Much of this is outlined in Seegers, *The Military*, as well as at "A Short History Of Military Intelligence Division". Online, available at: http://uk.geocities.com/sadf_history2/mihistory.html.
38 Republic of South Africa, *Report of the Commission of Inquiry into Matters Relating to the Security of the State* RP102/1971 (Pretoria: Government Printers, 1971): 10 [hereafter Potgieter Report].
39 According to Seegers, DMI counter-intelligence alerted Security Branch to the ARM instigators of the station-bomb days prior to the attack being launched, but Van den Bergh later claimed that no such intelligence had been shared: Seegers, 130–131. By implication, Van den Bergh may have wanted the attack to come off, in order to provide justification for the subsequent draconian approach to internal security that was initiated following this bomb.
40 Seegers, *The Military*, 131; Rocklyn Williams, *Back To The Barracks: The Changing Parameters of Civil–Military Relations under the Botha and De Klerk Administrations* (Colchester: University of Essex, 1992): 62. Williams' PhD study is an excellent source of analysis for many of the issues covered in this book, not the least of which because of Williams' own background as an ANC operative. Indeed, given that Williams was writing at the time of the transition, it is most telling that much of his analysis would ring true over the proceeding decade's investigations into the apartheid state's covert structures and activities, including especially those propagated by DMI. Alongside other excellent studies – such as Seegers', Chris Alden's *Apartheid's Last Stand: The Rise and Fall of the South African Security State* (London: MacMillan Press Ltd, 1996), Terry Bell's and Dumisa Ntsebeza's *Unfinished Business: South Africa, Apartheid and Truth* (Observatory (South Africa): RedWorks, 2001), or Stephen Ellis' and Tsepo Sechaba's *Comrades Against Apartheid: The ANC and the South African Communist Party in Exile* (London: James Currey Ltd, 1992), to pick but a few – Williams' work provides a great appreciation for the issues discussed in this book.
41 Seegers, *The Military*, 131.
42 Williams, 62.
43 See Sanders, 27–29, on this point.
44 International Defence and Aid Fund, *BOSS: The First 5 Years* (London, 1975): 10.
45 See, for example, Jeffrey T. Richelson, *The U.S. Intelligence Community* (Second Edition) (New York: Ballinger, 1989): 282–283. For a detailed – if unusual – assessment of US intelligence interests vis-à-vis apartheid South Africa, see Richard Cummings, "A Diamond Is Forever: Mandela Triumphs, Buthelezi and de Klerk Survive, and ANC on the U.S. Payroll", *International Journal of Intelligence and Counterintelligence* (Summer 1995). On Switzerland – with whom apartheid intelligence services had strong relations – see Peter Hug, *Military, Armaments Industry, and Nuclear Relations between Switzerland and South Africa and the UN Apartheid Debate of 1948–1994*. University of Bern NRP 42+ – Switzerland-South Africa Study. Online, available at: www.snf.ch/NFP/NFP42+/HugE.pdf.

46 Potgieter Report, 9.
47 James M. Roherty, *State Security in South Africa: Civil-Military Relations under P.W. Botha* (London: M.E. Sharpe Inc, 1992): 71.
48 *TRC2:3*, Appendix 12.
49 International Defence and Aid Fund, *BOSS: The First Five Years*, 10; Kenneth W. Grundy, *The Militarization of South African Politics* (London: I.B. Taurus, 1986): 42.
50 International Defence and Aid Fund, *BOSS: The First Five Years*, 10.
51 Seegers, *The Military*, 127; International Defence and Aid Fund, *South Africa: The BOSS Law* (London: IDAF, 1969): 1.
52 Republic of South Africa, *Establishment of a New Department of State – Bureau for State Security*. Government Notice No. 808 (16 May 1969): s1–2.
53 Its exact mandate was to:

> (*a*) collect, evaluate, correlate and interpret national security intelligence for the purpose of (i) detecting and identifying any threat or potential threat to the security of the Republic ... (*c*) to prepare and to interpret, for the consideration of the Council, a national intelligence estimate relating to any threat to the security of the Republic, and in this regard to advise the Council of any other intelligence at its disposal which may have an influence on any State policy relating to the combating of any such threat ... (*e*) to make recommendations to the Council on intelligence priorities
> (Republic of South Africa, Security Intelligence and State Security Council Act (No 64 of 1972): s2)

54 Grundy, *The Militarization of South African Politics*, 43.
55 IDAF (1975), 15.
56 J. Barber, "BOSS in Britain". *African Affairs* 82:328 (July 1983): 328.
57 Republic of South Africa, *Report of the Commission of Inquiry into Matters Relating to the Security of the State*, 46.
58 Deon Geldenhuys, *The Diplomacy of Isolation: South Africa's Foreign Policy Making* (Johannesburg: SAIIA, 1984): 147.
59 *Security Intelligence and State Security Council Act*, s3; Geldenhuys, *The Diplomacy of Isolation*, 141.
60 Grundy, *The Militarization of South African Politics*, 42–43.
61 Seegers, *The Military*, 131; Stephen Talbot, "The CIA and BOSS: Thick as Thieves", Ellen Ray, William Schaap, Karl Van Meter, and Louis Wolf (eds), *Dirty Work 2: The CIA in Africa* (Secaucus (NJ): Lyle Stuart Inc, 1979): 269.
62 Cawthra, *Brutal Force*, 38–39.
63 This really was par for the course in South Africa: all three key premiers – Vorster, Botha and De Klerk – between the 1960s and 1990s had their "favourite" agency for providing the national intelligence brief and dominating the other two. These were, respectively, BOSS, DMI and the NIS. The heads of each agency in their time would also serve as an unofficial "national security advisor" to the Prime Minister/President.
64 Hilton Hamann, *Days of the Generals: The Untold Story of South Africa's Apartheid-era Military Generals* (Cape Town: Zebra Press, 2001): 7–8.
65 Seegers, *The Military*, 139–143.
66 Alette J. Norval, *Deconstructing Apartheid Discourse* (London: Verso, 1996): 181–182.
67 Republic of South Africa, *Report of the Commission of Inquiry into Matters Relating to the Security of the State*, 33, 34.
68 Maj-Gen B. Mortimer, *Submission IRO The Former SADF: SA Defence Force Involvement in the Internal Security Situation in the Republic of South Africa*, (Pretoria:

SANDF Nodal Point, 1997). Online, available at: www.justice.gov.za/trc/hrvtrans/submit/sadf.htm: 4.
69 The term securocrat refers to those security officials who directed and controlled the national and counter-revolutionary strategies as core elements in the bureaucracy; it is not known who first coined the term, but it has always uniquely referred to the mid- and high-level South African officials involved in the apartheid security strategies.
70 *Security Intelligence and State Security Council Act*, s5.
71 *Security Intelligence and State Security Council Act*, s4.
72 Cawthra, *Brutal Force*, 37.
73 Grundy, *The Militarization of South African Politics*, 49.
74 South Africa was run with every element of society geared towards fighting the war – resulting in the total and integrated co-ordination of every sector of society into a nationally managed security architecture (whose aspects would include the military, political, social, welfare, economic, etc.) to oversee the implementation of this "total national strategy".
75 For an examination of the role of the securocrats in the decision-making process in South Africa, see Robert I. Rotberg, "Decision Making and the Military in South Africa", Robert I. Rotberg, Henry S. Bienen, Robert Legworld, and Garvin Maasdrop (eds), *South Africa and Its Neighbours: Regional Security and Self-Interest* (Lexington: D.C. Heath and Co, 1985): 13–26.
76 Suffice it to say that as a security state, the executive and Cabinet made every effort to blur or destroy any orders which directly linked them to illegal or covert actions by the security forces – this is not to say that there is not more than ample documentary evidence to tie the apartheid government between 1961 and 1989 to security force illegal activities (the vast majority of which were carried-out by the various intelligence services) but, rather, that such ties are extremely complicated and caught in a myriad of obfuscations, "grey orders" and destroyed evidence. The author based his entire doctoral thesis around this question – with particular regard to the use of assassination as a tool of the apartheid government's anti-liberation strategy the point being that determining responsibility (and culpability) for the actions of the apartheid intelligence and security forces remains both extremely difficult and extremely controversial, even more than two decades after the collapse of the apartheid security regime. See K.A. O'Brien, *The Assassins' Web: South Africa's Counter-revolutionary Strategy, Securocracy and Operations (with particular reference to the Special Tasking of Security Force Units) 1978–1990* (University of Hull, 2000); and Republic of South Africa. *Report of the Truth and Reconciliation Commission*, 1:2 "Historical Context: Gross Human Rights Violations in Political and Historical Perspective". Online, available at: www.polity.org.za/govdocs/commissions/1998/trc/1chap2.htm and all further chapters in that report.
77 Ellis and Sechaba, 93.
78 Allister Sparks, "South Africa Caught in Security Web", *Washington Post* (31 December 1986): A14.
79 Ellis and Sechaba, 93; "South Africa: The Security Line-up", *Africa Confidential*, 28:12 (10 June 1987): 2.; Williams, 179.
80 *SADF Submission*, 58.
81 *SADF Submission*, 59–60; and as quoted in Howard Varney, *Submission to the Truth and Reconciliation Commission: The Caprivi Trainees* (4 August 1997). Online, available at: www.truth.org.za/submit/caprivi.htm: C6.1.
82 *SADF Submission*, 10.
83 M. Hough and M. Van der Merwe, *Selected Official South African Strategic Perceptions 1976–1987*, Ad hoc Publication No. 25, Pretoria: Institute for Security

Studies University of Pretoria, May 1988: 9–10; James Selfe, "South Africa's National [Security] Management System," in Jacklyn Cock and Laurie Nathan, (eds), *Society at War: The Militarisation of South Africa* (New York: St. Martin's Press, 1989): 152.
84 Grundy, *The Militarization of South African Politics*, 15, 49, 53; Ellis and Sechaba, 93; "South Africa: The Security Line-up", 4; Rocklyn Williams, *Back To The Barracks: The Changing Parameters of Civil-Military Relations under the Botha and De Klerk Administrations* (Colchester: University of Essex, 1992): 179.
85 *ANC Submission*, 4.7.1.
86 *SADF Submission*, 76.
87 De Kock, 94, 145.
88 Operating above the National Joint Management Centre, the powerful OSP housed – in addition to the Bureau of Information – the NIS, the National Priorities Committee (responsible for budgetary considerations), and the Commission for Administration (which controlled the state bureaucracy): Alden, 223/45.
89 *SADF Submission*, 77.
90 *SADF Submission*, 75–76.
91 Seegers, *The Military*, 135; Cawthra, *Brutal Force*, 90.
92 Stephen Ellis, "The Historical Significance of the South African Third Force", *Journal of Southern African Studies*, 24:2 (June 1998): 267.
93 Seegers, *The Military*, 137.
94 Seegers, *The Military*, 137.
95 Gavin Cawthra, *Policing South Africa: The SAP and the Transition from Apartheid* (London: Zed Books, 1993): 88; Ellis, "Third Force", 267; Denis Herbstein and John Evenson. *The Devils Are Among Us: The War for Namibia* (London: Zed Books Ltd, 1989): 65.
96 *SADF Submissions*.
97 As referenced in Sanders, 41.
98 Seegers, *The Military*, 138, 221; "Intelligence officer says he knew about Stratcom", *Weekly Mail and Guardian*, 21 July 1995; "The Secrets of Stratcom", *Weekly Mail and Guardian*, June 23 1995.
99 Ellis, "Third Force", 268.
100 John D'Oliveira, *Vorster – the Man* (Johannesburg: Ernest Stanton, 1977): 125.
101 Ellis, "Third Force", 267.
102 *TRC2:2*, 165. For an extensive examination of the Selous Scouts – alongside other Rhodesian Security Force units – see Peter Stiff and Ron Reid-Daly, *Selous Scouts: Top Secret War* (Alberton (South Africa): Galago, 1987) and its update Ron Reid-Daly, *Pamwe Chete: The Legend of the Selous Scouts* (Weltevreden Park (South Africa): Covos-Day Books, 1999); see also J.K. Cilliers, *Counter-Insurgency in Rhodesia* (London: Croom Helm, 1985).
103 African National Congress, *Statement to the Truth and Reconciliation Commission* [hereafter *ANC Submission 1*] (August 1996). Online, available at: www.anc.org.za/ancdocs/misc/trcall.html#6 (downloaded 4 August 2010): 6.3.1.
104 Ellis and Sechaba, 116.
105 Winter, 568–569.
106 For discussions of the activities of BOSS abroad, see James Barber, "BOSS in Britain", *African Affairs* 82:328 (July 1983): 311–328; and Winter, *Inside BOSS*. See also note 1 concerning Winter's reliability.
107 Winter maintains that the reason the BOSS assassination unit was known as the "Z-Squad" was because "Z is the final letter in the alphabet. It's South Africa's 'final solution'" (Winter, 312).
108 Van den Bergh allegedly called the unit the "Z-Squad" because, with "Z" being the last letter of the alphabet, these men were "the ultimate force in fighting communism and South Africa's final option".

109 Winter, 560–561.
110 Winter, 559; Talbot, 269.
111 Winter, 563, 566.
112 Winter, 308–309.
113 Winter, 563.
114 Mondlane may have been killed by the Portuguese PIDE: Winter, 564.
115 Dolinchek later worked for the NIS and was involved in the Seychelles coup attempt – see Klaas de Jonge, *The Truth Commission Files: The Seychelles Case* (Netherlands Institute for Southern Africa). Online, available at: www.contrast.org/truth/html/seychelles.html (downloaded 6 December 1998); Williams, *Back to the Barracks*, 228; and Winter, 565. This allegation was made by Eugene De Kock, *A Long Night's Damage: Working for the Apartheid State*. As told to Jeremy Gordin (Saxonwold (South Africa): Contra Press, 1998): 198. Such specific operations will generally not be treated throughout this study except where they relate to the overall motif of understanding the role played by intelligence in South Africa's modern history.

3 "Total Strategy" and the "securocratisation" of the government, 1972–1978

1 The author has explored this issue elsewhere – see Kevin A. O'Brien, "Counter-intelligence for Counter-revolutionary Warfare: The South African Police Security Branch", *Intelligence and National Security* 16:3 (Autumn 2001): 27–59. For the main texts by these theorists which were used by the securocrats, see André Beaufre, *A Strategy of Action*. Translated R.H. Barry (London: Faber and Faber, 1967); Robert Thompson, *Defeating Communist Insurgency: Experiences from Malaya and Vietnam* (London: Chatt and Windus, 1967); David Galula, *Counter-insurgency Warfare: Theory and Practice* (New York: Frederick A Praeger, 1965); John J. McCuen, *The Art of Counter-revolutionary Warfare: A Psycho-Politico-Military Strategy of Counter-insurgency* (Harrisburg: Stackpole Books, 1965); and Samuel P. Huntington (ed.), *Changing Patterns of Military Politics* (New York: The Free Press of Glencoe, Inc, 1962).
2 Williams, *Back to the Barracks*, 63.
3 Williams, *Back to the Barracks*, 67.
4 For an examination of the lead-up, actions and consequences of Operation SAVANNAH, as well as the significant US–South African co-operation, see Robin Hallett, "The South African Intervention in Angola", *African Affairs* 77:312 (July 1978): 347–386.
5 Mark Phillips, "The nuts and bolts of military power: the structure of the SADF", Jacklyn Cock and Laurie Nathan (eds), *Society At War: The Militarisation of South Africa* (New York: St Martin's Press, 1989): 20–21.
6 Neta Crawford, "The Domestic Sources and Consequences of Aggressive Foreign Policies: The Folly of South Africa's 'Total Strategy'", *Southern African Perspectives* 41 (February 1995): 9–10; Williams, *Back to the Barracks*, 67.
7 For a good overview of the Rhodesian security and intelligence community, see Henrick Ellert, "The Rhodesian Security and Intelligence Community 1960–1980: A Brief Overview of the Structure and Operational Role of the Military, Civilian and Police Security and Intelligence Organizations which Served the Rhodesia Government during the Zimbabwean Liberation War", Ngwabi Bhebe and Terence Ranger (eds), *Soldiers in Zimbabwe's Liberation War* (Johannesburg: Heinemann, 1995): 87–103; and Ken Flower, *Serving Secretly: An Intelligence Chief on Record – Rhodesia Into Zimbabwe 1964 to 1981* (London: John Murray, 1987).
8 Stephen Burgess and Helen Purkitt, *The Roll-back of South Africa's Chemical and*

246 *Notes*

Biological Warfare Program. USAF Counterproliferation Center, Air University. (April 2001): 8.
9. For an extensive examination of the SADF's intelligence and special operations capabilities, see Kevin A. O'Brien, "Special Forces for Counter-revolutionary Warfare: The South African Case", *Small Wars and Insurgencies* 12:2 (Summer 2001): 79–109.
10. Ellis and Sechaba, 66.
11. For a history of the PAC-APLA (Azanian People's Liberation Army, the military wing of the PAC), see Tom Lodge, "Soldiers of the Storm: A Profile of the Azanian People's Liberation Army", J.K. Cilliers and Markus Reichardt (eds), *About-Turn: The Transformation of the South African Military and Intelligence* (Midrand: Institute for Security Studies, 1996): 105–117.
12. Inigo Gilmore, "Apartheid Minister Approved Killings", *The Times* (30 November 1996): 14.
13. The "Information Scandal" in 1977–1978 surrounded the murder of a leading National Party politician and the web of corruption and misuse of funds within the Department of Information, led by Dr Connie Mulder (tipped as the man to succeed Vorster as prime minister), which was revealed by journalists investigating the murder; Van den Bergh had worked with Mulder on establishing a détente policy for the region through a secret slush fund to "win over or buy out" African, European and North American opinion-makers. The scandal emerged after it was revealed that participants in the Department of Information had used the slush fund for their own aggrandisement; it was Van den Bergh's attempts to protect Mulder, often through intimidation of government investigators, that led to his own fall in this scandal. The SADF used the scandal against Mulder to the benefit of their own patron, Defence Minister Botha. For a good account, see Geldenhuys, *The Diplomacy of Isolation*, 84–88. See also Sparks, *The Mind of South Africa*, 308; M. Rees and C. Day, *Muldergate: The Story of the Information Scandal* (London: Macmillan, 1980); and Sanders, 94–107.
14. Sparks, *The Mind of South Africa*, 308.
15. Talbot, 270.
16. Robert Schrire, *Adapt or Die: The End of White Politics in South Africa* (London: Hurst and Company, 1992): 42.
17. As a symbol of this co-operation, the DCDP and SSC Secretariat, in order to facilitate this co-ordination, would later redraw the military's area commands in 1983 to coincide with the DCDP's nine development regions internally: Alden, 94.
18. Mark Swilling and Mark Phillips, "State Power in the 1980s: From 'Total Strategy' to 'Counter-revolutionary Warfare'", Cock and Nathan, 136.
19. Alden, 83.
20. For a discussion of South African strategy-making generally, see Roherty, *State Security*, 41–44.
21. Williams, *Back to the Barracks*, 75.
22. Alden, 170.
23. As quoted in Geldenhuys, *The Diplomacy of Isolation*, 140.
24. Republic of South Africa, *White Paper on Defence and Armaments Production* (Pretoria, 1975): 7.
25. Republic of South Africa, *White Paper on Defence and Armaments* (Pretoria, 1977): 1.
26. Ibid, 4.
27. Cawthra, *Brutal Force*, 31.
28. Roherty, *State Security*, 69.
29. Williams, *Back to the Barracks*, 68.
30. Republic of South Africa, *Truth and Reconciliation Commission Hearing Held at*

Durban on Monday, 4 August 1997. Online, available at: www.truth.org.za/ HRVtrans/caprivi/caprivi1.htm (downloaded 25 August 1999): 37 [hereafter *Caprivis Hearing*].
31 Williams, *Back to the Barracks*, 68.
32 Fraser, as quoted in Williams, *Back to the Barracks*, 74.
33 Selfe, "South Africa's National [Security] Management System", 150; *ANC Submission*, 4.7.
34 Robert H. Davies and Dan O'Meara, "The State of Analysis of the Southern African Region: Issues Raised by South African Strategy", *Review of African Political Economy* 29 (1983): 125. In July 1989, Davies was himself targeted for "elimination" by the CCB but the "project" was withdrawn: Jacques Pauw, *In Heart of the Whore: The Story of Apartheid's Death Squads* (Halfway House: Southern Book Publishers, 1991): 183.
35 Roger Southall, "Restructuring Intelligence for Post-Apartheid South Africa", Mike Hough (ed.), *Security and Intelligence in a Post-Apartheid South Africa – Strategic Review for Southern Africa*, XIV:2 (October 1992): 3–4.
36 Seegers, *The Military*, 186/84.
37 Williams, *Back to the Barracks*, 62.
38 Williams, *Back to the Barracks*, 132; SANDF Nodal Point, Appendix H to Part 3.
39 Williams, *Back to the Barracks*, 132.
40 Williams, *Back to the Barracks*, 139.
41 Williams, *Back to the Barracks*, 133.
42 *SADF Submission*, 50.
43 *SADF Submission*, 80.
44 For a good general examination of special forces world-wide, see Roger A Beaumont, *Military Elites* (New York: The Bobbs-Merrill Company, Inc, 1974). See also Roger A. Beaumont, *Special Operations and Elite Units, 1939–1988* (Greenwood Pub Group, 1988).
45 The use of the term "special forces" does not, in all cases, denote all units attached to the SADF that engaged in unconventional warfare and special operations; a differentiation is clearly made between those units that engaged in clandestine operations, and those that engaged in covert operations. For the purposes of this study, "clandestine operations" refers to those operations carried out by uniformed soldiers of the SADF engaged in operations such that their activities can be neither confirmed nor denied, but such that these operations are not done in the public eye; in contrast, "covert operations" refers to those operations carried out by non-uniformed soldiers and/or civilians such that their involvement in such operations can be plausibly denied and such that these operations are not carried out in the public eye, unless so done for propaganda purposes.
46 Pseudo-operations also had another more sinister application: personnel disguised as guerrillas would enter peasant villages to see what kind of reception they received; if it was warm, the village would be punished for its pro-insurgent stance. This also served – especially if the villagers believed that the operators were insurgents – to encourage the villagers away from supporting the guerrillas. See Stiff and Reid-Daly, *Selous Scouts*, 175–181.
47 Herbert M. Howe, "The South African Defence Force and Political Reform", *Journal of Modern African Studies* 32:1 (1994): 33–38.
48 Williams, *Back to the Barracks*, 230.
49 For an excellent study of the Rhodesian conflict, see J.K. Cilliers, *Counter-Insurgency in Rhodesia* (London: Croom Helm, 1985). For other studies which bear examining for this case, see R.G. Coyle and C.J. Millar, "A Methodology for Understanding Military Complexity: The Case of the Rhodesian Counter-Insurgency Campaign", *Small Wars and Insurgencies* 17:3 (Winter 1996):

360–378; M. Evans, *Fighting Against Chimurenga: An Analysis of Counter-Insurgency in Rhodesia 1972–9*. Local Series 37 (Salisbury: The Historical Association of Zimbabwe, 1981). For specific examinations by insiders, see Stiff and Reid-Daly, *Selous Scouts* and its update Reid-Daly, *Pamwe Chete: The Legend of the Selous Scouts* (Weltevreden Park (South Africa): Covos-Day Books, 1999); Ken Flower, *Serving Secretly: An Intelligence Chief on Record, Rhodesia into Zimbabwe, 1964 to 1981* (London: John Murray, 1987); Chris Cocks, *Fireforce: One Man's War in the Rhodesian Light Infantry* (Weltevreden Park (South Africa): Covos-Day Books, 1997); and Barbara Cole, *The Elite: The Story of the Rhodesian Special Air Service* (Transkei: Three Knights Publishing, 1984).
50 Seegers, *The Military*, 185.
51 This included training in urban and rural counter-insurgency techniques, bushcraft (partly provided by San and Bushmen indigenous forces), tracking (similarly taught by San and Bushmen personnel), counter-terrorism techniques, paramedical support, and other specialist techniques. For a good description of the selection and training process undergone by potential Recce recruits, see Harry McCallion, *Killing Zone: A life in the Paras, the Recces, the SAS and the RUC* (London: Bloomsbury, 1995): 74–105. McCallion – whose real name is Harry Gough – served for a period at the end of the 1970s in the Recces and, while his book is a useful examination of Recce selection and training, corroborative interviews suggest that much of his descriptions of Recce operations are questionable.
52 Williams, *Back to the Barracks*, 11ƒ28i.
53 Republic of South Africa. *Report of the Truth and Reconciliation Commission*, 2:2 "The State Outside South Africa Between 1960 and 1990". Online, available at: www.polity.org.za/govdocs/commissions/1998/trc/2chap2.htm (downloaded 25 August 1999): s177; Appendix 50 [hereafter *TRC2:2*].
54 All Recce information drawn from Paul Els, *We Fear Naught But God: The Story of the South African Special Forces* (Welteverden Park (South Africa): Covos Day Books, 2000) – noted by many former Recces to be "the most accurate" accounting of their units; Ellis and Sechaba, 104–105; Williams, *Back to the Barracks*, 146ƒ36; *SADF Submission*, 48; Davies and O'Meara, "Total Strategy", 195; the controversial Peter Stiff, *The Silent War: South African Recce Operations 1969–1994* (Alberton: Galago Publishing Ltd, 1999); confidential interviews, former Recce officer, August 1996 and March 1997; confidential interview, former SADF Commandant, spring 2000; and *TRC2:2*, Appendix 50–54. See Kevin A. O'Brien, "Special Forces for Counter Revolutionary Warfare",79–109 for a summary of these units and their operations.
55 Breytenbach later said that the formation of 32 Battalion was "cynically motivated": it was thought that the loss of too many white SADF personnel in Angola would cause demoralisation amongst the SADF and the white community back home, leading to political embarrassment and loss of support for the government. Black soldiers, especially foreign nationals, lost in combat would not have even remotely the same impact on the political support for the government. Williams, *Back to the Barracks*, 146ƒ36. For the personal history of the founding and initial operations of 32 Battalion, see Jan Breytenbach, *Forged in Battle* (Cape Town: Saayman and Weber, 1986); for a later account, see Jan Breytenbach, *They Live By The Sword* (Alberton: Lemur Books, 1990), and Jan Breytenbach, *The Buffalo Soldiers: The Story of South Africa's 32-Battalion 1975–1993* (Alberton: Galago Publishing Ltd, 2002); and *TRC2:2*, Appendix 56.
56 Williams, *Back to the Barracks*, 147.
57 Davies and O'Meara, "Total Strategy", 195; Williams, *Back to the Barracks*, 146ƒ36.

58 SADF Special Forces manual, as cited by Williams, *Back to the Barracks*, 146.
59 Williams, *Back to the Barracks*, 214.

4 Hydra: the rise of the national intelligence and counter-revolutionary structures, 1978–1983

1 James Roherty, "Managing the Security Power Base in South Africa", *South African International Quarterly* (Oct 1984): 61. For an in-depth look at the Information Scandal, see M. Rees and C. Day, *Muldergate: The Story of the Information Scandal* (London: Macmillan, 1980).
2 Geldenhuys, *The Diplomacy of Isolation*, 149; Sanders, 121.
3 Grundy, *The Militarization of South African Politics*, 44; Williams, *Back to the Barracks*, 130.
4 Williams, *Back to the Barracks*, 130.
5 Williams, *Back to the Barracks*, 130.
6 Williams, *Back to the Barracks*, 131.
7 Sanders, 124.
8 Geldenhuys, *The Diplomacy of Isolation*, 75; Grundy, *The Militarization of South African Politics*, 91.
9 This scramble in Angola and the relationship-of-circumstances between the CIA and BOSS/DMI is well documented in John Stockwell, *In Search of Enemies: A CIA Story* (New York: W.W. Norton & Company, Inc., 1978). Stockwell had been the CIA station chief in Kinshasa and the head of the CIA operation in Angola. See also Stephen Talbot, "The CIA and BOSS: Thick as Thieves", Ray *et al.*, *Dirty Work 2*, 266–275.
10 Grundy, *The Militarization of South African Politics*, 44.
11 "South Africa: The Security Line-up", 3.
12 Williams, *Back to the Barracks*, 142.
13 A confidential interview with a former NIS officer appeared to indicate contradictory information, however: sometime in 1985/1986, the SSC directed that a special unit – designated "K" (as in *koverte*, Afrikaans for "covert") – should be established within NIS for operational purposes. Divided into four sections (Command, Internal Covert, External Covert, and Operational Intelligence), this unit was devised to "replace the diplomatic missions and their intelligence networks overseas" should these ever be shut down due to sanctions; it was also reportedly designed to survive a post-apartheid transition, much as the SADF's CCB was designed to do. It was allegedly involved in the initial clandestine contacts with the ANC, first in Dakaar and, later, in Switzerland. "K" was alleged to have been terminated in 1990: interview, former NIS officer, London 1998. Initially, no information was found to corroborate this and it was believed that this unit could have related to the operational interests of the Co-ordinating Intelligence Committee ("KIK" in Afrikaans – see further in this study); however, in 2002, former NIS agent Riaan Labuschagne published his book *On South Africa's Secret Service: An Undercover Agent's Story* (Alberton (South Africa): Galago Books, 2002): 178–180, 230), which also noted the existence of "Directorate K" under the NIS as "the best-kept secret of pre-democratic South Africa". Labuschagne noted that "K" was "tasked to conduct any covert action required by National Intelligence or the [SSC]" and "by the early 1990s, had become a microcosm of NIS". Categorically an operational covert intelligence unit – which the NIS and Barnard always denied existed (see Barnard's submission and testimony to the Truth and Reconciliation Commission in the late 1990s) – it "was not restricted by any of the statutes that governed the greater South African intelligence community" and, allegedly, had agents with "executive powers" (i.e. law enforcement and the right to kill). The rest of Labuschagne's

account of "K" corroborates the original information provided to the author – presenting an intriguing point within this history.

14 Republic of South Africa, *Truth and Reconciliation Armed Forces Hearings – SADP*. Online, available at: www.truth.org.za/HRVtrans/forces/sap.htm (downloaded 25 August 1999): 88 [hereafter *Armed Forces Hearings – SAP*].
15 James Adams, *The New Spies: Exploring the Frontiers of Espionage* (London: Pimlico, 1994): xvi.
16 Loch K. Johnson, *America's Secret Power: The CIA in a Democratic Society* (Oxford: Oxford University Press, 1989): 59–73.
17 Ellis, "Third Force", 277–278.
18 *TRC2:3*, Appendix 37.
19 Ellis, "Third Force", 278.
20 As translated from Afrikaans in Williams, *Back to the Barracks*, 143; original *Die Burger* 17 February 1992.
21 Ellis, "Third Force", 277–278.
22 *TRC2:7*, 528.
23 Republic of South Africa, *State Security Council Hearing – Submission of Dr Niel Barnard*. Online, available at: www.truth.org.za/HRVtrans/security/ssbarn.htm (downloaded 24 April 2000) [hereafter *Barnard Submission*].
24 *TRC2:3*, Appendix 7–9.
25 Williams, *Back to the Barracks*, 143.
26 Seegers, *The Military*, 163, 183; *State Security Hearings*, 27.
27 Don Foster, *Detention and Torture in South Africa* (London: James Currey 1987): 31.
28 J.D. Van der Vyver. "State Sponsored Terror Violence". *South African Journal on Human Rights*, 4:1 (March 1988): 67.
29 In 1982, for example, 130 people were detained under section 29; in 1984, 280; in 1985, 406: Foster, op. cit., 32–33.
30 It must be pointed out that the South African courts had the ultimate say in whether an individual made justified use of this provision: Nicholas Haysom, "Licence to Kill Part I: The South African Police and the Use of Deadly Force", *South African Journal on Human Rights*, 3:1 (March 1987): 18.
31 For an extensive discussion of the ANC's intelligence and security apparatus, see Ellis, Stephen, "*Mbokodo*: Security in ANC Camps 1961–1990", *African Affairs* 93:371 (April 1994); ANC, *Submission 1* – 6.3; African National Congress, *Further Submissions and Responses by the ANC to Questions raised by the Commission for Truth and Reconciliation* [hereafter *ANC Submission 2*]; *Operations Report: the Department of Intelligence and Security of the African National Congress* [hereafter *ANC DIS Operations Report*] (12 May 1997). Online, available at: www.anc.org.za/ancdocs/misc/trc2d.html (downloaded 16 May 1997); African National Congress, *Further Submissions and Responses by the ANC to Questions raised by the Commission for Truth and Reconciliation – Appendix One: ANC Structures and Personnel, 1960–1994* [hereafter *ANC Structures*] (12 May 1997). Online, available at: www.anc.org.za/ancdocs/misc/trc2a.html) (downloaded 8 April 2010); and Tsepe Motumi, "The Spear of the Nation – The Recent History of Umkhonto we Sizwe (MK)", J.K. Cilliers and Markus Reichardt (eds), *About-Turn: The Transformation of the South African Military and Intelligence* (Midrand: Institute for Defence Policy, 1996): 92–93. Much of what follows in this section is derived from these sources.
32 ANC, *Submission 1* – 6.3.1 "Context of Security and Intelligence Operations".
33 ANC, *DIS Operations Report* – 1.
34 For an insightful discussion of how the ANC saw the apartheid state's efforts, capabilities and successes at penetrating its ranks, see ANC, *Submission 1* – 6.3.
35 ANC, *DIS Operations Report* – 2.2; ANC, *Submission 1* – 6.3.3.2; Ellis, "*Mbokodo*", 288–289.

36 This is outlined extensively in ANC, *Structures, passim.*
37 Ellis, "*Mbokodo*", 285.
38 ANC, *DIS Operations Report* – 1.
39 Williams, *Back to the Barracks*, 148.
40 Hough and Van der Merwe, 6; Grundy, *The Militarization of South African Politics*, 52.
41 Annette Seegers, "South Africa's National Security Management System, 1972–90", *Journal of Modern African Studies* (1991): 253–254.
42 Seegers, "South Africa's National Security", 254.
43 Seegers, "South Africa's National Security", 254–255.
44 Robert M. Price, *The Apartheid State in Crisis: Political Transformation in South Africa 1975–1990* (New York: Oxford University Press, 1991), 254.
45 Price, *Apartheid State*, 254.
46 Williams, *Back to the Barracks*, 154.
47 Alden, 10.
48 Williams, *Back to the Barracks*, 76.
49 As quoted in Roherty, *State Security*, 44*f*24.
50 Ellis, note to author, 4 June 2000.
51 Robert Davies and Dan O'Meara, "Total Strategy in Southern Africa: An Analysis of South African Regional Policy since 1978", *Journal of Southern African Studies* 11:2 (April 1985): 192; Robert D'A. Henderson, "South African Intelligence under de Klerk", *International Journal of Intelligence and Counterintelligence* 8:1 (Spring 1995): 56.
52 SWATF included six ethnic battalions and one (911) multi-ethnic battalion, as well as Namibian national servicemen. In the same vein, the South-West African Police was created in April 1981. Cawthra, *Brutal Force*, 34; *SADF Submission*, 10.
53 *SADF Submission*, 5.
54 Republic of South Africa, *Report of the Commission of Inquiry into Matters Relating to the Security of the State.*
55 Seegers, "South Africa's National Security", 256.
56 For a discussion of the roles of the intelligence and security forces in the negotiations towards full democracy, as well as the continuing destabilisation of the country before and after the April 1994 all-party elections, see Robert d'A Henderson, "South African Intelligence Under de Klerk"; and Kevin A O'Brien, "South Africa's Evolving Intelligence and Security Structures", *International Journal of Intelligence and Counterintelligence* 9:2 (Summer 1996): 187–232.
57 Williams, *Back to the Barracks*, 154.
58 Seegers, *The Military*, 162–169.
59 Seegers, "South Africa's National Security", 257.
60 Seegers, *The Military*, 162.
61 TBVC is short for Transkei, Bophutatswana, Venda and Ciskei, the four "independent" black homelands, all of which had their own defence forces and (most) intelligence services.
62 Williams, *Back to the Barracks*, 154; Seegers, "South Africa's National Security", 257; Republic of South Africa. *Report of the Truth and Reconciliation Commission*, 2:2 "The State Outside South Africa Between 1960 and 1990". Online, available at: www.polity.org.za/govdocs/commissions/1998/trc/2chap2.htm (downloaded 25 August 1999): 166 [hereafter *TRC2:2*].
63 Alden, 75.
64 Seegers maintains, contrary to Williams, that GIKOM assisted VEIKOM in its day-to-day activities and was not a separate committee within the JMC structure: Seegers, "South African's National Security", 258*f*21.
65 Williams, *Back to the Barracks*, 156, 158–159; Seegers, "South Africa's National Security", 258–259.

66 Seegers, "South Africa's National Security", 258.
67 Seegers, "South Africa's National Security", 257; Williams, *Back to the Barracks*, 156. Interestingly, Alden believes that the SAP's "lack of training in counter-revolutionary warfare" kept them from playing more of a central role in the regional JMCs: Alden, 76/83.
68 "South Africa: The government in the shadows", *Africa Confidential* 28:14 (8 July 1987): 3.
69 Price, *Apartheid State*, 253.
70 Williams, *Back to the Barracks*, 180.
71 De Kock, 92.
72 Williams, *Back to the Barracks*, 169.
73 Williams, *Back to the Barracks*, 156.
74 Seegers, "South Africa's National Security", 257.
75 In the early 1980s, the SSC had substituted the term "Revolutionary Onslaught" for "Total Onslaught": Seegers, *The Military*, 164.
76 Seegers, "South Africa's National Security", 257–258.
77 Seegers, "South Africa's National Security", 263.
78 Williams, *Back to the Barracks*, 157.
79 Williams, *Back to the Barracks*, 161–162.
80 De Kock, 91.
81 Williams, *Back to the Barracks*, 155.

5 Carrot and stick: the domestic COIN paradigm, 1980–1985

1 William Minter, *Apartheid's Contras: An Inquiry into the Roots of War in Angola and Mozambique* (London: Zed Books, 1994), 45.
2 Ellis and Sechaba, 161.
3 Ivor Sarakinsky, "State, Strategy and Extra-Parliamentary Opposition in South Africa, 1983–1988", *Politikon* 16:1 (June 1989): 72.
4 Ellis and Sechaba, 144.
5 Republic of South Africa State Security Council, *Riglyne vir n totale strategie teen die UDF: Tiende monitorverslag 1 April 1985 tot 31 Julie 1985* [Guidelines for a Total Strategy Against the UDF: Tenth Monitoring Report"], translated (15 August 1985).
6 Republic of South Africa State Security Council, *Riglyne vir n Strategie teen die Rewolsionere Oorlog teen die RSA* [Guidelines for a Strategy Against the Revolutionary War Against the RSA], translated (28 April 1986).
7 Ellis and Sechaba, 143.
8 For an understanding of the "street committee system" and the UDF's alternative governance structures, see Price, *Apartheid State*, 202–209.
9 Ellis and Sechaba, 144–145.
10 Roherty, *State Security*, 39–41.
11 Haysom, 5; National Party of South Africa, *National Party Submission to the TRC*. Online, available at: www.truth.org.za/submit/np-truth.htm (downloaded 12 November 1996).
12 Ellis and Sechaba, 160; Williams, *Back to the Barracks*, 170.
13 Williams, *Back to the Barracks*, 225.
14 Williams, *Back to the Barracks*, 225.
15 Ellis, "Third Force", 271.
16 As quoted in Hough and Van der Merwe, 109.
17 Republic of South Africa Department of Defence, "The South African Special Forces – Building on a Proud Tradition". Online, available at: www.mil.za/SANDF/Army/Special_Forces/sa_special_forces_brigade.htm (downloaded 5 March 2000).

18 Ellis, "Third Force", 271; Pauw, *Heart of the Whore*, 122–123.
19 Williams, *Back to the Barracks*, 225.
20 Herbstein and Evenson, 66.
21 Once captured, the guerrilla was faced with two hard choices: either face prosecution, which would most likely result in capital punishment, or work for the security forces; many chose the latter. One of the prime techniques used to "turn" guerrillas was by forcing them to kill an ANC or SWAPO member, either through capture or assassination, in order to implicate them and prevent them from returning to their comrades; however, there were still occasionally *askaris* who did return to the ANC. Often times, the *askaris* who were believed to be considering re-defection would simply be murdered by their officers: Ellis and Sechaba, 116.
22 For a detailed examination of the SAP's intelligence and security structures and operations, see O'Brien, "Counter-intelligence for Counter-revolutionary Warfare", 27–59.
23 *Vrye Weekblad* (9 March 1990), as quoted in Williams, *Back to the Barracks*, 225.
24 Republic of South Africa, *Report of the Truth and Reconciliation Commission*, 2:3 "The State inside South Africa Between 1960 and 1990". Online, available at: www.polity.org.za/govdocs/commissions/1998/trc/2chap3.htm (downloaded 7 November 1998): Appendix 5; African National Congress, *ANC Submission to the Truth and Reconciliation Commission*. Online, available at: www.anc.organisation.za/ancdocs/misc/trcall.html (downloaded 12 October 1996): 4.9.1 [hereafter *ANC Submission*]; Ellis, "Third Force", 274; Republic of South Africa, *State Security Council Hearing – Submission of Dr Niel Barnard*. Online, available at: www.truth.org.za/HRVtrans/security/ssbarn.htm (downloaded 24 April 2000); Pauw, *Heart of Darkness*, 195; confidential interview, former NIS officer, London (26 October 1998).
26 Herbstein and Evenson, 66.
26 Herbstein and Evenson, 61.
27 Cawthra, *Policing South Africa*, 92.
28 The *Flechas* ("Arrows") were a special operations unit formed by the Portuguese PIDE in Angola and dedicated to pseudo-operations; by 1974, it numbered approximately 1,000 personnel. Many of its members fled to Rhodesia to work for the Central Intelligence Organisation following the April 1974 Lisbon coup. Luís A.S. Inocentes, "Counterinsurgency Operations", John P. Cann (ed.), *Memories of Portugal's African Wars, 1961–1974* (Contributions To War Studies, Number One) (June 1997): 41.
29 These pseudo-operations often went too far: in one recorded incident in March 1982, *Koevoet* members masquerading as SWAPO guerrillas killed eight people in the village of Oshipanda, Ovamboland, only for the purpose of "demonstrating" a SWAPO atrocity. Cawthra, *Policing South Africa*, 93.
30 *TRC2:2*, 117; Herbstein and Evenson, 79.
31 De Kock, 72–73.
32 Seegers, *The Military*, 225.
33 Herbstein and Evenson, 75; *Koevoet* members used to wear shirts which boasted "Murder is our business and business is good": Mick Slatter, "The Terrorists Return", *Africa Report* 39:4 (July/August 1994): 60.
34 Ellis, "Third Force", 268.
35 Herbstein and Evenson, 76; *TRC2:2*, 101.
36 Seegers, *The Military*, 225; Herbstein and Evenson, 68, 70.
37 Ellis, "Third Force", 269.
38 Herbstein and Evenson, 61; De Kock, 82.
39 For a description of his career and life, see De Kock, op. cit.
40 "South Africa: The Security Line-up", *Africa Confidential* 28:12 (10 June 1987): 2.

41 Republic of South Africa. *Truth and Reconciliation Armed Forces Hearings – SAP*. Online, available at: www.truth.org.za/HRVtrans/forces/sap.htm: 99 [hereafter *Armed Forces Hearings – SAP*].
42 Anthony Minnaar, "The PEBCO Three, Cradock Four (Goniwe) and Motherwell Killings", Charles Schutte, Ian Liebenberg and Anthony Minnaar (eds), *The Hidden Hand: Covert Operations in South Africa* (Revised Edition) (Pretoria: HSRC, 1998): 287.
43 Pauw, *Heart of the Whore*, 63.
44 *Armed Forces Hearings – SAP*, 99; Pauw, *Heart of the Whore*, 47.
45 Nofemala had been on death-row for other murders and used this information as a bargaining chip to have his sentence commuted. Coetzee had been discharged from the SAP and, fearing prosecution for numerous murders when Nofemala began to reveal all, in 1989 fled to London where he "defected" to the ANC. His revelations to journalist Jacques Pauw formed the basis of Pauw's book *In The Heart of the Whore*, and led President De Klerk to appoint the *Commission of Inquiry Into Certain Murders* (Harms Commission) in 1990.
46 Mamsela was probably the most vicious *askari* ever, confessing to more than 40 killings during his time at Vlakplaas under Dirk Coetzee and in Cronje's unit: Pauw, *Heart of Darkness*, 46, 182.
47 This is what happened with one particular famous case, that of Oliver "Sweet" Sambo, who was killed by the Komatipoort Security Branch during interrogation; C1 operatives "disposed" of his body: De Kock, 214–215.
48 Pauw, *Heart of Darkness*, 59.
49 Ellis, "Third Force", 269.
50 Pauw, *Heart of Darkness*, 30; Patrick Laurence, *Death Squads: Apartheid's Secret Weapon*, (London: Penguin Books, 1990), 61.
51 As quoted in Pauw, *Heart of Darkness*, 36.
52 "De Kock Says he Does not Know how Many People he Killed", SAPA, 20 September 1996; De Kock, 135.
53 "My Strategy is to Keep Talking and Stay Alive, says De Kock after Four Days", *Saturday Star* (Johannesburg), 21 September 1996.
54 "De Kock Once Asked to Kill ANCWL Leader: Court Told", SAPA, 8 October 1996.
55 For a detailed examination of this, see O'Brien, "Counter-intelligence for Counter-revolutionary Warfare, 27–59; and Kevin A. O'Brien, "The Use of Assassination as a Tool of State Policy: South Africa's Counter-revolutionary Strategy 1979–1992 (Part II)", *Terrorism and Political Violence* 13:2 (Spring 2001): 107–142.
56 De Kock himself admitted to this figure: David Welsh, "Right-Wing Terrorism in South Africa". *Terror from the Extreme Right* (Special Issue of *Terrorism and Political Violence*) 7:1 (1995): 243; Laurence, *Death Squads*, 61.
57 "Prime Evil", SABC (1996 – exact date/time unknown) (Producer Jacques Pauw).
58 Pauw, *Heart of the Whore*, 85.
59 "Prime Evil", SABC.
60 De Kock, 99.
61 Bill Keller, "A Glimpse of Apartheid's Dying Sting", *New York Times* (19 February 1995). Online, available at: www.nytimes.com/1995/02/20/world/a-glimpse-of-apartheid-s-dying-sting.html.
62 Mark Israel, "Counter-exile Activities: Covert Action in the United Kingdom", Schutte *et al.*, 347.
63 *ANC Submission*, 5.2.
64 "Z-Squad Incorporated" may simply have been the extension of the BOSS assassination capability, now resident within "G" Section. Williams, *Back to the Bar-*

racks, 146; "The Case of 'Dulcie September'". Gillian Slovo, the daughter of Slovo and First, confronted Craig Williamson in his office in Pretoria. Such direct confrontations also became part of national reconciliation in the post-apartheid era.

65 C1 had previously, in 1981, targeted Janet's husband Marius, also a white ANC activist, however the mission had been called-off at the last moment because of a warning to Schoon from British intelligence. "Vlakplaas's orders for foreign ops came from the top: witness", SAPA, 21 February 1996; Pauw, *Heart of the Whore*, 59.

66 Chris McGreal, "Amnesty for Bombers who Blasted London ANC office", *Guardian* (16 October 1999); De Kock, 82–86.

67 Longreach even used the same address and phone-number as GMR for the first year of its life. "South Africa: The Network of a Master Spy", *Africa Confidential* 2:8 (15 April 1987): 1; Peta Thornycroft, "Palme's Murder Still a Mystery", *Weekly Mail and Guardian* (4 October 1997). This is discussed extensively in Tor Sellström, *Sweden and National Liberation in Southern Africa (A Concerned Partnership (1970–1994))* (Oslo: Nordic Africa Institute, 1999): 556–572.

68 "Former Rhodesian Crack Soldier Implicated in Palme's Murder", SAPA-AP, 29 September 1996.

69 "Man Fingered as Palme Killer Unknown to Swedish Investigators", SAPA-AFP, 29 September 1996; "White Did Not Kill Swedish PM: S. African Agent", SAPA-AFP, 30 September 1996.

70 "Alleged Palme Assassin Thrice Tried to Kill Joshua Nkomo", SAPA-DPA, 2 October 1996. For an account of these operations, see Peter Stiff, *See You In November: Rhodesia's No-holds-barred Intelligence War* (Alberton (South Africa): Galago Books, 1985): 281–282; and Reid-Daly, 388–396.

71 "Investigators Want to See Swede in Cyprus about Palme's Murder", SAPA-AFP, 2 October 1996. At this time, the death of Palme, a fervent anti-apartheid activist, has never been attributed to any individual.

6 The assassins' web: the growth of counter-revolutionary warfare intelligence, 1979–1985

1 Williams, *Back to the Barracks*, 62.
2 *TRC2:2*, 149; *TRC2:3*, Appendix 40.
3 Seegers, *The Military*, 186–187.
4 Louise Flanagan, "Covert operations in the Eastern Cape", Schutte *et al.*, 197; *ANC Submission*, 3.7; *TRC2:3*, 39.
5 Seegers, *The Military*, 186.
6 Seegers, *The Military*, 186/87.
7 As quoted in James M. Roherty, *State Security in South Africa: Civil-Military Relations under P.W. Botha* (London: M.E. Sharpe Inc, 1992): 128.
8 See particularly William Minter, *Apartheid's Contras: An Inquiry into the Roots of War in Angola and Mozambique* (London: Zed Books, 1994); Victoria Brittain, *Hidden Lives, Hidden Deaths: South Africa's Crippling of a Continent* (London: Faber and Faber, 1988); Robert S. Jaster, *South Africa and its Neighbours: the Dynamics of Regional Conflict*. Adelphi Papers 209 (London: International Institute for Strategic Studies, 1986); Joseph Hanlon, *Beggar Your Neighbour* (London: James Currey, 1986); Phyllis Johnson and David Martin, *Apartheid Terrorism: The Destabilization Report* (London: The Commonwealth Secretariat, 1989).
9 Ellis and Sechaba, 95. For what is probably one of the most comprehensive accounts of the "border war" in Angola and Namibia from its beginnings, see

256 *Notes*

William Steenkamp, *South Africa's Border War 1966–1989* (Gibraltar: Ashanti Publishing Ltd, 1989).
10 Robert Price, "Pretoria's Southern African Strategy", *African Affairs* 83:330 (January 1984): 25.
11 Hasu H. Patel, "Zimbabwe: Regional Security in Southern Africa", *Survival* XXX:1 (January/February 1988): 38.
12 As quoted in Hough and Van der Merwe, 121.
13 Minter, 126.
14 Seegers, *The Military*, 185.
15 Confidential interview, SADF officer, June 1995.
16 *SADF Submission*, 72.
17 Williams, *Back to the Barracks*, 132; *TRC2:2*, 158.
18 Williams, *Back to the Barracks*, 144.
19 Williams, *Back to the Barracks*, 144.
20 Reid-Daly, 470–474.
21 Minter, 125.
22 Williams, *Back to the Barracks*, 215.
23 Minter, 198.
24 De Kock, 72.
25 *TRC2:3*, Appendix 42.
26 *TRC2:3*, Appendix 43.
27 Hallett, "The South African Intervention in Angola", 349–350.
28 Williams, *Back to the Barracks*, 144.
29 Williams, *Back to the Barracks*, 144.
30 Richard Dale, "The Armed Forces as an Instrument of South African Policy in Namibia", *Journal of Modern African Studies* 18:1 (1980): 69.
31 *TRC2:2*, 289.
32 Howe, 33–38.
33 *ANC Submission*, 4.7.3.2, 4.9.
34 *ANC Submission*, 4.9.
35 The term "Marion" was chosen apparently because *Inkatha* was to be the "marionette" controlled by the SADF: Bob Drogin, "South African regime trained squad to kill activists, witness says", *Houston Chronicle* (14 March 1996): 28.
36 "Former Finance Minister Linked to Operation Marion", SAPA, 3 May 1996.
37 Human Rights Watch (Africa) 14 March 1995: 3 [hereafter HRW]. As a result of the KwaMakuthu Massacre, 18 people were charged in 1995 with 13 counts of murder, four of attempted murder and one of conspiracy to commit murder; these included former Defence Minister Malan, former SADF Chief Gen Jannie Geldenhuys, former CSI V-Adm Dries Putter, former DCSI Chief Gen Neels van Tonder, former Army Chief Gen Kat Liebenberg, former DMI Chief Gen Tienie Groenewald, former DST2 Director Brig Cornelius van Niekerk, former DMI officer Cmdt Jan van der Merwe, former DMI officer Col Dan Griesel, former SADF Natal Command intelligence officer Lt-Col Johannes Victor, former Special Forces instructor Maj Jakes Jacobs, former DMI officer Brig John More, former Security Branch officer Col Louis Botha, and *Inkatha* executives M.Z. Khumalo, Peter Msane, Prince Mkhize, Scelo Dlovu, Hloni Andreas Mbuyazi, Alex Vulindlela Biyela, and Martin Khanyile. The result of the trial was that three – Groenewald, Victor, and Griesel – were discharged due to a lack of evidence, and the rest were acquitted: see "Malan goes free", *Weekly Mail and Guardian* (11 October 1996). See also SAPA Reports 29 October, 2 November 1995, SAPA Report 23 May 1996.
38 "Malan Trial: Inkatha Training 'Most Sensitive Operation'", SAPA, 18 March 1996.

39 "KATZEN" was an amalgam of the first three letters of the chief of the army General Kat Libenberg's and last three letters of Van der Westhuizen's names: Louise Flanagan, "Covert Operations in the Eastern Cape", Schutte *et al.*, 194; *ANC Submission*, 4.7.3.3.
40 Sam Sole, "The Hammer Unit and the Goniwe Murders", Schutte *et al.*, 273–276.
41 The killing of the Cradock Four had been authorised at a meeting of the SSC on 19 March 1984 following a request by Barend du Plessis (the Minister for Black Education) that they be "removed" due to "inciteful" behaviour; in response on 7 June 1985, Brigadier van der Westhuizen sent a signal from the provincial JMC to the Secretary of the Strategy Branch, requesting permission that "the abovementioned persons [Goniwe and Calata] be permanently removed from society, as a matter of urgency": see Chris McGreal, "Can We Remove these Men?", *Guardian* (28 May 1999); Ellis, "Third Force", 275; Mungo Soggot, "Proof at last: Apartheid Cabinet Ordered Goniwe killing", *Weekly Mail and Guardian* (28 May 1999).
42 Anthony Minnaar, "The 'Third Force' in Retrospect", Schutte *et al.*, 61.
43 Sole, "The Hammer Unit and the Goniwe Murders", 279. It is noteworthy that this killing led, in turn in December 1989, to the deaths of three security policemen, killed by the C1 unit at Vlakplaas, after these individuals threatened to go public about their involvement in the Cradock killings. Authorised by Brigadier Nick van Rensburg (commander of the Security Branch "C" Section) and Colonel Gideon Nieuwoudt (head of the Port Elizabeth Security Branch) as a means of covering their involvement in the Cradock killings, the incident later became known as the Motherwell Bombing; ironically, the ANC accepted responsibility for the attack, which had been made to look like an anti-security forces ANC operation by the C1 team. See De Kock, 120–121; and "De Kock Implicates Himself in 1989 Car Bombing", SAPA, 13 May 1996; De Kock, 170–172; "De Kock Ordered Deaths of 3 PE Policemen, Informer: Prosecutor", SAPA, 16 November 1995.
44 De Kock, 130; Pauw, *Heart of Darkness*, 178–179; Anthony Minnaar, "The PEBCO Three, Cradock Four (Goniwe) and Motherwell Killings", Schutte *et al.*, 284–285.
45 *TRC2:3*, 241.
46 *TRC2:2*, 187.
47 *Vrye Weekblad* (9 March 1990), as quoted in Williams, *Back to the Barracks*, 225.
48 Pauw, *Heart of Darkness*, 224; Laurence, *Death Squads*, 30.
49 For an account of these operations, see Stiff, *See You In November*, 281–282; and Reid-Daly, *Pamwe Chete*, 388–396.
50 Williams, *Back to the Barracks*, 225.
51 Williams, *Back to the Barracks*, 225–226.
52 "Basson Supplied Toxic Substances: Court", SAPA (2 May 2000).
53 Pauw, *Heart of the Whore*, 210; Williams, 226.
54 "Basson Supplied Poisons to Kill Prisoners – Court", SAPA (3 May 2000).
55 Williams, *Back to the Barracks*, 226.
56 Williams, *Back to the Barracks*, 227.
57 "Seniors Should Take Rap for Killings, Assassin Tells Basson Trial", SAPA (11 May 2000).
58 Williams, *Back to the Barracks*, 227.
59 Williams, *Back to the Barracks*, 227.
60 *TRC2:2*, 381.
61 *TRC2:2*, 382.
62 For what is probably the best discussion of not only the CCB but South African "death-squads" in full, see Pauw, *Heart of the Whore*; see also Pauw's subsequent

book *Into the Heart of Darkness: Confessions of Apartheid's Assassins* (Johannesburg: Jonathan Ball Publishers, 1997), in particular 224–234. Finally, see also Laurence, *Death Squads.*
63 Republic of South Africa, *Commission of Inquiry into Certain Alleged Murders* (Harms Commission) (Pretoria, Government Printer 109/1990): 37.
64 Laurence, *Death Squads*, 30. During testimony to the Harms Commission (the "Commission of Inquiry into Certain Murders" of 1990), General Joubert, by then Deputy Chief-of-Staff, Intelligence, stated that the undertaking of projects of an extreme political or military sensitivity all had to be approved by General Geldenhuys and Minister Malan; this statement was supported by Major-General Jan Klopper (the Chief of Air Staff Operations in 1990) and former SADF Chief General Constand Viljoen. See Williams, *Back to the Barracks*, 226.
65 *Armed Forces Hearings – SADF*, 48.
66 *Armed Forces Hearings – SADF*, 53.
67 *Commission of Inquiry into Certain Alleged Murders*, 35.
68 *TRC2:2*, 387–398.
69 Confidential interview, former Special Forces officer, Britain, March 1997.
70 *SADF Submission*, 48.
71 *Armed Forces Hearings – SADF*, 46; Varney, D21.1.
72 RSA, *Commission of Inquiry into Certain Alleged Murders* (Pretoria, 1990): 35.
73 Williams, *Back to the Barracks*, 228–229.
74 Pauw, *Heart of the Whore*, 152; Laurence, *Death Squads*, 28–29.
75 Laurence, *Death Squads*, 32.
76 Pauw, *Heart of the Whore*, 159.
77 Laurence, *Death Squads*, 73; Williams, *Back to the Barracks*, 229.
78 Williams, *Back to the Barracks*, 229.
79 Ellis, "Third Force", 279–280.
80 Pauw, *Heart of the Whore*, 151–152; Williams, *Back to the Barracks*, 229.
81 Williams, *Back to the Barracks*, 228.
82 Williams, *Back to the Barracks*, 228.
83 John F. Burns, "Cape Town Death-Squad Inquiry Opens", *New York Times*, March 6, 1990, A3; Laurence, *Death Squads*, 24–25.
84 Pauw, *Heart of Darkness*, 226; Williams, *Back to the Barracks*, 229.
85 Williams, *Back to the Barracks*, 229–230.
86 Pauw, *Heart of Darkness*, 228; Williams, *Back to the Barracks*, 226.
87 Williams, *Back to the Barracks*, 226.
88 Williams, *Back to the Barracks*, 232*f*39.
89 See Greg Nott, "The David Webster Inquest and the CCB", Schutte *et al.*, op. cit.
90 Pauw, *Heart of the Whore*, 130–134. Subsequently during the Truth and Reconciliation Commission hearings, in August 1997, Mark Nielsen who claims to have worked for the CCB and for DMI, applied for amnesty for killing Webster; he also applied for amnesty for his role in Lubowski's assassination, although he says his role was only to supply the AK-47 rifle for that killing. "Prisoner Seeks Amnesty for Webster Killing", *Cape Argus Times* 7 August 1997.
91 Williams, *Back to the Barracks*, 229.
92 John F. Burns, "Pretoria Minister Halts Covert Unit", *New York Times*, February 27, 1990: A10.

7 Crossing the Rubicon: "the gloves come off" for a total counter-revolutionary strategy, 1985–1990

1 Ellis, "Third Force", 273.
2 Ellis, "Third Force", 273.

3 *TRC2:2*, 441–444. So negative was the general reaction to the raid that an elaborate propaganda exercise had to be mounted to justify the operation; orchestrated by Craig Williamson, it included the planting of stories in newspapers such as the *Citizen* and *Sunday Times,* pointing at "massive arms caches discovered" by the security forces prior to the raid. In 1996, former C1 commander De Kock revealed that his team had planted the arms-cache "discovered" and used to justify the raid, with the knowledge of Foreign Affairs Minister Pik Botha. "De Kock claims on cross-border raids are shocking: Pik Botha", SAPA, 19 September 1996; Roherty, *State Security*, 129; *SADF Submission*, 67; *TRC2:2*, 445–447.
4 *Caprivis Hearing*, 57.
5 Ellis, "Third Force", 264, 273.
6 Ellis, "Third Force", 273.
7 Sarakinsky, 72.
8 As quoted in Price, *Apartheid State*, 255.
9 Sparks, *The Mind of South Africa*, 357.
10 Williams, *Back to the Barracks*, 153.
11 Beresford, "The President, the Generals and the Murdered Teacher" *Guardian*, date unknown.
12 Seegers, "South Africa's National Security", 268.
13 Denis Herbstein, "Spy Master and Spy: Old spies don't die…", *Africa Report* 39:2 (March/April 1994): 45.
14 Seegers, "South Africa's National Security", 269.
15 "Any operational area" included all areas where the security forces were deployed "on service in the prevention or suppression of terrorism": Republic of South Africa, *Defence Act* (No 44 of 1957, as amended): s103*ter*.
16 Simon Baynham, "Political Violence and the Security Response", Jesmond Blumenfeld (ed.), *South Africa in Crisis* (London: RIIA, 1987): 108.
17 "South Africa: The Security Line-up", *Africa Confidential* 28:12 (10 June 1987): 1.
18 Pieter H. Groenewald, "Counter-revolutionary Action in South Africa: 1984–1990", *American Review* (Johannesburg) 10:2 (1991): 18.
19 Seegers, "South Africa's National Security", 261f26.
20 Johnson and Martin, 63, 106; *SADF Submission*, 67, 71.
21 Williams, *Back to the Barracks*, 152.
22 *State Security Hearing*, 2.
23 Swilling and Phillips, "State Power in the 1980s", 143.
24 Groenewald, 19.
25 As quoted in Swilling and Phillips, "State Power in the 1980s", 144–145.
26 Swilling and Phillips, "State Power in the 1980s", 145; *State Security Hearings*, 21.
27 Swilling and Phillips, "State Power in the 1980s", 146.
28 Sparks, *The Mind of South Africa*, 358.
29 *State Security Hearing*, 8–9.
30 *Armed Forces Hearings – SAP*, 96.
31 Ellis, "Third Force", 278–279.
32 *State Security Hearing*, 9; *Armed Forces Hearings – SAP*, 73–76, 90.
33 Testimony by Major Crafford, *Armed Forces Hearings – SAP*, 103.
34 Testimony by Brigadier Osthuizen and Brigadier Schoon, *Armed Forces Hearings – SAP*, 96, 97.
35 Colin Hossack, "State Security Council Members Knew Very Well what 'Eliminate' Meant", *Africa News Service* (30 October 1998).
36 *TRC2:3*, 451–452.
37 Cawthra, 220.
38 *Armed Forces Hearings – SADF*, 43–44.
39 *Armed Forces Hearings – SADF*, 44.

40 *TRC2:3*, Appendix 5; *ANC Submission*, 4.9.1; Pauw, *Heart of Darkness*, 195; confidential interview, London (26 October 1998).
41 Ellis, "Third Force", 274; *Barnard Submission*.
42 *TRC2:3*, 461.
43 *TRC2:3*, 463–464.
44 *TRC2:3*, 465, 498.
45 *TRC2:3*, 469.
46 *TRC2:3*, 465.
47 *TRC2:3*, 504.
48 *TRC2:3*, 460.
49 *TRC2:3*, 467.
50 *TRC2:3*, 473.
51 *TRC2:3*, 508.
52 *TRC2:3*, 476.
53 *TRC2:3*, 484.
54 *TRC2:3*, 499.
55 *TRC2:3*, 509.
56 *TRC2:3*, 488.
57 *TRC2:3*, 492.
58 De Kock, 95.
59 Overall information taken from *TRC2:3*, 457–509.
60 Williams, *Back to the Barracks*, 177.
61 Seegers, "South Africa's National Security", 261.
62 Williams, *Back to the Barracks*, 154.
63 Meyer had previously chaired the *Geveilstaf*, which became the NJMC: Seegers, "South Africa's National Security", 258.
64 Alden, 223.
65 Alden, 224.
66 Seegers, "South Africa's National Security", 261.
67 *Armed Forces Hearings – SADF*, 44, 50.
68 Williams, *Back to the Barracks*, 176.
69 Williams, *Back to the Barracks*, 176.
70 Williams, *Back to the Barracks*, 178–179.
71 Williams, *Back to the Barracks*, 179.
72 Groenewald, 19.
73 Patrick Laurence, "South Africa's 'Third Force' Soon in the Dock", *The Star International Weekly* (Johannesburg) 30 December 1994: 15. See also John Battersby, "A Secret Network to Preserve White Power", *The Christian Science Monitor* 24 August 1992: 6–7; Paul Taylor, "S. Africa's Past Horrors Pose Questions About Future Justice", *The Washington Post* 4 March 1995: A1, A22; and Allister Sparks, "Answers are Needed about NP's Secret Operations", *The Star International Weekly* (Johannesburg) 29 June–5 July 1995: 11.
74 State Security Council, "*Vergadering van die Staatsveiligheidsraad in Tuynhuys, Kaapstad op Maandag, 12 Mei 1986 om 09h30*", as quoted in De Kock, 280.
75 "Malan's Counsel Objects to Documents in KwaMakuthu Trial", SAPA, 7 August 1996.
76 *TRC6:4*, 584.
77 Battersby, 6–7.
78 Ellis, "Third Force", 273–274.
79 *Caprivi Hearings*, C1.4.
80 *Caprivis Hearing*, 124.
81 *Caprivis Hearing*, 59.
82 This could have included anything from "breaking a window to killing an ANC or PAC member": De Kock, 99, 151.

83 Alden, 219.
84 Ellis, "Third Force", 275.
85 Sparks, *The Mind of South Africa*, 356, 358.
86 "KwaMakuthu: Defence calls Gen to Define Military Terms", SAPA, 26 August 1996.
87 Ellis, "Third Force", 275.
88 "KwaMakuthu: Defence calls Gen to Define Military Terms", SAPA, 26 August 1996.
89 Paul Moorcroft, *African Nemesis: War and Revolution in Southern Africa 1945–2010* (London: Brassey's UK, 1990): 372.
90 Seegers, *The Military*, 248–249.
91 Seegers, *The Military*, 251.
92 *Barnard Submission*.
93 *Barnard Submission*.
94 Seegers, *The Military*, 253.
95 Jacklyn Cock, "Introduction", Cock and Nathan, 11; Roherty, *State Security*, 127.
96 Roherty, *State Security*, 136.
97 The securocrats believed this hard-core and criminal element constituted no more than 3 per cent of the opposition, and that if it could be eliminated then the resistance would subside: Roherty, *State Security*, 136.
98 Roherty, *State Security*, 132; "South Africa: The Security Line-up", 1.
99 "South Africa: The Security Line-up", 1.
100 "South Africa: The Security Line-up", 1.
101 Sparks, *The Mind of South Africa*, 358.
102 Sparks, *The Mind of South Africa*, 358.
103 Seegers, *The Military*, 309–310.
104 Sparks, *The Mind of South Africa*, 364.
105 An excellent overview and insights into all of this is provided in Chester Crocker, *High Noon in Southern Africa: Making Peace in a Rough Neighborhood* (Johannesburg: Jonathan Ball, 1993).
106 *National Party Submission*.
107 See Henderson, "South African Intelligence", 58–59. Elements within DMI allegedly faked several United Nations Transitional Assistance Group (UNTAG) radio-messages indicating that SWAPO were planning yet another armed incursion in the same manner as they had done in March 1989; the exposure of this hoax led to severe embarrassment for both Foreign Minister Botha and new State President De Klerk.
108 On this matter, see Sanders, *Apartheid's Friends*, *passim*; and Bob Woodward, *Veil: The Secret Wars of the CIA, 1981–1987* (New York: Simon & Schuster, 2005): 248, 256.
109 Alden, 243–244.
110 As quoted in Henderson, "South African Intelligence", 63/40.
111 Henderson, "South African Intelligence", 72/66.
112 Seegers, *The Military*, 263.
113 An excellent account of these can be found in Sparks, *Tomorrow Is Another Country*, especially chapter 3.
114 Alden, 267.
115 Williams, *Back to the Barracks*, 213.
116 For an interesting assessment of Botha's successes and failures in furthering reform, see Schrire, 115–123.

8 Negotiating a settlement: reform and retrenchment for all, 1990–1994

1. Mark Shaw, "Spy meets spy: Negotiating new intelligence structures", Steve Friedman and Doreen Atkinson (eds), *The Small Miracle: South Africa's Negotiated Settlement*. South African Review 7 (Johannesburg: Raven Press, 1994): 257–259.
2. Ellis, "*Mbokodo*", 295, 296. Indeed, O'Malley's biography of Mac Maharaj notes an incredible list of senior ANC and SACP members suspected or reported to the NEC and/or *Mbokodo* at various times as being agents of not only the apartheid state but also British and American intelligence (see Padraig O'Malley, *Shades of Difference: Mac Maharaj and the Struggle for South Africa* (New York: Viking, 2007): 268).
3. The ANC would institute no fewer than four high-level investigations into these abuses – alongside mutinies by MK cadres – in its camps, including the Stuart (1984), Jobodwana (1990), Skweyiya (1992) and Motsuenyane (1993) Commissions: see Ellis, "*Mbokodo*", 279–284 for a discussion of the commissions and their conclusions. The fact of these commissions also meant that, when it came to submitting amnesty applications to the post-apartheid Truth and Reconciliation Commission (TRC) in 1996–1997, the ANC maintained that one of the reasons its cadres were not required to was because these commissions had already investigated all human rights abuses in the ANC's exile structures – a point which would prove to be contentious, to say the least.
4. Ellis, "*Mbokodo*", 292; see also Paul Trewhela, "A Literature of Wolves", *Searchlight South Africa* 2:4 (No. 8) (January 1992): 68. It is very interesting to note, in contrast, that Ronnie Kasrils – former head of MK Intelligence and Special Operations – in his autobiography states that "whatever might be thought about interrogation methods in Communist countries, I found that Soviet and East German training emphasised the need to depend on brain work and not beatings to arrive at the truth": Ronnie Kasrils, *"Armed and Dangerous": My Underground Struggle Against Apartheid* (Oxford: Heinemann Educational, 1993): 257.
5. ANC, *DIS Operations Report* – 2.3.
6. Seegers, *The Military*, 280–281; African National Congress, *Operations Report: the Department of Intelligence and Security of the African National Congress*. Online, available at: www.anc.org.za/ancdocs/misc/trc2d.html (downloaded 16 May 1997).
7. Tim Jenkin, "Talking To Vula: The Story of the Secret Underground Communications Network of Operation Vula", *Mayibuye* (May – October 1995).
8. O'Malley, *Shades of Difference*, 267–270, 275–277.
9. Jenkin, "Talking To Vula".
10. Henderson, 'South African Intelligence Under de Klerk', 68.
11. Patti Waldmeir, *Anatomy of a Miracle* (London: Penguin Books, 1997): 195.
12. Mark Shaw, "Biting the Bullet: Negotiating Democracy's Defence", Friedman and Atkinson (eds), *The Small Miracle*, 231–232.
13. Sparks, *The Mind of South Africa*, 401.
14. "SANDF Chief of Staff Testifies in De Kock Trial", SAPA, 23 November 1995; "ANC Leaders' Arrests Led to Closure of Operation Vula", SAPA, 24 November 1995.
15. Ellis, "Third Force", 286.
16. Sparks, *The Mind of South Africa*, 400; Jenkin, "Talking To Vula".
17. Williams, *Back to the Barracks*, 235.
18. Waldmeir, 145. Whether such earlier meetings actually took place – and where and involving who – remain shrouded in mystery, not the least of which by its

Notes 263

alleged participants (including Mbeki and Zuma). Barnard used to travel regularly – and clandestinely – to Lusaka, where the ANC's leadership were based, and British intelligence reported contacts in London in the mid-1980s.

19 Alden, 267. For a discussion of the secret negotiations, see Sparks, *Tomorrow Is Another Country*, 21–119 *inter alia* – and 109–119 specifically concerning the Lucerne meetings.
20 This is discussed in great detail by Mandela himself in his autobiography *Long Walk To Freedom* (London: Little, Brown and Company, 1994): 522–545. It is also extremely interesting to understand Barnard's take on the meetings, which can be read at John Carlin, "Interview: Dr Neil Barnard", *The Long Walk of Nelson Mandela* – PBS Frontline (May 1999). Online, available at: www.pbs.org/wgbh/pages/frontline/shows/mandela/interviews/barnard.html. See also Sparks, *Tomorrow Is Another Country*, 36–56.
21 Sanders, 247.
22 Henderson, "South African Intelligence", 57.
23 Alden, 279; Seegers, *The Military*, 266–267.
24 Henderson, "South African Intelligence", 72. An excellent accounting of the CODESA negotiations – the first round of which occurred in December 1991 and, following their initial collapse, were resumed as CODESA-II on 15–16 May 1992 – can be found in Waldmeir, *Anatomy of a Miracle*, 191–195, 202–204. See also Doreen Atkinson, "Brokering a Miracle? The Multiparty Negotiating Forum", Friedman and Atkinson (eds), *The Small Miracle*, 13–43.
25 Henderson, "South African Intelligence", 65.
26 Henderson, "South African Intelligence", 68. More extensively, see O'Malley, *Shades of Difference*, 267–270. See also Jenkin, "Talking to Vula".
27 Henderson, "South African Intelligence", 59.
28 Seegers, *The Military*, 273; Henderson, "South African Intelligence", 60–61.
29 Henderson, "South African Intelligence", 69.
30 Eddie Koch, "A NIS Spy Centre?", *The Weekly Mail* (12–18 June 1992): 2.
31 Henderson, "South African Intelligence", 72.
32 Henderson, "South African Intelligence", 70–71.
33 "Baboon Foetus Placed at Tutu's House to Bewitch Him", SAPA (12 May 2000).
34 Laurence, *Death Squads*, 11, 12.
35 Laurence, *Death Squads*, 11, 12.
36 Ellis, "Third Force", 283.
37 Ann Eveleth, "Stratcom Never Died, Says ex-Cop", *Weekly Mail and Guardian* 18 August 1995.
38 As quoted in Ellis, "Third Force", 278.
39 *TRC2:7*, 499.
40 Henderson, "South African Intelligence", 78, n90.
41 *TRC2:7*, 499–501.
42 See Harms Commission, op. cit.
43 Laurence, *Death Squads*, 25.
44 Laurence, *Death Squads*, 29.
45 Laurence, *Death Squads*, 27.
46 Pauw, *Heart of the Whore*, 254–255.
47 "Mail Bugging Trial Continues", *Weekly Mail and Guardian* (27 December 1995); Pauw, *Heart of Darkness*, 133; "Prime Evil", SABC.
48 Ellis, "Third Force", 295. Henderson noted that this "Inner Circle" claimed to be a 'formal covert group' composed of former securocrats from across the security forces, which had decided that "de Klerk's reform process was 'running out of control'" and "demanded a 'turn back' from CODESA" or else De Klerk would "face the consequences". See Henderson, "South African Intelligence", n72.

264 Notes

49 Republic of South Africa, *White Paper on Intelligence* (October 1994): 18–19 [hereafter *White Paper*].
50 *White Paper*, 17–18; Confidential interview, October 2008.
51 Henderson, "South African Intelligence", 73. Ellis also defined it more simply as "a substantial, organised group of security officials or former officials intent on perpetrating violence in the service of a counter-revolutionary strategy": Ellis, "Third Force", 263.
52 For comprehensive overviews of the "Third Force", see *TRC2:6*, Appendix. See also Charles Schutte, Liebenberg, Ian and Minnaar, Anthony (eds), *The Hidden Hand: Covert Operations in South Africa* (Revised Edition) (Pretoria: HSRC, 1998); Pauw, *Heart of Darkness*; Ellis, "Third Force", 261–300; and Eugene De Kock (as told to Jeremy Gordin), *A Long Night's Damage: Working for the Apartheid State* (Saxonwold (South Africa): Contra Press, 1998).
53 Henderson, "South African Intelligence", 73.
54 Ellis, "Third Force", 293.
55 The National Peacekeeping Force (NPKF) was intended to be an independent crowd-control and community policing entity, under the direct control of the TEC, to allow both the SAP and the SADF to leave those most volatile areas where its presence contributed to the volatility – its development and deployment were plagued with problems, and it only deployed once (into the East Rand in a very dangerous situation) before being withdrawn to barracks and disbanded: see Shaw, "Biting the Bullet", 244–245.
56 Ellis, "Third Force", 286–287. The best assessment of this remains volume 2, chapter 7 of the TRC's Final Report. Online, available at: www.justice.gov.za/trc/report/finalreport/Volume%202.pdf, and volume 6, section 4 – Appendix. Online, available at: www.justice.gov.za/trc/report/finalreport/vol. 6_s4.pdf. See also Sparks, *Tomorrow Is Another Country, passim*.
57 Ellis, "Third Force", 285.
58 De Kock, 189.
59 De Kock, 190.
60 Ellis, "Third Force", 269.
61 "Prime Evil", SABC; De Kock, 244.
62 Ellis, "Third Force", 285.
63 John Battersby, "A Secret Network to Preserve White Power," *Christian Science Monitor* (24 August 1992); Sparks, *Tomorrow Is Another Country*, 174.
64 *ANC Submission*, 3.7; *TRC2:3*, 39.
65 "Vlakplaas and MI Responsible for Transkei Coup: Affidavit", SAPA, 11 July 1995; De Kock, 179–183.
66 Flanagan, "Covert operations in the Eastern Cape", 197.
67 *Armed Forces Hearings – SADF*, 33.
68 Sparks, *Tomorrow Is Another Country*, 172–173; Henderson, "South African Intelligence", 77.
69 *ANC Submission*, 4.9.
70 See TRC, "Political Violence in the era of Negotiations and Transition 1990–94", volume 2 chapter 7–94; Sparks, *Tomorrow Is Another Country*, 140–142.
71 Henderson, "South African Intelligence", 77.
72 De Klerk maintained later that "a written report did not exist" and that Steyn had only briefed him orally on his findings in December 1992 – see "F.W. de Klerk rejects TRC allegations", SAPA (16 January 1997). Steyn would also reveal later that the "SADF counter-intelligence organisation and the counter-intelligence of the former [NIS] were utilised to gather intelligence regarding these covert activities" – "Steyn Denies He Fingered Generals to De Klerk", SAPA (17 January 1997).

73 *Staff Paper Prepared for the Steyn Commission on Alleged Dangerous Activities of SADF Components* (December 1992) – in author's possession. See also *TRC2:7*, 19–21; Chiara Carter, "Apartheid Army's Deadly Secrets", *Sunday Independent* (30 April 2006). Online, available at: www.iol.co.za/index.php?set_id=1&click_id=13&art_id=vn20060430083249898C116766&singlepage=1; "South African Apartheid Probe Flooded with Allegations", AFP (31 January 1997); Stefaans Brümmer, "De Klerk 'Knew of Third Force Activities'", *Electronic Mail and Guardian* (16 January 1997); and "Shocks from the Steyn Report", *Electronic Mail and Guardian* (31 January 1997).

74 It is noteworthy that those the SADF leadership recommended should be retired included General Thirion, whom the Steyn Report specifically recommended for exemption from action, and excluded other names – including those of the three generals who drew up the list – against whom it was initially reported that Steyn had recommended that action *should* be taken. See *TRC2:7*, 22; Ellis, "Third Force", 290; Henderson, "South African Intelligence", 77; and Sparks, *Tomorrow Is Another Country*, 173–174. Subsequently, Steyn released a statement to the TRC noting that he had "only advised de Klerk to order a criminal investigation after 23 officers had already been suspended or compelled to take early retirement" and that he "denied he made any specific recommendations to former State President F.W. de Klerk": "Steyn Denies He Fingered Generals to De Klerk", SAPA (17 January 1997).

75 Henderson, "South African Intelligence", 77–78.

76 *TRC2:7*, 22–23; "F.W. de Klerk rejects TRC allegations", SAPA (16 January 1997).

77 Carter, "Apartheid Army's Deadly Secrets", notes that it was "insider intelligence provided by both military and [NIS] agents" which proved so decisive in Steyn's assessments.

78 *Reports of the Commission of Inquiry Regarding the Prevention of Public Violence and Intimidation* (RJ Goldstone, Chairman): the illegal importation, distribution and use of firearms, ammunition and explosives by the SAP, SADF, ANC and IFP (5 October 1993); on security force involvement and alleged misconduct by the SAP (26 November 1993); Fourth Interim Report on hit squads and the SAP Internal Stability Division (6 December 1993); on attacks on members of the SAP, Self Defence and Protection Units of the IFP or ANC, and the murder of IFP members (21 April 1994). In particular, the report of 18 March 1994 entitled *Interim Report on Criminal Political Violence by Elements within the South African Police, the Kwazulu Police and the Inkatha Freedom Party'*, *by the Commission of Inquiry regarding the Prevention of Public Violence and Intimidation* detailing "third-force activities" and criminal political violence of the ANC, IFP, and elements within the SAP and KwaZulu Police in KwaZulu(-Natal) is essential.

79 Henderson, "South African Intelligence", 78, n92.

80 De Kock was found guilty of six counts of murder, one of attempted murder, and numerous other counts of assault, fraud, arms trafficking, narcotics trafficking, and sentenced to two life sentences plus 212 years. At 11:50pm on 10 May 1997 (the deadline for amnesty applications), De Kock submitted an application for amnesty to the Truth Commission. De Kock's amnesty application was expected to provide even more insight than the evidence at his trial had regarding the apartheid regime's covert machinery. See Jim Day, "De Kock Reveals Plan to Murder Nujoma", *Electronic Mail and Guardian* 16 May 1997. Online, available at: pubweb.web.co.za/mg/news.

81 DMI developed plans to do the same thing it had done in Namibia – influencing the elections away from SWAPO using COMOPS (see Chapter 7) – in the 1992 Angolan national elections between the ruling MPLA government and the Jonas Savimbi's UNITA forces (which both Pretoria and Washington

266 *Notes*

had provided covert support to for more than 15 years), by preparing for a "military takeover" should UNITA lose the elections; the plans were never brought to fruition: see *SouthScan* 7:20 (22 May 1992): 146; *New Nation* (26 February – 4 March 1993): 1; and SAPA (27 February 1993).
82 Ellis' SADF source maintains that ECHOES was "officially 'aimed at combating verbal attacks on [SADF] duties and functions. Activity relates to the acquisition of information in relation to MK [Umkhonto we Sizwe] mainly and passing this to the media'", but ultimately involved "violence, blackmail and other illegal means": Ellis, "Third Force", 288.
83 ANC Submission, 4.9.
84 "SADF Will Not Comment On 'Project Echoes'", SAPA (12 November 1992); John Carlin, "SA Hit-Squad 'Linked to RUC'", *Independent* (London) (14 November 1992).
85 Ellis, "Third Force", 283–284.
86 See, for example, Bill Berkeley, "The Warlords of Natal", *The Atlantic Monthly* 273:3 (March 1994): 85–100; Ruth Elizabeth Tomaselli, "Inkathagate: Covert Funding – Overt Violence", *Covert Action*, 38 (Fall 1991): 39–43. See also 'Intelligence Officer Says he Knew about Stratcom', *Weekly Mail and Guardian* (21 July 1995); and 'The Secrets of Stratcom', *Weekly Mail and Guardian* (23 June 1995).
87 Henderson, "South African Intelligence", 70 and n59.
88 Henderson, "South African Intelligence", 71.
89 This is discussed in great detail in *TRC2:6 passim*.
90 *TRC2:6d*, 34–42.
91 Ellis, "Third Force", 288.
92 Henderson, "South African Intelligence", n64.
93 Henderson, "South African Intelligence", 78.
94 *TRC2:7*, 542–543.
95 This issue – De Klerk's weakness and the fact that he appeared to only instigate investigations into covert activities when forced to by "public smoking gun evidence" – is discussed in great detail in Henderson, "South African Intelligence", 52ff.
96 Rocklyn Williams, "All the President's Men," *Saturday Star* (Johannesburg) (11 July 1992): 11.
97 Ellis, "Third Force", 282.
98 Henderson, "South African Intelligence", 78, n92.
99 Henderson, "South African Intelligence", 79.
100 Henderson, "South African Intelligence", 76.
101 Henderson, "South African Intelligence", n81.
102 Given that these trials occurred at the time of the Truth and Reconciliation Commission (TRC) in the mid-to-late 1990s, many analysts felt, however, that placing such individuals on trial – and, therefore, abrogating this amnesty – was not so much an attempt to bring them to book, but rather a ploy to force these individuals (and others) to apply to the TRC for amnesty. Such a ploy may have worked: while Malan and his co-accused were on trial, other apartheid-era personalities – including Dirk Coetzee and former SSC superspy Craig Williamson – placed applications before the commission for amnesty in return for testifying. See SAPA Reports 14 March, 12 April 1996.
103 Ellis, "Third Force", 277–278.
104 For a discussion of these, see Sparks, *Tomorrow Is Another Country*; see also Henderson, "South African Intelligence", 51–89.
105 Ted Bauman, "The Key to a Peaceful South Africa", *The World and I* (October 1993). Online, available at: www.worldandi.com/specialreport/1993/october/Sa11159.htm.

106 As Ellis notes, this was "a case of wanting them inside, where they were at least under observation, rather than outside, where all manner of harm was possible": Ellis, "Third Force", 293.
107 Sparks, *Tomorrow Is Another Country*, 119.
108 Henderson, "South African Intelligence", n66.
109 Henderson, "South African Intelligence", 79.
110 Sparks, *Tomorrow Is Another Country*, 115; Henderson, "South African Intelligence", n66.
111 Republic of South Africa, *Transitional Executive Council Act* (Act 151 of 1993); Shaw, "Spy Meets Spy", 263.
112 Although the "independent homelands" of Transkei, Bophutatswana, and Venda had intelligence services (civilian and military), Ciskei did not; its International Research Bureau, which later became the Ciskei Intelligence Service, was disbanded in August 1991 due to (at best) questionable covert activities: see Sandy Africa, "The Role, Prospects and Expectations of the TBVC Intelligence Services During an Interim Government Period", *Strategic Review For Southern Africa: Security and Intelligence in a Post-Apartheid South Africa* XIV:2 (October 1992): 79. For a brief discussion of the PASS, also known as the PAC Intelligence and Security Department, see Tom Lodge, "A Profile of the Azanian Peoples' Liberation Army", Cilliers & Reichardt, 109.
113 Shaw, "Spy Meets Spy", 268–269.
114 Republic of South Africa, *Transitional Executive Council Act* (Act 151 of 1993); Shaw, "Spy Meets Spy", 263.
115 These – and the fall-out from each – are discussed in great detail in Sparks, *Tomorrow Is Another Country*.
116 Joe Nhlanhla, "The Modalities of Combining the SATBVC and Liberation Movements' Intelligence Services in a Changing South Africa", *Strategic Review for Southern Africa: Security and Intelligence in a Post-Apartheid South Africa* XIV:2 (October 1992), 66.
117 Republic of South Africa, *Constitution of the Republic of South Africa* (as drafted April 1996): s186(a).
118 *White Paper*, 6–7.
119 *White Paper*, 7.
120 Nhlanhla, "The Modalities of Combining the SATBVC and Liberation Movements' Intelligence Services in a Changing South Africa", 76.
121 *White Paper*, Annexure B: *Basic Principles and Guidelines of National Intelligence*.
122 *White Paper*, 2–3.
123 *White Paper*.
124 *White Paper*, 11. This code of conduct would reflect similar ones for SAPS and SANDF.
125 Ellis, "Third Force", 293.
126 Shaw, "Spy Meets Spy", 269.
127 Rex Gibson, "Memoirs of an Invisible Man", *Star International Weekly* (Johannesburg) (26 January–1 February 1995): 13.

9 Progress and problems: South Africa's new intelligence dispensation, 1994–2005

1 Waldmeir, 259.
2 This was certainly still the case in the period immediately following their unbanning and during the process of the ANC reorganising – and reintegrating – itself from a jailed-and-exiled liberation movement into a bona fide political party involved in negotiating the settlement; Waldmeir notes that, in July 1991 at the ANC's first conference inside South Africa since 1958, Alfred

Nzo (then outgoing ANC Secretary-General) berated the executive and the rank-and-file for

> Lacking enterprise, creativity and initiative ... happy to remain pigeonholed within the confines of populist rhetoric and cliché ... we have not utilised our full potential to mobilise millions of our people into effective action ... [we are in] danger of being removed from the leadership pedestal [the ANC] now occupies.
>
> (Waldmeir, 197)

This was a severely damning indictment of the ANC's negotiating position based on its strengths and weaknesses at that stage.

3 Much of the basis for confrontation and tensions between the ANC and Inkatha results not only from the deep-rooted antagonism between the two former liberation movements that developed over decades of apartheid, but as well from the fact that the IFP had long been covertly supported by the apartheid government in operations against the ANC. The revelation of this support in 1992 led to the so-called "Inkathagate" scandal, and resulted in allegations (evidence of which was found by the Goldstone Commission of 1991–1994) that the SADF-DMI and Special Forces had trained and equipped Inkatha hit squads in operations against the ANC. When the ruling National Party "struck a deal" with the ANC in 1990, Inkatha felt abandoned by the NP and reacted accordingly: Allister Sparks, "Answers are Needed about NP's Secret Operations", *Star International Weekly* (Johannesburg) 29 June–5 July 1995: 5; Henderson, "South African Intelligence", 69–70.

4 The NCPS, which was contributed to by the Ministries of Safety and Security, Defence, Correctional Services, Justice and Intelligence Services, rested on four "pillars": enhancing the effectiveness of the criminal justice process, reducing crime through environmental design, increasing public values and education, and confronting transnational crime; in addition, a key element of the NCPS was to be the improvement of information and intelligence collection relating to these aspects. It, in conjunction with the proposed Community Safety Plan, was supposed to play the most direct role in impacting on the personal safety and security of all South Africans: by ensuring the safe living of individuals within their communities, and the secure development of those communities; it has not – however – succeeded. "National Crime Prevention Strategy Unveiled", SAPA Report (22 May 1996).

5 Section 187 of the Constitution includes statements to the effect that, "The security services must act, and must teach and require their members to act, in accordance with the Constitution and the law, including customary international law and international agreements binding on the Republic" (s187(6)), as well as

> Neither the security services nor any of their members may perform their functions in a manner that (a) prejudices a political party interest that is legitimate in terms of this Constitution; or (b) furthers any private interest of a political party.
>
> (s187(7))

6 *White Paper*, 5. Most of these points arose out of the ANC's National Policy Conference statement entitled *ANC Policy Guidelines For A Democratic South Africa: A New Approach To Intelligence*, released on 31 May 1992.

7 Not the least of which by this author – see the author's earlier works at: Kevin A. O'Brien, "Controlling the Hydra: A Historical Analysis of South African

Intelligence Accountability", Hans Born and Loch K. Johnson (eds), *Who's Watching the Spies? Establishing Intelligence Service Accountability* (Potomac Books, 2005); and Kevin A. O'Brien, "South Africa's Evolving Intelligence and Security Structures", *International Journal of Intelligence and Counterintelligence*. 9:2 (Summer 1996): 187–232.

8 Annexure B, subsection 4 of the White Paper on Intelligence mandates the President or Minister to authorise "special activities" further to the missions of the NIA and SASS (Republic of South Africa, *National Strategic Intelligence Act* (Act 39 of 1994) (December 1994) [hereafter *NSI Act*] s2(1) and 2(2)) pursuant to the definition of the counter-intelligence mission as laid out in section 1(v) of the *NSI Act*. There is concern that this grants too much leeway for covert activities to the authorities, as has happened elsewhere (for example, the history of the US *National Security Council Act* 1947 and subsequent CIA covert activities).

9 See Chapter 8, note 112.

10 Republic of South Africa, *Intelligence Services Act* (Act 38 of 1994) (December 1994): s3(1)(a-g) [hereafter IS Act].

11 *White Paper*, 12–13.

12 Brendan Seery, "Out of the Cold and into the Light", *Star International Weekly* (Johannesburg) (16–22 March 1995): 11.

13 Annette Seegers, "The New Security in Democratic South Africa: A Cautionary Tale", *Conflict, Security and Development* 10:2 (May 2010): 271.

14 *IS Act*, s3(1).

15 At the time of writing (spring 2010), the current NIA head is Lizo Gibson Njenje (a previous ANC Intelligence deputy head, and later a Deputy Director General in both the NIA and SASS), the head of SASS is Rieaz "Moe" Shaik (a controversial figure who was previously a personal advisor to now-President Jacob Zuma and was previously a lead thinker in the ANC's approach to intelligence transformation during the transition, and later the Deputy National Co-ordinator of Intelligence – a profile can be read at Paddy Harper, "I Spy ... a Man Born to be in Intelligence", *Sunday Times* (South Africa) (10 October 2009). Online, available at: www.timeslive.co.za/sundaytimes/article145322.ece), and the Director General of the new State Security Agency (see Chapter 10) is Mzuvukile J. Maqetuka (another former ANC Intelligence leader, who after the transition served also as Deputy Director General of both the NIA and SASS, and later was the National Co-ordinator of Intelligence). See Chapter 10 for further discussion.

16 Sharon Chetty, "Meeting the Government's needs is Sigxashe's aim", *Star and SA Times* (20 December 1995): 7.

17 Shaw, "Spy Meets Spy", 265.

18 Jovial Rantao, "Civilian Management for the Police", *Star International Weekly* (Johannesburg) (13–19 July 1995): 5; SAPS Act, Chapter 10 "Independent Complaints Directorate", s50/53/54.

19 Lt Col C.R.C. Bester, *The Development Of Civil Military Relations In South Africa*. South African Army College (1999). Online, available at: www.mil.za/CSANDF/CJSupp/TrainingFormation/ArmyCollege/ArmyCollege1999/The%20Development%20.htm.

20 Confidential interview, October 2008.

21 This was the only security portfolio not given to an ANC official: Chris Whitfield, "De Klerk for Security Chairmanship", *Star International Weekly* (Johannesburg) (15–21 September 1994): 4.

22 *White Paper*, 15; National Intelligence Agency, *Guiding Principles of the new South African Intelligence Dispensation* (Pretoria, 1995), 19–20; NSI Act, s4(2).

23 Ministry of the Intelligence Services, *National Intelligence Co-ordinating Committee*. Online, available at: www.intelligence.gov.za/Functions/NICOC.htm.

24 "Fivaz Announces Agreement between Police and Intelligence Agencies"; "SAPS, NIA, SASS, SANDF to Fight Together Against Crime", SAPA Reports 10 May 1996.
25 IS Act, s31.
26 There are significant similarities in the intelligence structures and the legislation governing said structures in the British Parliamentary models of governing, such as Britain, Canada and Australia. At the same time, however, given South Africa's republican nature which grew out of a British Parliamentary system, there are certain aspects of the new dispensation that reflect a peculiarly South African requirement, given its political history and considerations for the future. Compared to the Canadian and British models, South Africa has retained a little of each in its Inspectors-General. Canada's Inspector-General of CSIS is authorised complete and total access to information without restriction under section 31(1)/(2) of the *CSIS Act* unless it involves a Cabinet secret; the Inspector-General then reports his findings to the Security Intelligence Review Committee (SIRC). In Britain, the position of Commissioner for each service was created under section 4(1) of the *British Secret Services Act* and 8(1) of the *British Intelligence Services Act*. The Commissioner is authorised complete and total access to information (BSS Act s4(4); BIS Act s8(4)) with the only restriction being that information of a sensitive nature shall not be included in reports to Parliament (*BIS Act* s4(7); *BSS Act* s8(7)).
27 *White Paper*, 14; ISC Act, s2(1)/(2), 3(1)(g). Its first chair was Lindwe Sisulu (now Minister of Intelligence) and its current chair is Dr Siyabonga Cyprian Cwele – both of the ANC.
28 Parliament of the Republic of South Africa website. Online, available at: www.parliament.gov.za/pls/portal30/docs/folder/parliamentary_information/publications/five/chapter6.htm.
29 *ISC Act*, s4(1)/(3).
30 *ISC Act*, s4(2)(a). The IG, however, is authorised to access information detailing sources.
31 Shaw, "Spying for Democracy", 2.
32 Section 2 of the *Intelligence Services Control Amendment Act* 1999.
33 *ISC Amendment Act 1999*: s2b.
34 Eddie Koch, "SA Intelligence World in Turmoil", *Weekly Mail and Guardian* (20 October 1995).
35 *ISC Amendment Act 2002*: s6.
36 Republic of South Africa, *Intelligence Services Control Act* (Act 40 of 1994) (December 1994): s7(1)/(2),(3)–(6) [hereafter ISC Act].
37 Patrick Laurence, "The Future of the NIA", *Focus* (17 March 2000). Online, available at: www.hsf.org.za/focus17/NIAfocus17.html.
38 Chamber of Mines of South Africa website. Online, available at: www.bullion.org.za/Level3/CoM/randera.htm.
39 "Care Needed In Selecting Intelligence IG: DA" – Parliament SAPA (17 June 2003). Online, available at: www.anc.org.za/anc/newsbrief/2003/news0618.txt; Ministry of the Intelligence Services, *Inspector General*. Online, available at: www.intelligence.gov.za/OversightControl/inspector_general.htm.
40 Intelligence officials said that the process of establishing the IG's office had been hampered by the illness of former Minister of Intelligence Joe Nhlanhla, who was later replaced by Lindwe Sisulu: "SA Intelligence Boss Throws In The Towel", *ZA*NOW* (28 January 2002).
41 Shaw, "Spy Meets Spy", 267.
42 *White Paper, Annexure A: "Code of Conduct for Intelligence Workers"*.
43 *IS Act*, s22(1).
44 *IS Act*, s15–18, 22(2), 23.

45 This code was in addition to the more traditional sections on violations of powers and duties as found in chapter III "Discipline" and section 22 "Offences" of the *IS Act*: Shaw, "Spy Meets Spy", 266.
46 National Intelligence Agency website. Online, available at: www.nia.org.za.
47 Koch, "SA Intelligence World in Turmoil".
48 "Nhlanhla Defends Employing Coetzee", SAPA (5 January 1996).
49 Ellis, "*Mbokodo*", 297.
50 James Adams, *The New Spies: Exploring the Frontiers of Espionage* (London, Pimlico, 1994): xii–xiii.
51 Shaw, "Spy Meets Spy", 265.
52 See Basildon Peta, "ANC Split Threatened as Leaders Face Spying Charges", *Independent* (London) (16 October 2003). Online, available at: www.independent.co.uk/news/world/africa/anc-split-threatened-as-leaders-face-spying-charges-583511.html; the commission's findings in J.J.F. Hefer, *Report of the Hefer Commission of Inquiry into Allegations of Spying against the National Director of Public Prosecutions, Mr B.T. Ngcuka* (20 January 2004). Online, available at: www.info.gov.za/otherdocs/2004/heferreport.pdf; Laurian Clemence, "Ngcuka was 'Probably Never' a Spy-Hefer", SAPA (21 January 2004). Online, available at: www.polity.org.za/article/ngcuka-was-x2018probably-neverx2019-a-spyhefer-2004–01–21; and the commission's documents at "O'Malley Archives: Hefer Commission". Online, available at: www.nelsonmandela.org/omalley/index.php/site/q/03lv03445/04lv04015/05lv04120.htm.
53 Despite criticisms of the author's original assessment on this point (see Kevin A. O'Brien, "South Africa's Evolving Intelligence and Security Structures", *International Journal of Intelligence and Counter-Intelligence* 9:2 (1996): 208–209; and Sanders, 300) concerning specifically the ANC-DIS's background and training, while the author has softened marginally his original assessment – while emphasising again the enlightenment which permeated the post-1990 ANC-DIS approach to achieving this new dispensation – the original assessment stands, which has been reinforced by many other observers since (see, for example, Stephen Ellis, "When the ANC Refuses To Listen", *Mail and Guardian* (6 November 2009); Lauren Hutton, "Spies, Lies And Secret Tapes", *ISS Today* (30 Mar 2009). Online, available at: www.issafrica.org/pgcontent.php?UID=18569; or Annette Seegers, "The New Security").
54 Trewhela, "A Literature of Wolves", 68.
55 Ellis, "*Mbokodo*", 289–294.
56 Confidential interview, October 2008.
57 See Paul Taylor, "S. Africa's Past Horrors Pose Questions About Future Justice", *Washington Post* 4 March 1995: A1, A22; Bill Keller, "Trial Offers a Glimpse of Apartheid's Dying Sting", *New York Times* 19 February 1995: A5. As well, see Ellis, "*Mbokodo*", 279–298.
58 For a discussion of the linkages between these criminal trials and the TRC processes, see Kevin A. O'Brien, "Truth and Reconciliation in South Africa: Confronting the Past, Building the Future?", *International Relations* (August 2000): 1–16. On the TRC specifically, see also Francois Du Bois and Antje Du Bois-Pedain (eds), *Justice and Reconciliation in Post-Apartheid South Africa* (Cambridge, MA: Cambridge University Press, 2008); James L. Gibson, *Overcoming Apartheid: Can Truth Reconcile a Divided Nation?* (New York: Russell Sage Foundation, 2004); Terry Bell (in collaboration with Dumisa Buhle Ntsebeza), *Unfinished Business: South Africa, Apartheid and Truth* (Observatory (South Africa): Redworks, 2001): Chapter 9–13; Antjie Krog, *Country of My Skull* (London: Random House, 1998); Richard A. Wilson, *The Politics of Truth and Reconciliation in South Africa: Legitimizing the Post-Apartheid State* (Cambridge: Cambridge University Press, 2001); and Elizabeth Stanley, "Evaluating the

272 *Notes*

Truth and Reconciliation Commission", *The Journal of Modern African Studies* 39:3 (2001): 525–546.

59 More than 2,500 were received on the final day alone for amnesty applications: "7700 amnesty applications received by midnight deadline Saturday", *SAPA* (10 May 10 1997). Initially, a large percentage of those applications received were from individuals already imprisoned for crimes, rather than those seeking amnesty from prosecution.

60 Indeed, it was only in the submission by former SAP Commissioner, Johan van der Merwe, that a senior member of the security forces not only claimed responsibility for the actions of those under his command, but also revealed considerable information about the covert activities carried out by the security forces: Inigo Gilmore, "Former Police Chief says Botha Ordered Bombing", *The Times* (23 October 1996): 14. Similarly, in testimony by former Minister of Defence Magnus Malans, he "accepted full responsibility for actions taken by troops under [my] command, including raids into neighbouring states when innocent civilians were killed": Ray Kennedy, 'Ex-Minister Takes Blame for Killings by Apartheid Troops', *The Times* (8 May 1997): 14.

61 See African National Congress, *Statement to the Truth and Reconciliation Commission* (August 1996). Online, available at: www.anc.org.za/ancdocs/misc/trcall.html, particularly s3.3 ("Just Struggle in the International Context") and s6 ("Did the ANC Perpetrate any Gross Human-Rights Violations?"); African National Congress, *Further Submission and Responses by the African National Congress to Questions Raised by the Commission for Truth and Reconciliation* (12 May 1997). Online, available at: www.anc.org.za/ancdocs/misc/trc2.html.

62 The ANC leadership did apply strongly for amnesty, though, including then-Deputy President Mbeki, Ministers Modise, Omar, Maharaj and Skweyiya, as well as approximately 30 other senior ANC leaders: David Beresford, "Hopes of Truth about 'Dirty War' against ANC", *Electronic Mail and Guardian* (13 May 1997).

63 Paul Taylor, "S. Africa's Past Horrors Pose Questions About Future Justice", *Washington Post* (4 March 1995): A1, A22.

64 These are discussed in detail in Ellis, "*Mbokodo*", *passim*.

65 This commission determined that at least 22 suspected spies had been executed, or allowed to die through neglect, in ANC camps in Angola, Zambia, Tanzania and Uganda: "Tutu begins Inquiry into Rights Violations", *Globe and Mail* (16 April 1996): A16.

66 For a discussion of these, see O'Brien, "South Africa's Evolving Intelligence and Security Structures", 187–232.

67 *Intelligence Services Control Amendment Act* (66–2002): s7(11)(h).

68 *ISC Amendment Act 2002*: s2.

69 *ISC Amendment Act 2002*: s4b.

70 This was clarified in the Act that "one Inspector-General may be appointed with regard to some of or all the Services as long as the activities of all the Services are monitored by an Inspector-General": *ISC Amendment Act 1999*: s5a/b.

71 *ISC Amendment Act 1999*: s5b.

72 *ISC Amendment Act 1999*: s7.

73 *ISC Amendment Act 1999*: s8–9.

74 *ISC Amendment Act 2002*: s7(7).

75 *ISC Amendment Act 2002*: s3c.

76 *ISC Amendment Act 2002*: s7(7) and s7(11)(a).

77 *ISC Amendment Act 2002*: s7(11)(h).

78 *General Intelligence Law Amendment Act* (66–2000): s18–22B.

79 *Intelligence Services Act* (65–2002): s5.

80 *Intelligence Services Act* (65–2002): s22.
81 *Intelligence Services Act* (65–2002): s12.
82 *Intelligence Services Act* (65–2002): s26.
83 *Electronic Communications Security (Pty) Ltd Act* (Act 68 of 2002): s7; Ronnie Kasrils, MP, "South African Intelligence Services: Towards Meeting The Challenges Of The 21st Century – Ten Priorities For Immediate Action" – Speech On The Occasion Of The Secret Services Debate (Cape Town, 23 June 2004). Online, available at: www.intelligence.gov.za/Speeches/BudgetVote2004.htm.
84 *Electronic Communications Security (Pty) Ltd Act* (Act 68 of 2002): chapters 2, 3.
85 *Electronic Communications Security (Pty) Ltd Act* (Act 68 of 2002): s7.
86 *General Intelligence Laws Amendment Act* 2003 (Bill 47 of 2003): 2(b).
87 *General Intelligence Laws Amendment Act* 2003 (Bill 47 of 2003): 8(c).
88 *General Intelligence Laws Amendment Act* 2003 (Bill 47 of 2003): 14.
89 Some of this is documented in the author's "South Africa's Evolving Intelligence and Security Structures", *International Journal of Intelligence and Counterintelligence* 9:2 (Summer 1996): 187–232. See also, for example, the scandals around former Police Commissioner Jackie Selebi and its links to senior NIA and ANC intelligence personnel (Sam Sole, "Barry Gilder and the Hot Frogs", *Mail and Guardian* (27 November 2009). Online, available at: www.mg.co.za/article/2009-11-27-barry-gilder-and-the-hot-frogs; "Jackie Selebi corruption trial resumes", SAPA (1 March 2010). Online, available at: www.mg.co.za/article/2010-03-01-jackie-selebi-corruption-trial-resumes; Stefaans Brümmer and Sam Sole, "I spy..", *Mail and Guardian* (22 May 2009). Online, available at: www.mg.co.za/article/2009-05-22-i-spy); the "coup" attempt against Mbeki allegedly organised by rival ANC factions working within the NIA and national intelligence structures – which, notably, saw the issue of apartheid-era moles within the ANC raise its head yet again, and was tied directly into Zuma's looming succession fight against Mbeki at a time that Zuma was on-trial for corruption tied to South Africa's mid-1990s massive arms purchase (Basildon Peta, "ANC Split Threatened as Leaders Face Spying Charges", *Independent* (London) (16 October 2003). Online, available at: www.independent.co.uk/news/world/africa/anc-split-threatened-as-leaders-face-spying-charges-583511.html); and – tied directly to the previous scandal – the appointment of leading MK/DIS intelligence operative Moe Shaik to the directorship of the NIA in mid-2009, following the conviction of his brother Schabir on fraud and related charges surrounding Zuma's role (Shaik was his financial advisor) in the 1990s arms purchase ("DA to Oppose Appointment of Mo Shaik as NIA Head", SAPA (30 August 2009). Online, available at: www.mg.co.za/article/2009-08-30-da-to-oppose-appointment-of-mo-shaik-as-nia-head; "Moe Shaik's Appointment Angers Opposition Parties", SAPA (3 October 2009). Online, available at: www.mg.co.za/article/2009-10-03-moe-shaiks-appointment-angers-opposition-parties), leading directly to the decision to appoint Lizo Gibson Njenje, a former head of operations at the NIA who was suspended with former spy boss Billy Masetlha in 2005, as head of the NIA in October 2009, at a time when Njenje was embroiled in a separate fraud investigation (Adriaan Basson, "Spy Boss Haunted by Tender Probe", *Mail and Guardian* (9 October 2009). Online, available at: www.mg.co.za/article/2009-10-09-spy-boss-haunted-by-tender-probe) – to highlight a few.
90 See Sam Sole, Pearlie Joubert, Stefaans Brümmer, "Inside Operation Destroy Lucifer", *Mail and Guardian* (19 June 2009). Online, available at: www.mg.co.za/article/2009-06-19-inside-operation-destroy-lucifer, and Sam Sole, "Spooks Haunt our Democracy", *Mail and Guardian* (22 May 2009). Online, available at: www.mg.co.za/article/2009-05-22-spooks-haunt-our-democracy.
91 See Kevin A. O'Brien, "The McBride Affair: South African Intelligence in

Crisis", *Jane's Intelligence Review* 11:1 (January 1999): 40–47 for a detailed discussion of this matter and its consequences. See also Republic of South Africa – Ministry of Defence and the Ministry for Intelligence Services, "Transformation Of Military Intelligence: Joint statement by the Minister and Deputy Minister of Defence and the Deputy Minister for Intelligence Services – Appointment of Ministerial Commission of Inquiry into the transformation of defence intelligence", 9 April 1998.

92 *IS Act*, s4(3)(a/b).

93 Masetlha was dismissed and prosecuted on two criminal charges: contravening the *Intelligence Services Oversight Act* by lying to intelligence Inspector-General Zolile Ngcakani about the origins of the hoax e-mails, and for committing commercial fraud by using NIA-funds to pay "others" involved in the hoax emails. The "others" included former NIA-Manager for electronic surveillance, Funokwakhe Madlala and IT salesman Muziwendoda Kunene. The NIA's Counterintelligence Manager Bob Mhlanga was transferred to the SAPS and Gibson Njenje, the NIA Deputy Director General of Operations, was suspended. As is noted in note 89, however, Njenje was subsequently reappointed as head of the NIA in October 2009. See Seegers, "The New Security", 274, n66.

94 *Intelligence in a Constitutional Democracy – Final Report to the Minister For Intelligence Services, The Honourable Mr Ronnie Kasrils, MP*. Ministerial Review Commission on Intelligence (10 September 2008). Online, available at: www.ssrnetwork.net/document_library/detail/4276/intelligence-in-a-constitutional-democracy-ndash-final-report-to-the-minister-for-intelligence-services-10-september-2008.

95 Indeed, as the ISS notes, "Since then, nothing has been seen or heard of the Commission's Report nor of the recommendations for tighter controls on the use of special powers that are detailed therein" – "Spies, Lies And Secret Tapes", *ISS Today* (30 March 2009). Online, available at: www.issafrica.org/pgcontent.php?UID=18569. On the commission, see "Kasrils: Ministerial Review Commission on Intelligence", *Polity.org.za* (1 November 2006). Online, available at: www.polity.org.za/article/kasrils-ministerial-review-commission-on-intelligence-01112006-2006-11-01; and the commission's final report *Intelligence in a Constitutional Democracy: Final Report to the Minister for Intelligence Services, the Honourable Mr Ronnie Kasrils, MP* (10 September 2008). Online, available at: www.issafrica.org/uploads/intelrpt.pdf. The Institute for Security Studies (South Africa) also began a project to review the future plans and priorities of South Africa's intelligence dispensation – see Lauren Hutton (ed.), *To Spy or Not To Spy? Intelligence and Democracy in South Africa*. ISS Monograph Series No. 157 (February 2009). Online, available at: www.iss.co.za/pgcontent.php?UID=2537; Lauren Hutton, "Intelligence and Accountability in Africa", Policy Brief No. 2 (June 2009). Online, available at: www.issafrica.org/uploads/jul09intelligenceaccount.pdf; and all seminars and reports from this project.

96 Seegers notes the relationship between private intelligence companies and the NIA's inabilities – a symbiotic and self-sustaining problem: Seegers, "The New Security ", 276–277.

97 Cwele's wife was arrested in drug-smuggling charges in January 2010: "S African Minister's Wife Sheryl Cwele on Drug Charges", *BBC News* (29 January 2010). Online, available at: http://news.bbc.co.uk/2/hi/africa/8488355.stm; the Minister claimed to have no knowledge of the activities.

98 Siyabonga Cwele, "Mobilising our Resources to Work Together to do More to Achieve National Security, State Security Minister", *South African Government Information* (2 October 2009). Online, available at: www.search.gov.za/info/

previewDocument.jsp?dk=%2Fdata%2Fstatic%2Finfo%2Fspeeches%2F2009%2F09100511351002.htm%40Gov&q=%28+%28cwele%29%3CIN%3ETitle+%29+%3CAND%3E%28+Category%3Cmatches%3Es+%29&t=S+Cwele+on+appointment+of+Mo+Shaik+as+Head+of+State+Security; and Nthambeleni Gabara, "SA's Civilian Intelligence Structures to Merge" (4 October 2009). Online, available at: http://freenetafrica.com/node/921.
99 Sam Sole, "Zuma's New Spy Purge", *Mail and Guardian* (5 February 2010). Online, available at: www.mg.co.za/article/2010-02-05-zumas-new-spy-purge. Laurie Nathan, an academic from University of Cape Town and formerly a member of the 2006 Ministerial Review Commission, has also commented on many of these issues in his paper *Lighting up the Intelligence Community: A Democratic Approach to Intelligence Secrecy and Openness* – Global Facilitation Network for Security Sector Reform Policy Paper (April 2009). Online, available at: www.ssrnetwork.net/documents/Publications/Intelligence/Intelligence%20Policy%20Paper.pdf.
100 Gaye Davis, "Spying Allegations: Who are the Silly Buggers?", *Weekly Mail and Guardian* (3 February 1996).
101 In addition, there were reported attempts by *Inkatha* to resurrect a paramilitary and intelligence capacity within both the IFP and the KwaZulu-Natal Police, using funds from Germany's Konrad Adenauer Foundation and, allegedly, the CIA: Paul Stober, Marion Edmonds, Eddie Koch and Ann Eveleth, "Inkatha's Secret German War Chest", *Weekly Mail and Guardian* (15 September 1995); Jeff Stein, "South Africa's Many 'Watergates' May Spill Over on the CIA", *Baltimore Sun* (20 March 1996); Koch, op. cit.
102 Indeed, in November 2001, Mbeki's office established a new Presidential Support Unit in the Ministry of Intelligence to provide logistical backing to the Presidency and former President Nelson Mandela. "'Spy unit' for Mbeki", *ZA*NOW* (22 February 2002). See also Stefaans Brümmer, "Inside the ANC's spy unit", *Mail and Guardian* (6 May 2001). Online, available at: www.mg.co.za/mg/za/archive/2001may/features/04may-spy.html. This issue is discussed in more detail in O'Brien, "South Africa's Evolving Intelligence and Security Structures", 208–211.
103 Confidential interview, April 1996.
104 See, for example, Laurie Nathan, "Organ Failure: A Review of the SADC Organ on Politics, Defence and Security", Liisa Laakso (ed.), *Regional Integration for Conflict Prevention and Peace Building in Africa; Europe, SADC and ECOWAS* (Helsinki: Department of Political Science, University of Helsinki, 2002): 40.

10 Conclusion: still fighting the war – the legacy of South Africa's intelligence history

1 Seegers, "The New Security", 278.
2 Interviews conducted over the last decade with senior intelligence officers in a number of Western countries have demonstrated a serious concern over both the functional state of South Africa's intelligence capabilities, and the corruption endemic in those institutions: confidential interviews, London, Washington, Ottawa, Berlin, Canberra – 1998–2010.

Bibliography

Government documents

Convention on the Prevention and Punishment of Crimes against Internationally Protected Persons, Including Diplomatic Agents, 13 I.L.M 42 (1974), entered into force 1977.

Cwele, Siyabonga. "Mobilising our Resources to Work Together to do More to Achieve National Security, State Security Minister". *South African Government Information* (2 October 2009). Online, available at: www.search.gov.za/info/previewDocument.jsp?dk=%2Fdata%2Fstatic%2Finfo%2Fspeeches%2F2009%2F09100511351002.htm%40Gov&q=%28+%28cwele%29%3CIN%3ETitle+%29+%3CAND%3E%28+Category%3Cmatches%3Es+%29&t=S+Cwele+on+appointment+of+Mo+Shaik+as+Head+of+State+Security.

Geneva Convention Relative to the Protection of Civilian Persons in Time of War, 75 U.N.T.S. 287, entered into force 21 October 1950.

Hague Convention (IV) Respecting the Laws and Customs of War on Land, With Annex of Regulations (18 October 1907).

Hefer, J.J.F. *Report of the Hefer Commission of Inquiry into Allegations of Spying against the National Director of Public Prosecutions, Mr B.T. Ngcuka* (20 January 2004). Online, available at: www.info.gov.za/otherdocs/2004/heferreport.pdf

Kirkham, James F., Sheldon G. Levy, and William J. Crotty. *Assassination and Political Violence: A Report to the National Commission on the Causes and Prevention of Violence* – vol. 8. Washington: Government Printing Office, October 1969.

Ministry of the Intelligence Services. *National Intelligence Co-ordinating Committee.* Online, available at: www.intelligence.gov.za/Functions/NICOC.htm.

Mortimer, Maj-Gen B. *Submission IRO The Former SADF: SA Defence Force Involvement in the Internal Security Situation in the Republic of South Africa.* Pretoria: SANDF Nodal Point, 1997.

National Intelligence Agency. *Guiding Principles of the New South African Intelligence Dispensation* (Pretoria, 1995), 19–20; NSI Act, s4(2).

Protocol Additional to the Geneva Conventions of 12 August 1949, and Relating to the Protection of Victims of International Armed Conflicts (Protocol I), 1125 U.N.T.S. 3, entered into force 7 December 1978.

Republic of South Africa. *Truth and Reconciliation Armed Forces Hearings – SADF.* Online, available at: www.truth.org.za/HRVtrans/forces/sadf.htm (no download date).

Republic of South Africa. *Truth and Reconciliation Armed Forces Hearings – SAP.* Online, available at: www.truth.org.za/HRVtrans/forces/sap.htm (no download date).

Republic of South Africa. *Truth and Reconciliation Commission Hearing Held at Durban on Monday, 4 August 1997*. Online, available at: www.truth.org.za/HRVtrans/caprivi/caprivi1.htm (no download date).

Republic of South Africa. *Truth and Reconciliation Commission State Security Hearings*. Online, available at: www.truth.org.za/HRVtrans/security/1securit.htm (no download date).

Republic of South Africa, *Establishment of a New Department of State – Bureau for State Security*. Government Notice No. 808. 16 May 1969.

Republic of South Africa. *Report of the Commission of Inquiry into Matters Relating to the Security of the State*. 1971.

Republic of South Africa. *Security Intelligence and State Security Council Act*. No 64. 1972.

Republic of South Africa. *White Paper on Defence and Armaments Production*. Pretoria. 1975.

Republic of South Africa. *White Paper on Defence and Armaments Production*. Pretoria. 1977.

Republic of South Africa. *Commission of Inquiry into Certain Alleged Murders*. Pretoria, Government Printer 109. 1990.

Republic of South Africa. *Interim Report on the Conduct of Members of 32 Battalion: 8 April 1992*. Goldstone Commission. 10 June 1992.

Republic of South Africa. *Report into Allegations Concerning Front Companies of the SADF and the Training by Inkatha Supporters at the Caprivi in 1986*. Goldstone Commission. 1 June 1993.

Republic of South Africa. *Report on Criminal Political Violence by Elements within the South African Police, the KwaZulu Police and the Inkatha Freedom Party*. Goldstone Commission. 18 March 1994.

Republic of South Africa. *Report of the Truth and Reconciliation Commission*, 2:1 "National Overview". Online, available at: www.polity.org.za/govdocs/commissions/1998/trc/2chap1.htm (downloaded 3 November 1998).

Republic of South Africa. *Report of the Truth and Reconciliation Commission*, 2:3 "The State inside South Africa Between 1960 and 1990". Online, available at: www.polity.org.za/govdocs/commissions/1998/trc/2chap3.htm (downloaded 7 November 1998).

Republic of South Africa. *Report of the Truth and Reconciliation Commission*, 2:4 "The Liberation Movements from 1960 to 1990". Online, available at: www.polity.org.za/govdocs/commissions/1998/trc/2chap4.htm (downloaded 7 November 1998).

Republic of South Africa. *Report of the Truth and Reconciliation Commission*, 2:5 "The Homelands from 1960 to 1990". Online, available at: www.polity.org.za/govdocs/commissions/1998/trc/2chap5.htm (downloaded 7 November 1998).

Republic of South Africa. *Report of the Truth and Reconciliation Commission*, 2:6a "Special Investigation into the death of President Samora Machel". Online, available at: www.polity.org.za/govdocs/commissions/1998/trc/2chap6a.htm (downloaded 7 November 1998).

Republic of South Africa. *Report of the Truth and Reconciliation Commission*, 2:6c "Special Investigation into Project Coast". Online, available at: www.polity.org.za/govdocs/commissions/1998/trc/2chap6c.htm (downloaded 7 November 1998).

Republic of South Africa. *Report of the Truth and Reconciliation Commission*, 2:6d

278 *Bibliography*

"Special Investigation into Secret State Funding". Online, available at: www.polity.org.za/govdocs/commissions/1998/trc/2chap6d.htm (downloaded 7 November 1998).

Republic of South Africa. *Report of the Truth and Reconciliation Commission*, 2:7 "Political Violence in the Era of Negotiations and Transition, 1990–1994". Online, available at: www.polity.org.za/govdocs/commissions/1998/trc/2chap7.htm (downloaded 7 November 1998).

Republic of South Africa. *Report of the Truth and Reconciliation Commission*, 3:2 "Regional Profile Eastern Cape". Online, available at: www.polity.org.za/govdocs/commissions/1998/trc/3chap2.htm (downloaded 7 November 1998).

Republic of South Africa. *Report of the Truth and Reconciliation Commission*, 3:3 "Regional Profile Natal and KwaZulu". Online, available at: www.polity.org.za/govdocs/commissions/1998/trc/3chap3.htm (downloaded 7 November 1998).

Republic of South Africa. *Report of the Truth and Reconciliation Commission*, 3:5 "Regional Profile Western Cape". Online, available at: www.polity.org.za/govdocs/commissions/1998/trc/3chap5.htm (downloaded 7 November 1998).

Republic of South Africa. *Report of the Truth and Reconciliation Commission*, 2:2 "The State Outside South Africa Between 1960 and 1990". Online, available at: www.polity.org.za/govdocs/commissions/1998/trc/2chap2.htm (downloaded 25 August 1999).

Republic of South Africa. *Report of the Truth and Reconciliation Commission*, 1:2 "Historical Context: Gross Human Rights Violations in Political and Historical Perspective". Online, available at: www.polity.org.za/govdocs/commissions/1998/trc/1chap2.htm (downloaded 30 April 2000).

Republic of South Africa. *State Security Council Hearing – Submission of Dr Neil Barnard*. Online, available at: www.truth.org.za/HRVtrans/security/ssbarn.htm (downloaded 24 April 2000).

Republic of South Africa – State Security Council, *Riglyne vir n totale strategie teen die UDF: Tiende monitorverslag 1 April 1985 to 31 Julie 1985* [Guidelines for a Total Strategy Against the UDF: Tenth Monitoring Report], 15 August 1985 (translated).

Republic of South Africa – State Security Council, *Riglyne vir n Strategie teen die Rewolsionere Oorlog teen die RSA* [Guidelines for a Strategy against the Revolutionary War against the Republic of South Africa], 28 April 1986 (translated).

United Nations General Assembly. *International Convention on the Suppression and Punishment of the Crime of Apartheid* (original 6 December 1971, A/RES/2768 (XXVI); 30 November 1973, A/RES/3068 (XXVIII).

United States Army. *The Law of Land Warfare*. Field Manual 27–10. Washington: Government Printing Office, 1956.

United State Congress. *Foreign Assistance Act*. Washington: Government Printing Office, 1974.

United States Congress. *US and Soviet Special Operations*. Washington: Congressional Research Service, 1986.

Books

Adams, James. *The New Spies: Exploring the Frontiers of Espionage*. London: Pimlico, 1994.

Alden, Chris. *Apartheid's Last Stand: The Rise and Fall of the South African Security State*. London: Macmillan Press Ltd, 1996.

Amnesty International. *South Africa: State of Fear*. London: Amnesty International, 1992.

Andradé, Dale. *Ashes To Ashes: The Phoenix Program and the Vietnam War – Cover for Assassination or Effective Counterinsurgency?* Toronto: Lexington Books, 1990.

Andrew, Christopher. *Defend The Realm: The Authorized History of MI5*. New York: Alfred A. Knopf, 2009.

Andrew, Christopher and Gordievsky, Oleg. *Inside the KGB*. Toronto: Hodder & Stoughton, 1990.

Asprey, Robert B. *War in the Shadows: The Classic History of Guerrilla Warfare from Ancient Persia to the Present*. London: Little, Brown and Company, 1994.

Barrell, Howard. *MK: The ANC's Armed Struggle*. London: Penguin Books, 1990.

Beaufre, André. *Introduction to Strategy*. Translated R.H. Barry. London: Faber and Faber, 1965.

Beaufre, André. *A Strategy of Action*. Translated R.H. Barry. London: Faber and Faber, 1967.

Beaumont, Roger A. *Military Elites*. New York: The Bobbs-Merrill Company, 1974.

Beaumont, Roger A. *Special Operations and Elite Units, 1939–1988*. Greenwood Pub Group, 1988.

Bell, J. Bowyer. *The Myth of the Guerrilla: Revolutionary Theory and Malpractice*. New York, 1971.

Bell, Terry and Ntsebeza, Dumisa Buhle. *Unfinished Business: South Africa, Apartheid and Truth*. Observatory (South Africa): Red Works, 2001.

Benson, Mary. *South Africa: The Struggle for a Birthright*. London: James Currey, 1966.

Berman, John Kane. *Political Violence in South Africa*. Johannesburg: SAIRR, 1993.

Bhebe, Ngwabi and Terence Ranger (eds). *Soldiers in Zimbabwe's Liberation War*. Johannesburg: Heinemann, 1995.

Blackburn, Douglas and Caddel, W. Waithman. *Secret Service in South Africa*. Reprinted from the 1911 Edition. Honolulu: University Press of the Pacific, 2001.

Blackstock, Paul W. *The Strategy of Subversion: Manipulating the Politics of Other Nations*. Chicago, 1964.

Blumenfeld, Jesmond (ed.). *South Africa in Crisis*. London: RIIA, 1987.

Bois, Francois Du and Antje Du Bois-Pedain (eds). *Justice and Reconciliation in Post-Apartheid South Africa*. Cambridge, MA: Cambridge University Press, 2008.

Bopela, Thula and Luthuli, Daluxolo. *Umkhonto we Sizwe: Fighting for a Divided People*. Alberton (South Africa): Galago Books, 2005.

Borraine, Alex. *A Country Unmasked: Inside South Africa's Truth and Reconciliation Commission*. Oxford: OUP, 2000.

Breytenbach, Jan. *Forged in Battle*. Cape Town: Saayman and Weber, 1986.

Breytenbach, Jan. *They Live By The Sword*. Alberton: Lemur Books, 1990.

Breytenbach, Jan. *The Buffalo Soldiers: The Story of South Africa's 32-Battalion 1975–1993*. Alberton: Galago Publishing Ltd, 2002.

Brittain, Victoria. *Hidden Lives, Hidden Deaths: South Africa's Crippling of a Continent*. London: Faber and Faber, 1988.

Burger, Marlene and Gould, Chandre. *Secrets and Lies: Wouter Basson and South Africa's Chemical and Biological Warfare Programme*. Cape Town: Zebra Press, 2002.

Burgess, Stephen and Helen Purkitt. *The Roll-back of South Africa's Chemical and Biological Warfare Program*. Alabama: USAF Counterproliferation Center, Air University, 2001.

Bibliography

Callwell, C.E. *Small Wars: Their Principles and Practices.* London: HMSO, 1906.

Cann, John P. (ed.). *Memories of Portugal's African Wars, 1961–1974.* Contributions to War Studies, Number One. London: King's College London, June 1997.

Cawthra, Gavin. *Brutal Force: The Apartheid War Machine.* London: International Defence and Aid Fund, 1986.

Cawthra, Gavin. *Policing South Africa: The SAP and the Transition from Apartheid.* London: Zed Books, 1993.

Cilliers, J.K. *Counter-Insurgency in Rhodesia.* London: Croom Helm, 1985.

Cilliers, J.K. and Reichardt, Markus (eds). *About-Turn: The Transformation of the South African Military and Intelligence.* Midrand: Institute for Security Studies, 1996.

Cock, Jacklyn and Nathan, Laurie (eds). *Society at War: The Militarisation of South Africa.* St. Martin's Press, 1989.

Cocks, Chris. *Fireforce: One Man's War in the Rhodesian Light Infantry.* Weltevreden Park (South Africa): Covos-Day Books, 1997.

Cohen, Eliot. *Commandos and Politicians: Elite Military Units in Modern Democracies.* Cambridge: Center for International Affairs, Harvard University, 1978.

Cole, Barbara. *The Elite: The Story of the Rhodesian Special Air Service.* Transkei: Three Knights Publishing, 1984.

Coll, Alberto R., Ord, James S. and Rose, Stephen A. (eds). *Legal and Moral Constraints on Low-Intensity Conflict.* International Law Studies Volume 67. Newport: Naval War College, 1995.

Crocker, Chester. *High Noon in Southern Africa: Making Peace in a Rough Neighborhood.* Johannesburg: Jonathan Ball, 1993.

Debray, Regis. *Revolution in the Revolution?* London: Penguin Books, 1968.

De Kock, Eugene. *A Long Night's Damage: Working for the Apartheid State.* As told to Jeremy Gordin. Saxonwold (South Africa): Contra Press, 1998.

Du Plessis, A. and Hough, M. *Selected Official Strategic Perceptions 1989–1992.* Ad hoc Publication No. 29. Pretoria: Institute for Strategic Studies University of Pretoria, 1992.

Dulles, Allen. *The Craft of Intelligence.* New York: Harper & Row, 1963.

Eades, Lindsay Michie. *The End of Apartheid in South Africa.* Westport: Greenwood Press, 1999.

Ellis, Stephen and Sechaba, Tsepo. *Comrades against Apartheid: The ANC and South African Communist Party in Exile.* London: James Currey, 1992.

Els, Paul. *We Fear Naught But God: The Story of the South African Special Forces.* Welteverden Park (South Africa): Covos Day Books, 2000.

Evans, M. *Fighting Against Chimurenga: An Analysis of Counter-Insurgency in Rhodesia 1972–9.* Local Series 37. Salisbury: The Historical Association of Zimbabwe, 1981.

Feit, Edward. *South Africa: The Dynamics of the African National Congress.* London, 1962.

Feit, Edward. *Urban Revolt in South Africa 1960–1964: A Case Study.* Evanston, 1971.

Flower, Ken. *Serving Secretly: An Intelligence Chief on Record, Rhodesia into Zimbabwe, 1964 to 1981.* London: John Murray, 1987.

Foster, Don. *Detention and Torture in South Africa.* London: James Currey 1987.

Frankel, Philip H. *Pretoria's Praetorians: Civil–Military Relations in South Africa.* Cambridge: CUP, 1984.

Frankel, Philip. *Soldiers in a Storm: The Armed Forces in South Africa's Democratic Transition.* Boulder: Westview Press, 2000.

Frankel, Philip, Pines, Noam, and Swilling, Mark (eds). *State, Resistance and Change in South Africa.* London: Croom Helm, 1988.

Friedman, Steve and Doreen Atkinson (eds). *The Small Miracle: South Africa's Negotiated Settlement.* South African Review 7. Johannesburg: Raven Press, 1994.

Galula, David. *Counterinsurgency Warfare: Theory and Practice.* New York: Frederick A Praeger, 1965.

Geldenhuys, Deon. *The Diplomacy of Isolation: South African Foreign Policy Making.* Johannesburg: SAIIA, 1984.

Geldenhuys, Deon and Gutteridge, William. *Instability and Conflict in Southern Africa: South Africa's Role in Regional Security.* London: Institute for the Study of Conflict, 1983.

Geldenhuys, Jannie. *A General's Story from an Era of War and Peace.* Johannesburg: Jonathan Ball Publishers, 1995.

George, Alexander (ed.). *Western State Terrorism.* New York: Routledge, 1991.

Giap, Vo Nguyen. *People's War, People's Army: The Viet Cong Insurrection Manual for Underdeveloped Countries.* New York: Frederick A. Praeger, 1962.

Gibson, James L. *Overcoming Apartheid: Can Truth Reconcile a Divided Nation?* New York: Russell Sage Foundation, 2004.

Goodman, David. *Faultlines: Journeys into the New South Africa.* Berkley: University of California Press, 1999.

Greeff, Jack. *A Greater Share of Honour.* Ellisras (South Africa): Ntomeni Publishers, 2001.

Grundy, Kenneth W. *Guerrilla Struggle in Africa: An Analysis and Preview.* New York, 1971.

Grundy, Kenneth W. *Soldiers without Politics: Blacks in the South African Armed Forces.* Berkley: University of California Press, 1983.

Grundy, Kenneth W. *The Militarization of South African Politics.* London: I.B. Taurus, 1986.

Guevara, Che. *Guerrilla Warfare.* Introduction by Harries-Clichy Peterson. London: Cassell and Company, Ltd, 1968.

Hamann, Hilton. *Days of the Generals: The Untold Story of South Africa's Apartheid-era Military Generals.* Cape Town: Zebra Press, 2001.

Hanlon, Joseph. *Beggar Your Neighbour.* London: James Currey, 1986.

Harvey, Robert. *The Fall of Apartheid: The Inside Story from Smuts to Mbeki.* Basingstoke: Palgrave Macmillan, 2001.

Havens, Murray Clark, Leiden, Carl and Schmitt, Karl M. *The Politics of Assassination.* Englewood-Cliffs: Prentice Hall Inc, 1970.

Heitman, Helmoed-Romer. *South African War Machine.* Johannesburg: Bison Books, 1985.

Herbstein, Denis and Evenson, John. *The Devils Are Among Us: The War for Namibia.* London: Zed Books Ltd, 1989.

Herman, Michael. *Intelligence Power in Peace and War.* Cambridge: Cambridge University Press, 1996.

Hoffman, Bruce and Taw, Jennifer Morrison. *A Strategic Framework for Countering Terrorism and Insurgency.* Santa Monica: RAND National Defense Research Institute, 1992.

Holland, Heidi. *The Struggle: A History of the African National Congress.* New York: George Braziller, 1990.

Hough, M. and Van der Merwe, M. *Selected Official South African Strategic Perceptions*

1976–1987. Ad hoc Publication No. 25. Pretoria: Institute for Security Studies University of Pretoria, May 1988.

Hug, Peter. *Military, Armaments Industry, and Nuclear Relations between Switzerland and South Africa and the UN Apartheid Debate of 1948–1994*. University of Bern. Online, available at: www.snf.ch/NFP/NFP42+/HugE.pdf.

Huntington, Samuel P. (ed.). *Changing Patterns of Military Politics*. New York: The Free Press of Glencoe, Inc, 1962.

International Defence and Aid Fund. *South Africa: The BOSS Law*. London: IDAF, 1969.

International Defence and Aid Fund. *BOSS: The First Five Years*. London: IDAF, 1975.

Ion, A. Hamish and Neilson, Keith (eds). *Elite Military Formations in War and Peace*. Westport: Praeger, 1996.

Jaster, Robert S. *South Africa and its Neighbours: the Dynamics of Regional Conflict*. Adelphi Papers 209. London: International Institute for Strategic Studies, 1986.

Johnson, Loch K. *America's Secret Power: The CIA in a Democratic Society*. Oxford: Oxford University Press, 1989.

Johnson, Phyllis and Martin, David. *Apartheid Terrorism: The Destabilization Report*. London: The Commonwealth Secretariat, 1989.

Jonge, Klaas de. *The Truth Commission Files: The Seychelles Case*. Netherlands Institute for Southern Africa. Online, available at: www.contrast.org/truth/html/seychelles.html (downloaded 6 December 1998).

Kalley, Jacqueline A, Schoeman, Elna, and Andor, L.E. (eds), *Southern African Political History: A Chronology of Key Political Events from Independence to Mid-1997*. Westport: Greenwood Press, 1999.

Karis, Thomas G. and Gerhart, Gail M. *From Protest to Challenge: A Documentary History of African Politics in South Africa, 1882–1990. Volume 5: Nadir and Resurgence 1964–1979*. Bloomington: Indiana University Press, 1997.

Kasrils, Ronnie. *"Armed and Dangerous": My Undercover Struggle against Apartheid*. Oxford: Heinemann Educational, 1993.

Kempton, Daniel., *Soviet Strategy Towards Southern Africa: The National Liberation Movement Connection*. New York: Praeger, 1989.

Kent, Sherman. *Strategic Intelligence for American World Policy*, revised edition. Princeton, NJ: Princeton University Press, 1966.

Kitson, Frank. *Gangs and Counter-Gangs*. London: Barrie and Rockliff, 1960.

Kitson, Frank. *Low Intensity Operations: Subversion, Insurgency and Peace-keeping*. London: Faber and Faber, 1971.

Kitson, Frank. *Bunch of Five*. London: Faber and Faber, 1977.

Krog, Antjie. *Country of My Skull*. Johannesburg: Random House, 1998.

Labuschagne, Riaan. *On South Africa's Secret Service: An Undercover Agent's Story*. Alberton (South Africa): Galago Books, 2002.

Laqueur, Walter. *Guerrilla Warfare: A Historical and Critical Study*. London: Transaction Publishers, 1998).

Laurence, Patrick. *Death Squads: Apartheid's Secret Weapon*. London: Penguin Books, 1990.

Lodge, Tom. *Black Politics in South Africa since 1945*. London: Longman, 1985.

McCallion, Harry. *Killing Zone: A Life in the Paras, the Recces, the SAS and the RUC*. London: Bloomsbury, 1995.

McCuen, John J. *The Art of Counter-revolutionary Warfare: A Psycho-Politico-Military Strategy of Counter-insurgency*. Harrisburg: Stackpole Books, 1965.

Malan, Magnus. *My Life with the SA Defence Force.* Pretoria: Protea Book House, 2006.

Mandela, Nelson. *Long Walk To Freedom.* London: Little, Brown and Company, 1994.

Manganyi, Noel and Du Toit, André. *Political Violence and the Struggle in South Africa.* London: Macmillan, 1990.

Mao Tse-tung. *Problems of Strategy in Guerrilla War Against Japan.* Peking: Foreign Language Press, 1965.

Mao Tse-tung. *On Guerrilla Warfare.* Trans Samuel B. Griffith. London: Cassell and Company Ltd, 1968.

Marchetti, Victor and Marks, John D. *The CIA and the Cult of Intelligence.* New York: Dell Publishing, 1980.

Meli, Francis. *South Africa Belongs to Us.* London: James Currey, 1989.

Minter, William. *Apartheid's Contras: An Inquiry into the Roots of War in Angola and Mozambique.* London: Zed Books, 1994.

Mockaitis, Thomas R. *British Counterinsurgency, 1919–1960.* London: Macmillan, 1990.

Moorcroft, Paul L. *African Nemesis: War and Revolution in Southern Africa, 1945–2010.* London: Brassey's, 1990.

Morris, Michael. *Terrorism: The first full account in detail of terrorism and insurgency in Southern Africa.* Cape Town, 1971.

Nathan, Laurie. "Organ Failure: A Review of the SADC Organ on Politics, Defence and Security". In Liisa Laakso (ed.). *Regional Integration for Conflict Prevention and Peace Building in Africa; Europe, SADC and ECOWAS.* Helsinki: Department of Political Science, University of Helsinki, 2002: 40.

Norval, Alette J. *Deconstructing Apartheid Discourse.* London: Verso, 1996.

O'Brien, Kevin A. "Controlling the Hydra: A Historical Analysis of South African Intelligence Accountability", Hans Born and Loch K. Johnson (eds), *Who's Watching the Spies? Establishing Intelligence Service Accountability.* Potomac Books, 2005.

O'Brien, Kevin A. "Fragmented Hydra: The Evolution of South Africa's Intelligence Community, 1960–2005", Mark Phythian, Stuart Farson, Peter Gill, Shlomo Shpiro. (eds), *National Approaches,* in Loch Johnson (series editor), *PSI Handbook of Global Security and Intelligence* (Praeger Security International, 2007).

O'Malley, Padraig. *Shades of Difference: Mac Maharaj and the Struggle for South Africa.* New York: Viking, 2007.

O'Meara, D. and S. Dlamini. *The Struggle for South Africa.* London: Zed Books, 1988.

D'Oliveira, John. *Vorster – the Man.* Johannesburg: Ernest Stanton, 1977.

Osanka, Franklin Mark (ed.). *Modern Guerrilla Warfare: Fighting Communist Guerrilla Movements, 1941–1961.* New York: Free Press of Glencoe, 1962.

Ostrovsky, Victor and Hoy, Claire. *By Way of Deception.* Toronto: Hodder and Stoughton, 1990.

Paget, Julian. *Counter-Insurgency Campaigning.* London: Faber and Faber Ltd, 1967.

Paret, Peter. *French Revolutionary Warfare from Indochina to Algeria: The Analysis of a Political and Military Doctrine.* London: Pall Mall Press, 1964.

Paret, Peter and Shy, John W. *Guerrillas in the 1960's.* Princeton Studies in World Politics 1. London: Pall Mall Press, 1962.

Pauw, Jacques. *In the Heart of the Whore: The Story of Apartheid's Death Squads.* Halfway House: Southern Book Publishers, 1991.

Pauw, Jacques. *Into the Heart of Darkness: Confessions of Apartheid's Assassins*. Johannesburg: Jonathan Ball Publishers, 1997.

Price, Robert M. *The Apartheid State in Crisis: Political Transformation in South Africa 1975–1990*. New York: Oxford University Press, 1991.

Pustay, John S. *Counterinsurgency Warfare*. New York: The Free Press, 1965.

Ransom, Harry Howe. *Central Intelligence and National Security*. Cambridge: Harvard University Press, 1958.

Ray, Ellen, William Schaap, Karl Van Meter, and Louis Wolf. (eds). *Dirty Work 2: The CIA in Africa*. Secaucus, NJ: Lyle Stuart Inc, 1979.

Rees, M. and Day, C. *Muldergate: The Story of the Information Scandal*. London: Macmillan, 1980.

Reid-Daly, Lieutenant-Colonel RF. *Pamwe Chete: The Legend of the Selous Scouts*. Weltevreden Park (South Africa): Covos-Day Books, 1999.

Richelson, Jeffrey T. *The U.S. Intelligence Community* (Second Edition). New York: Ballinger, 1989.

Reisman, W. Michael and Baker, James E. *Regulating Covert Action*. London, 1992.

Rivers, Gayle. *The Specialist: The Personal Story of an Elite Specialist in Covert Operations*. London: Guild Publishing, 1985.

Rogers, Anthony. *Someone Else's War: Mercenaries from 1960 to the Present*. London: HarperCollins Publishers, 1998.

Roherty, James M. *State Security in South Africa: Civil–Military Relations under P.W. Botha*. London: M.E. Sharpe Inc, 1992.

Rositzke, Harry. *The KGB: The Eyes of Russia*. London: Sidgwick and Jackson, 1981.

Ross, Robert. *A Concise History of South Africa*. Cambridge: CUP, 1999.

Rotberg, Robert I, Henry S. Bienen, Robert Legworld, and Garvin Maasdrop (eds). *South Africa and Its Neighbours: Regional Security and Self-Interest*. Lexington: D.C. Heath and Co, 1985.

Sampson, Anthony. *Mandela: The Authorised Biography*. London: HarperCollins Publishers, 1999.

Sanders, James. *Apartheid's Friends: The Rise and Fall of South Africa's Secret Services*. London: John Murray, 2006.

Schrire, Robert. *Adapt or Die: The End of White Politics in South Africa*. London: Hurst and Company, 1992.

Schultz, Richard H. Jr, Robert L. Pfaltzgraff, Jr, Uri Ra'anan (eds). *Guerrilla Warfare and Counterinsurgency: US-Soviet Policy in the Third World*. Toronto: D.C. Heath and Co, 1989.

Schutte, Charles, Liebenberg, Ian and Minnaar, Anthony (eds). *The Hidden Hand: Covert Operations in South Africa* (Revised Edition). Pretoria: HSRC, 1998.

Seegers, Annette. *The Military in the Making of Modern South Africa*. London: Tauris Academic Books, 1996.

Selfe, James. "South Africa's National [Security] Management System". In Jacklyn Cock and Laurie Nathan, (eds). *Society at War: The Militarisation of South Africa*. New York: St. Martin's Press, 1989: 149–156.

Sellström, Tor. *Sweden and National Liberation in Southern Africa (A Concerned Partnership (1970–1994))*. Oslo: Nordic Africa Institute, 1999: 556–572.

Sparks, Allister. *The Mind of South Africa: The Story of the Rise and Fall of Apartheid*. London: William Heinemann Ltd, 1990.

Sparks, Allister. *Tomorrow Is Another Country*. London: William Heinemann Ltd, 1995.

Steenkamp, Willem. *Borderstrike! South Africa into Angola*. Pretoria: Butterworths, 1983.

Steenkamp, Willem. *South Africa's Border War 1966–1989*. Gibraltar: Ashanti Publishing Ltd, 1989.

Stiff, Peter. *See You in November: Rhodesia's No-holds-barred Intelligence War*. Alberton (South Africa): Galago Books, 1985.

Stiff, Peter. *Nine Days of War and South Africa's Final Days in Namibia*. Alberton (South Africa): Lemur, 1991.

Stiff, Peter. *The Silent War: South African Recce Operations 1969–1994*. Alberton (South Africa): Galago Books, 1999.

Stiff, Peter. *Warfare by Other Means: South Africa in the 1980s and 1990s*. Alberton (South Africa): Galago Books, 2001.

Stiff, Peter. *The Covert War: Koevoet Operations Namibia 1979–1989*. Alberton (South Africa): Galago Books, 2004.

Stiff, Peter and Reid-Daly, Ron. *Selous Scouts: Top Secret War*. Alberton (South Africa): Galago, 1987.

Stockwell, John. *In Search of Enemies: A CIA Story*. New York: W.W. Norton & Company, Inc, 1978.

Swanepoel, PC. *Really Inside BOSS: A Tale of South Africa's late Intelligence Service (And Something about the CIA)*. Revised Edition. Derdepoortpark (Pretoria), 2008.

Thompson, Sir Robert. *Defeating Communist Insurgency: Experiences from Malaya and Vietnam*. London: Chatto and Windus, 1967.

Treverton, Gregory F. *Covert Action: The Limits of Intervention in the Postwar World*. New York: Basic Books, Inc, 1987.

Vanneman, Peter. *Soviet Strategy in Southern Africa: Gorbachev's Pragmatic Approach*. Stanford: Hoover Institution Press, 1990.

Waldmeir, Patti. *Anatomy of a Miracle*. London: Penguin Books, 1997.

Walshe, P. *The Rise of African Nationalism in South Africa: The African National Congress 1912–1952*. Berkley: University of California Press, 1971.

Walzer, Michael. *Just and Unjust Wars: A Moral Argument with Historical Illustrations*. New York: Basic Books USA, 1992.

Wilkinson, Paul. *Political Terrorism*. Studies in Comparative Politics. London: Macmillan Press, 1974.

Williams, Rocklyn. *Back To The Barracks: The Changing Parameters of Civil-Military Relations under the Botha and De Klerk Administrations*. Colchester: University of Essex, 1992.

Wilson, Richard A. *The Politics of Truth and Reconciliation in South Africa: Legitimizing the Post-Apartheid State*. Cambridge: Cambridge University Press, 2001.

Winter, Gordon. *Inside BOSS: South Africa's Secret Police*. London: Penguin Books, 1981.

Woodward, Bob. *Veil: The Secret Wars of the CIA, 1981–1987*. New York: Simon & Schuster, 2005.

Articles and papers

Adam, Heribert and Moodley, Kogila. "Political Violence, 'Tribalism', and Inkatha". *Journal of Modern African Studies* 30:3 (1992): 485–510.

Africa, Sandy. "The Role, Prospects and Expectations of the TBVC Intelligence Services During an Interim Government Period", *Strategic Review For Southern*

Africa: Security and Intelligence in a Post-Apartheid South Africa XIV:2 (October 1992): 79.

Africa, Sandy and Mlombile, Siyabulela. "Transforming the Intelligence Services: Some Reflections on the South African Experience". Project on Justice in Times of Transition – John F. Kennedy School of Government, Harvard University (15 October 2001). Online, available at: www.hks.harvard.edu/justiceproject/Africa,%20Mlombile%20WP.doc.

Barber, James. "BOSS in Britain". *African Affairs* 82:328 (July 1983): 311–328.

Berkeley, Bill. "The Warlords of Natal", *Atlantic Monthly* 273:3 (March 1994): 85–100.

Barrell, Howard. "The Turn to the Masses: the African National Congress' Strategic Review of 1978–1979". *Journal of Southern African Studies* 18:1 (March 1991): 64–92.

Bell, J. Bowyer. "The Future of Guerrilla Revolution in Southern Africa". *Africa Today* 19 (Winter 1972): 7–15.

Beres, Louis Rene. "Assassination and the Law: A Policy Memorandum". *Studies in Conflict and Terrorism* 18 (1995): 299–315.

Burns, David. "Insurgency as a Struggle For Legitimation: The Case of Southern Africa". *Small Wars and Insurgencies* 5:1 (Spring 1994): 29–62.

Claude, Inis L. "Collective Legitimization as a Political Function of the United Nations". *International Organizations* 20 (1996): 16–42.

Clifford-Vaughan, F. McA. "Terrorism and Insurgency in South Africa". *Journal of Social, Political and Economic Studies* 12 (1987): 259–275.

Coyle, R.G. and Millar, C.J. "A Methodology for Understanding Military Complexity: The Case of the Rhodesian Counter-Insurgency Campaign". *Small Wars and Insurgencies* 17:3 (Winter 1996): 360–378.

Cummings, Richard. "A Diamond Is Forever: Mandela Triumphs, Buthelezi and de Klerk Survive, and ANC on the U.S. Payroll", *International Journal of Intelligence and Counterintelligence* (Summer 1995).

Crawford, Neta. "The Domestic Sources and Consequences of Aggressive Foreign Policies: The Folly of South Africa's 'Total Strategy'". *Southern African Perspectives* 41 (February 1995).

Dale, Richard. "Melding War and Politics in Namibia: South Africa's Counterinsurgency Campaign, 1966–1989". *Armed Forces and Society* 20:1 (Fall 1993): 7–24.

Dale, Richard. "The Armed Forces as an Instrument of South African Policy in Namibia". *Journal of Modern African Studies* 18:1 (1980): 57–71.

Davies, Robert and O'Meara, Dan. "Total Strategy in Southern Africa: An Analysis of South African Regional Policy since 1978". *Journal of Southern African Studies* 11:2 (April 1985): 183–211.

Davies, Robert H. and O'Meara, Dan. "The State of Analysis of the Southern African Region: Issues Raised by South African Strategy". *Review of African Political Economy* 11:29 (Summer 1984): 64–76.

Ellis, Stephen. "*Mbokodo*: Security in ANC Camps 1961–1990". *African Affairs* 93:371 (April 1994): 279–298.

Ellis, Stephen. "The Historical Significance of the South African Third Force". *Journal of Southern African Studies* 24:2 (June 1998): 261–300.

Fall, Bernard B. "The Theory and Practice of Insurgency and Counterinsurgency". *Naval War College Review* LI:1 (Winter 1998): 46–78.

Fauvet, Paul. "Briefings: Roots of Counter-revolution – The Mozambique National Resistance". *Review of African Political Economy* 29 (1983): 108–121.

Fedorowich, Kent. "German Espionage and British Counter-Intelligence in South Africa and Mozambique, 1939–1944", *Historical Journal*, 48:1 (2005): 218.

Foster, DH, Sandler, D, and Davis, D.M. "Detention, Torture and the Criminal Justice Process in South Africa". *International Journal of the Sociology of Law* 15:2 (May 1987): 105–120.

Geldenhuys, Deon and Kotzé, Hennie. "Aspects of Political Decision Making in South Africa". *Politikon* 10:1 (June 1983): 33–45.

Gibson, Rex. "Memoirs of an Invisible Man", *Star International Weekly* (Johannesburg) (26 January – 1 February 1995): 13.

Groenwald, Pieter H. "Counter-revolutionary Action in South Africa 1984–1990". *American Review* (Johannesburg) 10:2 (1991): 17–26.

Groenwald, Pieter H. "The Development of the Security Situation in South Africa Since January 1990". *American Review* (Johannesburg) 10:3 (1991): 2–6.

Hallett, Robin. "The South African Intervention in Angola". *African Affairs* 77:312 (July 1978): 347–386.

Harper, Paddy. "I Spy ... a Man Born to be in Intelligence", *Sunday Times* (South Africa) (10 October 2009). Online, available at: www.timeslive.co.za/sundaytimes/article145322.ece.

Haysom, Nicholas. "Licence to Kill Part I: The South African Police and the Use of Deadly Force". *South African Journal on Human Rights* 3:1 (March 1987): 3–27.

Henderson, Robert D'A. "South African Intelligence Under de Klerk". *International Journal of Intelligence and Counterintelligence* 8:1 (Spring 1995): 51–89.

Herbstein, Dennis. "Spy Master and Spy". *Africa Report* 39:2 (March/April 1994): 44–45.

Hough, M. "Revolutionary Warfare in the RSA". *ISSUP Strategic Review* (May 1986): 1–19.

Howe, Herbert M. "The South African Defence Force and Political Reform". *Journal of Modern African Studies* 32:1 (1994): 29–52.

Isaacman, Allen. "Regional Security in Southern Africa: Mozambique". *Survival* XXX:1 (January/February 1988): 14–38.

Jenkin, Tim. "Talking To Vula: The Story of the Secret Underground Communications Network of Operation Vula". *Mayibuye* (May – October 1995).

Johns, Sheridan. "Obstacles to Guerrilla Warfare – a South African Case Study". *Journal of Modern African Studies* 11:2 (1973): 267–303.

Kasrils, Ronnie. "The Revolutionary Army: A Discussion Article". *Sechaba* (September 1988). Online, available at: www.anc.org.za/ancdocs/history/mk/rkmk.html (downloaded 1 March 2000).

Leklem, Erik and Boulden, Laurie. "Exorcising Project B: Pretoria Probes its Shady Chemical Past". *Jane's Intelligence Review* 9:8 (August 1997): 372–375.

Lewis, Bernard. "The Sources for the History of the Syrian Assassins". *Speculum: Journal of Medieval Studies* 27 (1952): 475–89.

Lopes, Mona. "The MNR: Opponents or Bandits?" *Africa Report* 31:1 (January/February 1986): 67–73.

Nathan, Laurie. *Lighting up the Intelligence Community: A Democratic Approach to Intelligence Secrecy and Openness*. Global Facilitation Network for Security Sector Reform Policy Paper (April 2009). Online, available at: www.ssrnetwork.net/documents/Publications/Intelligence/Intelligence%20Policy%20Paper.pdf.

O'Brien, Kevin A. "A Blunted Spear: The Failure of the ANC/SACP Revolutionary

War Strategy 1961–1990", *Small Wars and Insurgencies* 14:2 (Autumn 2003): 27–70.

O'Brien, Kevin A. "Counter-intelligence for Counter-revolutionary Warfare: The South African Police Security Branch", *Intelligence and National Security* 16:3 (Autumn 2001): 27–59.

O'Brien, Kevin A. "Special Forces for Counter-revolutionary Warfare: The South African Case", *Small Wars and Insurgencies* 12:2 (Summer 2001): 79–109.

O'Brien, Kevin A. "The Use of Assassination as a Tool of State Policy: South Africa's Counter-revolutionary Strategy 1979–1992 (Part II)", *Terrorism and Political Violence* 13:2 (Spring 2001): 107–142.

O'Brien, Kevin A. "Truth and Reconciliation in South Africa: Confronting the Past, Building the Future?", *International Relations* (August 2000): 1–16.

O'Brien, Kevin A. "The Use of Assassination as a Tool of State Policy: South Africa's Counter-revolutionary Strategy 1979–1992" (Part I), *Terrorism and Political Violence* 10:3 (Summer 1998): 34–51.

O'Brien, Kevin A. "Regional Security in Southern Africa: South Africa's National Perspective", *International Peacekeeping* 3:3 (Autumn 1996): 52–76.

O'Brien, Kevin A. "South Africa's Evolving Intelligence and Security Structures", *International Journal of Intelligence and Counterintelligence*. 9:2 (Summer 1996): 187–232.

O'Brien, Kevin A. "South Africa appoints new intelligence chief", *Jane's Intelligence Review* 14:5 (May 2002).

O'Brien, Kevin A. "The McBride Affair: South African Intelligence in Crisis", *Jane's Intelligence Review* 11:1 (January 1999): 40–47.

O'Brien, Kevin A. "Report on the Coup Attempt Uncovered by Defence Intelligence in South Africa: Aftermath and Implications", *African Defence Journal* (May/June 1998): 1, 22.

O'Brien, Kevin A. *The Assassins' Web: South Africa's Counter-revolutionary Strategy, Securocracy and Operations (with Particular Reference to the Special Tasking of Security Force Units) 1978–1990*. University of Hull, 2000.

Orkin, Mark. "'Democracy Knows No Colour': Rationales for Guerrilla Involvement Among Black South Africans". *Journal of Southern African Studies* 18:3 (September 1992): 642–669.

Oseth, Lt-Col John M. "Intelligence and Low-Intensity Conflict". *Naval War College Review* (November 1986): 19–35.

Patel, Hasu H. "Regional Security in Southern Africa: Zimbabwe". *Survival* XXX:1 (January/February 1988): 38–58.

Price, Robert. "Pretoria's Southern African Strategy". *African Affairs* 83:330 (January 1984): 11–32.

Roherty, James. "Managing the Security Power Base in South Africa". *South African International Quarterly* (October 1984): 56–65.

Sarakinsky, Ivor. "State, Strategy and Extra-Parliamentary Opposition in South Africa, 1983–1988". *Politikon* 16:1 (June 1989): 69–82.

Seegers, Annette. "Current Trends in South Africa's Security Establishment". *Armed Forces and Society* 18:2 (Winter 1992): 159–174.

Seegers, Annette. "South Africa's National Security Management System, 1972–90". *Journal of Modern African Studies*. (1991): 253–273.

Seegers, Annette. "The Military in South Africa: A Comparison and Critique (Review)". *South Africa International* 16:4 (April 1986): 192–200.

Seegers, Annette. "The New Security in Democratic South Africa: A Cautionary Tale", *Conflict, Security and Development* 10:2 (May 2010): 271.

Seegers, Annette. "Theories of Revolution: The Third Generation after the Eighties". *Politikon* 19:2 (June 1992): 5–25.

Shafer, D. Michael. "The Unlearned Lessons of Counterinsurgency". *Political Science Quarterly* 103:1 (1988): 57–80.

Slatter, Mick. "The Terrorists Return". *Africa Report* 39:4 (July/August 1994): 60–61.

Slovo, Joe. "The Armed Struggle Spreads". *Sechaba* 5/6 (December 1971/January 1972). Online, available at: www.sacp.org.za/people/slovo/astruggle.html (downloaded 2 March 2000).

Southall, Roger. "Restructuring Intelligence for Post-Apartheid South Africa", Mike Hough (ed.). *Security and Intelligence in a Post-Apartheid South Africa – Strategic Review for Southern Africa*, XIV:2 (October 1992): 3–4.

"South Africa: The Government in the Shadows", *Africa Confidential*, 28:14 (8 July 1987): 3.

"South Africa: The Security Line-up", *Africa Confidential*, 28:12 (10 June 1987): 2.

"South Africa: The Network of a Master Spy", *Africa Confidential* 2:8 (15 April 1987): 1.

Stanley, Elizabeth. "Evaluating the Truth and Reconciliation Commission". *Journal of Modern African Studies* 39:3 (2001): 525–546.

Taylor, Ian. "The Ambiguous Commitment: The People's Republic of China and the Anti-Apartheid Struggle in South Africa". *Journal of Contemporary African Studies* 18:1 (January 2000): 91–106.

Taylor, Paul. "S. Africa's Past Horrors Pose Questions About Future Justice". *Washington Post* 4 March 1995: A1, A22.

Tomaselli, Ruth Elizabeth. "Inkathagate: Covert Funding – Overt Violence", *Covert Action*, 38 (Fall 1991): 39–43.

Trewhela, Paul. "A Literature of Wolves". *Searchlight South Africa* 2:4 (No. 8) (January 1992): 62–69.

Van der Vyver, JD. "State Sponsored Terror Violence". *South African Journal on Human Rights* 4:1 (March 1988): 55–75.

Welsh, David. "Right-Wing Terrorism in South Africa". *Terror From the Extreme Right* (Special Issue of *Terrorism and Political Violence*) 7:1 (1995): 239–264.

Young, Eric T. "The Victors and the Vanquished: The Role of Military Factors in the Outcome of Modern African Insurgencies". *Small Wars and Insurgencies* 7:2 (Autumn 1996): 178–195.

Zulu, Paulus. "Behind the Mask: South Africa's Third Force". *Indicator South Africa* 10:1 (Summer 1992): 8–14.

Media sources (general and specific)

South African Press Agency (SAPA), 1987–2010.
Eastern Cape News Agency (ECNA), 1994–2000.
Mail and Guardian (Pretoria), 1987–2010.
Star and SA Times (Pretoria), 1996–2010.
The Star (Johannesburg), 1990–2010.
Business Day (Pretoria), 1994–2000.
"Alleged Palme Assassin Thrice Tried to Kill Joshua Nkomo". SAPA-DPA. 2 October 1996.

"ANC Leaders' Arrests Led to Closure of Operation Vula". SAPA. 24 November 1995.

"Baboon Foetus Placed at Tutu's House to Bewitch Him". SAPA. 12 May 2000.

Basson, Adriaan. "Spy Boss Haunted by Tender Probe". Mail and Guardian. 9 October 2009. Online, available at: www.mg.co.za/article/2009-10-09-spy-boss-haunted-by-tender-probe.

"Basson Supplied Poisons to Kill Prisoners – Court". SAPA. 3 May 2000.

"Basson Supplied Toxic Substances: Court". SAPA. 2 May 2000.

Battersby, John. "A Secret Network to Preserve White Power". Christian Science Monitor. 24 August 1992.

Beresford, David. "Hopes of Truth about 'Dirty War' against ANC". Electronic Mail and Guardian. 13 May 1997.

Brümmer, Stefaans. "De Klerk 'Knew of Third Force Activities'". Electronic Mail and Guardian. 16 January 1997.

Brümmer, Stefaans. "Inside the ANC's Spy Unit". Mail and Guardian (6 May 2001). Online, available at: www.mg.co.za/mg/za/archive/2001may/features/04may-spy.html.

Brümmer, Stefaans and Sam Sole. "I Spy..". Mail and Guardian. 22 May 2009. Online, available at: www.mg.co.za/article/2009-05-22-i-spy.

Burns, John F. "Pretoria Minister Halts Covert Unit". New York Times. 27 February 1990.

Burns, John F. "Cape Town Death-Squad Inquiry Opens". New York Times. 6 March 1990.

Carlin, John. "SA Hit-Squad 'Linked to RUC'". Independent (London). 14 November 1992.

Carlin, John. "Interview: Dr Neil Barnard". The Long Walk of Nelson Mandela – PBS Frontline. May 1999. Online, available at: www.pbs.org/wgbh/pages/frontline/shows/mandela/interviews/barnard.html.

Carter, Chiara. "Apartheid Army's Deadly Secrets". Sunday Independent. 30 April 2006. Online, available at: www.iol.co.za/index.php?set_id=1&click_id=13&art_id=vn20060430083249898C116766&singlepage=1.

Chetty, Sharon. "Meeting the Government's Needs is Sigxashe's Aim". Star and SA Times. 20 December 1995: 7.

Clemence, Laurian. "Ngcuka was 'Probably Never' a Spy-Hefer". SAPA. 21 January 2004. Online, available at: www.polity.org.za/article/ngcuka-was-x2018probably-neverx2019-a-spyhefer-2004-01-21.

"Counsel for De Kock Admits Client is Guilty of Five Murders". SAPA. 5 August 1996.

"DA to Oppose Appointment of Mo Shaik as NIA Head". SAPA. 30 August 2009. Online, available at: www.mg.co.za/article/2009-08-30-da-to-oppose-appointment-of-mo-shaik-as-nia-head.

Davis, Gaye. "Spying Allegations: Who are the Silly Buggers?". Weekly Mail and Guardian (3 February 1996).

Day, Jim. "De Kock Reveals Plan to Murder Nujoma". Electronic Mail and Guardian. 16 May 1997. Online, available at: pubweb.web.co.za/mg/news.

"De Kock claims on cross-border raids are shocking: Pik Botha". SAPA. 19 September 1996

"De Kock Gave COSAS Booby-Trapped Grenades: Witness". SAPA. 22 January 1996.

"De Kock Implicates Himself in 1989 Car Bombing". SAPA. 13 May 1996.
"De Kock Not Guilty of Trying to Kill Dirk Coetzee: Counsel". SAPA. 6 August 1996.
"De Kock Once Asked to Kill ANCWL Leader: Court Told". SAPA. 8 October 1996.
"De Kock Ordered Deaths of 3 PE policemen, Informer: Prosecutor". SAPA. 16 November 1995.
"De Kock Says he does not Know how Many People he Killed". SAPA. 20 September 1996.
"De Kock Tells Court he Regrets Killing Victims". SAPA. 19 September 1996.
"De Kock Tells How he Killed Nyanda's Brother in Swaziland". SAPA. 16 September 1996.
"De Kock Wanted to Kill 'Traitor' Coetzee, Court Hears". SAPA. 31 January 1996.
Drogin, Bob. "South African Regime Trained Squad to Kill Activists, Witness Says". *Houston Chronicle*. 14 March 1996: 28.
Ellis, Stephen. "When the ANC Refuses To Listen". *Mail and Guardian*. 6 November 2009.
Eveleth, Ann "Stratcom Never Died, Says ex-Cop". *Weekly Mail and Guardian*. 18 August 1995.
"Ex-Security Policeman Coetzee Not Interested in Amnesty". SAPA. 30 January 1996.
"Former Finance Minister Linked to Operation Marion". SAPA. 3 May 1996.
"Former Rhodesian Crack Soldier Implicated in Palme's Murder". SAPA-AP. 29 September 1996.
"F.W. de Klerk rejects TRC allegations". SAPA. 16 January 1997.
Gilmore, Inigo. "Apartheid Minister Approved Killings". *The Times*. 30 November 1996.
Hossack, Colin. "State Security Council Members Knew Very Well what 'Eliminate' Meant". *Africa News Service*. 30 October 1998.
Hutton, Lauren. "Spies, Lies and Secret Tapes", *ISS Today*. 30 Mar 2009. Online, available at: www.issafrica.org/pgcontent.php?UID=18569.
Hutton, Lauren. (ed.). *To Spy or Not To Spy? Intelligence and Democracy in South Africa*. ISS Monograph Series No. 157 (February 2009). Online, available at: www.iss.co.za/pgcontent.php?UID=2537.
"Intelligence Officer Says he Knew about Stratcom'. *Weekly Mail and Guardian*. 21 July 1995.
"Investigators Want to See Swede in Cyprus about Palme's Murder". SAPA-AFP. 2 October 1996.
"Jackie Selebi corruption trial resumes". SAPA. 1 March 2010. Online, available at: www.mg.co.za/article/2010-03-01-jackie-selebi-corruption-trial-resumes.
Keller, Bill. "Trial Offers a Glimpse of Apartheid's Dying Sting". *New York Times*. 19 February 1995. Online, available at: www.nytimes.com/1995/02/20/world/a-glimpse-of-apartheid-s-dying-sting.html.
Kennedy, Ray. 'Ex-Minister Takes Blame for Killings by Apartheid Troops'. *The Times*. 8 May 1997: 14.
Koch, Eddie. "A NIS Spy Centre?". *Weekly Mail*. 12–18 June 1992: 2.
Koch, Eddie. "SA Intelligence World in Turmoil". *Weekly Mail and Guardian*. 20 October 1995.
"KwaMakuthu: Defence calls Gen to Define Military Terms". SAPA. 26 August 1996.
Laurence, Patrick. "South Africa's 'Third Force' Soon in the Dock". *Star International Weekly* (Johannesburg). 30 December 1994: 15.

McGreal, Chris. "Amnesty for Bombers who Blasted London ANC office". Guardian. 16 October 1999.
"Mail Bugging Trial Continues". Weekly Mail and Guardian. 27 December 1995
"Malan's Counsel Objects to Documents in KwaMakuthu Trial". SAPA. 7 August 1996.
"Malan Goes Free". Weekly Mail and Guardian. 11 October 1996.
"Malan Trial: Inkatha Training 'Most Sensitive Operation'". SAPA. 18 March 1996.
"Man Fingered as Palme Killer Unknown to Swedish Investigators". SAPA-AFP. 29 September 1996.
"Moe Shaik's Appointment Angers Opposition Parties". SAPA. 3 October 2009. Online, available at: www.mg.co.za/article/2009-10-03-moe-shaiks-appointment-angers-opposition-parties.
"My Strategy is to Keep Talking and Stay Alive, Says De Kock after Four Days". Saturday Star (Johannesburg). 21 September 1996.
"National Crime Prevention Strategy Unveiled". SAPA Report. 22 May 1996.
"Nhlanhla Defends Employing Coetzee". SAPA. 5 January 1996.
Peta, Basildon. "ANC Split Threatened as Leaders Face Spying Charges". Independent (London). 16 October 2003. Online, available at: www.independent.co.uk/news/world/africa/anc-split-threatened-as-leaders-face-spying-charges-583511.html.
"Prime Evil". SABC (1996 – exact date/time unknown) (Producer Jacques Pauw).
"Prisoner Seeks Amnesty for Webster Killing". Cape Argus Times. 7 August 1997.
Rantao, Jovial. "Civilian Management for the Police". Star International Weekly (Johannesburg). 13–19 July 1995: 5.
"SADF Will Not Comment on 'Project Echoes'". SAPA. 12 November 1992.
"S African Minister's Wife Sheryl Cwele on Drug Charges". BBC News (29 January 2010). Online, available at: http://news.bbc.co.uk/2/hi/africa/8488355.stm.
"SANDF Chief of Staff Testifies in De Kock Trial". SAPA. 23 November 1995.
"Secret Killings: Project COAST". Panorama BBC1 2220h 14 July 1998 (Producer Peter Molloy).
Seery, Brendan. "Out of the Cold and into the Light". Star International Weekly (Johannesburg). 16–22 March 1995: 11.
"Seniors Should Take Rap for Killings, Assassin Tells Basson Trial". SAPA. 11 May 2000.
"Shocks from the Steyn Report". Electronic Mail and Guardian. 31 January 1997.
Soggot, Mungo. "Proof at Last: Apartheid Cabinet Ordered Goniwe Killing". Weekly Mail and Guardian. 28 May 1999.
Sole, Sam. "Barry Gilder and the Hot Frogs". Mail and Guardian. 27 November 2009. Online, available at: www.mg.co.za/article/2009-11-27-barry-gilder-and-the-hot-frogs.
Sole, Sam. "Spooks Haunt our Democracy". Mail and Guardian. 22 May 2009. Online, available at: www.mg.co.za/article/2009-05-22-spooks-haunt-our-democracy.
Sole, Sam. "Zuma's New Spy Purge". Mail and Guardian (5 February 2010). Online, available at: www.mg.co.za/article/2010-02-05-zumas-new-spy-purge.
Sole, Sam, Pearlie Joubert, Stefaans Brümmer. "Inside Operation Destroy Lucifer". Mail and Guardian. 19 June 2009. Online, available at: www.mg.co.za/article/2009-06-19-inside-operation-destroy-lucifer.
"South African Apartheid Probe Flooded With Allegations". AFP. 31 January 1997.

Sparks, Allister. "South Africa caught in security web". Washington Post. 31 December 1986: A14.
Sparks, Allister. "Answers are Needed about NP's Secret Operations". Star International Weekly (Johannesburg). 29 June–5 July 1995: 5.
"'Spy unit' for Mbeki". ZA*NOW (22 February 2002).
Stein, Jeff. "South Africa's Many 'Watergates' May Spill Over on the CIA". Baltimore Sun (20 March 1996).
"Steyn Denies He Fingered Generals to De Klerk". SAPA. 17 January 1997.
Stober, Paul, Marion Edmonds, Eddie Koch and Ann Eveleth. "Inkatha's secret German War Chest", Weekly Mail and Guardian (15 September 1995)
Taylor, Paul. "S. Africa's Past Horrors Pose Questions about Future Justice". Washington Post. 4 March 1995: A1, A22.
"The Secrets of Stratcom". Weekly Mail and Guardian. 23 June 1995.
Thornycroft, Peta. "Palme's Murder Still a Mystery". Weekly Mail and Guardian. 4 October 1997.
"Truth or Tragedy". Ch4 (UK) (1998 – exact date/time unknown).
"Two Life Sentences, 212 Years' Imprisonment for De Kock". SAPA. 30 October 1996.
"Tutu Begins Inquiry into Rights Violations". Globe and Mail. 16 April 1996: A16.
"Vlakplaas and MI Responsible for Transkei Coup: Affidavit". SAPA. 11 July 1995.
"Vlakplaas Men to Appear in Supreme Court". SAPA. 18 October 1996.
"Vlakplaas's Orders for Foreign Ops Came from the Top: Witness". SAPA. 21 February 1996
"White Did Not Kill Swedish PM: S. African Agent". SAPA-AFP. 30 September 1996.
Whitfield, Chris. "De Klerk for Security Chairmanship". Star International Weekly (Johannesburg). 15–21 September 1994: 4.
Williams, Rocklyn. "All the President's Men". Saturday Star (Johannesburg). 11 July 1992: 11.
"Woman Tells of Missing ANC Boyfriend Allegedly Killed by Police". SAPA. 20 November 1995.

Internet sources (general)

African National Congress. ANC Second Submission to the TRC – Part 1. Online, available at: www.anc.org.za/ancdocs/misc/trc2.html (downloaded 16 May 1997).
African National Congress. ANC Submission to the Truth and Reconciliation Commission. www.anc.organisation.za/ancdocs/misc/trcall.html (downloaded 12 October 1996).
African National Congress. Freedom Can Be Won: A Call to the South African People (1970). Online, available at: www.sacp.org.za/docs/hitory/canbewon.html (downloaded 2 March 2000).
African National Congress. Final Resolution on Strategy and Tactics: ANC 48th Annual Conference (July 1991). Online, available at: www.anc.org.za/ancdocs/history/conf/stratact48.html (downloaded 1 March 2000).
African National Congress. List of MK Operations. www.anc.org.za/ancdocs/misc/trc2c.html (downloaded 16 May 1997).
African National Congress. Message to the People of South Africa on the Occasion

of the 20th Anniversary of the Formation of Umkhonto we Sizwe, December 16, 1981. Online, available at: www.anc.org.za/ancdocs/history/or/or81–19a.html (downloaded 1 March 2000).

African National Congress. Operation Mayibuye (11 July 1963). Online, available at: www.anc.org.za/ancdocs/history/mk/mayibuye.html (downloaded 2 March 2000).

African National Congress. Operations Report: the Department of Intelligence and Security of the African National Congress. Online, available at: www.anc.org.za/ancdocs/misc/trc2d.html (downloaded 16 May 1997).

African National Congress. Seventy-Five Years of Struggle. Online, available at: www.anc.org.za/ancdocs/history/mk/forward.html (downloaded 2 March 2000).

African National Congress. Strategy and Tactics of the ANC (May 1969). Online, available at: www.anc.org.za/ancdocs/history/stratact.html (downloaded 2 March 2000).

African National Congress. "Umkhonto we Sizwe – Born of the People", Statement of the National Executive Committee of the African National Congress on the 25th Anniversary of the Formation of Umkhonto we Sizwe, December 16, 1986. Online, available at: www.anc.org.za/ancdocs/history/or/or86–16.html (downloaded 1 March 2000).

African National Congress. Umkhonto we Sizwe (MK) operations report. Online, available at: www.anc.org.za/ancdocs/misc/trc2b.html (downloaded 16 May 1997).

Bauman, Ted. "The Key to a Peaceful South Africa". The World and I. October 1993. Online, available at: www.worldandi.com/specialreport/1993/october/Sa11159.htm.

Bester, Lt Col C.R.C. The Development Of Civil Military Relations In South Africa. South African Army College (1999). Online, available at: www.mil.za/CSANDF/CJSupp/TrainingFormation/ArmyCollege/ArmyCollege1999/The%20Development%20.htm.

Gabara, Nthambeleni. "SA's Civilian Intelligence Structures to Merge" (4 October 2009). Online, available at: http://freenetafrica.com/node/921.

Hutton, Lauren. "Intelligence and Accountability in Africa". Policy Brief No. 2 (June 2009). Online, available at: www.issafrica.org/uploads/jul09intelligenceaccount.pdf.

Intelligence in a Constitutional Democracy: Final Report to the Minister for Intelligence Services, the Honourable Mr Ronnie Kasrils, MP. (10 September 2008). Online, available at: www.issafrica.org/uploads/intelrpt.pdf.

"Kasrils: Ministerial Review Commission on Intelligence". Polity.org.za (1 November 2006). Online, available at: www.polity.org.za/article/kasrils-ministerial-review-commission-on-intelligence-01112006–2006–11–01.

Laurence, Patrick. "The Future of the NIA". Focus. 17 March 2000. Online, available at: www.hsf.org.za/focus17/NIAfocus17.html.

National Party of South Africa. National Party Submission to the TRC. Online, available at: www.truth.org.za/submit/np-truth.htm (downloaded 12 December 1996).

National Party of South Africa. Second Submission of the National Party to the Truth and Reconciliation Commission. Online, available at: www.truth.org.za/submit/np2.htm (downloaded 15 April 1997).

"O'Malley Archives: Hefer Commission". Online, available at: www.nelsonmandela. org/omalley/index.php/site/q/03lv03445/04lv04015/05lv04120.htm.

"SA Intelligence Boss Throws in the Towel". ZA*NOW. 28 January 2002.

"The Case of 'Dulcie September'". The Truth Commission Files. Netherlands Institute of Southern Africa (NIZA), November 1997. Online, available at: www.contrast.org/truth/html/dulcie_september.html (downloaded 6 December 1998).

"The Chemical Warfare Case". The Truth Commission Files. Netherlands Institute for Southern Africa, November 1997. Online, available at: www.contrast.org/truth/html/chemical_biological_weapons.html (downloaded 6 December 1998).

Varney, Howard. Submission to the Truth and Reconciliation Commission: The Caprivi Trainees. 4 August 1997. Online, available at: www.truth.org.za/submit/caprivi.htm (no download date).

Index

accountability 211–20
Adult Education Consultants (AEC) 117, 125
Advisory Committee on Special Secret Projects 192
African National Congress (ANC): and armed struggle 7, 19–22; control of apartheid security apparatus 211; Department of Intelligence and Security (ANC-DIS) 173, 176, 197–9, 207–10, 218, 219–20; Department of National Intelligence and Security (ANC-NAT) 21, 76–8, 172, 177; electoral victory 2, 204; external support 8; founding of 5; infiltration of 36–7; intelligence in exile 76–8; National Executive Committee (ANC-NEC) 130, 152, 231; in key intelligence service positions 228, 230–1; negotiations with NIS 176–7, 195–6; participation in TRC 221–2; politicisation of intelligence 227–31; Politico-Military Council (PMC) 21 96–7; restructuring intelligence and security 172–3; Revolutionary Council 21; unbanning of 175; underground networks 174–6
African Resistance Movement (ARM) 6, 20, 23
Africa Risk Analysis Consultants (ARAC) 117
Afrikaner Resistance Movement (AWB) 184
Afrikaner-nationalist forces, threat from 15–16
Afrikaners, problems confronting 3–6
amnesty 194–5, 221–2
Anglo–Boer Wars 14
Angola 8, 30, 35, 43, 44, 45, 46, 48, 60, 75, 78, 98, 105, 117, 118, 121–2, 123–4, 166, 167, 174
anti-apartheid movements, infiltration of 36–7, 38–9
apartheid leadership, participation in TRC 221
apartheid: founding of 4–6, 7, 17–19; intelligence dispensation during 7–9, 9–10; shards if 181–2
Area Defence Policy 43, 49
armed struggle: end of 172–6; launch of 5–6, 7; and SAP/ANC 19–22
assassinations 9, 38–9, 44, 68, 74–5, 82, 105–6, 108–15, 137, 141, 145–6, 181–3, 198
autonomous intelligence capability, British resistance to 14–19

Azanian people's Liberation Army (APLA) 20, 45, 60, 62, 221

"Badger Unit" 183
Barnard, Dr Lukas Niel 66, 68, 71, 72, 168, 170, 176, 177, 179, 196, 197, 205
Battle of the Intelligence Brief 63–4
Biko, Steve 114
"Binnekring" 183
Black Consciousness Movement (BCM) 114
Black Councils 98, 164
Boer republics, intelligence capability 13–17
Boesak, Rev Allan 96, 137
Boipatong massacre 188–9
bombings 6, 20–1, 91, 99, 114, 120, 135, 204
Bophutatswana 87, 117, 179, 184
Bophutatswana Internal Intelligence Service 74, 197, 208, 210
Botha, P.W. 28, 30–1, 49, 51, 63–4, 83–4, 114, 139, 140–1; fall of 169–70; rise of 41–6; "Rubicon speech" 143–4; triumph of 45–6
Botswana 39, 53, 75, 124, 134, 139, 149
Britain: antipathy towards 4–5; intelligence relationship with 14–19, 24, 26, 43, 76; legacy of 7; policing model 14, 15, 34
Broederbond 15, 28, 177
Bureau for State Security (BOSS) 10, 25–9; direct targeting capabilities 38–9; downfall of 51–4; establishment of 6; reorganisation of 129; end of 63–76
Bureau for State Security Act No 104 (1978) 64, 74

Cabinet: Committee for Security Affairs (CCSA) 178, 179; Committee on Security and Intelligence (CCSI) 178, 211–12, 214; Constitutional Affairs Committee 93; Economic Affairs Committee 93; power of 6, 10, 30–1, 83–4; reshuffle (1991) 180; Secretariat 84; Social Affairs Committee 93
centralised intelligence services 25–9
Chief of Staff Intelligence (CSI) 70, 71–2
CIA 24, 58, 65–6, 68
Ciskei 86, 117, 162, 179, 184
Ciskei Intelligence Service 75, 210
Civil Co-operation Bureau (CCB), SADF 54, 56, 58, 67, 103, 116–17, 132–5; in abeyance 181, 182–4; disbanding of 188; founding of 162; operations 135–7; origins and development of 128–35

Co-ordinating Intelligence Committee (KIK), SSC 103, 125, 150, 152, 153-4, 155, 178, 185, 194, 219; Counter-revolutionary Information Task Team 72
code of conduct 216-17
Coetsee Commission (1978) 52, 64-5
Cold War 8, 16, 17-18, 47, 48, 76, 99, 173; end of 166-7, 199
colonial occupation 5
colonial policing model 14, 15, 34
Commonwealth 16, 19, 76, 81
Commonwealth Eminent Persons' Group (EPG) 143-4
Communications Committee (KOMKOM) 76, 156
Communist threat 5, 16, 17-18, 47, 48, 69, 120, 164
"Comsec" 226-7
Congress of South African Trade Unions (COSATU) 96
Constitution 80, 200, 201, 214, 217, 230; and intelligence dispensation 205-7; proposals for reform of 95-6
contra-mobilisation 118-28
Convention for a Democratic South Africa (CODESA) 177, 178
Counter Insurgency Committee (TIK) 86
counter-insurgency 34-9
counter-insurgency training 49-50
counter-intelligence 34-9, 53; SAP capabilities 103-15
counter-revolution 7-9
counter-revolutionary activities: growth of state capabilities 98-103; legal basis for 74-5
counter-revolutionary strategy 138-46; failing of 163-8; and JMCs 154-9
counter-revolutionary warfare: covert capability for 161-3; integrated approach to 159-63
covert capability 116-18, 161-3
covert operations: De Klerk's weak grasp on 192-6; DMI 116-18; indiscriminate use of 69-70; reigning in 179-84
"Craddock Four" 127, 138
Criminal Procedure Act (1977) 75
criminal prosecutions 220-1

De Klerk, F.W. 52, 69-70, 84, 134, 169, 170, 172, 177-82, 187, 188-91, 204-5; weak grasp on covert operations 192-6
de Kock, Col Eugene 106, 108, 109-10, 111, 114-15, 161, 186-7, 220
death squads 109-11, 181-3
Defence Act No. 44 (1957) 22-3, 142
Defence Staff Council 43
"Delta-40" 103, 129
democratic elections 2, 125, 187, 204
Department of Constitutional Affairs 197
Department of Constitutional Planning and Development (CDPD) 46, 163, 176
Department of Foreign Affairs and Information 66
Department of Foreign Affairs, Foreign Intelligence Bureau 208
Department of National Security (DONS) 66
destabilisation, intelligence for 118-28

Directors General 214, 215-16, 228
"dirty tricks" operations 33
document security 18
domestic violence 69-70
double agents 7, 173
Dynamic Teaching, African Information Systems (PTY) Ltd 117

economically motivated violence 183-4
Electronic Communications Security (Pty) Ltd 226, 230
Electronic Communications Security (Pty) Ltd Act (2002) 226
electronics security 226-7
End Conscription Campaign 97
Erasmus Commission 38, 64
Executive Outcomes 183
exile, ANC intelligence in 76-8
exiles, return of 183-4
external threats 43-4, 48, 98-9, 184

Fascism 15, 16
Forcas Armadas Populares de Libertação de Angola (FAPLA) 98, 105, 123
foreign counter-intelligence 111-15
Freedom Charter 97
Frente de Liberaçao de Moçambique (FRELIMO) 39, 120, 122
Frente Nacional de Liberaçao de Angola (FNLA) 60, 105
front companies 33, 117-18, 134-5, 183
Frontline States: destabilisation of 98-9, 118-28; as buffer zone 75-6; SAP in 34-9
Further Indemnity Act No 151 (1992) 194-5

General Intelligence Law Amendment Act (2000/2003) 226, 227
GME Pty Ltd 183
Goldstone Commission 182, 187-91, 193
Government of National Unity (GNU) 7, 177, 204-5
guerrilla strategy 19-22
guerrillas (*askaris*) 36-7, 103, 106, 108-11, 187

Harms Commission (1990) 132, 181, 182, 186, 187, 190, 193
heads of Combined Services (HOCS) Committee 212
Hefer Commission 219
human rights abuses 69, 106, 160, 173, 195, 218, 221-2

illegal operations 56
indemnification 142, 194-5
Indemnity Act No 35 (1990) 194
"information scandal" 45-6, 63, 64, 66
Inkatha 99, 125-6, 162, 163
Inkatha Freedom Party (IFP) 183, 187-8, 189, 191-2, 204, 205, 209, 215
"Inkathagate" 191-2
Inspectors-General 215-16, 225-6
integration 199, 217-20, 221; versus destruction 207-111
intelligence activities, legal basis for 74-5
intelligence and security establishment, overview of 3-11
intelligence assessments 72-3, 140, 212, 219

intelligence capability formation 100–3
intelligence co-ordination 23–4, 72, 74, 91, 212, 214
intelligence community, guaranteeing support of 9–10
intelligence dispensation 7–9; 1910–1948 13–17; apartheid era 7–9; building new 196–202; and constitution 205–7; oversight and accountability 211–20; role during early days of apartheid 17–19; reshaping 223–6
intelligence establishment, expanding 25–9
intelligence function: establishing 22–5; re-examining 199
intelligence history 11–12; legacy of 233–6
intelligence personnel (1994–1995) *208*
Intelligence Records Bureau 16
intelligence restructuring 207–11, 222–7
Intelligence Review Board 226
Intelligence Service and State Security Council Act (1987) 74
Intelligence Services Act (1994/2002) 206, 207, 209–10, 214, 216–17, 226, 228
Intelligence Services Control Act (1994) 206, 214, 223
Intelligence Services Control Amendment Act (1999) 223, 225, 226
Intelligence Services Council on Conditions of Employment 226, 227, 230
intelligence structures: evolution of 218; rationalisation of 72; and targeting 148–59
intelligence structuring 172–3
intelligence training 77, 175, 219–20, 226
intelligence-led policy 69–70
intelligence-led targeting 147–8
intelligence-sharing 17–18, 19, 24, 26, 212, 214
intelligence: ANC's approach to 76–8; for destabilisation 118–28; development of 52–4; end of 207–10; new environment (1994–1995) 204–7; parliamentary oversight of 214–15; philosophy of 199–202; politicisation of 227–31; post-apartheid era 10–11; and TEC 197–9
Interim Constitution 197, 206
internal contra-mobilisation 125–8
internal intelligence collection 24
Internal Intelligence Service Act (1982) 74
internal protest movement, establishment of 96–8
Internal Security Act (1972) 74, 75
internal targeting 44–5, 153–4
internal threats 15–16, 24, 48, 184; UDF as 96–8
international events 166–8
international isolation 41, 81, 167–8, 178
international sphere, ANC/SACP emphasis on 21–2
International University Exchange Fund (IUEF) 114

Joint Co-ordinating Intelligence Committee (JCIC) 198, 199, 212
Joint Counter-Insurgency Committees (GTKs) 86
Joint Intelligence Centre (GIS) 87, 90, 154
Joint Management Centres (JMCs) 66, 86–92; Communications Committee COMCOM/KOMKOM 87; Constitutional/Economic/Welfare Committee (CESCOM/SEMKOM) 87, 156; and counter-revolutionary strategy 154–9; Daily Management Committee/Executive Committee 87; Joint Intelligence Committee (JICOM/GIKOM) 87, 88, 90; Liaison Committee 87; NIS withdrawal from 164; Secretariat 87; Security Committee (SECCOM/VEIKOM 87, 90
Joint Operations Centre (JOC) 32, 87, 154
Joint Security Staff (Geveilstaf/GVS) 88, 91, 103, 148–9, 155, 161, 195
Joint Standing Committee on Intelligence (JSCI) 214–15, 223–5
Joubert Plan 128, 147–8

KGB 24, 219
Khan Commission 53, 182, 190, 191–2, 193
Koevoet 35–6, 58, 122–3, 187; emergence of 104–7; formation of 101, 103; in South Africa 108–11
KwaZulu Police Force (KZP) 126, 190
KwaZulu-Natal (KZN) 126, 162, 219

legal basis, intelligence/country-revolutionary activities 74–5
Lesotho Liberation Army (LLA) 121–2, 124
Lisbon, coup in 65–6
Longreach Pty Ltd 114–15, 117–18

"McBride affair" 228
Malan, Gen. Magnus 46, 47, 71, 101, 104, 119–20, 132, 140, 154, 157, 159–60, 180, 191, 220
Mandela, Nelson 20, 143–4, 169, 175, 177, 186, 205, 217, 218–19
Mass Democratic Movement (MDM) 97
Matthews Commission 229
Mbeki, Thabo 1, 176, 177, 210, 219
Mbokodo 78, 172, 173, 229
MI5/MI6 16–18; Security Liaison Offices 17
militarisation: of politics 80; of society 50, 80, 100, 154, 167
Military Intelligence Division (DMI), SADF 10, 42; and Civil Co-operation Bureau 128–37; Combined Operations 52; covert capabilities 116–18; creation of 16, 23; decline of 19; development of 51–4; Directorate Covert Collection (DCC) 52, 53–4, 56, 116–18, 188–9; Directorate Special Tasks (DST) 52, 75, 117, 121–8; end of 210–11; expansion of 52–4; fall of 177–81; influence of 30–1, 42–5, 80; intelligence sharing 72; Intelligence Staff Council 52–3; interpretation 52; as lead agency 64–5, 68–9, 70–1; polluted intelligence 195; reorganisation of 50; and Special Branch 23–4, 28–9; special operations units 100–1; Special Tasks units 120–2; Sub-Division, Counter-Intelligence (SDCI) 52, 53; Sub-Division, Intelligence Operations (SDIO) 52, 53–4; Sub-Division, Military Intelligence (SDMI) 52–3; triumph of 45–6; *see also* Special Forces
military training 175
"moles" 7, 36–7, 173, 174, 178, 218, 221

Montsuenyane Commission (1990) 222
Morogoro Conference (1969) 77
Movimento Popular de Libertação de Angola (MPLA) 34, 44, 66, 120, 121, 123
Mozambique 35, 44, 48, 75, 117, 118, 121–2, 124–5
Mugabe, Robert 129

Namibia 34, 35–6, 43, 48, 56–7, 59, 60, 82, 99, 104–6, 117, 118, 121–2, 124, 125, 133, 136–7, 166, 167, 168, 174
Natal 86, 99, 108, 122, 125–6, 128, 191
National Academy of Intelligence 226
National Co-ordinating Mechanism (NCM) 84, 178
National Communications Centre (NCC) 227, 230; Office for Interception Centres (OIC) 227, 230
National Crime Prevention Strategy (1996) 206, 209
National Early Warning Centre 212
National Intelligence Agency (NIA): Director General 214; factionism 222, 231; Inspector General 215–16; politicisation of 229; setting-up of 207, 208–10
National Intelligence Co-ordinating Committee (NICOC) 178, 199, 210–11, 212, 214
National Intelligence Estimates 212
National Intelligence Priorities 212
National Intelligence Service (NIS) 10: establishment of 129; information on ANC 218–19; integration of 207–8; negotiations with ANC 176–7, 195–6; negotiations with NAT 173; rise of 63–76, 177–81; under GNU 207–10; withdrawal from JMCs 164
National Intelligence Service Act (1988) 74
National Joint Management Centre (NJMC) 32, 149, 155–6, 179; External Working Group 155
National Joint Operations Centre 32
National Management Centre 66
National Party (NP): declaration of apartheid of 4–5, 7; hostility to 50; loss of power 204–5
National Security Committee (NSC) 178
National Security Council Act (1981) 74
National Security Management System (NSMS) 30, 49, 84, 155–7; abolition of 178; activation of 100; implementation of 80–4; and National Welfare Management System 92–3; structure of 84–6
National Security Strategy 29
National Service 49
National Strategic Intelligence Act (1994) 206, 207, 210, 226, 229
National Strategic Intelligence Amendment Act (2002) 226
National Strategy Concept against the Revolutionary Onslaught (1986) 147
National Welfare Management System (NWMS) 92–3, 155, 157
negotiated settlement: ANC in 21–2, conditions for 69–70; external pressure for 166–8; National Party in 204–5; NIS role in 209; search for 176–96
new political landscape 169–70

New York Accords (1988) 174
newly independent states, support for ANC 8
Nhlanhla, Joe 21, 78, 173, 177, 199, 200, 209, 217–18
Nkomati Accord (1984) 124, 176
Nkomo, Joshua 115, 130
nuclear weapons programme 8

office of state president (OSP) 33, 179, 211; Bureau of Information 178
"oil spot" technique 145, 165
Operation BIBLE 173, 174, 178, 219
Operation DISA 121, 122
Operation DRAMA 122, 123
Operation ETANGO 124
Operation EZUVA 124
Operation Flair 177
Operation Hammer 49–50
Operation K 35–6
Operation KATZEN 92, 126–7, 162
Operation MARION 123, 126, 127, 162
Operation Mayibuye 20
Operation MAYONNAISE 118
Operation ORPHEUS 127
Operation PASTOOR 189
Operation SAVANNAH 30, 43
Operation Shishita 77
Operation VULA 174–6, 178, 179, 182, 198, 219
Operation Winter 44
Opposition United Party 19
Ossewa-Brandwag (OB) 15
Ovambo, SAP in 34–6
oversight 211–20, 223, 225, 229

Palme, Olaf 114–15
Pan African Congress (PAC) 6, 20, 37, 175
Pan-African Security Service (PASS) 197, 204–5, 208, 209, 219–20
Pan Afrika Industrial Investment Consultants CC (PAIIC CC) 117
Parliamentary Joint Standing Committees on Defence and Intelligence 211
People's Courts 98, 140
People's Liberation Army of Namibia (PLAN) 34, 98–9, 104, 105, 122, 123
people's war, quest for 21, 74, 98, 140, 174
Pikoli Review Commission (1996) 223
Police Act No. 7 (1958) 18, 24, 142
Policia Internacional e de Defesa do Estado (PIDE) 26, 65–6
policing model 14, 15, 34
political reform 145, 163–4, 176
political history, impact on security 3–6
politicisation of intelligence 10–11, 18–19, 71–2, 202, 227–31
politics, SADF influence 42–6
Port Elizabeth Civic Organisation (PEBCO) 127
post-apartheid era, intelligence function 10–11
Potgieter Commission 26, 28–9, 47, 48, 84
Prevention of Violence and Intimidating Act No 139 (1991) 187
private intelligence sector 26, 217
private military companies 183
professional standards 219–20

Index 299

Project ANCOR/KAMPONG 125
Project Barnacle 130–1
Project ECHOES 191, 192
Project VALLEX 125
Promotion of National Unity and Reconciliation Act No 34 (1995) 194–5, 221
propaganda 21, 33, 53, 77, 87, 135, 136–7, 155
Provincial Intelligence Co-ordinating Committees (PICOCs) 212
"pseudo" operations 35, 36–7, 56, 103, 104–6, 108–11, 118
Public Safety Act (1953) 74
Public Service Amendment Act (1969) 25
Public Service Commission 64

Reconstruction and Development Programme (RDP) 207–8
reform apartheid 46, 50–1, 145
regional contra-mobilisation 122–5
Regulation of Interception of Communications and Provision of Communication-related Information Act (2002) 227
Report on the National Security Situation (1975) 80
Republican Intelligence (RI) 5, 22–5,
Resistência Nacional Moçambicana (RENAMO) 120, 121, 122, 123, 124, 126
revolution 7–9; containing and countering 159–63
revolutionary onslaught 93, 138–42
revolutionary war 95–8; fears of 81–2
Rhodesia 35, 36, 44, 48, 57, 58, 59, 82, 98, 118, 119; *see also* Zimbabwe
right-wing groups 25, 160, 179, 180, 184, 185, 189, 196, 198, 202, 204–5, 232
rural counter-insurgency capabilities 45

Sabotage Act (*General Law Amendment Act*) (1962) 20, 74
sanctions regime 8, 76, 114, 178, 192
Secret Services Account Amendment Act No 142 (1992) 192
Secret Services Evaluation Committee 192
Security Branch (SAP-SB) 10, 18–19, 23, 36–7, 42; CI 103, 108–11, 181, 187, 188; "C" section 150–1; and DMI 23–4, 28–9; end of 210–11; "G" Section 103, 111–15; intelligence sharing 72; in Namibia 34–9; re-emergence of 76; resurgence of 103–15; Sections 107; specialist operations units 101; transfer of 187; transformation of 177
Security Intelligence and State Security Council Act (1972) 25–6, 28, 29, 47, 74
security: changing paradigm 75–6; impact of political history 3–6; new paradigm of 199–202; restructuring 172–3
securocracy, rise of 29–34, 41–6
Selous Scouts 36, 44, 58, 129
"separate development" policy 45
Sharpeville Massacre (1960) 6, 19–20, 99
signals intelligence 226–7
Simonstown Beraad Accords (1982) 72–3
society, militarisation of 50, 80, 100, 154, 167
socio-economic issues 50–1, 93, 145, 164–5
socio-political reform 50–1, 145, 165
sources, protection of 214–15
South Africa Army 35; Citizen Force units 43, 49; "Hammer" COIN units 43, 50, 54, 56, 127, 128, 160; internal operations 100; Pathfinders 56, 60; Reserve 43
South African Air Force 35
South African Communist Party (SACP): and armed struggle 7, 19–22; launch of armed struggle 5–6; unbanning of 175; underground networks 74–6
South African Defence Force (SADF): Chief of Staff, Intelligence (CSI) 54, 60; as corporate actor in domestic policies 42–5; creation of intelligence capability 22–3; curtailing activities of 179–81; deployment to townships 100; Directorate Covert Collection (DCC) 181; dismissal of officers 189–90; Parachute Battalion 58, 59; Reconnaissance Commandos 54, 56–7, 58, 59–60, 62, 101, 122–3, 129–30, 143; Signals Intelligence Unit 53; special operations units 101; "third force" capabilities 159–61; *see also* Civil Co-operation Bureau; Military Intelligence Division (DMI); Special Forces
South African National Academy of Intelligence (SANAI) 230
South African National Defence Force (SANDF) 210–11, 228; Intelligence Division 210
South African Police (SAP): in Boipatong massacre 188–9; counter-intelligence capabilities 103–15; and counter-intelligence/counter-insurgency 34–9; Crime Combating and Investigation Division (SAP-CCID) 177, 208, 210; commissioner of 25; Crime Information Service (SAP-CIS) 177, 187; Criminal Investigations Branch 187; Detective Branch 15, 18; dismissal of officers 190–1; infiltration of 18; Internal Stability Unit (ISU) 159–60, 161; Namibia Division 34–9; prior to 1948 14–16; Riot Unit 34; special operations units 101; "third force" capabilities 159–61; Uniform Branch 18; *see also Koevoet*; Security Branch (SAP-SB)
South African Police Service (SAPS) 208, 209; Civilian Ministerial secretariat 210; National Crime Investigation Service (NCIS) 210, 215–16
South African Police Services Act (1995) 206
South African Secret Service (SASS) 207–8, 222; Director General 214; Inspector General 215–16
South African Students' Organisation (SASP) 39
South West African Peoples' Organisation (SWAPO) 34–5, 44, 66, 99, 101, 103, 104–5, 118, 120, 122, 123, 124, 125, 133, 136–7, 167, 168, 174, 187, 191
South-West African Police (SWAPOL) 75, 104
South-West African Territorial Force (SWATF) 75
"sovereignty" 19
Soweto Uprising (1976) 7, 21, 45, 46, 51, 69, 75–6, 143
Special Forces, SADF 42, 52, 54–7, 75, 104, 147–8; Civil Co-operation Bureau (CCB) 52; destabilisation strategies 120–2; DMI control of 116–17; General Office

Index 301

Special Forces *continued*
  Commanding (GOC) 60; influence on JMCs 158; internal operations 100–1; origins and development 58–62; target identification workgroup 149
state opponents, targeting 7–8, 9–10, 38–9
State Security Advisory Board (SSAB) 23–4
State Security Agency (SSA) 230
State Security Commission 23
State Security Council (SSC) 26, 28, 49, 66; (1968–1972) 29–34; Administration Branch 32; Joint Security Staff 103; National Co-ordinating Committee 155; National Intelligence Interpretation Branch (NIIB) 32, 65; formation of 72, 81; inadequacy of 84; inter-departmental committees (IDCs) 32, 86; power of 6, 83; restructuring 194; Secretariat 32, 86; Strategic Planning Branch (SPB) 32; strategy documents 147; termination of 178; Working Committee 32, 33, 86, 178; *see also* Co-ordinating Intelligence Committee; Stratkom
states of emergency 69, 138–46; conditions for lifting 165
Steyn Commission 182, 187–91, 193
Strategy and tactics of the ANC 20
Strategy for Combating of ANC (1986) 147
Stratkom 32, 33–4, 155; *KomOps* 33, 100
"street committees" 98, 140
study, aims of 11–12
Super-ZAPU 121–2, 124
Suppression of Communism Act (1950) 20
Swaziland 110–11, 117, 123, 124–5

Tanzania 39, 174, 222
targeting processes and authorities 151–3
Terrorism Act (1967) 20, 74, 75
"Third Force" 49, 215, 217, 227; establishment of 159–61; unleashing of 185–7; reigning-in of 179–96
threat perception, restructuring 141–2
Total Counter Revolutionary Strategy 30, 41, 142–6, 159
"Total National Strategy" 30, 41, 46, 64, 68, 70; and NSMS 78–93; origins of 49–51; summary of 47–9
"Total Onslaught" 5, 28–9, 32, 33, 46, 47, 50, 68–9, 147
townships: alternative governance 98, 140, 164; violence in 99–100, 142–3, 156–7, 183–4
training: counter-insurgency 49–50; intelligence 77, 175, 219–20, 226
Transitional Executive Council (TEC) 177, 197–9; Sub-Council on Intelligence (SCI) 197–8, 201, 205
Transitional Executive Council Act 198
transitional period 2–3, 7, 10–11
Transkei 86, 117, 179, 184, 188, 189
Transkei Intelligence Service 74, 197, 204–5, 207–8, 210
Trewits 74, 103, 108, 161; establishment of 148–51; internal targeting 153–4; target processes and authorities 151–3
Tricameral Parliamentary system 95–6

Truth and Reconciliation Commission 160, 182, 220–2
Tutu, Archbishop Desmond 137, 222
"Twelve Point Plan" (1979) 83–4, 96

Uganda 166, 174, 222
Umkhonto weSizwe (MK) 5–6, 20–1, 35, 45, 76–7, 126, 163, 198; Revolutionary Council (RC) 78; Special Operations Units 21, 78, 96–7, 99–100; underground networks 174–6
unconventional operations 58–9
underground networks 174–6
underground structures, ANC 21–2
União Nacional para la Independência Total de Angola (UNITA) 105, 120, 121, 122, 123–4
Union Defence Force (UDF) 14–16, 175
United Democratic Front (UDF), as internal revolutionary threat 96–8
Unlawful Organisations Act (1960) 20

Vaal Triangle Uprising (1984) 97, 99
van den Bergh, Henrik 19, 20, 24, 25, 26, 28, 38–9, 46, 63, 64
Veikoms 86, 87, 90, 152, 154, 156, 179
Venda 86, 117, 179, 184
Venda National Intelligence Service 197, 208, 210
vigilantes 74, 122, 125, 145, 162, 164
violence, legitimisation of 141
Vlakplaas "C" Section 108–11, 182–4, 186–7
Vlakplaas CI death-squad 130, 161–2
Vlok, Adriaan 140, 159, 161, 180, 181–2
Vorster, B.J. 25, 26, 28, 30, 36, 46, 63

Waldmeir, Patti 204, 175
welfare issues 93
West: Gorbachev's rapprochement with 166–7; intelligence relationship with 8, 26, 76, 167
White Paper on Defence (1973/1977/1979) 47, 48, 84
White Paper on Defence: Defence in a Democracy (1995) 206
White Paper on Intelligence (1994) 184, 200–1, 205, 206–7, 235
White Paper on the Rationalisation of the Public Service and Related Institutions (1980) 64
"win hearts and minds" (WHAM) approach 31, 35, 43, 54, 57–8, 93, 165
World War II 16

Xhosa Resistance Movement (XWB) 126–7

Z-Squad Incorporated 114
"Z-Squads" 38–9, 103, 129
Zambia 44, 53, 123, 134, 174, 189, 222
Zimbabwe 118, 121, 130
Zimbabwe African National Union (ZANU) 35, 120, 122
Zimbabwe African People's Union (ZAPU) 109, 115
Zimbabwe People's Resistance Army (ZIPRA) 35
Zuma, Jacob 1, 78, 173, 177, 210, 219, 228, 229

eBooks – at www.eBookstore.tandf.co.uk

A library at your fingertips!

eBooks are electronic versions of printed books. You can store them on your PC/laptop or browse them online.

They have advantages for anyone needing rapid access to a wide variety of published, copyright information.

eBooks can help your research by enabling you to bookmark chapters, annotate text and use instant searches to find specific words or phrases. Several eBook files would fit on even a small laptop or PDA.

NEW: Save money by eSubscribing: cheap, online access to any eBook for as long as you need it.

Annual subscription packages

We now offer special low-cost bulk subscriptions to packages of eBooks in certain subject areas. These are available to libraries or to individuals.

For more information please contact webmaster.ebooks@tandf.co.uk

We're continually developing the eBook concept, so keep up to date by visiting the website.

www.eBookstore.tandf.co.uk